14-1

Ralph,
Merry Christmas 1987
With affection,
Ken & Marilyn

D0208038

FREE IN THE FOREST

FREE IN THE FOREST

*Ethnohistory of the Vietnamese
Central Highlands 1954–1976*

Gerald Cannon Hickey

*New Haven and London
Yale University Press*

Published with the generous assistance of the Earhart Foundation.

Designed by Sally Harris
and set in Monophoto Bembo type by
Asco Trade Typesetting Ltd., Hong Kong.
Printed in the United States of America by
Vail-Ballou Press, Binghamton, N.Y.

Library of Congress Cataloging in Publication Data
Hickey, Gerald Cannon, 1925–
    Free in the forest.

    Bibliography: p.
    Includes index.
    1. Montagnards (Vietnamese tribes)—History.
2. Central Highlands (Vietnam)—History.
3. Insurgency—Vietnam—Central Highlands.
4. Ethnicity.   I. Title.
DS556.45.M6H52   959.7   81–11595
ISBN 0–300–02437–1   AACR2

10 9 8 7 6 5 4 3 2 1

CONTENTS

ILLUSTRATIONS

Unless otherwise indicated, photographs were taken by the author.

PREFACE

Early in 1963 I was approached by the RAND Corporation about returning to Vietnam with the possibility of continuing research on the people of the central highlands. I was at the time near the end of my temporary appointment in the Southeast Asia Studies Program at Yale University, and there were other academic possibilities. I had completed my portion of the book *Ethnic Groups of Mainland Southeast Asia* (the coauthors were Frank Le Bar and John Musgrave), and Yale University Press had accepted the manuscript of *Village in Vietnam* for publication. Most of my colleagues advised me to remain at a university and pursue an academic career. An exception was Paul Mus, the noted savant of Far Eastern civilization who had been born in Vietnam and who had taken an active political role in trying to end the Indochina war through peaceful negotiations. He thought such a decision should be based on whether or not one chose to participate in the events of history, and he described to me some of the events arising out of his own involvement. The intent, I think, was to illustrate the elements of drama, frustration, and peril that such a role might hold. I shall be ever grateful for his wise words.

My interest in the people of the central highlands was first stimulated in 1953 when I was in Paris on a fellowship to research the ethnology of Indochina. This interest was heightened in 1956 when, as a member of the Michigan State University Vietnam Advisory Group, I had the occasion to visit the highlands and begin actual field research. I also became acquainted with some of the younger highland leaders and their rising spirit of ethnonationalism, a response to Saigon's attempts to integrate them into the Vietnamese cultural sphere. I sailed from Saigon in December 1959 with a strong desire to learn more about the central highlands, its people, and its problems.

By 1963, with insurgency sweeping the Vietnamese countryside, there was considerable concern in Washington over the disaffection of the mountain people (who occupied what was considered a "strategic region") from the Saigon government. It was this situation that prompted the offer from RAND to return to Vietnam and conduct research among the highland people. Under an arrangement with RAND and the Advanced Research Projects Agency (ARPA), which was financing some RAND projects in Vietnam, I continued research in the highlands from February 1964 until March 1973.

Despite the violence of the Vietnam war during that period, I was able to gather ethnographic data with a focus on the historical emergence of an interethnic group leadership (part of which is represented in the kinship charts in this volume). I also functioned as an unofficial intermediary between the highland leaders and Saigon (particularly the American mission). Some time was devoted to historical research at the National Museum and the Institute of Historical Research. Several visits to Phnom Penh enabled valuable contacts with Khmer officials and dissident highland leaders. In 1972 I became a member of the National Academy of Science's Committee for the Study of the Effects of Herbicides in Vietnam and conducted research on the use of these chemicals in the highlands (the results are summarized in this volume).

After leaving Vietnam I went to Cornell University as Visiting Associate Professor of Indochinese Studies in the Southeast Asia Program and the Department of Anthropology. Between 1975 and 1977, a fellowship from the Woodrow Wilson International Center for Scholars located at the Smithsonian Institution, Washington, D.C., allowed me to continue research at the Library of Congress, the State Department, the Defense Department, and the U.S. Army Center of Military History. Much of the manuscript was completed at the Wilson Center.

In gathering data on the ethnohistory of the central highlands from 1954 I was assisted by highland people too numerous to mention, but I would like to extend particular thanks to Y Thih Eban, Touneh Han Tho, Nay Luett, and Y Char Hdok. Others who helped were Michael Benge, Dr. Pat Smith, researchers of the Summer Institute of Linguistics, the priests of the Missions Etrangères de Paris, and members of the Christian and Missionary Alliance. Logistical support was generously provided by the U.S. Agency for International Development; the U.S. Special Forces; the U.S. Military Assistance Command, Vietnam; and the ARPA Research and Development Field Unit. In Saigon, my efforts to represent the views of highland leaders were aided by Ton That Tien, Tran Nhu Trang, Janice Hopper, Virginia Callahan, Ambassador Ellsworth Bunker, Eva Kim, William Colby, Nicholas Thorne, Philip Habib, John Kirk, and Thomas Burke. I would like to express my gratitude to Joan Allen, Guido (Yogi) Ianiero, George Tanham, and Rita McDermott of the RAND Corporation for their support during the war years in Vietnam. I also would like to thank Arthur T. Hadley for financial assistance during the final phase of my work in Vietnam.

The Earhart Foundation of Ann Arbor, Michigan, generously provided valuable support in funding a fellowship for Touneh Han Tho to spend a period as my research assistant in Washington and in granting a subvention for the final preparation of this book and the companion work. Mary Connor assisted with the preparation of the manuscript, which was typed by Joan Allen, Tazu Warner, Rosalie Fonoroff, and Dorothy Hager. The maps were drafted by Christopher Mueller-Wille, Dan Greenway, and William Hezlep. Nguyen Van Tam did the kinship charts. Michael DeMetre assisted with the photographs. At Yale University Press, the professional guidance of Adrienne Suddard and Edward Tripp has been invaluable in transforming the manuscript into the book.

I would like to thank my family, particularly my mother and my sisters, Catherine and Carole, for their support during the long period of research and writing.

Finally, I would like to express my most heartfelt gratitude to the people of the central highlands for their unfailing kindness, their courage, and for everything I learned from them.

INTRODUCTION

On 21 July 1954, the final session of the Geneva Conference witnessed the signing of a cease-fire that brought to an end the fighting that had raged in Indochina since 1945. For all their historical significance, the agreements will be remembered as very curious. To begin with, the first part of the document, the "Agreement on the Cessation of Hostilities in Vietnam," which provided for the cease-fire (with a demarcation line at the 17th parallel dividing Vietnam into two "temporary regroupment areas") was signed by only military, *not diplomatic*, representatives of the French and the Viet Minh. The "Final Declaration," which formed the second part of the agreements, concerned political arrangements, and in a vaguely worded passage called for general elections to be held on 21 July 1956. However, despite the fact that there were at the conference delegations from France, Britain, the United States, the Soviet Union, the People's Republic of China, Cambodia, Laos, the State of Vietnam (whose head was the former emperor, Bao Dai), and the Democratic Republic of Vietnam (whose head was Viet Minh leader Ho Chi Minh), *no one signed* the Final Declaration. It was in effect an unsigned treaty.[1]

Furthermore, *Vietnam*, the political and territorial entity that was the subject of the agreements, had never existed as such prior to 21 July 1954. The borders had been established by the French and there were large areas within them that historically had never known Vietnamese rule. This was true of much of the central highlands, the southern portion of the mountain range we know in English as the Annam Cordillera or Annamite Chain. (The French call it the Chaine Annamitique, while the Vietnamese know it as the Trường Sơn, "Long Mountains".) Although this region

1. Joseph Buttinger, *A Dragon Embattled*, 2 vols. (New York: Frederick A. Praeger, 1967), 2: 824–39; Bernard Fall, *Vietnam Witness 1953–66* (New York, London, and Washington: Frederick A. Praeger, 1966), pp. 69–76.

xiii

geographically has come to be known as the "Vietnamese central highlands," in the past the Vietnamese controlled only the eastern fringe. (This
is discussed in the companion volume, *Sons of the Mountains: Ethnohistory of
the Vietnamese Central Highlands to 1954.*) At the time of the Geneva
Agreements the central highlands were, as a result of a 1950 French decree,
classified as a Crown Domain directly under Bao Dai but not part of the
State of Vietnam. For the people of that mountain region, the decision at
Geneva to include their homeland as part of an ill-defined Vietnamese zone
south of the 17th parallel would prove momentous in the years to come.

The highlanders are radically different from the lowland Vietnamese
in that they speak languages of the Mon Khmer and Austronesian
(Malayopolynesian) linguistic stocks and physically resemble other
Southeast Asians of similar linguistic affiliation, such as the Cambodians,
Malays, and Indonesians. Although divided into many ethnic groups (see
appendix A for population figures), the highlanders share many sociocultural characteristics that historically have set them apart from the more
advanced Cham, Khmer, and Vietnamese. This book traces the ethnohistory of the central highlands and its people from 1954 (following the
Geneva Agreements) to 1976 (the formation of the Socialist Republic of
Vietnam). A major thesis here, as in the first book, is that for a long period
of time the mountain people have been developing a common ethnic
identity. It has been a process of sociocultural change attributable to a
number of interrelated economic, political, religious, and geographic factors, all of which are reflected in the events of history. An examination of
the events prior to 1954 reveals that contact among the highlanders
themselves and with the outside world was a major catalyst in sustaining
the process of ethnicity. It calls to mind a similar phenomenon that
occurred among some indigenous groups in the Americas who were
identified by Europeans with whom they came into contact as "Indians"
and who in time came to identify themselves collectively as such.
However, in the case of the highlanders no comparable term has been
adopted. Outsiders with whom they have had contact invariably had
generic designations (sometimes pejorative) for them.[2] Since the early

---

2. The Vietnamese always used the name, *mọi* ("savage"), until recent times when political
expediency replaced it with *Đồng Bào Thượng* ("highland compatriots") and *Dân Tộc Thiểu Số*
("ethnic minorities"). Borrowing from the Vietnamese, the French for a long time referred to the
highlanders as "les Mois," finally changing to their own *Montagnards* ("highlanders" or "mountaineers"). The Cambodians called all upland people *phnong* ("savages"). The highlanders have some
common designations for certain lowland people. The Vietnamese are known as *Yuan*, and the Lao as

1950s, for example, the French term *Montagnards* ("mountaineers" or "highlanders") has gained wide acceptance in the West—particularly among journalists—but not among the highlanders themselves. Many upland groups have in their languages generic expressions for all of the upland people, and in recent years the Jarai term *Ana Chu* meaning "Sons of the Mountains" has gained favor among highland leaders (see below).

Pre-1954 ethnohistory also reveals the importance of leadership, specifically the emergence of an intergroup elite, to the process of ethnicity. It is the leaders who are recorded in histories; it is the leaders with whom the outsiders must deal in contact situations; and it is the leaders who define such contact for their own people. Ultimately it is they who are the prime movers in ethnonationalism.

The archeological record and historical lexicostatistics contain evidence of primordial ties the highlanders had with the Cham, Khmer, and Vietnamese, whose societies were transformed by the Indian and Chinese great traditions. The first glints of evidence of contact are found in Cham historical accounts from as early as the fifth century concerning tribute paid by their rulers to the Court of Peking. These accounts describe highland products such as precious woods, elephant tusks, and rhinoceros horns, thereby suggesting some Cham-highlander trade. The first explicit mention of highlanders in any historical records is found in Cham epigraphs of the mid-twelfth century which relate how their armies penetrated the highlands. Oral legends preserved by some of the upland groups that had submitted to Cham domination describe changes in their leadership and the tributary relations their chiefs had with the Cham kings. Historical accounts of the Khmer and Vietnamese focus on the tributary relations their rulers had with two powerful Jarai shamans—the King of Fire and the King of Water. These relations ended in the mid-nineteenth century when Norodom ascended the throne of Cambodia in 1859 and when the French conquered Vietnam during the reign of Tu Duc (1848–1883).

The arrival of the first French missionaries at Kontum in the middle of the nineteenth century ushered in an era of ever-increasing contact among

---

Lao. Those highland people who have had contact with the Khmer call them *Kur*. For the Cham, however, there are several designations. The Koho-speaking groups as well as the Mnong, Bahnar, Jarai (west of Cheo Reo), and Rhadé (west of M'drak) call them *Prum*, while the eastern Jarai and Rhadé, the Chru, and Roglai refer to them as *Cham*. On the western side of the mountains, the French are known as *Prang*, and on the eastern side, they are called *Tay* (a Vietnamese term). The Chinese are known as *Khách* on the western side and *Lo* on the eastern side of the mountains. Indians (usually merchants in towns) are called *Yawa*.

the highlanders themselves and between them and the outside world. Toward the end of the century when the French administration assumed control over the central highlands (invoking the tributary relations between the Court of Hue and the Kings of Fire and Water as a rationale for them to act as protectors of Annam to justify this move) highland leadership began to undergo vast changes. Initially the French settled on a strategy of using the local chiefs (some of whom had been identified in the accounts of French explorations) as intermediaries between the colonial administration and the indigenous population. In addition to their traditional responsibilities the chiefs were now burdened with such things as collection of taxes and organizing corvée labor for French projects— notably the construction of "penetration routes" aimed at opening the region for economic exploitation. The French presence also meant the first towns at Ban Me Thuot, Kontum, and Dalat, and a few primary schools. The children of the chiefs were predominant among the students, and by the 1920s they became the first highland teachers, civil servants, and technicians. They represented a new type of leader—one who had familiarized himself with the language and ways of the colonial administration while retaining his ties and identity with the village society from which he came. But the intrusion of the French, their land-grabbing, corvées, and taxes, stirred an undercurrent of resentment and with it, the first real manifestation of highland ethnonationalism in the form of the bizarre Python God movement that swept large parts of the mountain country in the late 1930s.

World War II brought a relatively quiescent period to the mountains. On 9 March 1945, however, the Japanese took over the administration of Indochina, plunging the highlanders into a long night of international conflict. The world that had existed prior to that date vanished forever. With the ensuing Indochina war the highlanders became "a people in between," as some joined the French and some the Viet Minh, but most found themselves unwitting victims of the struggle. Nonetheless, during the war, highland leadership underwent significant changes for two reasons: the French decided to improve secondary-level education and there was an increase in marriages among elite families both within and among ethnic groups.

In an attempt to win greater support among the highlanders, the French decided to improve secondary schools by establishing the Collège Sabatier in Ban Me Thuot and providing scholarships to the prestigious Lycée

Yersin in Dalat. Most of those who benefited were of the elite families. At the Collège Sabatier the Rhadé students included Y Thih Eban (see chart 5.2) and Y Ju Eban, two founders of the Bajaraka Movement (discussed in chapter 2); Y Chon Mlo Duon Du, later a controversial leader; and the flamboyant militant, Y Kdruin Mlo (2.24), who preferred calling himself Philippe Drouin. Other Rhadé students were Y Mo Eban (5.7), Y Klong Adrong, and Y Jut Buon To (1.19). The last two are now in the United States. The Jarai at the school included Rcom Anhot (3.12) and Nay Blim (2.25), both of whom would later serve in the National Assembly; and Nay Luett (2.26), the future Minister for Development of Ethnic Minorities. Others were Rcom Pioi (2.21), who became a teacher and subsequently an army officer (his brother Rcom Briu followed the Viet Minh and later rose to the rank of general in the Communist forces); and political activists Ksor Dun (5.8), Rcom Perr (3.13), and Siu Nay. One Bahnar student was Hiup (1.20), grandson of Ber, the first highland civil servant, and another was Hiup's brother-in-law, Paul Nur (1.13), who would become the first Minister for Development of Ethnic Minorities. Two Mnong Rlam at the school were (known by their Rhadé names) Y Tang Phok and Y Char Hdok, who would receive a bachelor's degree in the United States. Another was Bun Sur, who later would study in Paris and become a province chief in Cambodia. The Chru students included Touneh Yoh (4.10), Touneh Ton (4.14), and Touneh Han Tho (4.2), who now is in the United States. From the Sre came two brothers, Toplui Pierre K'Briuh and Toplui K'Broi (4.11,12) both of whom would receive American bachelor's degrees.

In 1952, head of state Bao Dai began granting young qualified highlander students scholarships to the Lycée Yersin, one of the best secondary schools in Southeast Asia. Among those who obtained scholarships were Touneh Yoh, Touneh Han Tho, Toplui K'Briuh, Toplui K'Broi, Bun Sur, Ksor Dun, Rcom Anhot, and Nay Luett.

Strong bonds of friendship were formed among the young highlanders at both schools. Although intermarriage among elite families already was taking place, these new friendships resulted in an increased number of intermarriages. Each of the genealogies presented in charts 1, 2, 3, 4, and 5 began to enlarge, and it was inevitable that they would link together. The result was one vast kin network extending over a wide territory and incorporating elite families of the Bahnar, Sedang, Rengao, Jarai, Rhadé, Mnong Rlam, Sre, Lat, Chru, and Bru. In addition, a new spirit of ethnonationalism arose among this group of young highlanders, who were soon to emerge as the leaders. They would prove an effective force in the dark days that lay ahead.

With the Geneva Agreements the highlanders found themselves under Vietnamese rule and contact between the two groups quickened, resulting in a dramatic new phase of ethnonationalism that initially was political in character and then became militant. With the 1955 establishment of the Republic of Vietnam under President Ngo Dinh Diem, highland leaders became enraged when their people were classified as "ethnic minorities" in their own mountains. Anxious to build South Vietnam into a viable political entity, Diem concluded that the ethnic minorities (highlanders, Cham, Khmer, and Chinese) would have to be assimilated into the Vietnamese cultural sphere. The 1957 Land Development Program was designed to attain the dual goals of developing the highlands economically and bringing modernization to the highlanders by resettling massive numbers of Vietnamese in the region. The reaction of the highland leaders was a political movement that was more spirited than sophisticated, but significantly it was the first time that ethnonationalism had taken the form of political activism, and Diem's attempts to shatter it were of no avail.

Despite the intrusions of the land development scheme, the period following the Geneva Agreements was a relatively peaceful time when the highland villagers could move along the trails and farm their fields without fear. It would be remembered as a happy time. It ended all too soon at the beginning of the 1960s when the renewed Communist insurgency brought dark clouds of conflict, and the highlanders again found themselves "a people in between." Late in 1961, as security crumbled in highland provinces, the American Central Intelligence Agency (CIA) launched a village defense program in Darlac, and it soon proved successful. This represented the first direct American involvement with the highlanders (which made the Saigon government uneasy). When in mid-1962 the program was taken over by the U.S. military it was changed into an offensive operation, setting the course for future American strategy in Vietnam. In the hope that the Americans were supporting their cause, some of the highland leaders became active in the program. They failed to realize that the Americans' interest in the highlands had nothing to do with ethnonationalism—the Americans, like the French, were simply using the highlanders for their own ends.

By 1964, insurgency was rapidly intensifying into war. Suddenly, in

September a new movement organized by some highland leaders and officers of the Royal Khmer Army from neighboring Cambodia appeared. This movement was responsible for violent mutinies in five upland Special Forces camps, settlements that had grown out of the village defense scheme. As if reflecting the tenor of the times, highland ethnonationalism had become militant, and it was an unexpected turn that produced shock in Saigon and Washington. After the trouble in the camps subsided (the rebels set up their headquarters across the border in Cambodia), the Vietnamese government made lukewarm efforts to gain the support of the nonrebel highland leaders. With United States forces moving into the mountains in increasing numbers, security of the region became a primary concern in Washington, thus American pressure was exerted on the Saigon government to satisfy the demands of the highlanders. Negotiations with the rebels were begun, but dragged on without any accommodation ever being reached. Some social and economic programs were announced, but implementation was slow. There also was a small measure of progress made in giving the highlanders more political participation both in Saigon and in provincial administration. Early in 1966, a ministry with vague responsibilities for "ethnic minority development" was established with Paul Nur (1.13) as minister.

Although the rebel and nonrebel leaders shared the same ethnonationalist ideals and maintained communication, the division weakened the highlander cause at a time when concerted efforts and manifest solidarity were important. The Vietnamese officials would only negotiate seriously with anyone who clearly had a mandate and the Americans were uneasy in situations where the locus of power was not very well defined. Furthermore, the highland people now needed strong leadership to sustain them as the Vietnam war swept into the mountain country like a typhoon. Unlike the Indochina war, this conflict was waged with the most modern weaponry. Jet fighters appeared from nowhere all too often when innocent villagers were going about their daily business. Even worse were the B-52s which could neither be seen nor heard, unleashing destruction hitherto undreamed of by the people of the mountains. The Communists mounted night assaults on villages, breaching the weak defenses within minutes and using grenades (and in one case flamethrowers) against the women and children huddled in bunkers. Only the towns had some degree of security, and with the Tet Offensive early in 1968, Ban Me Thuot, Pleiku, Kontum, and Dalat were engulfed by the war.

A glimmer of hope in the gathering darkness came with the June 1971 appointment of Nay Luett (2.26), a courageous and dedicated leader, as minister for ethnic minority development. Gathering around him colleagues such as Touneh Han Tho and Toplui Pierre K'Briuh, Luett turned the ministry into a center of ethnonationalism where mountain country leaders gathered and participated in planning. In an atmosphere of new enthusiasm they set out to bolster their threatened social and economic programs and devise relief efforts for the highland victims of the war. The leaders also seriously discussed the selection of a common name for all their people, and *Ana Chu*, "Sons of the Mountains," seemed the likely choice. It was a time when the process of ethnicity was reaching a point of culmination, but time was running out.

Despite new enthusiasm and renewed hope, Nay Luett and his colleagues were well aware that the worsening war could threaten the very existence of their people. United States military units were rapidly withdrawing, leaving the defense of the region in the hands of ill-trained, badly led Vietnamese troops who, Nay Luett was convinced, had no will to fight for the highlands. He therefore proposed the formation of a 50,000-man highland military force, but the Vietnamese and Americans would not consider the idea. He also proposed a plan to regroup all of the surviving highlanders in the provinces of Kontum, Pleiku, Darlac, Phu Bon, Tuyen Duc, and Lam Dong, but the Saigon government was cool to the scheme primarily because many Vietnamese military and civilian officials coveted the rich land in places like Darlac.

Then suddenly on 30 March 1972, the Communists launched a sweeping, devastating offensive. As their troops attacked strategically important places in the highlands, the fighting and B-52 bombing drove whole ethnic groups from their traditional territories. Overwhelmed by the violence and an inundation of refugees, social and economic programs that had taken years to build, crumbled overnight. The disruption was such that in the wake of the offensive, the existing ethnolinguistic maps of the highlands were no longer valid. When Luett and his colleagues realized that at least 200,000 highlanders had probably perished in the war thus far and 85 percent had been forced to leave their villages, it became painfully clear that the struggle for survival had now eclipsed the struggle to maintain ethnic identity.

Ironically, the series of events that led directly to the fall of South Vietnam began in the highlands on 10 March 1975, when the Communists, with collusion of some highland leaders, attacked and captured Ban Me Thuot. This led to the fateful decision by a group of Vietnamese generals to abandon Kontum and Pleiku, precipitating what probably was the worst bloodbath of the war and the total collapse of the Saigon military forces. On 1 May 1975, the Communist troops entered the capital and the Vietnam war was ended. Peace, however, did not return to the highlands. It soon became apparent that the oft-promised autonomy for the highlanders was only a propaganda ploy. Worse still, Hanoi immediately began implementing plans to resettle large numbers of Vietnamese in upland "economic zones." There also were announcements in rhetoric reminiscent of the Diem era about programs to settle the "nomadic" mountain people in "sedentary villages." At the same time all of the highland leaders from the ministry and those who had been active in provincial administrations and programs were captured and incarcerated either in jails or "reeducation camps." Those leaders who managed to elude captivity along with young highlanders from the Army, the Special Forces, and other paramilitary groups, fled into the forest where they organized a resistance movement.

In July 1976 (22 years after the Geneva Agreements), the two Vietnams were unified into the Socialist Republic of Vietnam. Now the Hanoi regime would be free to isolate and Vietnamize the highlands. In the villages the highlanders will experience a transformation of their traditional ways and an ebbing of their ethnic identity, but as long as there are Sons of the Mountains who have chosen to carry on their way of life free in the forest, that ethnic identity will continue to exist.

1 TIME BETWEEN THE WARS

By September 1954 the guns of the Indochina War had at last fallen silent and, with this, French rule in Vietnam was ended forever. Vietnam itself, however, was divided once more as it had been throughout most of its history. North of the 17th parallel, Ho Chi Minh headed a government in Hanoi again, and the Democratic Republic of Vietnam (usually called North Vietnam) began to evolve along Communist lines. Initially, the situation south of the Demilitarized Zone was less clear. As Ngo Dinh Diem (who had agreed to form a new government in June 1954) secured his control of the administration by the end of 1954, it became increasingly apparent that a non-Communist government would hold sway in the south. This was realized in October 1955, when the Republic of Vietnam (better known as South Vietnam) came into being.

These events were to bring sweeping changes for the people of the mountains. The central highlands became part of the territory of South Vietnam, i.e., the Republic of Vietnam, and the highlanders, now officially designated Đồng-Bào Thượng or "Highland Compatriots," found themselves—along with the Cham, Khmer, and Chinese—in the new category of "ethnic minorities." As part of his goal to attain national integration, Diem adopted a policy of assimilating the ethnic minorities into the Vietnamese cultural sphere. This involved decrees and practices designed to impose on the highlanders the social institutions and cultural traits of the Vietnamese. It was an effort at erasing ethnic boundaries, and it was to have a profound effect in the highlands for many years to come.

Nonetheless, the 1954–58 period was to be remembered as a period of peace when the highland people could move along paths and roads and work their fields without fear, when the young could plan to establish families, clear new lands, and build new houses. By and large it was a relatively happy time, that time between the wars.

DIEM'S CONSOLIDATION OF POLITICAL AUTHORITY IN SOUTH VIETNAM

With his appointment as prime minister in June 1954, Diem became head of the government and, following the enactment of the Geneva Agreements in July, found himself ruling all territory south of the 17th parallel. By September, however, it was evident that his real authority was minimal. Part of the reason was that, in the south, power did not rest in the state. The French policy of "divide-and-rule" had dispersed power among competing factions—the army, the police, the secret service, and interest groups such as French and Chinese business circles or Vietnamese landlords with extensive holdings in the Mekong river delta. In addition, considerable power had been put in the hands of the Binh Xuyen (originally a band of river pirates that developed into a Mafia-like organization that controlled gambling and vice as well as the police and security forces in Saigon) and two relatively new religious movements with territorial enclaves, the Hoa Hao and Cao Daists. Furthermore, the Viet Minh had not withdrawn all of its political cadres, and these cadres, because of their triumph over the French, enjoyed a certain prestige among the population. Also, Diem had inherited a national economy badly disrupted by the war. There was widespread damage to systems of communication, and vast areas of paddy fields had been abandoned by peasants who fled to the urban areas.

Diem's first priority was to gain control of the army, and his struggle to do so brought out both the inherent weakness of his opponents and his reliance on the United States for his survival. Although economic interests remained well entrenched in South Vietnam, the French military presence there had long been dependent on American financial support, and there had been a concomitant shift in political influence. After the signing of the Geneva Agreements, the United States began to put pressure on France to liquidate all traces of colonialism in Vietnam, such as support of the Binh Xuyen, Hoa Hao, and Cao Daist armies or the role of chief of state created for Bao Dai. By September 1954, Vietnamese, French, and American representatives had worked out some diminution of French control. On 7 September, General Ely, high commissioner and commander of French forces in Indochina, turned over the Norodom Palace, seat of the high commissioner, to Diem (who renamed it the Independence Palace). Four days later, responsibility for the administration of justice, the police, security, public safety, and civil aviation was vested in the Diem government. It also was agreed in principle that as of 1 January 1955 Vietnam would have the right to issue its own currency. Command of the National Army was transferred from the French to the Diem government. The United States Military Assistance Advisory Group (MAAG), which had been formed to supervise the delivery of arms and equipment to the French army, assumed the task of training the Vietnamese army. All parties agreed that aid funds from the United States would go directly to the Vietnamese government. Finally, France agreed to withdraw its Expeditionary Corps on request from the Vietnamese government.

September also marked the beginning of a turbulent period for the Diem government. Early in the month, General Nguyen Van Hinh, chief of staff of the Vietnamese army and son of former Prime Minister Nguyen Van Tam, began making public statements against Diem. The resultant conflict almost led to a coup d'état by Hinh, in league with Binh Xuyen leader Le Van Vien, that would have brought Bao Dai back from France to head the government. But Diem, demonstrating a remarkable ability at political maneuvering, rallied support from Hoa Hao and Cao Daist leaders—it was rumored that American funds were used to purchase their loyalties—particularly from General Trinh Minh The, leader of a Cao Daist faction that was considered a "third force" between the Communists and French collaborators during the Indochina War. Meanwhile, growing American influence and support for Diem was eroding Bao Dai and General Hinh's positions, and by 1 October Diem felt strong enough to reject Bao Dai's "advice" that he take General Hinh and Le Van Vien into the cabinet. Bao Dai thereupon summoned Hinh to France for "consultation." With this "victory," Diem's position at the beginning of 1955 was considerably stronger than it had been six months previously, but it still was far from unshakable.

Diem's next priority was to remove the Binh Xuyen, Hoa Hao, and Cao Daists from the political arena, and his strategy was to play the leaders of these "sects" against one another. He had retained the support of some Hoa Hao and Cao Daist leaders, and in January 1955 he won to his side Colonel Nguyen Van Hue, chief of staff under the Hoa Hao general Tran Van Soai. Soon after, the Cao Daist General Trinh Minh The rallied to Diem's side, bringing with him a force of 5,000 men.

Diem then moved against the Binh Xuyen in an effort to break their control of the Saigon police force and security service. When, late in January, it came time to renew the license permitting operation of the

Grand Monde, the Binh Xuyen gambling casino in Cholon which was the primary source of Binh Xuyen revenues, the government refused to do so. In retaliation for this and similar harassments by Diem, a group of Binh Xuyen, Hoa Hao, and Cao Daist leaders formed a "spiritual union" and dispatched a delegation to Cannes to convince Bao Dai that he should remove Diem. On 22 March they issued an ultimatum to Diem, demanding that a new national government be formed within five days. Diem cautiously rejected it on 24 March (and was reported to have quickly bought the loyalty of General Nguyen Thanh Phuong, commander-in-chief of the Cao Daist forces). On 28 March Diem ordered paratroop units (some of which were composed of members of the Nung ethnic group from the highlands of northern Vietnam) into the Binh Xuyen headquarters. Armed conflict would have taken place if it had not been for the intervention of General Ely, who feared for the safety of the numerous French civilians in Saigon.

April 1955 was a month of crisis for Diem. Some of his strong supporters quit the government, forcing him to form a junta with his brothers Ngo Dinh Nhu and Ngo Dinh Luyen as well as other kinsmen. Then Bao Dai, taking advantage of the fact that parts of the Mekong river delta and the western provinces remained in the hands of the Hoa Hao and Cao Daists, issued a decree making pro-French General Nguyen Van Vy the chief of staff. At the same time, he issued an invitation to Diem to come to Cannes for "consultation." Diem refused, and on 23 April, when everyone expected him to resign, he announced that general elections would be held within three or four months. On 27 April, the government issued an order stating that, after a forty-eight-hour time limit, the Binh Xuyen troops would be forbidden to circulate in Saigon-Cholon. The following day the government and Binh Xuyen troops clashed near the Binh Xuyen headquarters between Saigon and Cholon, causing extensive damage to the area and inflicting heavy casualties on the civilian population. Diem's forces won the day. This was followed by an attempt on the part of General Vy to seize control of the army, but he was blocked by General Ty and two colonels, Tran Van Don and Duong Van Minh (both of whom would be leaders in the 1963 coup d'état that toppled Diem). These two colonels were popular with the Vietnamese military and, the next day, were promoted to the rank of brigadier general. Diem's army pursued the Binh Xuyen units into Saigon's suburbs while government army elements clashed with Hoa Hao forces in the delta. The Cao Daists elected to surrender. Again Diem had emerged victorious.

Diem's victory over the opposition consolidated his political position and won him new support from the Americans. At the same time, the French position in Vietnam steadily weakened, and the demise of colonialism became increasingly apparent. In May 1955 General Ely was relieved of his command, and a new American ambassador, G. Frederick Reinhardt, arrived in Saigon. Also in May, the French command agreed to withdraw its forces from the Saigon-Cholon area. Diem, meanwhile, set about laying the groundwork for the removal of Bao Dai. In June he got the Council of the Royal Family in Hue to deprive Bao Dai of his prerogatives, and the council also proposed that Diem be elected president. On 7 July, Diem set the date for general elections for 23 October 1955. It was to be a contest between Bao Dai and Diem and the results were predictable. Diem won by an overwhelming majority (he claimed some 98.3 percent of the total vote cast).[1] After the election, he proclaimed the Republic of Vietnam.

Presidential ordinances dated 23 January 1956 created a Constitutional Assembly to draft a new constitution for the Republic of Vietnam. Elections for membership were held on 4 March 1956, with four of the 123 seats to go to highlanders (see map 2). Those elected to fill them were Hiar (1.7), the Bahnar teacher from Kontum; Y Ut Nie Buon Rit, the noted Rhadé teacher from Ban Me Thuot; Ramah Pok, a Jarai from Pleiku; and K'Kre (4.5), a Sre-Chru from Dalat. The new constitution was completed and promulgated by President Diem on 26 October 1956, at which time the Constitutional Assembly became the first legislative assembly for a term of three years. On 29 December the assembly approved the appointment of Nguyen Ngoc Tho as vice president.[2]

THE POLICY OF ASSIMILATION

In his efforts to make the new state viable, Diem faced a number of social and economic problems. As was the case with many newly independent states in post-World War II Southeast Asia, one of the major challenges was

1. Joseph Buttinger, *Vietnam: A Dragon Embattled*, 2 vols. (New York: Frederick A. Praeger, 1967), 2: 851–72; Dennis J. Duncanson, *Government and Revolution in Vietnam* (New York and London: Oxford University Press, 1968), pp. 220–22; Bernard Fall, *Viet-Nam Witness 1953–66* (New York: Frederick A. Praeger, 1966), pp. 141–59.

2. National Institute of Administration, *Viet Nam Government Organization Manual 1957–58* (Saigon: National Institute of Administration Research and Documentation Division, 1958), pp. 27–32.

to achieve a national integration of the many and varied ethnolinguistic groups. Diem's response was to try assimilating the ethnic minorities (the highlanders, Cham, Khmer, and Chinese) into the Vietnamese cultural sphere. There was in his adoption of this policy an element of Vietnamese chauvinism. In addition, his policy reflected the notion, prevalent in many Southeast Asian capitals at the time, that in order to attain national integration, ties to kin groups, villages, religious sects, and ethnic groups (particularly ethnic minorities) must be replaced by loyalty to the state. Clifford Geertz has argued that "considered as societies, the new states are abnormally susceptible to serious disaffection based on primordial attachments."[3] He added that these "primordial attachments" (a term he borrowed from Edward Shils) have come to be regarded as competing with civil attachments to the state.[4] Neither Geertz nor Shils feels that the two loyalties are intrinsically antithetic. For them, these primordial attachments are part of the fabric of the society and therefore can also be part of the fabric of the new state. For Geertz, what is required is an "integrative revolution" that would bring about an adjustment of primordial and civil attachments, making them compatible. Ethnicity, in this event, would be legitimized, so that the solidarity and "consciousness of kind" associated with it are extended into the "developing social order" of the new state. The individual, in effect, retains his ethnic identity and comes to develop a loyalty to the state. Without this integration, Geertz warns, there can be a disaffection leading to political disintegration, partition, or irredentism.

Unfortunately, leaders in many of the new states failed to recognize this, seeing ethnicity (particularly in the case of minorities) as something to be done away with in order to have national integration. This view was—and still is—held not only by political leaders but also by many social scientists. Connor points to a tendency among scholars concerned with "nation-building" theories either to ignore ethnic diversity or to treat ethnic identity "as merely one of a number of impediments to effective state-integration." "To the degree that ethnic identity is given recognition," Connor continues, "it is apt to be a somewhat unimportant and ephemeral nuisance that will unquestionably give way to a common identity uniting

---

3. Clifford Geertz, "The Integrative Revolution: Primordial Sentiments and Civil Politics in the New States," in *Old Societies and New States*, ed. Clifford Geertz (New York: The Free Press, 1963), pp. 105–57.
4. Edward Shils, "Primordial, Personal, Sacred and Civil Ties," *British Journal of Sociology* 8, no. 2 (1957): 130–45.

all inhabitants of the state, regardless of ethnic heritage, as modern communication and transportation link the state's various parts more closely." Noting that if this process of "modernization were effective, the number of states troubled by ethnic disharmony would be on the decrease," he cites the contrary evidence of ethnic minority political movements among the Basques, Catalans, Bretons, Scots, and South Tyroleans in the well-established European states.[5] Numerous other examples could be drawn from other parts of the world.

In the same vein, Barth writes that culture contact and change are becoming more widespread "as dependence on the products and institutions of industrial societies spreads in all parts of the world." But, he adds, "the important thing to recognize is that a drastic reduction of cultural differences between ethnic groups does not correlate in any simple way with a reduction in the organizational relevance of ethnic identities or a breakdown in boundary-maintaining processes."[6] In other words, modernization does not mean increased assimilation. Diem's attempts to integrate the highland ethnic minority through a process of assimilation, therefore, could result in contributing to the rise rather than the demise of ethnic identity. This, as will be discussed below, is exactly what happened.

In a conversation concerning Diem's policy for assimilating the highlanders, former Vice President Nguyen Ngoc Tho pointed out that, from the time he assumed the role of prime minister in June 1954, Diem felt that French influence in the central highlands (see maps 3 and 4) had to be eliminated. The Crown Domain instituted by the French was in Diem's words a "legal fiction" which only gave the appearance of Vietnamese control while, in reality, the French maintained their hegemony over the region, using the Crown Domain to keep the "Kinh" (Vietnamese) out of the highlands so the French could "develop plantations and exploit the valuable minerals." It was therefore essential to do away with the Crown Domain as the first step toward integrating the highlands into the national framework. Afterward the administration of the region would have to be reorganized, and then the "primitive highland people would have to be civilized," i.e., Vietnamized. Diem believed that the highlanders were "intelligent enough to be assimilated into the Vietnamese type of village

5. Walker Connor, "Nation-Building or Nation-Destroying?", *World Politics* 24 (April 1972): 320.

6. Fredrik Barth, ed., *Ethnic Groups and Boundaries: The Social Organization of Culture Difference* (Boston: Little, Brown, 1969), intro. pp. 32–33.

life," though he was wary of the Rhadé, who, because they had "Cham blood" tended to be "devious." Nguyen Ngoc Tho stressed that Diem saw economic development as another means of integrating the highlands into the state and envisaged this taking place in a "progressive way—neither too rapidly nor too slowly." Since the region was sparsely populated, Diem deemed it necessary to move Vietnamese from the overpopulated coastal provinces, where "there is too much sand and not enough soil," into the uplands. The Vietnamese settlers would have a role in the economic development, and they would also bring Vietnamese culture to the indigenous people. Barely a month after becoming prime minister, Diem got Bao Dai to surrender his special powers in the administration of the highlands and eight months later, on 11 March 1955, put the central highlands (still with the French designation PMS from *Pays Montagnard du Sud*) under the administration of the Saigon government. That same day he promulgated Decree No. 61 appointing a government delegate for the highlands and replacing all of the French résidents with Vietnamese province chiefs. The new delegate was Ton That Hoi, the former Quan Dao in Ban Me Thuot, who took up residence in Dalat.

Establishing a Vietnamese administration in the highlands was to prove no easy task. There already was a shortage of trained personnel for all levels of the administration in the lowlands due to the failure of the French to prepare the Vietnamese for independence. To make matters more difficult, there were very few Vietnamese who had had any administrative experience in the upland regions. Furthermore, the remote uplands held no allure for the average Vietnamese, who still regarded the mountains as the abode of evil spirits, the place where "poisoned water" (*nuóc độc*) flowed in the streams, a region peopled by savages.

The program launched by the French after their return to train more highlanders for the administration was still in an incipient stage of development. The Collège Sabatier in Ban Me Thuot had at this time only around sixty students, and in 1954 the French had begun sending a few highlanders to the School of Administration founded the year before in Dalat. Among the first students in the Highland Section there were Touprong Hiou (4.4), a Chru who had been serving as sector chief at Dran; Ya Yu Sahau, a Chru school teacher; and Y Blu Nie Buon-Drieng, a Rhadé who held several administrative posts at Ban Me Thuot.

American aid at this time was being administered in Vietnam by the United States Operations Mission (USOM), an outgrowth of the old Special Technical and Economic Mission which was later subsumed in the

Agency for International Development (AID). In April 1955 Michigan State University, which had a contract with AID, signed an agreement with the Vietnamese government to provide professors and other specialists in police and public administration. Some of the professors were assigned to the School of Administration to assist in developing its program. The school was moved from Dalat to Saigon in July 1955 and its name changed to the National Institute of Administration. One part of the Day Program of the Preparatory Section (a two-year program) was composed of members of ethnic groups from the northern (they were refugees) and central highlands.[7] The group that began training for the 1955–56 period included Y Dhuat Nie Kdam, a Rhadé who became a well-known administrator in Darlac; Y Chon Mlo Duon Du, also a Rhadé who later became active in the Ministry for Development of Ethnic Minorities; and Rcom Rock (3.11), a Jarai from Cheo Reo. The Third Class for the 1956–57 period had Pierre Yuk (1.12), who became active in the Kontum administration; and two young Chru leaders, Touneh Han Din (4.3) and Touneh Yoh (4.10). The 1957–58 group also had two Chru: Boui Ngai, who later became an administrator in the Danhim valley; and Touneh Han Tho (4.2), who became the best trained highland administrator.

But these small gains in administrative training were accompanied by some disruptive changes in the highland education system. Early in 1955 the Directorate of Education for the Southern Highlands, which had been under the secretary general of the Crown Domain, was taken over by the Vietnamese and in October 1956 was put under the Department of Education. The 1959 government manual stated that "the directorate aims at promoting the national culture, spreading the use of the Vietnamese language in the Highlands, and developing the various branches of study to help the mountaineers contribute to the work of national reconstruction."[8] Subjects such as French history and geography were replaced by Vietnamese history and geography, and Vietnamese language instruction replaced not only French but also training in the mother tongues. According to one Rhadé teacher, Y Toeh Mlo Duon Du (5.1), the newly appointed Vietnamese inspector for education in the highlands had all of the teaching materials in the Rhadé language burned.

In August 1955 the secondary schools in the highlands were turned over

---

7. Nghiem Dang, "The National Institute of Administration," in *Viet Nam: The First Five Years*, ed. Richard Lindholm (East Lansing, Michigan: Michigan State University Press, 1959), pp. 63–65.
8. National Institute of Administration, *Viet Nam Government*, pp. 172–73.

to the Vietnamese government. According to Touneh Han Tho, the Collège Sabatier was renamed the Nguyen Du School and the curriculum became Vietnamese. Vietnamese also became the language of instruction, forcing most of the highland students who were not versed in the language to leave school. Sre students K'Briuh (4.11) and his brother K'Broi (4.12); Mnong students Bun Sur, Rhadé Y Gum Buon Ya (who later became a medical doctor), and Nay Ba; a Jarai (who later studied in Japan), all went for further study at the Lycée Yersin, which continued to be run by the French Cultural Mission.

While reducing French influence in the highlands, Diem resorted to a French-created institution, the Oath Ceremony, which he held at Ban Me Thuot in June 1955 to achieve a public display of support by leaders from various ethnic groups. Among the highland "chiefs" summoned for it were Siu Anhot, the King of Fire; Nay Nui (2.11), the elderly Jarai leader; Y Ut Nie Buon Rit, the Rhadé who was the first highland schoolmaster; Y Blieng Hmok, a Rhadé civil servant; and Touprong Hiou (4.4), the Chru leader. The format of the celebration was basically the same as it had been in the past. Diem sat in the place of honor that previously had been occupied by French résidents (such as Sabatier) and officials (such as Admiral Decoux, Admiral d'Argenlieu, and High Commissioner Bollaert), as well as by Bao Dai. The elephants "saluted" and the president, after having alcohol from a jar poured over his feet, sipped from several jars. But now the oath of loyalty was sworn not to France or to Bao Dai but to the Republic of Vietnam.

The central highlands had officially become a part of the national territory of the Republic of Vietnam on 23 October 1955, the day of the Bao Dai–Diem elections. Three days later a presidential order awarded the National Order Medal Fourth Class to Ama Kham Suk, the teknonymous designation for Y Keo Khue, the nephew of the old Muong-Lao chief Khunjanob, who had been the first chief in the Darlac area to collaborate with the French at the end of the nineteenth century.[9] Khunjanob's sister had married a Mnong Preh, and Y Keo was their son. When Khunjanob retired as judge of the Highland Law Court in 1930 (he died in 1953), Y Keo (Ama Kham Suk) replaced him.

The same presidential order awarded National Order Medals Fifth Class

9. Ngô Đình Diệm, "Sắc-lệnh: So 12-TTP," Decree Number 12-TTP (Saigon, 11 November 1955), personal papers of Touneh Han Dang, Saigon, Vietnam.

to Y Ut Nie Buon Rit, the Rhadé who was the first highland schoolmaster; Y Blieng Hmok, a Rhadé civil servant; K'Kre, member of the Dalat city council; and Touneh Han Dang, the Chru leader who had served for a long time as judge in the highlander law court in the Danhim valley.

Changes in the Vietnamese military organization during this period affected the highlander military personnel. The Vietnamese army that Diem took over in 1954 numbered 200,000, but the United States Defense Department, which was providing military aid (including the MAAG advisors), wanted it reduced to 85,000. Discussion with Diem resulted in agreement on an army of 150,000, the level at which it remained until 1961. Duncanson notes that due to French tradition and American advice, the Vietnamese army was organized with a conventional command structure. There was a general staff and a field army divided into three corps (in 1962 it increased to four corps) and seven divisions (in 1962 this was increased to nine divisions). Most divisions were subdivided into two-battalion regiments instead of brigades.[10]

According to Touneh Han Tho, by the end of 1955 the highlander units that had been in the French army were being reorganized and integrated into the National Army. The highlanders were in the 4th Military Zone, and the 7th Battalion (composed primarily of Chru, Sre, and Maa), numbering around one thousand men, was integrated into a regiment of the National Army. The battalion's headquarters was moved from Dalat (where Bao Dai had wanted it near his palace) to the airfield (servicing Dalat) at Lien Khuong. Captain Touprong Ya Ba (4.9), the Chru battalion commander, was replaced by a Vietnamese captain in January 1956, but the new commander did not actually assume his new post until April.

At the beginning of 1956, when Tai-speaking refugees from the northern highlands began arriving in the Lien Khuong area, the 7th Battalion was ordered to assist them by clearing the forest for settlements and paddy fields. Touneh Han Tho related how his half-brother Touneh Han Tin (4.13), a lieutenant, joined with a Vietnamese lieutenant interested in the highland people to organize some village-improvement projects in the Danhim valley (e.g., an irrigation project in the village of Cado). The two lieutenants then wrote to Lt. Col. Huynh Cong Tinh, deputy commander of the 4th Military Zone, asking for the use of highland military personnel to participate in the village projects. On 25 June 1956 Lt. Col. Tinh wrote a

---

10. Duncanson, *Government*, pp. 289–90.

letter of approval and also notified the military commanders in Haut Donnai province to begin projects to help the highland villagers. Diem, on a visit to the area, was impressed with these efforts and asked Lt. Col. Tinh to submit a report to him concerning highland village projects. A report was prepared by Tinh's secretary, Nguyen Van Long (who used the pseudonym Nguyen Trac Di, under which he later wrote many works on the highlanders for the government), and Touneh Han Tho claims that this led to the formation of the Nha Công-Tác Xã-Hội Miền Thượng (literally "Bureau for Highland Social Work" though usually called the Bureau for Highland Affairs) on 3 July 1957. It was located in Dalat, and Lt. Col. Huynh Cong Tinh became director (the following year he was named province chief of Dong Nai Thuong as Haut Donnai was now called).

SOME MOVEMENT TO NORTH VIETNAM

While these changes were occurring in South Vietnam, highlanders sympathetic to the Viet Minh were moving to North Vietnam in accordance with the Geneva Agreements. In 1957 I was told by some Rhadé that between 5,000 and 6,000 had "gone north" with the Viet Minh, although, in view of data gathered since that time, these figures would seem high.[11] Other sources estimated that around 6,000 highlanders went north with the Viet Minh (out of a total of 140,000); they were mostly Viet Minh military personnel and their families.[12] In North Vietnam these "regroupees" from the southern minorities became the responsibility of a newly formed Minority Committee under the direction of General Chu Van Tan, who was a Nung leader in the Viet Minh movement. The Minority Committee also was responsible for the autonomous zones in the northern highlands.

  Hiar (1.7), a retired Bahnar school teacher, related how one of his best students, Thieng (1.18), was among those from Kontum who elected to go north with the Viet Minh. Thieng was born in 1921, of a Bahnar mother and Vietnamese father from Bong Son in Binh Dinh province. After

  11. This, and other information gathered in a 1957 field trip to the highlands, was contained in the Michigan State University Vietnam Advisory Group, "Preliminary Research Report on the PMS," Saigon 1957, mimeographed, p. 22.
  12. "L'Héroique et lamentable exode d'un million de réfugiés du nord," *Horizons*, Edition Spéciale, 1956, p. 6.

studying with Hiar at the Franco-Bahnar school in Kontum, he continued his studies at the Collège de Qui Nhon. In 1943 he returned to Kontum, married a Vietnamese girl, and was serving as director of a new school in Dak To when the Japanese occupied the province. He returned to Kontum, which was soon taken over by the Viet Minh. When Thieng went north in 1954, he was accompanied by a Bahnar student named Theuh. Hiar reported that in 1956 he received a letter (delivered by hand) from Thieng, who informed his former teacher that he was in Russia studying medicine. Later, Hiar added, there was a rumor in Kontum that Thieng had become a doctor. Thieng's brother, Tul, became the second husband of Pher (1.22), the daughter of Ber (1.10), who was the first highlander in the French colonial civil service.

It appears that some of the highlanders going north went overland, but many of them also journeyed to Qui Nhon where they boarded ships for the voyage to North Vietnam. One of these was Nay Bam, a Hroy (a subgroup of the Jarai), who defected from the Viet Cong in 1971 and was interviewed in Saigon in 1972. He was born in 1939 in the village of Buon Lai Hoi in the mountains of western Phu Yen province (now Phu Khanh province). He recalled that when he was a small boy he saw French troops come into his village searching for Viet Minh. Around 1952 the first Viet Minh cadre came to the village. All were Vietnamese, and initially they only indulged in anti-French propaganda, stressing how the French had exploited the highlanders, using them for corvée. They also related how French troops stole chickens and pigs from the highland villagers.

Subsequently the Viet Minh established the first school in the village, with Vietnamese instructors teaching the Hroy languages, which they spoke fluently and for which they had devised an alphabet. There was no instruction in Vietnamese. The pupils also studied "Highland Culture" which for the most part consisted of singing and dancing. Bam studied at the school for two years, becoming literate in the Hroy language. During this period the village was bombed by French aircraft once and, although no one was injured, a house was burned. On several occasions, however, French army troops came to the village searching for the Viet Minh (who had gone into the forest). The officers were French while the rest of the troops were highlanders, Cambodians, and Moroccans. Bam noted that the officers behaved well, but he claimed that some of the soldiers forced village girls into the forest where they raped them.

After the Geneva Agreements the Viet Minh urged the villagers to go with them to North Vietnam. It was, they said, a beautiful place where the government would assist them in settling. If the villagers remained in the south, the Viet Minh warned, the French would come and burn their houses. Of the approximately two hundred villagers (some forty households), Bam, one other young man named Y Ho, and a Rhadé visitor from M'drak named Y Pum were the only ones to go north. Together they walked over the mountain trails to the port city of Qui Nhon where they boarded a French ship bound for North Vietnam. Bam recalled that there were around eighty highlanders on the ship, including Bahnar, Jarai, Rhadé, Mnong, Jeh, Sedang, Hre, Katu, Cua, Keyong (this may be a subgroup of the Halang), and some Koho-speaking people (see map 2). They landed at Ninh Giang where they remained for one month before going to the newly founded Southern Ethnic Minorities School at Gia Lam, close to Hanoi. There were 400 students from the central highlands as well as Cham and Khmer students. The six-year program that Bam followed included Vietnamese language (no other language was taught), and studies in Vietnamese culture, history, and geography. During his time there, he met Nay Der (2.12) and Nay Phin (2.19), both of whom had gone with the Viet Minh in 1945.

Another Jarai who went north in 1954 was Ksor Wen. He defected from the Viet Cong in March 1968 and was interviewed in July 1972. He had been born in the Mount Ju area south of Cheo Reo around 1938. One day in 1949 the Viet Minh entered his village and took him away with them. They told his kinfolk that he would only be gone for six months while he went to school (he did not return until 1965). Between 1949 and 1954, he worked as a courier for the Viet Minh. Following the Geneva Agreements, Ksor Wen was sent with other Jarai to Qui Nhon where they were put on a Polish ship enroute to Haiphong. After they disembarked, they were taken immediately to the Southern Ethnic Minorities School, where they remained for a primary school education. Wen recalled that there were around 4,000 students, and the highland groups represented included the Jarai, Rhadé, Bahnar, Bru, Pacoh, Cua, Katu, Sedang, Halang, Jeh, Sre, Maa, Mnong (several subgroupings including Chil), Tring, Lat, Chru, Stieng, and Chrau. He described the same curriculum as Nay Bam, adding that they also received political indoctrination (much of which was anti-Ngo Dinh Diem propaganda). In addition, at the advanced level, they had training in use of compasses and map reading (he noted that most of the maps were made in China or Russia). Ksor Wen recalled that the time at the minorities school was pleasant. The students were well-treated, and each received a monthly stipend. They were free to leave the school during leisure time, and he particularly liked visiting Haiphong to view the odd-shaped islands in the Bay of Along. He also pointed out that from time to time Ho Chi Minh and other high ranking officials would visit the school and chat with the students.

The case of another highlander moving north was reported in a U.S. Department of State document.[13] A highlander named Y Lon, who had been trained in North Vietnam, was captured in the south in October 1960 (see below). Although his name would suggest he was Rhadé, Y Lon was born in the Toumorong valley in northern Kontum province, so he probably was Sedang. He had served with the French army in Toumorong. In 1954 he joined the Viet Minh. He went to Qui Nhon where he sailed on a Polish ship for North Vietnam. He related that there were between 6,000 and 7,000 highlanders on board, most of them members of the Viet Minh 120th Regiment commanded by Y Bloc Eban, a Rhadé who had joined the Viet Minh in 1945 and later rose to a relatively high position in the Communist regime. In the north, Y Lon was sent to the school for ethnic minorities at Gia Lam, where he remained until he was sent back to South Vietnam.

The Central Normal School for Ethnic Minorities to which many highlanders were sent had opened in March 1955 with 410 students from ethnic groups of the northern and central highlands. Its goal was to turn out teachers and political cadres from the upland ethnic minorities throughout Vietnam.[14] According to Fall, one of the outstanding students at the school was Y Ngong Nie Kdam, the Rhadé medical technician who had joined the Viet Minh in 1945.[15] Fall writes that he had gone to Russia for further training (he also became a ranking highland leader in the Communist party in Vietnam).

To all appearances, the Hanoi regime's policy toward the ethnic minorities differed drastically from that in the south. It seemed to be a policy of allowing the minorities to maintain their ethnic identity rather than trying to assimilate them as the Saigon administration was attempting to do with

13. Department of State, *A Threat to the Peace: North Viet-Nam's Effort to Conquer South Viet-Nam*, two parts (Washington: Department of State, 1961), part I, p. 29, part II, pp. 30–32.

14. Larry Jackson, "The Vietnamese Revolution and the Montagnards," *Asian Survey* 9, no. 5 (1969): 320.

15. Bernard Fall, *The Two Vietnams: A Political and Military Analysis* (New York: Frederick A. Praeger, 1963), p. 152.

the highlanders, Cham, Khmer, and Chinese. In January 1955 Ho Chi Minh appeared before a gathering of 600 delegates representing 65 minority groups from all over Vietnam and announced plans for autonomous zones to be established in the northern highlands. On 29 April 1955 the Thai-Meo zone was inaugurated. It was named for the Tai-speaking and Meo (Hmong) groups inhabiting the zone which covered an area of 19,000 square miles (nearly one-third of the total area of North Vietnam) in the northwestern portion of the country. In May 1955 an administrative committee with 24 members (2 Vietnamese and 22 minority people) was formed to run the zone. Vietnamese, however, held 51 percent of the administrative posts in the zone. On 10 August 1956 a second autonomous zone called Viet-Bac was established in the northeastern portion of the uplands. Chu Van Tan, director of the Minority Committee, was named president of the zone. In this zone, 72 percent of the administrative positions were held by members of minority groups. In March 1957 a third zone called Lao-Ha-Yen (because it was in the Lao Kay-Yen Bay area of highland Ha Giang province) was formed. Its highly diverse ethnic makeup, however, made it ungovernable and in March 1959 it was quietly abolished.[16]

"SOCIOECONOMIC DEVELOPMENT" IN THE HIGHLANDS

In South Vietnam, Ngo Dinh Diem faced a number of social and economic problems in his effort to build a new national entity. One of the most pressing problems resulted from the vast influx of refugees from the north following the Geneva Agreements. By the time this movement ended, it involved between 900,000 and one million people. According to the General Commission for Refugees, some 15,000 northern highland people were among the refugees. Of these, 15,000 were Nung (most of them part of a French army division), 1,000 Muong, 2,000 Tai-speaking people (Black Tai, White Tai, and Tho), and 600 Yao.[17]

One way the Saigon government hoped to cope with the refugee problem was to settle large numbers of them (all of the Muong, Yao, and Tai-speaking groups in addition to many Vietnamese) in the central

16. Jackson, "The Vietnamese Revolution," pp. 321–22.
17. Buttinger, *Vietnam: A Dragon Embattled*, 2: 900.

highlands. It was noted previously that from the time he became premier Ngo Dinh Diem was concerned about integrating the highlands into the new state. He envisaged this being done through economic development. Bui Van Luong, who served as Commissioner General for Agricultural Development (also as Minister of the Interior and Minister of the Economy), pointed out in a 1971 interview in Saigon that Diem drew heavily on the 1952 Bao Dai scheme for economic development of the central highlands. One aspect of the Bao Dai scheme that particularly appealed to Diem was the relocation of large numbers of Vietnamese into the mountains to provide labor for the economic development. This would relieve population pressures on the coastal plain of central Vietnam. The highlands also would be a likely place to settle many of the refugees from North Vietnam. Moreover, Diem thought that having anti-Communist Catholic refugees in the sparsely populated areas would bring a measure of security against Viet Cong infiltration and movements. Luong noted too that the Vietnamese priests in Dalat and Djiring (see map 3) were very favorable to the influx of northern Catholic refugees to swell their congregations. Luong added that another aspect of the Bao Dai scheme that Diem liked was the idea of "settling highlanders in permanent villages" (a reflection of the erroneous notion that the highland people were nomadic or seminomadic).

A decree dated 12 July 1955 created the Directorate of Economy for the Highlands of Central Vietnam, to be located in Dalat. Initially, it was under the delegate for the highlands (Ton That Hoi), but on 1 January 1956 it was put under the Department of National Economy. Among other things, one of the main functions of the directorate was to implement the economic development programs for the highlands.[18]

Ordinance No. 57 dated 22 October 1956 initiated a new land reform program in South Vietnam. The aim was to increase agricultural production, permit a more equitable distribution of land, and make it possible for tenants to become small landowners. This legislation also provided the basis for new "land development" programs. The Commissariate General for Land Development was established on 23 April 1957. This agency was organized like a ministry directly under control of the president and vice president. The official government report on land development stated that the primary aim of land development was to bring large areas of the

---

18. National Institute of Administration, *Viet Nam Government*, pp. 172–73.

Mekong river delta and the central highlands under cultivation so they could contribute to the national economy.[19] It claimed that of the 5,700,000 hectares in the central highlands only 109,000 had been exploited by the French administration. The report noted that under the land reform law the Vietnamese settlers in the highlands could be given title to the lands they farm.

The report also stressed the security aspects of the program, noting that the sparsely populated parts of the highlands near the western border were amenable to being used as "hideouts for Communists and subversive elements." Therefore, the report added, "the creation of land development centers with settlers having experience in the anti-Communist struggle will greatly contribute to an effective control system in these regions and assure security in the villages of the hinterlands."

In addition to resettling northern refugees and people from overcrowded lowland areas, the Land Development Program for the highlands included among its goals the transformation of the agricultural methods and lifestyle of the indigenous population. The report stated:

> The Land Development policy is to incite them [the highlanders] to group in centers chosen by reason of their closeness to their old habitat and to get used, little by little, to a sedentary life with new agricultural methods, such as clearing with machinery, use of chemical fertilizers, cultivation of industrial plants, etc., to take advantage of social organizations such as dispensaries, maternity hospitals, schools, etc., in a word to have a steadier and easier life.

Financing of the Land Development Program was done through the national budget, with loans made available from the National Agricultural Credit Office to those being settled. There also was assistance from foreign states, particularly the United States and France. Some American aid was direct, with dollars made available for purchase of machinery and fertilizers. Indirect American aid was channeled through counterpart funds for subprojects. French technical aid was administered through the Colombo Plan. Material assistance was given by voluntary agencies, such as the Catholic Relief Services and CARE.[20] By late 1956 implementation of the Land Development Program had begun. Bui Van Luong recalled how Col. Le Van Kim, who had been chief of staff for the 4th Infantry

---

19. Republic of Vietnam, Commissariat General for Land Development, *The Work of Land Development in Vietnam up to June 30, 1959* (Saigon, 1959), pp. 3–7.

20. Ibid., p. 9.

("Montagnard") Division during the Indochina War, was appointed the government representative for the program in the highlands. Given his extensive experience with highlanders during the war, it was thought that he would be adept at administering the program. His headquarters was established at Ban Me Thuot.

A report dated 22 January 1957 and prepared by a member of the USOM Agricultural Division staff recommended that "there should be a clear, just policy regarding Montagnard rights."[21] It noted that "the Montagnard tribes by tradition have certain rights to the land," adding that "it is our understanding that such rights have never been formally defined and recorded." Pointing out that failure to take the highlanders' land claims into consideration could result in disaffection to the Communists, the report suggested three "major steps." The first was "payment of ownership rights," and the second was "opening of newly cultivated lands to the Montagnards as well as to the Vietnamese and in a manner suitable to their customs." The third was "teaching through dialect-speaking agents permanent cultivation techniques."

The views expressed in this report did not reflect those of either most American officials in Saigon or some influential foreign advisors to President Diem. In his assessment that the western provinces and the central highlands were "serving only as hideouts to hostile guerrillas" the Chief of the Division of Refugee Resettlement for USOM reflected the prevalent lack of knowledge of these regions so removed from Saigon.[22] Similarly, Wolf Ladejinsky, an advisor to Diem, described the central highland as a wilderness "little more than Bao Dai's hunting preserve" where "virtually none but nomadic tribesmen lived."[23]

On 16 February 1957 an agreement for American support of the "P.M.S. Land Development" project was signed by the acting director of USOM and a high-ranking Vietnamese official.[24] It described the P.M.S. as an area in which "ninety percent of the inhabitants are tribespeople who

21. "Policy Regarding Land Development Projects," mimeographed, United States Operations Mission (Saigon, January 1957), p. 5.
22. Alfred L. Cardinaux, "Commentary: Alfred L. Cardinaux on Father Harnett," in *Viet Nam: The First Five Years*, ed. Richard Lindholm (Lansing, Michigan: Michigan State University Press, 1959), p. 87.
23. Wolf Ladejinsky, "Agrarian Reform in Free Viet-Nam," *Viet-Nam in World Affairs*, Special Issue, 1960, p. 158.
24. Foreign Operations Administration, United States of America, "Project Proposal and Approval Summary, P. M. S. Land Development" (Saigon, 16 February 1967).

practice a rudimentary and extremely wasteful type of cultivation." The United States agreed to provide $1,053,070 for fiscal year 1957 while the Vietnamese agreed to contribute the piaster equivalent of $2,288,992 (these were counterpart funds generated by the U.S.-financed commercial import program). Scheduled to begin in March, the project called for resettlement in 1957 of 2,500 families (approximately 12,500 people) in 25 villages on 3,730 hectares of "land belonging to the National Domain." These new villages would be located near Ban Me Thuot and Buon Ho in Darlac, An Khe and Kannak in Binh Dinh, and Cheo Reo in Pleiku. The initial settlers were to be from overpopulated portions of the central coast, with each family receiving five hectares. Another goal of this first phase in the Land Development project was to be an "attempt to aid autochtonous highlanders." This would be achieved by "orienting the highlanders towards grouping into communities and rational exploitation of their lands."

According to Bui Van Luong, the Highland Land Development Program was launched with an "agricultural fair" at Ban Me Thuot on 22 February 1957. Organized by Le Van Kim, there were floats, bands, speeches, highlanders in their "native costumes," and an elephant race. The gala air, however, was shattered when a would-be assassin broke through the crowd and fired a pistol at Ngo Dinh Diem. The bullet missed the president, but struck the minister of agriculture, seriously wounding him. The captured assailant was described as a "Communist agent bent on killing Diem." It was then clear to me that the program would have problems.

While in Paris on a fellowship in 1953–1954, I was able to gather considerable data on the highlanders in various library collections. Most of the available material had been written by French missionaries, administrators, and military personnel, and it included folklore and history (much of which was reported in the earlier volume). In March 1956 I went to South Vietnam with the Michigan State University Vietnam Advisory Group (MSUG). As part of MSUG's studies of government ministries to recommend reforms, I traveled to Ban Me Thuot, Pleiku, and Kontum in June 1956 with the goal of interviewing some civil servants in the Provincial Information Service. My Vietnamese assistant and I flew on Air Vietnam to Ban Me Thuot where we conducted interviews (most of the personnel were Vietnamese). I was also able to visit surrounding Rhadé villages and begin taking some ethnographic notes and some photographs as well.

For the first time I experienced the unfailing hospitality of the highlanders. Also, for the first time I saw the rousseauean late afternoon scene in a highland village when the air is still and a thin veil of smoke from the evening cooking fires settles amidst the longhouses and luxuriant foliage all around. Villagers walk in silence, returning from the forest and fields with their backbaskets laden with wild fruits, vegetables, and edible flowers. Villagers also gather by the nearby stream to bathe, while downstream the elephants frolic in the water against a backdrop of rich green bamboo groves.

Long-established Rhadé Kpa villages normally have between 20 and 40 longhouses, invariably oriented in the same direction. Like all houses of highlanders, they are constructed on piling (which prevents wild animals from entering as well as allowing good ventilation and in some cases is a measure against flooding). The Rhadé houses also reflect the common highland pattern of employing locally available building material (roofing of tin and aluminum were later to be used widely as a result of American programs). The frame of the house commonly is of solid hardwood logs in the case of the Rhadé (elephants are required to haul them). Bamboo is used extensively for floors (in Rhadé houses there is one layer of bamboo logs over which split bamboo is placed, providing a floor mat), partitions, and external walls. Roofs are of thick thatching. Many windows (which can be closed with bamboo screens) allow light and ventilation in most highland houses.

I was to realize later that the Rhadé houses, with their striking scale, style, and construction, are the most impressive in the highlands. The large hardwood frame is of hand-hewn logs that are fit together on the ground and then raised as barns were on American farms in the past. Divination determines the site of the house and also is involved in house construction among the Rhadé. When a location has been adjudged favorable, an offering of seven grains of rice, wrapped in cloth on which alcohol and chicken blood have been poured, is made to the spirits. Hardwood timber is selected not only for its fine quality but also with regard to omens. For example, a tree on which a certain type of orchid grows is avoided, and if, with the first strikes of the ax, water runs, the tree is not felled.

A propitiatory offering precedes construction and, if an elephant is used in transporting logs, a ritual is held to protect the animal from accidents. Prior to the placement of the large columns which constitute the piling and main support of the structure, a chicken is offered. Use of "male" and "female" bamboo in certain combinations is well defined in the construction. When the house is three-quarters completed, a ritual offering is made to the spirits, and when the principal hearth is finished, a chicken or a pig is slaughtered. When the house stands ready for the family to move in, a three-day celebration is held with a pig and buffalo sacrificed to honor the mistress of the house.

While these ideational principles are important in the house site and construction, the final ritual honoring the mistress of the house signals the importance of social organization in the floor plan and social use of the house. Most houses in the highlands are shared by more than one nuclear family (parents and children), and some aspects of the kinship system, particularly prescribed residence, affect the house form and interior floor plan. Generally, among those highland groups that have unilineal descent, i.e., descent traced through either the female line (matrilineal descent) or the male line (patrilineal descent), the living arrangements in the house tend to be more rigidly defined than they are among those who trace descent through both the male and female lines (bilateral descent). For those with unilinear descent there is a prescription for the married children to remain either with the wife's parents (matrilocal residence the rule when descent is matrilineal) or with the husband's parents (patrilocal residence the rule when descent is patrilineal).

Among those with bilateral descent—this includes the Mon Khmer-speaking Bahnar, Rengao, Sedang, Halang, Jeh, and Hre, as well as the Austronesian-speaking Jarai Arap and Jarai Tabuan (see map 2)—the pattern is for married children to reside temporarily with both sets of parents (ambilocal residence), eventually settling with one or the other depending on where they are needed. Many of them establish their own households (neolocal residence).

The Rhadé, Jarai, Roglai, Chru, Mnong, Sre, Lat, and Chrau-speaking people have matrilineal descent. In each of those groups a house is occupied by an extended family, consisting of parents and their married daughters with their families. In most instances these groups have longhouses, the length of which is determined by the number of nuclear families in the residence. The Bru, Pacoh, Katu, Stieng, and Maa have patrilineal descent, but they do not have longhouses.

At the front of the Rhadé house there is a large log veranda (*adring*) reached by ascending steps hewn in a log or a wood plank, very often decorated with carved female breasts. Verandas of varying sizes are found

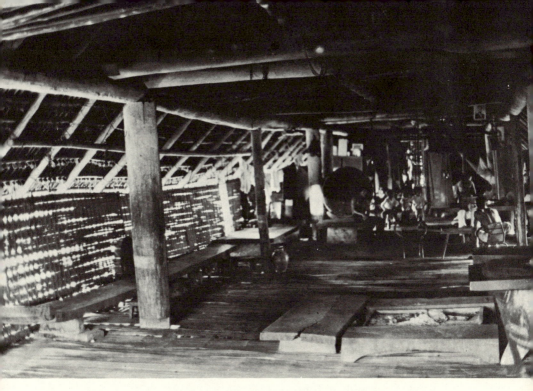

The main room (*tung gah*) of a Rhadé house in the vicinity of Ban Me Thuot

in most highland houses and they serve a variety of functions. Tools and chicken baskets are stored there, and the veranda provides an excellent place for sunning paddy, cotton, coconut shells (used for kindling), and the many kinds of roots and bark used in making alcohol. A common highland scene is a woman or girl husking paddy on the veranda. This is done by placing the paddy in a hardwood mortar and pounding it with a long-handled wooden pestle.

The female breast motif is repeated on the beam over the main portal and the crossbeam in the center of the house, along with lizards and buffalo horns. Immediately inside there is a large room (*tung gah*) which contains a hearth and benches of varying length hewn from hardwood logs. A large drum, used on ceremonial occasions, is suspended from the rafters. As in all highland houses, the area along the walls is devoted to storage, and in this large room family belongings are kept. Bins contain paddy for the family's use, and there are baskets, the most common of which are those with shoulder straps so the basket can be worn like a knapsack to carry such things as paddy, wild fruits and vegetables, purchases from the market, firewood, and gourds of drinking water. As in most highland houses, there are the inevitable alcohol jars and gongs, both highly prized prestige items that reflect the relative wealth of the family.

Jars for making alcohol vary in size and in quality. Generally, the older jars are considered to be of great value and many of them are said by the highlanders to date "from the time of the ancestors." Most of the old jars have a worn dark brown or black glaze, and some would surely command a good price in the world antique market. Occasionally one also encounters large blue and white porcelain jars which have excellent glazes and art work. The Rhadé differentiate between "male" and "female" old jars, and both the Rhadé and Bahnar have myths that describe the ancient jars as once having been live animals that inhabited swampy areas. Upon being struck with arrows, they were transformed into jars. Normally the old jars never leave the house, but among the Stieng highly valued *srung* jars are very often part of the bride price, so they move from one family to another. Newer jars usually have a light brown glaze and a dragon motif on the side. They are produced in coastal cities by the Vietnamese and shipped to the highlands in trucks.

Jar alcohol is normally prepared through a process of fermenting rice, and occasionally some highlanders make it using maize. During the Vietnam War it was discovered that the bulgur wheat distributed through the American aid program made quite palatable alcohol. Among the Rhadé Kpa, the first step in the alcohol preparation is to mix a ferment (*k'pei*) consisting of rice flour, wild ginger root, and bark from two kinds of local trees. The second step begins by boiling partially husked rice, which is then spread on a large circular flat basket and placed on the veranda to dry in the sun. After it is dried, some of the ferment is powdered and mixed with it. The third phase involves placing a mixture of rice bran and broken husks on the bottom of a deep basket, then pouring the mash of cooked rice and ferment over it. The remainder of the basket is filled with more bran and husks, and the basket is left to stand for a day or two. The contents of the basket are poured into a jar, which is sealed with banana leaves and allowed to stand for at least one week.

Jars of alcohol are integral parts of all highland ceremonies and celebrations (which often take place in the house). Traditionally, all of the highlanders were animists with large pantheons of spirits of varying kinds. Most groups have spirits they call *yang*, or a cognate word thereof, regardless of whether their language is of the Austronesian or Mon Khmer stocks. The religious practitioners include shamans and sorcerers, and some groups have witchcraft. Family heads and village leaders organize and often officiate at rituals, which are held on innumerable occasions. Rituals mark every phase of a highlander's life as well as the planting cycle. When sickness or misfortune strikes, rituals are held to propitiate the spirits, and ritual welcomes are accorded visitors to a village.

Throughout the highlands there is a similarity in the format of ceremonies associated with the spirits. All of them involve invocations to explicit deities, accompanied by offerings of food and a jar (or jars) of alcohol. Some offerings may involve slaughtering a small animal such as a chicken or goat but an important ritual requires that a pig or buffalo be killed. Buffalos are tied to a stake and slaughtered slowly with sabers and/or spears. The flesh and blood of the animals are served in the feasting, which also involves all of the guests drinking alcohol through bamboo tubes directly from the jar.

All during such rituals, a row of men play the gongs, and their haunting music often can be heard when walking through a highland village. The Rhadé Kpa have three types of gongs, all of metal with upturned rims. The very large gong, called *char*, gives off a resonant sound when struck with the wooden hammer. Small in size but similar in appearance are the *knah* gongs that always are in sets of six, with each gong having a name that indicates its relative size. The third type of gong is called *ching*, which has a circular indentation in the center where it is struck. In the past, these gongs were obtained in Cambodia and Laos; those made in Cambodia are called *ching kur* while those of Lao manufacture are known as *ching lao*. In recent times, the Rhadé have bought only Vietnamese gongs (*ching yuan*), which they consider inferior both in strength and sound.

Many Rhadé rituals take place in the main room of the house. The area immediately inside the entrance is *wang bhok* where visitors are welcomed. *Wang tung* is the middle section of the room where rituals take place and jars of alcohol are tied to stakes. The rear of the room, *tung mnie*, is where the females gather during the celebrations. This does not imply that they play a lesser role, however, because in the highland societies with matrilineal descent (the Rhadé, Jarai, Chru, Roglai, Mnong, Sre, Lat, and Chrau-speaking people) women play an important role. The women take the men in marriage, and the couple resides at the bride's house. The eldest female in residence is the head of the household and has ownership of all the family goods (house, harvests, animals, and land). At rituals held in the

Stieng women fishing with hand-traps

house, she normally has an important role, such as making the offering of gratitude to Yang Mdie, the Rhadé Rice Spirit in a postharvest ceremony.

The section of the Rhadé house to the rear of the main room consists of a long corridor containing hearths on one side and on the other a series of small compartments (*adu pit*) where family members sleep. The first compartment is occupied by the eldest female and her husband and children, while each remaining compartment is allotted to the other females and their families. The last compartment is reserved for single adult females. At the rear of the house is a small entrance used only by household members.

In each compartment there are the personal belongings of the occupants. Clothes are kept in baskets. Here one is apt to see the long-handled ax with a small, very sharp blade that is the most common artifact in the highlands. Highlanders carry these axes with them as they move through the forest both for protection and for cutting any wild edible fruit or vegetable they may encounter. These axes are used also to fell trees, split wood, hew timber, cut and shave rattan, dig roots out of the fields, clear brush, and break earth.

Traditionally highlanders produced their own weapons, tools, mats, baskets, and clothes. Cotton is still widely grown, and while some highland women make dyes, most thread and dyes now are purchased in local markets. Weaving, however, still is a woman's activity and the Rhadé looms are set up either in the main room or under the house (where wood is stored and where pigs often are penned). Men weave mats and baskets and make tools and weapons.

Hunting, trapping, and fishing have always been sources of important food supplements in the highlanders' diets. Wildlife abounds in the highlands. Big game includes tigers, elephants, panthers, several kinds of wild oxen (including gaurs and koupreys), and various types of bears. In the past there were rhinoceros, but none has been seen since the 1940s and they are thought to be extinct. Deer are plentiful as are wild boars, porcupines, jackals, otters, mongooses, hares, skunks, and squirrels (including flying squirrels). There are many different kinds of wild cats, among them three types of civets—madagascar civets, binturongs, and palm civets. Langurs, macaques, gibbons, and the common Rhesus monkey swing through the forests. On the edges of some lakes and rivers there are crocodiles and other reptiles, including several types of lizards, pythons, and cobras. Rats are trapped, roasted, and eaten. There also is a great variety of birds, among them numerous kinds of pheasants, quails, falcons, herons, ducks, hawks, eagles, vultures, harriers, cranes, rails, coots, painted snipes, and owls.

Traditionally, crossbows, spears, sabers, and knives were used in warfare and in hunting, although now the highlanders are apt to use firearms if they are obtainable. Still in use are various kinds of traps and snares and fish traps fashioned out of split bamboo and rattan. Fishing nets are made in the villages, and they also can be purchased in the market towns. Many highland villages have one or more specialists in working metals purchased from Chinese and Vietnamese merchants (although during the Vietnam War metals from American army junk piles and also from bomb craters were used). These specialists produce spearheads, knives, sabers, ax blades, plowshares, and other metal parts of farm tools. All of these weapons and tools are stored on the rafters of the house.

As in all highland villages, the Rhadé rely on their fields and kitchen gardens for their rice, vegetables, and fruits. Highlanders farm upland dry rice in swiddens, and where there is relatively level land and available water sources they cultivate wet-rice in paddies. Although the swidden method varies from one highland group to another and even within individual groups, there are some basic common characteristics. Essentially, it is a system of rotating agriculture wherein during the dry season (for high-landers located in areas affected by the southwest monsoon this would be January through March, while for those in the path of the northeast monsoon it would be from June to August) a given field is cleared, and the cut wood and brush are dried and burned. After the rains begin, the field is farmed. The duration of the farming period depends on the adjudged fertility of the soil. Following the farming period, the field is left to fallow until a new growth has appeared, and then it is cultivated again.

The selection of a new swidden is never haphazard, and highlanders rely upon a knowledge of the forest and soils passed down through generations. The Rhadé, for example, consider red soil good for growing rice but avoid sandy soil. The Rengao judge greyish soil to be the best for upland dry rice. The Bru and Katu view the presence of large trees to be a sign of soil fertility while the Jarai regard the excrement from a certain type of worm as an indication that the earth is ideal for rice farming. Some groups combine their careful scrutiny of soil and flora with divination; among the Mnong Chil, for example, some men sleep on the prospective site and will farm the area if they have a "favorable dream."

In all of the highland groups the division of farm labor is the same. Men fell the trees (usually, large trees are left standing) while the women and children cut the brush. Men rake the debris into piles and burn it, carefully guarding the fires. There is some variation in planting. With some groups the men broadcast the seeds, and with others they make holes with dibble sticks, after which the women follow to plant the seeds.

Paddy fields are found in relatively level marshy areas, valley bottom land, volcanic depressions, and on hillside terraces. The Lat, who live in the vicinity of Dalat (the name means "Lat Water"), are the only highlanders who practice wet-rice cultivation exclusively. Located at a high elevation, their paddy terraces sweep up the slope of Lang Bian Mountain. To the southeast, the Chru have paddy fields on bottom land and in terraces. They have an elaborate irrigation system that taps water from the tributaries feeding the Danhim river and channel it through a system of canals and dikes. Every Chru village has a "water chief," who is responsible for mustering villagers to clear the canals and repair the dikes before each planting season.

Highlanders farm numerous secondary crops in the swiddens, some-times in paddy fields, and in the kitchen gardens located close to the houses.

The Rhadé Kpa devote a section of the swidden to maize while the Jarai and Katu plant maize between the rows of dry rice. Another common crop is tobacco, which most often is grown near the house. Kitchen garden crops include squash, gourds, peanuts, tomatoes, various kinds of beans, lettuce, pumpkins, lemon grass, taro, ginger, onions, mushrooms, carrots, garlic, yams, cabbage, chili peppers, cucumbers, pineapples, manioc, and sugar cane. Banana trees abound in the villages, and usually there are some lime, orange, coconut, guava, jackfruit, grapefruit, papaya, mango, and avocado trees. Kapok trees and areca palms with betel vines climbing the trunks are found in many villages. Coffee trees often grow near some of the Rhadé Kpa houses, and the Hre and Cua like to cultivate tea plants in their gardens.

When we finished interviewing in the Ban Me Thuot area we decided to visit Lac Thien (called Poste du Lac by the French) farther south. Along Route 21, there was a succession of Rhadé villages of the Bih subgroup. It was interesting to note that away from the influence of the town, most of the men wore only their traditional loincloths while the women went about in long skirts but were bare above the waist. A small river had to be crossed on a ferry poled by men, and the country became thick with forests. Suddenly there was the lake at Lac Thien, beautiful in a primeval setting of green mountains, reflecting the blue sky in its still waters (there were crocodiles in the marshes at one end).

The Vietnamese district information officer took us to a nearby Mnong Rlam village, where we were invited to a buffalo sacrifice. Seated on floormats in the main room of a longhouse, we drank from the jars (the mixture had a smokey flavor) as an elderly man poured water into it to measure the prescribed amount of libation. Chanting an invocation, the eldest woman of the longhouse placed bracelets around our wrists (this turned out to be a common part of celebrations to welcome visitors in societies with matrilineal descent).

Afterward the district chief insisted we visit Bao Dai's hunting lodge, located on a promontory above the lake. It presented a stark contrast to the Mnong Rlam village. The dirt road suddenly gave way to a concrete drive lined with flowers and ahead loomed a French-style chalet. Inside there was a large main room with comfortable furniture and in one corner was a small bar. Hung along the walls were game trophies—a gaur head and elephant tusks. A tiger skin covered the floor by the fireplace. A sizable generator supplied electricity for lights and air conditioners in the bed-rooms (where neatly curtained windows looked out over the lake) as well as for a walk-in freezer for game in the basement.

From Ban Me Thuot we flew to Pleiku (the small airport was located near the large Catecka tea plantation and also served Kontum). The Jarai Hodrung, like the Rhadé, trace descent through the female line and married couples reside in the wife's parents' house. The Jarai longhouses, however, are not as solidly constructed as those of the Rhadé. Many of the Jarai in the vicinity of Pleiku farm paddy fields located in volcanic depressions, and they also have large herds of cattle that graze on the plain of the Pleiku plateau.

Although the visit to Kontum was brief, we were able to visit villages adjacent to the town. The Bahnar Jolong and Rengao trace descent through both the male and female lines (bilateral descent). Residence consequently is not rigidly defined. Both Bahnar and Rengao houses are rectangular and constructed on piling. There is a large room with a hearth for receiving visitors and holding rituals. Several rooms behind are family quarters. The traditional Bahnar houses are of wood and bamboo with thatched roofs. In the Kontum area most of the villagers are Christian and the houses have covered verandas, tile roofs, and mud and straw wattled walls, reflecting outside (particularly Vietnamese) influence. Non-Christian villages have the traditional men's house in the center of the settlement. Constructed on piling, these structures have high, sloping thatched roofs often graced with symbolic decorations. Inside there are several hearths but no partitions. Young, unmarried men and boys sleep in the men's house, and it also is a gathering place for village males. The elders convene there, and the walls often are covered with skulls and other symbols of ritual sacrifices. In many villages the men's house is taboo for females.

Agriculture in the immediate vicinity of Kontum is unique in the highlands. Along the Bla river the Bahnar Jolong and Rengao have extensive fields on higher ground where they cultivate rainfed rice on permanent fields. These fields are farmed for five or six years, after which they are left to fallow. When wild growth appears, the fields are fenced in and used for pasturage.

When I next went to the highlands in March 1957, it was at a time when Vietnamese government programs for altering the mountain people's way of life were just beginning. On the drive up Route 20 from Saigon the scenery changed from the lush, fluvial countryside near Bien Hoa to the sometimes harsh terrace zone with its twisted forests. As Route 20 continued in a northeasterly direction, it began to ascend the Blao plateau, and at Kilometer 113 there were curious huge rocks and the first highland villages of the Maa. On the plateau were thick forests, scattered Maa villages, and the tea estates with their neat rows of glistening plants following the gentle contours of the land. We stopped at the National School of Agriculture, Forestry, and Animal Husbandry (built with American aid in 1955). There were eleven Rhadé students from the vicinity of Ban Me Thuot being trained in a program designed to bring modern farming methods to the highland people. These students were accepted at the school with only a primary school certificate while the Vietnamese were required to have secondary school diplomas. Training for the highlanders was described by the school's director as "practical," i.e., it focused on the use of light agricultural machines, chemical fertilizer, and rotation of crops. The highland students leaving the school would become "agricultural agents," each in charge of a ten-family "model village" to which highlanders would be moved. Among other things the agents would maintain model gardens in some villages. The director explained that by the end of 1957 there would be thirty "model villages," and with their modern farming methods they would be examples for the highlanders of the standard of living they might achieve. Each model village would have two hundred families, and each family would receive two hectares (each resettled Vietnamese family was to receive five hectares). The director also explained that primary school education for highland villages was being revamped. All instruction would be in Vietnamese. With the assistance of USOM, a 1,600,000 piasters (the official rate at that time was 35 piasters to the American dollar) project was being launched to create 117 primary school classes in Kontum and Pleiku to bring Vietnamese education to the highland villagers.

From Blao, Route 20 continued to ascend past extensive tea estates to Djiring, after which it wound through thickening rain forest which suddenly gave way to pine forests in the cooler air of the higher elevations. With its profusion of chalets, Dalat might have been a town in the French Alps, and the Vietnamese seemed curiously out of place (the children had a healthier color than they did in Saigon). The marketplace, its stalls crammed with tempting fresh vegetables, reflected the town's function as a center for truck gardening. Highlanders could be seen here and there carrying portions of tree barks, on which sprays of orchids grew, to the market where Vietnamese buyers transported them to Saigon.

The Chief of the Regional Directorate for Agriculture outlined the goals of the agricultural development program being implemented. He first pointed out that the population of the mountain region was sparse and that the highlanders only used the swidden method, which he considered "backward and wasteful." His plan was to set aside 200 hectares in each province for resettlement of 200 highland families. Each family would receive one hectare for farming under the guidance of Vietnamese and highlander agricultural agents. If the highlanders refused to move to the new villages, the province chief would ban swidden farming, leaving them no alternative but to move.

Early in April 1957 I organized a field research trip into the highlands (with Frederick Wickert of the MSUG staff) to gather data on indigenous land tenure systems. Among the Vietnamese and Americans in Saigon there was a current notion that it was not necessary to worry about highlanders' land claims in implementing the Land Development Program because they had no land tenure systems. Wickert and I intended gathering preliminary information to demonstrate that such tenure systems did indeed exist, and we also hoped to discuss with highland leaders some ideas for resolving the land question. Approval for this research was obtained from Wesley Fishel, Chief Advisor for MSUG, and also from the Vietnamese government. The communication from the Secretary of State at the Presidency, however, recommended that anyone going to the highlands to study Vietnamese-highlander relations should talk only with the province chiefs rather than with "local people" in order "to avoid any possible misunderstanding." [25]

Riding in a jeep-station wagon with a Vietnamese driver who called himself Masourin, we drove north from Saigon on Route 13 to reach Route 14, passing through the territory that had been described by some of the French explorers (such as Gautier) in the late nineteenth century (see map 3). Route 14 was in bad condition due to the neglect of the war years. It wound over the dry, rolling country of the Stieng, passing Mount Bara, which rose like a large mound covered with scrubby growth. Farther

25. Nguyen Huu Chau, the Secretary of State at the Presidency to the Chief Advisor of MSUG (Saigon, 2 April 1957).

north, there were massive rain forests of mixed growths that crowded one another in the struggle to reach the sunlight. Tangled vines and orchids clung to the massive hardwood trees. At Trois Frontières (named for the three frontiers of Cochinchina, Annam, and Cambodia that once converged here), there was the weathered monument to Henri Maitre, the French explorer and writer who in 1912 had been slain by the much-feared Mnong chief Pu Trang Lung in a nearby village. There also was a small nondescript settlement of wood and thatched houses and shops, one of which was a restaurant boasting a menu of venison and other wild game.

As Route 14 continued northeast in the direction of Ban Me Thuot, the forest gave way in places to Rhadé villages with their rows of longhouses and granaries on the edge of the settlements. Children (some of them nude) scampered about, and on the large verandas of the main entrances to the houses, women worked, weaving cloth or husking rice. Along the road, highland men, women, and children walked in single file. The men carried crossbows and machetes while the women had backbaskets filled with gourds of water, produce from the forest, or firewood. As the vehicle passed, they invariably stopped and bowed, a gesture of respect that the French had expected.

Route 14 entered Ban Me Thuot from the south, passing through Buon Ale-A, where the Christian and Missionary Alliance was located (see map 6). On the hillside by the road stood the three "Italian villas" that Gordon Smith had constructed in 1950. Looking like the "villas" one might have seen in California or Florida in the 1930s and 1940s, these houses seemed impressive in this setting. In front of them, a carefully trimmed lawn graced with a large traveler palm swept down to the edge of Route 14. Farther on, the road passed the sumptuous hunting lodge of Bao Dai. It was a large rambling building in a European style (referred to by the local highlanders as "le palais"), set in a tropical garden and surrounded by a high wall. In the town the road was shaded by magnificent gnarled old trees. On the right side was the provincial administrative headquarters, a collection of masonry buildings with tile roofs. They reflected a French provincial style adapted to the tropics: a veranda with rococo touches, French windows, and high ceilings with fans. The former *résidence* was built on piling and had a large veranda hidden by multicolored bougainvilleas.

Farther along was the sports stadium where the Oath Ceremonies were held and where the recent "agricultural fair" had taken place. Behind the

stadium was the impressive guest lodge of Bao Dai (called the Grand
Bungalow), a large, hardwood adaptation of a Rhadé longhouse. It was
now occupied by the American military advisors (MAAG) to the 23rd
Division, whose headquarters were located nearby. As a result the Grand
Bungalow had taken on the look of an American military garrison. Part of
the garden had become the "motor pool" with rows of jeeps and other
military vehicles, and there were the innumerable signs identifying offices,
quarters, the mess hall, and clubs. There were the inevitable high fence and
military policemen guarding the only entrance. Close by was the former
Groupe Scholaire Antomarchi (now called the Nguyen Du School), consisting of some frame buildings interspersed with Rhadé longhouses that
served as dormitories. The school director's house resembled a French
chalet.

Beyond the stadium to the north was the Vietnamese quarter, the center
of which was the market, a crowded collection of stalls and stands covered
by a roof. Around it were the usual Chinese two-storied shop houses built
of masonry and low, one-storied Vietnamese shops with tile roofs. There
also were some Indian shops, almost always specializing in cloth. Some of
the Chinese and Vietnamese vendors catered exclusively to highlanders,
selling new alcohol jars, sets of gongs, fish nets, and metal for making
implements and weapons. The Vietnamese residential section was a jumble
of small frame houses crowded together.

Wickert and I were received hospitably by the American military
advisors, who provided lodging. Immediately, we began interviewing
some of the provincial officials, beginning with the Vietnamese province
chief. He lamented that the highlanders working in the administration
were trained in French and were not literate in Vietnamese (it is noted
below that several of the highland civil servants had studied in Hue and Qui
Nhon). As a result, the province chief noted, "one Vietnamese clerk is
worth three highland clerks." The highlanders, he emphasized, must learn
the Vietnamese language and ways (such as wearing Vietnamese clothes).
The province chief explained that he had no contact with the Highland
Law Court, relying instead on his highland assistants Y Blieng Hmok,
Y Dhuat Nie Kdam, and Y Blu Nie Buon Drieng to deal with any
problems arising in the court or in any of the villages. One current problem
concerned the Vietnamese traders (about thirty of them) that the province
chief allowed to circulate in Darlac. They offered villagers attractive
articles the highlanders could not afford and this led to conflicts. Also, the

A Rhadé proprietress of clan land

province chief was annoyed at what he described as the highlanders' belief that they owned all of the land and everything on it. Conflict ensued when Vietnamese sought to settle on land or fish in some of the streams.

We met with the three highland assistants the province chief had mentioned. As was noted previously, Y Blieng Hmok had studied in Qui Nhon and subsequently worked in the French administration. When the Viet Minh assumed control of the highlands in August 1945, Y Blieng was one of the highland leaders who joined them. Not long after, however, he returned to his civil service post at Ban Me Thuot. Y Dhuat Nie Kdam had received training in Hue, and in 1954 Y Blu Nie Buon Drieng was among the first highlanders to study at the Administration School in Dalat. All three, therefore, were well versed in the Vietnamese language. From them we obtained information on the Rhadé land tenure system.

According to Rhadé legend, the original owners of all land were members of the Nie Kdam clan, but since they did not work hard in their fields they were forced in time to relinquish land to other clans (all Rhadé clans are organized into two phratries—the Eban, which includes clans with other names such as Hmok, Ayun, Buon Krong, Mlo, Hdok, Kbuor, Knul (or Knuol), and Hwing, and the Nie, which includes clan names beginning with "Nie" and the Buon To). Clans claim certain territory, the boundaries of which are known to members. The guardian of this territory is the *po lan* (proprietor of the land), and this normally is the eldest female of that part of the clan that claims ownership and lives in the territory. She protects the land for the clan, designating who can farm, hunt, fish, and cut timber in the territory. She also has a number of duties, such as marking the boundaries of the land, periodically performing rituals for clan ancestors, and dealing with any violations of clan land.

Wickert and I were warmly welcomed by the American missionaries, Reverend N. Robert Ziemer and Reverend Edward Mangham. (Gordon Smith, who had founded the mission, and his family had moved to a new mission they were organizing for the World Evangelization Crusade in Danang.) We discussed the relations between the highlanders and Vietnamese, and the two missionaries outlined some of the complaints they had received from Rhadé in their congregation. They concerned the claim that Vietnamese were settling on land owned by the Rhadé, the collapse of the village medical program organized by the French, the superimposition of a Vietnamese administrative system on Rhadé villages without regard for indigenous leadership, and what the Rhadé considered the arrogant attitude of the Vietnamese in general. The missionaries also agreed to provide us with Rhadé interpreters to visit villages. We interviewed in Buon Ale-A, Buon Kosier, and Buon Pan Lam, all in the vicinity of Ban Me Thuot. The villagers, like the Rhadé civil servants, emphasized that they did not claim all of the land but only certain territories that were well delineated.

Although our interviews were focused on land tenure and other aspects of Rhadé society, the interviewees invariably began to complain about the Vietnamese. As the missionaries had indicated, they were concerned about Vietnamese taking land claimed by Rhadé. In mid-1956 northern Vietnamese refugees were settled in two large villages (Ha Lan A and Ha Lan B), located along Route 14 thirty-two kilometers north of Ban Me Thuot. The villagers cited cases of these settlers and other squatters moving onto land that Rhadé villagers had cleared in preparation for planting. There also was resentment among the villagers and civil servants over what they considered discrimination against them in the administration. Those working in the provincial services had been trained by the French, and now that the administration was Vietnamized they felt alienated. The large influx of Vietnamese was clearly a threat to the Rhadé, who feared that they would soon be outnumbered.

The Rhadé villagers also volunteered information on the "Viet Minh" (as they continued to call the Viet Cong). They said that "many" (estimates were around 5,000 to 6,000) from Darlac went north after the Geneva Agreements. They also said that Rhadé and Vietnamese guerrillas were operating in the more remote parts of the province. There were reports of Vietnamese cadremen completely adapting to Rhadé ways, such as wearing loincloths and breaking their teeth (which the Rhadé traditionally did in a puberty rite). Communist propaganda continued with the same theme of "autonomy for the highlanders" as it had during the Indochina War. Broadcasts in Rhadé and Jarai were being beamed to the highlands on Radio Hanoi.

Over an incredibly bad road, we journeyed to Ban Don where we met with Y Keo (Ama Kham Suk), the nephew of Khunjanob and judge for the Ban Me Thuot highlander law court. He was a pleasant, stout man who wore a Lao sarong and lived in a Lao style house. He proudly displayed his French medals and awards and explained that he traveled to Ban Me Thuot for five days each month to hear cases at the court. He also outlined the land tenure system of the Rhadé, relating it to the kinship system as the others had done. As we were leaving, elephants were gathering by the house, and Y Keo pointed out that they would soon form a trade caravan to go to southern Laos, inquiring whether we might be interested in joining it.

Back in Ban Me Thuot, I met with Father Roger Bianchetti, a member of the Kontum Mission, who was training young highlanders to cultivate coffee and process the beans for sale. He echoed the same views as the American missionaries concerning the highlanders' complaints about the Vietnamese. He made the observation that the highlanders felt like "conquered people."

Leaving Ban Me Thuot on Route 14 in the direction of Pleiku, Wickert and I stopped near the northern Vietnamese refugee villages to visit the small group of young Americans sponsored by the International Voluntary Services (IVS), a private organization that had been founded in 1953. The purpose of IVS was to recruit trained technicians to work in rural development projects, and in 1956 IVS signed a contract with USOM for volunteers to come to Vietnam. The small group in the highlands included the first volunteers to arrive, and they had begun work in February 1957. Initially they had agricultural and nursing programs for the Vietnamese settlers, and subsequently they began working among the highland villagers. Eventually they organized the Ea Kmat Seed Propagation Center near Ban Me Thuot, and it grew into an important agricultural development station.

North of Buon Ho (see map 4) Route 14 ran through the heavily wooded, rocky Mount Dreh pass (where in 1954 the French army Mobile Group 100 had suffered its last ambush by the Viet Minh). Jarai villages began to appear along the road as it ascended a green and undulating plateau that swept up to the Hodrung peak (a sacred place for the Jarai who believe that it was at this peak that their ancestors emerged from the subterranean world). Not far from the peak was the town of Pleiku, which in 1957 was a small town with only several thousand inhabitants. Much of it was hidden under pines, the only trees in the vicinity. The province chief's house (the former *résidence*) was built on piling and had a large veranda. Nearby was a collection of Jarai Hodrung longhouses. A Vietnamese settlement had sprung up along Route 14, with open-front shops, a small market, and a gasoline station.

In Pleiku, Wickert and I met with provincial officials to discuss their views on the current situation and land development. The Vietnamese province chief (who not long after was killed in an automobile accident) described relations between lowland and highland people as being very good. Highlanders in the civil service participated in social gatherings with the Vietnamese. The province chief himself went to highland village celebrations, where he ate the food (noting that he did this in spite of it not being "sanitary") but he only pretended to drink from the jars. It was, he felt, necessary to show respect (although he admitted that he did not like their habit of going about half naked, and he wished that the men would wear trousers instead of the brief loincloth). The province chief declared that land tenure was a problem because the Jarai (whom he described as the only ethnic group in the province) only claim the land they are farming and they move constantly because of their farming methods.

Interviews with highland civil servants and villagers proved the province chief wrong. In addition to the Jarai, Pleiku also had numerous Bahnar. Farming methods varied from swidden to permanent paddy farming. Permanently used land, such as paddy fields, gardens, and house sites, is considered family property and is inherited through the female line. A family has usufruct of its swiddens whether they are being farmed or are fallowing.

As in Darlac, many of the highland villagers and civil servants we encountered complained about ill treatment by the Vietnamese. Vietnamese soldiers sometimes entered villages to steal animals. In the Pleiku market, Vietnamese would pluck fruits and vegetables from the highlanders' backbaskets. Illiterate highlanders were constantly being cheated by merchants because they could not understand the numbers on the new piaster notes. As in Darlac, some of the civil servants expressed the view that they were relegated to an inferior status by the Vietnamese officials.

North of Pleiku, Route 14 ran close to Lake Tenneung, a placid body of water located in a deep depression. According to Jarai legend, a Cham army invading the highlands was drowned in this lake. Beyond the lake, the road entered the twisting Mount Pao pass and descended into the valley where Kontum stood on the bank of the Bla river. Kontum had the look of being an older town than any other in the highlands. It also had a certain charm. Although none of the streets were paved, the row of shop-houses by the old market were of weathered masonry and a few had rococo carvings. The tile roofs looked as if they had endured many rainy seasons. The residential section had wide streets, and the Vietnamese houses were large, with wattled mud walls painted white or powder blue. Each house was set in a sizable plot, much of which was devoted to extensive vegetable gardens, fruit trees, and patches of flowers. Some of the Bahnar villages, such as Kon Rohai, were really part of the town, and their houses with wattled walls and tile roofs (but still built on piling) reflected the long years of Vietnamese influence in Kontum.

At the northern edge of the town along Route 14, the newly arrived American MAAG detachment was housed in tents. In the evening they showed movies on an outdoor screen, attracting many Vietnamese and highlanders (who, by their reactions, clearly sympathized with the Indians in the western movies).

The province chief complained about the lack of trained highlanders for positions in the administration. The result was that only one of the four district chiefs was a highlander. He also voiced discontent over the way the highlanders (whom he described as "lazy") farmed. It was destructive, and he planned to end it by launching a forest conservation program. Tea, coffee, and pepper estates could be established in the province.

We went to pay our respects to Bishop Paul Seitz, head of the Kontum Mission. The bishop came down the steps of the large, rambling Norman-style mission headquarters to greet us. A storm was just beginning, and he presented a dramatic figure with his black soutane, greying beard, and penetrating eyes. In his book-lined office we discussed the relations between the highlanders and Vietnamese in Kontum. The two groups had lived in proximity for many years in Kontum, and the bishop felt that it had been beneficial for the highlanders. They had retained their way of life but had learned many things from the Vietnamese, such as better gardening and farming methods (he noted that there was extensive permanent field cultivation by highlanders in the vicinity of Kontum). The highlanders, he felt, must develop both socially and economically to avoid being overwhelmed by the more advanced Vietnamese.

As in Ban Me Thuot and Pleiku, the highland villagers and civil servants were most cooperative in providing information on their land tenure systems. The Jarai near Kontum had the same tenure as the Pleiku Jarai. The Bahnar Jolong, however, had village territories in which the residents farmed. The use of this territory (land, streams, and trees) was carefully controlled by the village elders (*kra*). Fields close to Kontum that were farmed permanently, however, belonged to individuals and families. The Sedang also had village territories similar to those of the Bahnar.

The most impressive highlander encountered in Kontum was Paul Nur (1.13), a man with a brooding air, who was bitter about the Vietnamese treatment of highland people. He was serving as a schoolmaster, and he cited examples of highland civil servants and teachers being accorded second class status by the Vietnamese. He also said that male villagers were expected to do corvée on roads for twenty to thirty days a year. Although they were supposed to receive 40 piasters a day, they never received any compensation.

In order to obtain some data on Sedang land tenure we traveled northward along Route 14. Above Kontum the road passed through thickly wooded country past some Bahnar villages. At Kon Horing, a large Sedang settlement near the road, the schoolmaster provided information on land tenure. We also obtained additional data in Dak To and in villages north of that town. The French priests from the Kontum Mission lived in villages in this area. Their style of life was little different from that of the highlanders around them. In one village the French priest kindly invited us to share his meal of wild boar. In addition to discussing some Sedang customs and some aspects of land tenure, he related the story of how he had hidden three downed U.S. airmen during World War II.

From Dak To we returned to Kontum and then drove south on Route 14 to the juncture of Route 7 near Pleiku and proceeded to Cheo Reo. Route 7 wound down from the plateau in a southeasterly direction through country that was only sparsely forested but had many escarpments and curiously shaped hills. Located at the confluence of the Ayun and Apa rivers, Cheo Reo was little more than a collection of Jarai villages, most of them established by members of the elite Rcom clan, the first to settle in this area. There were a few small administrative buildings (Cheo Reo was a district headquarters), a school, and some Vietnamese shops built of wattled walls and thatched roofs. We were greeted by Nay Moul (2.17), a husky man with a thick, large face (he was one of the first highlanders to join the French army in 1931). He had married Rcom H'ban, daughter of the famed Jarai chief Nay Nui (2.11). Both are good examples of the Jarai belief that certain individuals are favored by a spirit called Yang Rong and consequently have charisma (*dhut*). Such persons are described as *knuih* and are predestined to leadership. With both, this charisma was manifest in unusual physical strength and courage. This charisma enabled Nay Nui to marry a woman of the prestigious Rcom clan, and when this union proved auspicious he arranged for Nay Moul to marry his daughter, thus establishing a pattern in Cheo Reo for men of the Nay clan to wed women of the Rcom clan.

We gladly accepted Nay Moul's invitation to stay at the very large longhouse that Nay Nui had built many years before (the old chief lived across the river with a daughter). While there, we gathered information on the land tenure system of the Jarai in the Cheo Reo area. Essentially it is the same as that of the Jarai Hodrung at Pleiku; paddy fields, gardens, and house sites belong to the family and are passed down through the female line while families have a usufruct of swiddens, both those being farmed and those fallowing.

I also obtained some information on the King of Fire and the King of Water. Nay Moul related that the former resided in a village north of Cheo Reo not far from Route 7. Every dry season he made a tour of villages in the region to perform rituals aimed at bringing rain for the crops and warding off epidemics.

From Cheo Reo we returned north on Route 7 to the juncture of Route 19, which we took to the coast. Toward the end of the Indochina War in 1954, the French army Groupe Mobile 100 had suffered a series of Viet Minh attacks on this road. Now, three years later, there still were burned-out hulks of military vehicles almost hidden in the green forest growths along the road. Here and there were small concrete memorials to the fallen. We reached Qui Nhon and went south along the magnificent coast via Nhatrang to Saigon.

Since Ban Me Thuot was scheduled to be the site for some of the first Land Development Centers, I decided to focus further investigation on the matter of land tenure on some of the Rhadé villages and clans involved. In May 1957 I returned to Ban Me Thuot, accompanied by Price Gittinger, a staff member of the USOM Agricultural Divison, who was conducting most of the research for the proposed land reform program. At Ban Me Thuot we consulted with Colonel Le Van Kim, director of the Land Development Program in the highlands. An alert, intelligent man with considerable wartime experience in the region, Kim was very well aware of the problems involved in his program because of Rhadé land claims. He had become familiar with the Rhadé land tenure system, so he had formed a committee consisting of himself, several of his Vietnamese officers (who were learning to speak Rhadé), the district chief, and some notables from local Rhadé villages. The Rhadé village of Buon Kroa near Ban Me Thuot was to be the site of the first Land Development Center. When the agricultural fair was held in February 1957, the committee agreed to pay the village 10,000 piasters for five hectares to use as a demonstration plot to indicate that implementation of the program was beginning.

Gittinger and I met with Rhadé civil servants and village leaders to discuss the possibility of land being sold or leased to the government. The consensus was that the government could take any land not claimed. Clan land, however, was inalienable according to Rhadé tradition, but it might be leased. They pointed out that some of the French plantations were on clan or village land leased for ninety-nine years (a *bail emphythéotique*). They also noted that most of the land around Buon Kroa belonged to the Eban clan, and the current guardian (*po lan*) was an elderly woman named H'deo Eban.

We went to Buon Kroa, and the villagers provided an elephant to transport us through the thick forest to the swidden where the villagers were busy planting their crops. We found H'deo Eban in the middle of a field being sown that day, sitting amidst some jars of alcohol. Nearby, some men were striking gongs that provided a rhythm for rows of men who moved along making holes with dibble sticks in the reddish soil. Behind them, women followed, stooping to drop seeds from a bamboo tube into the holes. Then, with the solid end of the tube they pushed dirt into each hole and tamped the soil. As we began discussing the land question with H'deo Eban, the gong players and some of the planters came to join in the conversation.

H'deo Eban was annoyed because some of the Eban land had been taken for land development and she had never been consulted by Le Van Kim's committee. She and the others pointed out that in the past payments had been made to land guardians and villages for plantation lands. Since 1954, however, these payments had ceased. One man stated, "The government is stronger than we, so we must do what it wants, just as we had to do what the French wanted." H'deo Eban finally agreed to meet with Kim's committee to discuss leasing Eban land, although she was vague about what the compensation might be. One villager noted that most Rhadé were unfamiliar with cash, and traditionally land was rented for such things as a pig, a large old jar, or a woman's skirt.

Gittinger and I then consulted with various Rhadé and Vietnamese officials (including Y Keo, the judge living in Ban Don). All agreed that a commission of Vietnamese and Rhadé be formed to negotiate with local village notables and clan land guardians to work out the land question. We returned to Saigon and in June 1957 submitted separate reports. Gittinger's report focused on Rhadé land rights, particularly in the Buon Kroa situation. He recommended that the Rhadé land claims be honored and, where Vietnamese were to be settled on clan lands, the guardians be given compensation. Le Van Kim's committee was cited as one means of coping with these claims. He also pointed out that a failure to resolve such land claims would generate discontent among the highlanders, making them more susceptible to Communist propaganda. In addition, he recommended that "USOM, on its side, should support such a general land tenure accord, and should make it a condition of its continuing support for land development projects." [26]

My report contained the same recommendation concerning the need to resolve highlander land claims, and it also favored the formation of a commission such as the one organized by Le Van Kim. Furthermore, it summarized the findings on land tenure and related aspects of the various ethnic groups' social organization, on agriculture, and on Communist activities that had been gathered during both field trips. It also presented some of the views expressed by the province chiefs and the highlanders regarding the Vietnamese. Included were some historical data that had been gathered at the National Museum in Saigon. Since this report was to

26. J. Price Gittinger, "Tenure in Ban Me Thuot Land Development Projects: Situation and Recommendations (Summary)," mimeographed (Saigon, 18 June 1957).

be sent to President Diem and other government officials, it was decided to have a French version.[27]

According to Wesley Fishel, Chief Advisor of the MSUG, Diem was very upset by my report, particularly the section about the highlanders' attitudes toward the Vietnamese. (Typical of the direct quotations were: "The Vietnamese talk equality, but they don't mean what they say. In their hearts they want to dominate us. They are colonialists. The French were bad at the mouth, but in their hearts they were good" and "The Vietnamese think they all are mandarins."). Diem arranged a flight to Ban Me Thuot, where, forewarned of his purpose, the province officials had some Rhadé notables whom they dressed in Vietnamese clothes greet him with a few Vietnamese words at the airstrip. Diem returned to Saigon and told Fishel that the report was inaccurate. The highland people, he said, loved the Vietnamese and desired to emulate them.

But the harshest criticism of my report (and Gittinger's as well) came from Wolf Ladejinsky, a land reform "expert" for Diem. He had been telling Diem that it was the richest region in Vietnam. At the MSUG offices he ranted that the report "was the worst ever issued" by the group. "How do you expect the government to deal with these children?" was his comment regarding my recommendations for revolving land claims. I retorted that if he operated on the premise that the highlanders were "children" he would not get far in any dealings with them. Then he added, "They look out the window and say 'I own all the land I see'," to which I responded that such a statement only demonstrated that he had not read the report. Gittinger's report was withdrawn by USOM and locked in a safe. My report, however, was allowed by Fishel to circulate without changes. Nonetheless, both Gittinger and I were in disfavor (one of the few who supported our views was Bernard Fall). Worst of all, it was quietly agreed in the American mission that the Land Development Program would move ahead without regard for highlander land claims.

According to Bui Van Luong, it was understood in Saigon that compensation to the highlanders for land expropriated by the government (this would not be a lease but a forced sale) would be in the form of a water buffalo or a jar of rice alcohol. Reports from Ban Me Thuot, however, indicated that Le Van Kim was making cash payments for land, and by mid-1957 he already had expended some 30,000 piasters in Darlac province.

27. Michigan State University Vietnam Advisory Group, "Preliminary Research."

This information annoyed President Diem and his brother Nhu, who felt that there was no need for negotiation or compensation. Kim was removed from his post (subsequently he became director of the new Military Academy in Dalat).

The Land Development Program moved ahead. The centers were called Đinh Điền, the same term used historically for civilian settlements in the Vietnamese "advance southward." Now, in many respects, the "advance westward" that had characterized the eighteenth century expansion of the Vietnamese into the Mekong river delta was continuing in the highlands. The settlers included northern Catholic refugees, landless peasants from the coastal plain, Civil Guard personnel with their dependents and demobilized soldiers. As in the historical advance southward, there also were social undesirables and political exiles. Many moved voluntarily and some were lured to the highlands with promises of fertile land and ideal agricultural conditions. There were those, however, who were forcibly relocated.

As of July 1959 there were 37 Land Development Centers—21 in Pleiku, 8 in Darlac, 2 in Kontum, and 6 in newly established Quang Duc province. They had a total of 44,109 inhabitants, and 11,016 hectares had been cleared. In addition to growing some rice and kitchen garden secondary crops, the settlers also were cultivating rubber, ramie, kenaf, coffee, and cotton.[28]

Although the highlander resettlement scheme was considered to be part of the Land Development Program, it actually had begun in 1955 when six new settlements containing some 1,894 inhabitants were established (it is not clear whether or not they were war refugees). By 1956 there were nine new villages with 2,800 people. With the 1957 Land Development Program the resettlement of highlanders increased, and as of 1958 there were 38 new communities in Darlac, Pleiku, Kontum, and Quang Duc provinces with 26,191 inhabitants (see map 5).[29]

As part of the effort to bring Vietnamese culture to the highlands, many place names were changed during this period. Cheo Reo became Hau Bon and Ban Me Thuot was now called Lac Giao (no one used either of these new names). Djiring was changed to Di Linh and Blao to Bao Loc. The

28. Huy Sơn, "Công cuộc dinh điền ở Cao Nguyên" (Resettlement Program in the Highlands), *Sáng Dội Miền Nam* (Southern Brightness) 2, no. 7 (1960): 10–13.

29. Republic of Vietnam, *Seven Years of the Ngo Dinh Diem Administration, 1954–1961* (Saigon, Information Printing Office, 1961), p. 115; République du Vietnam, *Bilan des réalisations gouvernementales, 1954–1962* (Saigon, Présidence de la République, 1962), pp. 132–34.

highlander law courts were not officially abolished, but Touneh Han Dang related how the judges' stipends were discontinued. The intent apparently was to let the courts languish in the hope that they would fade away so that Vietnamese laws could be put into effect among the highlanders.

Some of the Vietnamese provincial administrators had their own means of trying to alter highland traditions. In Darlac, the province chief forbade the Rhadé to wear loincloths when they entered the town, requiring them to be garbed in skirt and trousers. In Pleiku, officials ordered Jarai refugees to build their new houses on the ground, Vietnamese style, rather than on piling as was their custom.

2 RISING ETHNONATIONALISM AND INSURGENCY

The peace that had come to the highlands after the Geneva Agreements was all too brief. Ethnonationalism, which for a long time had been steadily growing, suddenly intensified in 1958 with the appearance of a movement named "Bajaraka," a combination of the key letters of Bahnar, Jarai, Rhadé, and Koho, reflecting a following drawn from the major ethnic groups. With a flag designed to appeal to all of the people of the central highlands, Bajaraka was the first explicitly political movement that had ever arisen in the mountain country. Its birth marked the beginning of a long, sometimes violent period of dissidence.

The end of the decade also witnessed a reappearance of the Communist insurgency that had been as widespread as the Viet Minh movement during the Indochina War and that since 1954 had been quiescent while it reorganized and recruited. The Diem government called these insurgents the "Việt Cộng" (a shortened version of "Việt Nam Cộng Sản" or "Vietnamese Communists"). In December 1960 the movement formally proclaimed itself to be "The National Liberation Front of South Vietnam" (usually known as the NLF) and described itself as being indigenous to South Vietnam, independent of Hanoi (this proved to be a fiction). As fighting between the Viet Cong and government forces spread, the highlanders again found themselves caught in the cross fire. The sounds of violence, the appearance of refugees on the roads, and the burning villages all signaled the end to that fleeting afternoon of tranquillity between the wars.

THE BAJARAKA MOVEMENT

The Diem government's attempt to erase ethnic boundaries as a means of attaining national integration was singularly unsuccessful. When, within

47

the framework of "nation-building," such strategies as the Land Development Program were formulated in Saigon, there was never the slightest suspicion that they might trigger dissidence among the highlanders. As a matter of fact there was a great deal to indicate that Diem and other high officials in the government felt that the highlanders ought to be grateful for the opportunity to learn Vietnamese ways. Among many of the Americans in Saigon—including some of the MSUG political scientists—the Vietnamese government's approach to the minorities was viewed as efficacious: "nation-building" could be achieved more effectively by replacing ethnic loyalties with ties to the state. My own view, reflected in my report on the highlands, was that forced assimilation would only generate resentment. It would be more advisable to allow the highlanders and other ethnic minorities to retain their ethnic identities and work out for themselves a well-defined place in the national framework. This would be an "integrative revolution," to use Geertz's terms, that would bring about an adjustment of primordial—in this case ethnic—ties and civil attachments.[1]

One group of young, educated highlanders felt the policies of the Diem government reinforced, rather than reduced, their sense of ethnic identity, particularly the common identity of being highlanders. The result was the first indigenous ethnonationalist movement to appear in the central highlands. Barth sees such young leaders as "agents of change," members of a "new elite," i.e., persons "with greater contact and more dependence on the goods and organizations of industrialized societies," and observed that "in their pursuit of participation in wider social systems to obtain new forms of value" such agents of change had three strategies open to them.[2] The first was to become incorporated in the larger society. The second was to accept "minority status," in which case they would "accommodate to and seek to reduce their minority disabilities by encapsulating all cultural differentiae in sectors of nonarticulation, while participating in the larger system of the industrialized group in the other sectors of activity." Their third choice was to emphasize their ethnic identity, "using it to develop

1. Clifford Geertz, "The Integrative Revolution: Primordial Sentiments and Civil Politics in the New States," in *Old Societies and New States*, ed. Clifford Geertz (New York: The Free Press, 1963), pp. 105–57.

2. Fredrik Barth, *Ethnic Groups and Boundaries: The Social Organization of Culture Difference* (Boston: Little, Brown, 1969), pp. 32–33.

new positions and patterns to organize activities in those sectors formerly not found in their society."

According to his analysis, in the first strategy an ethnic group would probably "remain as a culturally conservative, low-articulating ethnic group with low rank in the larger social system." The second would "probably lead to an eventual assimilation of the minority." The third strategy "generates many of the interesting movements that can be observed today, from nativism to new states." The highlander agents of change settled on the third choice.

Early in 1955 a group of highlanders, most of them employed in the provincial and education services, began to meet in the Rhadé village of Buon Ale-A (where the Christian and Missionary Alliance church was located) to discuss their grievances against the new government of Ngo Dinh Diem and their hopes for the future of the highland people. One of the group's organizers was a young Rhadé named Y Thih Eban (5.2), a stocky man with an easygoing manner that masked intense feelings about the survival of the highlanders. Born in 1932, Y Thih had been brought up in Buon Ale-A and had spent considerable time with Y Plo Eban, the talented Rhadé teacher who joined the Viet Minh in 1945 and died when he left with the Viet Minh after the return of the French. In discussing his own background, Y Thih continually referred to the strong influence Y Plo's spirit and courage had had on his development.

Y Thih received his primary education at the Groupe Scolaire Antomarchi in Ban Me Thuot and the Franco-Jarai School in Pleiku. After receiving his Primary School Certificate in 1949, he completed a one-year clerical training course at the Collège Sabatier. He became a Christian in 1950, joining the Protestant congregation in Buon Ale-A, and married H'wick Nie Hrah, daughter of the respected Rhadé teacher Y Toeh Mlo Duon (5.1). It was Y Toeh's son Y Ham Nie Hrah (5.4) who won Gordon Smith's praise as his most adept Bible student and who went on to become in 1956 the first highlander to be ordained a pastor in the Christian and Missionary Alliance.

In 1950 Y Thih became an accountant in the Darlac Provincial Health Service, then under the direction of a French army physician. In 1955 Y Thih's family was touched by the violence of war for the first time. His sister was serving as a nurse in the Pleiku Province Hospital and her husband was employed in the Public Works. When Kontum fell to the

Viet Minh, an assault was launched on Pleiku, and Y Thih's sister and her husband were killed.

After the Geneva Agreements, Y Thih found himself increasingly concerned about the future of the highland people. As the Vietnamese influx in Darlac began, his concern turned to anxiety. He sought other highlanders who felt as he did and did not have to look very far. There were the same discontents and fears among his fellow highlanders who were employed in the provincial services. In the Health Service they included Y Say Mlo Duon Du, Chief of the Personnel Office (his sister's son, Y Wang Mlo Duon Du, had joined the Viet Minh and remained with them); Y Dhua Buon Dap, a clerk; and Y Mot Nie Kdam, a male nurse in the Anti-Malaria Unit. All were Rhadé. In addition there were two Bahnar, Paul Doi and Michel Dong, both clerks in the province hospital. In the Education Service there was Y Mo Eban (5.7), an affinal kinsman of Y Thih's wife.

This was the beginning of the Bajaraka ethnonationalist movement. Blumer has described the initial stage in the formation of a specific social movement as arising when people are restless and uneasy: "They are susceptible to appeals and suggestions that tap their discontent, and hence, at this stage, the agitator is likely to play an important role."[3] Y Thih was just such an agitator, bringing together other highlanders in small group meetings in Buon Ale-A. At the first meetings, held early in 1955, they exchanged examples of discrimination against highlanders and outrages by the Vietnamese army. For example, military personnel would enter villages to carry away animals, fruits, and garden produce. They even entered houses to steal sleeping mats, blankets, and personal belongings. In one incident, when the villagers complained, the soldiers boasted that now that the Vietnamese ruled the highlanders they could do as they pleased.

After several such meetings, the group began to discuss courses of action, finally settling on a plan to form a secret organization called Le Front pour la Libération des Montagnards, which they referred to as the FLM. Y Mot Nie Kdam was elected president, and Y Thih became secretary, while Y Say Mlo Duon Du assumed the role of treasurer. Late in March 1955 Y Thih wrote a long letter in Rhadé to President Diem outlining what the highlanders expected of the government. It requested an official govern-

---

3. Herbert Blumer, "Collective Behavior," in *Principles of Sociology*, ed. Alfred McClung Lee (New York; Barnes & Noble, 1969), p. 103.

ment policy of respect for highlander customs and traditions. The highlanders should also be allowed the flag that had been authorized for them
under the Crown Domain of Bao Dai. The letter contained a plea for equal
treatment of highlanders and Vietnamese in the civil service and called for a
settlement of the highland people's land claims. Y Thih warned that there
might be Communists among the northern refugees moving into the
highlands. Y Thih addressed a closing comment to Diem himself: "You are
a father like a tiger and a mother like a tigress; you care for us, but at the
same time you claw us." (This use of analogies drawn from their own
milieu was characteristic of the highlanders.) The letter was sent by regular
post, and copies were disseminated among the provincial services in the
highlands. There was no response or reaction, however, and Y Thih and his
group could not determine whether or not Diem had received the letter.

The FLM group continued to meet during 1956, although no activities
were undertaken. At the beginning of 1957 the Health Service was reorganized and most of the FLM members were transferred to other
provinces. But, instead of weakening their small movement, this change
served to spread the FLM net over a wider area as the dispersed members
recruited new members. They all, in effect, became agitators. Y Thih was
sent to Pleiku, where he immediately formed a new "secret committee" of
other highlanders who shared his views. Among them were Y Bham
Enuol, assistant to the Chief of Agricultural Services, and Y Ju Eban, a
fellow worker in the hospital administration. Y Bham was born at Buon
Ale-A in 1913. He studied at the Franco-Rhadé School and later at the
Christian and Missionary Alliance Bible School. In the early 1940s
Emperor Bao Dai had launched a program to provide advanced agricultural training for highlanders and Y Bham, accompanied by another
Rhadé, Y San Nie, was sent to Tuyen Quang in northern Vietnam for a
three-year course of studies at the Ecole Nationale d'Agriculture. On his
return to Darlac, Y Bham was given the position of Technical Agent in the
Provincial Agricultural Service. He soon gained the reputation of being a
very capable and reliable civil servant, so he was given civil service status in
the Cadre Indochinois of the colonial administration. Y Ju Eban was born
around 1935 in the village of Buon Tong Ju near Ban Me Thuot. After his
education at the Franco-Rhadé School, he took a position in the administration as a clerk.

The new members in Pleiku included two Jarai: Siu Sipp, who worked in the Pleiku district administration, and R'mah Liu, a secretary in the Province Hospital. Siu Sipp was born around 1927 at Plei Jut near Pleiku. After primary school he joined the French army, attaining the rank of sergeant. He had just left the army and taken a position in the administration when he met Y Thih. R'mah Liu was born around 1929 at the important village of Plei Kly, south of Pleiku town on Route 14. He had studied at the Franco-Jarai School and the Collège Sabatier before joining the administration.

Of the other members in the original FLM group, Y Dhua Buon Dap was transferred to Dong Nai Thuong province while Paul Doi and Michel Dong moved to the hospital at Kontum. They, like Y Thih, began to recruit new members of the FLM. At the same time, the Ban Me Thuot group continued to function and expand in membership.

According to Y Thih, recruitment for the FLM was relatively easy among highlanders who were exposed to the new Vietnamese presence because they were usually discontent. This was particularly true of educated highlanders, most of whom were employed in the administration as civil servants or teachers. They were French-trained, which now was a liability, and they experienced a strong feeling of alienation in the new Vietnamese scheme of things. Discontent also was spreading among highland students. Touneh Han Tho reports that in 1955, when he was studying at the Collège d'Adran in Dalat, he and his fellow highlanders would meet in their rooms to talk about the changes taking place in the region. (They heard much about this from their parents when they visited home.) The following year, when he was at the Lycée Yersin, Han Tho and other highland students decided to form some kind of organization. One of those advocating some kind of action was Nay Luett (2.26), the brightest of the highland students at the Lycée.

Nay Luett was born in May 1935 in Bon Me Hing, south of Cheo Reo, to a village family of modest means. His mother, Nay Hyoi, was a Jarai Mdhur and his father, Kpa Tlam, was a Hroy. As a child, he displayed a remarkable brightness, which was interpreted as a manifestation of *kdruh* (the charisma attributed to the spirits). This attracted the attention of Nay Moul (2.17), the Jarai leader in Cheo Reo. He arranged with Luett's parents to take the boy to live at the large Rcom longhouse. Luett studied at the Cheo Reo primary school and then at the Franco-Bahnar School in Kontum and in Ban Me Thuot at the Collège Sabatier. Nay Moul made it possible for him to enter the Lycée Yersin. He also arranged a marriage between Luett and his daughter Rcom Hom, in keeping with the pattern of Nay males marrying Rcom females.

Recruitment among the educated highlanders was successful not only because of their discontent but also because they either knew one another or knew about one another. Many had attended the same schools— particularly in Kontum and Ban Me Thuot. In addition, there were interlacing bonds of friendship, and there also was an increasing number of marriages taking place among the elite families of the Bahnar, Jarai, Rhadé, Chru, Lat, and Sre (as the kinship charts indicate). These interpersonal relationships as well as the common awareness of their highlander ethnic identity in the face of their growing domination by the Vietnamese, whom they regarded as aliens in the highlands, provided the basis for the strong esprit de corps that Blumer feels is so important in the initial phase of any social movement.[4]

Early in 1958 the Ban Me Thuot and Pleiku groups merged, and a new central committee was formed. According to Y Thih, everyone reasoned that since Y Bham Enuol was the eldest (he was born in 1913) he should be president. The vice president was Y San Nie, who had studied at the agriculture school in Tuyen Quang with Y Bham. Y Thih was named secretary general, Siu Sipp became treasurer, and Y Ju Eban was appointed liaison agent with the other provincial committees. Y Bhan Kpuor, a Rhadé lieutenant in the army, became representative for the highland military personnel, and Lt. Touprong Ya Ba (4.9) was appointed commander of the FLM's Etat Major (military headquarters).

Y Dhon Adrong was named representative of the highland students. He had been born in Buon Emap, near Ban Me Thuot, around 1933. After completing his primary school training at the Groupe Scolaire Antomarchi, he was accepted at the Lycée Yersin in Dalat and gained the distinction of being the first highlander to receive the First Baccalaureat. He taught in Ban Me Thuot and in the mid-1950s was named Director of Primary Education at Lac Thien (Poste du Lac) district in southern Darlac.

Representatives for each highland province also were selected. Paul Nur (1.13) was the only representative of Kontum, but Pleiku had a delegation that included Siu Plung (1.23), Rahlan Yik, Siu Djit, and Siu Ja. The Darlac delegation was headed by Y Bih Aleo, a former civil servant who also had been in the Garde Indochinoise and had followed the Viet

4. Ibid., pp. 105–08.

Minh, later becoming a Viet Cong leader. Also in the Darlac delegation were Y Du Nie and Y Mo Eban (5.7). Dong Nai Thuong province was represented by two Chru—Touneh Yoh (4.10) and Touneh Phan, a clerk in the medical service—and a Lat named K'Teh from the Dalat Police Service.

Below the province level there was a committee for each district, and within the district a committee for each canton. A canton normally had about nine villages within its boundaries, and each village had a committee. Y Thih claimed that at this time the movement had an estimated 200,000 followers. Among them were civil servants, school teachers, military personnel, members of the police force, students, and ordinary villagers.

On 1 May 1958 the central committee gathered in Pleiku to decide future strategy. Addressing the gathering in Rhadé, which was understood by many of the educated highlanders who had studied in Ban Me Thuot, Y Thih proposed that they call their organization the Bajaraka Movement, a name derived from the key letters in Bahnar, Jarai, Rhadé, and Koho. This was accepted, as was Y Thih's design for a Bajaraka flag. The flag featured a red circle dualistically symbolizing the "red soil of the highlands" and "the blood shed by the highland people in their struggle for survival" set on a green background representing "the green highland forests." At the upper left corner were four white stars for the four highland provinces of Kontum, Pleiku, Darlac, and Haut Donnai. (They preferred the French designation Haut Donnai rather than the Vietnamese Dong Nai Thuong.) The five points on each star represented the five districts in each highland province.

Afterward the grievances of the highlanders against the central government were aired and duly recorded.[5] First, they expressed resentment at the loss of the semiautonomy they had enjoyed under the French, and they noted that this change of status had taken place without their having been consulted. Subsequent complaints were listed under explicit headings, such as "economic" (which included land-grabbing and cheating by Vietnamese traders), "political" (the superior attitude of the Vietnamese), "administrative" (lower salary and status for highlanders in the civil service), "military" (Vietnamese enlisted men given higher status than highlander officers, no highlander had been accepted for training as a

5. They were later presented in Y Bham Enuol, "Extraits de l'histoire des hauts-plateaux du centre Viet-Nam (Pays Montagnards du Sud-Indochinois)," mimeographed (Zone d'Organisation, 1956), pp. 7–10.

commissioned or noncommissioned officer since 1955), and "security" (highland villagers had more to fear from the Vietnamese army than from the Viet Cong). Additional headings were "justice" (resentment at the abolishment of the highlander law courts), "culture and language" (discontinued training in highland languages, inadequate schools), and "social welfare and public health" (a highlander only received 25 piasters per day for the same work done by a Vietnamese for 45 piasters, highlanders were badly treated in the province hospitals).

At this meeting Y Bham Enuol presented a formal request for highlander autonomy. He also announced that the minutes of the meeting would be included in a letter that would be sent to all highlanders working in the administration. The meeting, in many respects, signaled the progression of the movement from its initial phase into a stage of formalization. The esprit de corps, so essential to this progression, had been generated in the first phase. Related to this, the in-group (highlanders) and the out-group (Vietnamese) had been defined. By early 1958 the morale of the movement was developing significantly. At the meeting the wrongs and injustices were aired and recorded, and there was ample expression of what Blumer calls the "conviction of the rectitude of the purpose of the movement," a conviction intrinsic to morale.[6] There also was an increased structuring of leadership and formulation of group ideology. As Blumer points out, "without an ideology, a social movement would grope along in an uncertain fashion and could scarcely maintain itself in the face of pointed opposition from outside groups." Although it was not stated explicitly at the meeting, the essence of the Bajaraka ideology was the maintenance of the highlander ethnic identity. This was strongly manifest in Y Bham's call for highland autonomy. It also was symbolically expressed in the Bajaraka flag, which interestingly did not contain such items as an elephant's head or crossbow as did the French-formulated seals and military unit emblems.

As the Bajaraka Movement became more active, it was inevitable that the Vietnamese security police would become aware of its existence. According to Touneh Han Tho, one source of information on the movement's activities was indiscretion by some of the highlanders in the gendarmerie. The school for training the Gendarmerie Nationale in Dalat had been started by the French in the early 1950s and the program had been continued by the Diem government. Some forty highlanders—one of

6. Blumer, "Collective Behavior," pp. 108–11.

whom was Siu Plung (1.23)—had graduated from the school by 1958, and some of them joined the Bajaraka Movement. In May 1958 they began circulating letters written in the local highland languages outlining the goals of the movement. At this time Han Tho was working in the Di Linh (Djiring) administration as part of his training at the National Institute of Administration. One of the letters fell into the hands of the Vietnamese because the highlanders had naively written on the envelope in French, "Not to be seen by Vietnamese." It was translated by a highlander in the office, and its contents were transmitted to the provincial security service and to Saigon.

Touneh Han Tho claims that when news of the dissident activities in Dong Nai Thuong province reached Saigon, it was decided to bring about some immediate administrative changes as one means of coping with the situation. The result was a decree dated 19 May 1958 dividing Dong Nai Thuong into the provinces of Tuyen Duc, with its administrative center in Dalat, and Lam Dong, which had Bao Loc (Blao) as its capital (see map 5).

One South Vietnamese report claims that delivery of this letter to the security service precipitated an investigation.[7] Some "foreigners" also were implicated. This report asserts that in 1957 a member of the U.S. Embassy staff named Francis S. (a reference to Francis Sherry of the CIA staff), "who made frequent hunting trips in the highlands, made contact with Y Bham, Y Thih, and Y Preh" (Y Preh Buon Krong, affiliated with the Christian and Missionary Alliance in Buon Ale-A). The report also states that in September 1957 Y Bham met secretly with "foreign Catholic priests" and with "advisory officers" in Ban Me Thuot, Pleiku, and Kontum.

Y Thih related how, early in 1958, members of the Bajaraka committee in Ban Me Thuot drew up a petition intended for President Diem asking for autonomy. First, however, they showed it to Father Roger Bianchetti of the Kontum Mission. He advised against their asking for autonomy on the grounds that the highland people were, in his opinion, not ready for it. He warned that if they sent the request to the president they might find themselves "in a wasps' nest." They therefore decided not to send the petition.

The first Bajaraka effort at taking direct action to gain the movement's

7. Nguyễn Trắc Dĩ, "Tìm hiểu phong-trào F.U.L.R.O. (1958–1969)," (Understanding the F.U.L.R.O. Movement [1958–1969]), mimeographed (Saigon: Bộ Phát-Triển Sắc-Tộc, 1959), pp. 5–10.

goal of autonomy took place in early August 1958, when Y Bham decided to write a letter (in French) appealing to the heads of the American, British, French, Indian, and Laotian diplomatic missions in Saigon to intervene with the Vietnamese government on behalf of the highlanders. The letter outlined some of the highlanders' grievances. Also, emphasizing that the highland people had shed blood in the struggle against "the enemy," the letter called on these diplomatic leaders to support the cause of highland autonomy.

The letters were entrusted to Y Ju Eban and Nay Luett (2.26), the son-in-law of Jarai leader Nay Moul. It is noted above that in 1957 Luett was active in organizing the highland students at the Lycée Yersin. In discussing the events of this period, Luett recalled going to Pleiku in June 1958 and meeting Y Thih and Y Bham. He was attracted to their views and joined the Bajaraka Movement. He agreed to assist in delivering the letters, so he and Y Ju went to Saigon. Henry G. Lefever of the Mennonite Central Committee accompanied the two highlanders to the U.S. Embassy where they met with Ambassador Durbrow. Luett and Y Ju explained their mission to Durbrow, who promised to discuss the highlanders' complaints with Vietnamese government officials. Luett and Y Ju duly delivered the letters to the other embassies. Nay Luett pointed out with a shrug that nothing came of this effort.

In September 1958 two of Paul Nur's cademen were arrested in Dak To, north of Kontum, and this aroused indignation among the members of the Bajaraka Movement. On 8 September an ad hoc Liberation Committee issued a letter in French addressed to President Diem and signed by Y Bham. It protested the arrests and asked that officials be sent from Saigon to resolve the problems in the highlands. Y Mot Nie Hrah and Y Dhon Adrong carried the letter to Saigon where they delivered it to Independence Palace. They also distributed copies of the letter to highland members of the National Assembly. Copies also were sent to the province chiefs in the highlands.

These actions precipitated the Bajaraka Movement's first crisis. The government security forces moved quickly to arrest those leaders they considered "dangerous." Y Thih Eban, Y Bham Enuol, Y Ju Eban, and Siu Sipp were arrested in Pleiku. Paul Nur was detained in Kontum, and Nay Luett was taken into custody in Cheo Reo. Touneh Yoh, who was taking the Special Course for Highlanders at the National Institute of Administration, was arrested at the Ministry of the Interior where he was getting practical experience. Y Bih Aleo was detained briefly but released because he was in a provincial committee rather than the central committee. Y Thih reported that he was taken to Independence Palace in Saigon to be questioned by President Diem. However, the president was not available, so he was returned to Pleiku. There, Ton That Dinh, commander of the Second Military Corps (he later was a member of the junta that overthrew Diem), met with Y Thih and asked why they had delivered the earlier letter to the American ambassador. Y Thih replied that they did it "because it is the Americans who are driving the automobile." All of the arrested Bajaraka leaders were sent to Dalat and put in underground solitary cells for three months.

On 12 October 1958 Y Dhon Adrong and Y Bih Aleo sent President Diem a request, signed by 1,000 highlanders, for the release of the prisoners. They also organized a demonstration in Ban Me Thuot. An estimated crowd of 2,000 streamed into the town from surrounding villages, and a Bajaraka leader addressed them, enumerating the grievances of the highland people. Armored units of the 23rd Division moved in to disperse the crowd. On 27 October the province chief organized a meeting of Vietnamese and highlanders from the civil service at the Lido Cinema in Ban Me Thuot to demonstrate solidarity between the two groups. At one point a Rhadé named Y Wang, who worked in the provincial administrative office, stood up and stated that if the Vietnamese and highlanders were "brothers" it had to be proven with deeds and not just words.

On 26 November 1958 the jailed Bajaraka leaders were taken to Hue. According to Nay Luett, Y Bham was put in the Criminal Section of the prison, where conditions were very harsh. The others were in the Political Section, and conditions were not much better. Quarters were cramped and food was sparse—six grams of rice and some dried fish each day. Paul Nur requested an extra ration of rice with which he intended brewing some alcohol, but he filled out the request incorrectly. It appeared that he was trying to cheat, so he was banished to the Criminal Section. For those in the Political Section, conditions improved slowly and they were allowed to leave the compound for several hours in the evening. Y Thih used the time to attend religious services in a nearby Protestant church.

Diem was outraged at the highlanders' attempts to organize an autonomy movement. Touneh Han Tho claims that Vietnamese staff members of the presidency, some of whom had gone to the National Institute of Administration with him, heard Diem refer to the highlanders as *chúng nó* (a pejorative usage of *they*). When he became particularly angry, he could be heard shouting about the *bọn thượng* (highland gang).

Vindictive in his attempts to crush ethnonationalism among the highlanders, Diem immediately abolished the Highlander Students' Section at the National Institute of Administration. The Bureau for Highland Affairs was moved from Dalat to Hue. Highlanders in the civil service and the military forces in the uplands were dispersed in the lowlands. Y Dhuat Nie Kdam, Y Chon Mlo Duon Du, Ya Yu Sahau, Boui Ngai, Touneh Han Tin (4.13), Touneh Han Tho (4.2), Rcom Rock (3.11), Rcom Perr (3.13), Siu Plung (1.23), and Pierre Yuk (1.12) were all sent to Quang Tri and Danang. Some one hundred military officers and noncommissioned officers were sent to Hue for "re-education," after which they were sent to provinces in the Mekong river delta. Y Pem Knuol, Rcom Hin, and Touprong Ya Ba (4.9) were assigned to posts in Saigon. Highland army officers were ordered to take Vietnamese names. Touprong Ya Ba became Truong Son Ba (Truong Son is the Vietnamese designation for the Annam Cordillera) and Y Pem Knuol took the name Nguyen Van Phien. According to Touneh Han Tho, the civil servants were told to assume Vietnamese names but refused to do so. Fearing some kind of general uprising among the highlanders, the government at this time ordered provincial officials to seize all traditional weapons, such as crossbows, spears, and knives.

There also were some legal and administrative results from the Bajaraka affair. A decree dated 12 December 1958 and a memorandum dated 28 May 1959 stated that the highlanders had a right to enjoy only the produce of the land they cultivated, implying thereby that they did not have the right of ownership. Administrative changes were ordered with the aim of bringing more Vietnamese functionaries and military personnel into the region. A 23 January 1959 decree created the province of Quang Duc out of territory that had belonged to Bien Hoa and Darlac. Construction of a new capital named Gia Nghia was begun in a remote forested area southeast of former Poste Maitre in the Mnong country (see maps 3 and 5). Land Development Centers were clustered around it.

In September 1959 Diem ordered the release of Y Bham and Paul Nur. Y Bham returned to Ban Me Thuot where he began to agitate for a revival of the Bajaraka Movement. Both Y Bham and Nur were soon arrested again. According to Y Thih, Y Bham was taken to the Ban Me Thuot police headquarters where electric charges were put under his arms, temporarily paralyzing him. Some of the American missionaries were allowed into the jail to care for him.

In the next National Assembly elections, held on 30 August 1959, there were only two seats for highlanders, as against four in the previous assembly. The two delegates were Hiar (1.7) from Kontum and Y Ut Nie Buon Rit from Ban Me Thuot. Both were well-known teachers and neither had participated in the Bajaraka Movement.

There also was a tendency at this time for the government to purposely underestimate the highlander population in order to minimize the importance of this segment of the population. In 1958 the government reported that the highlander population totaled 455,592.[8] The combined highlander populations in Dong Nai Thuong, Pleiku, Kontum, and Dalat city (Darlac province was not reported at all) was estimated at 253,815, while the figure for the uplands of the coastal provinces was fixed at 211,777. This compares with the 1943 census conducted by the French which reported a total highland population of one million. Of this total, 494,000 lived in Darlac, Kontum, Pleiku, Haut Donnai (later called Dong Nai Thuong), and Phan Rang.[9]

KHMER AND CHAM ETHNONATIONALIST MOVEMENTS

During this period, when ethnonationalism was spreading among the highlanders, movements similar to Bajaraka were forming among the Cham and Khmer Krom (the Khmer living in Kampuchea Krom or "Lower Cambodia," i.e., the Mekong river delta provinces in Vietnam).[10] Diem's policy of assimilation of ethnic minorities was also applied to the Cham and Khmer—and to the Chinese. Attempts to impose Vietnamese cultural institutions on both groups generated a great deal of resentment, and, as in the highlands, ethnonationalist movements resulted.

Ever since their "advance southward" had taken them into Cambodian territory in the Mekong river delta, the Vietnamese had been regarded as alien invaders by the Khmer Krom. When Diem abolished the use of the

8. Bộ Kinh-Tế Quốc-Gia (Ministry of the National Economy), *Việt-nam Niên-Giám Thống-Kê* (Statistical Yearbook of Vietnam), vol. 7 (Saigon, Viện Quốc-Gia Thống-Kê, 1959), pp. 18–21.

9. *Annuaire des etats-associés: Cambodge, Laos, Vietnam, 1953* (Paris: Editions Diloutremer et Havas, 1953), pp. 66–67.

10. In 1973 the Ministry for Development of Ethnic Minorities estimated that the Khmer Krom numbered around 500,000 and the Cham population between 50,000 and 60,000.

Khmer language and did away with Khmer schools, Khmer Krom antagonism deepened. Many Khmer Krom moved to Cambodia, and those who remained in Vietnam sent their children to study in Phnom Penh. One result of this situation was a wave of ethnonationalism among the Khmer Krom that eventually gave rise to the Struggle Front of the Khmer of Kampuchea Krom, usually known as the KKK.[11]

This movement had its beginnings in the late 1950s when a Khmer Krom monk named Samouk Seng, a mystic who had spent considerable time among the monks, hermits, healers, and sorcerers in the Seven Mountains area in the southwest corner of the Mekong river delta, founded the Can Sen So (White Scarves).[12] Named for the white scarves (inscribed with cabalistic symbols) favored by its members, this organization had as its goal the preservation of Khmer ethnic identity. Although the White Scarves Movement was small, the Cambodian government apparently saw it as a potential counterforce to the Khmer Serei, a dissident movement begun by Son Ngoc Thanh, an activist in the struggle against the French. Thanh left Cambodia after the Geneva Agreements because he considered Prince Norodom Sihanouk, the new head of state, to be a collaborator. Based in Vietnam, the Khmer Serei began conducting guerrilla operations on the Cambodian side of the border. The Cambodian government, therefore, lent support to the White Scarves.

In 1961 when Chau Dara, another Khmer Krom monk from the Seven Mountains, assumed leadership of the White Scarves, he improved the internal structure of the movement and increased recruitment among the Khmer Krom in South Vietnam. The name was changed to the Struggle Front of the Khmer of Kampuchea Krom. Chau Dara demanded that the Vietnamese government accord better treatment for the Khmer Krom and grant this minority more rights. In time his demands became more extreme. For example, at one point he asked that the Vietnamese allow "Lower Cambodia" to be put under the sovereignty of the Phnom Penh government. As the movement grew, it built an armed force estimated to be around 1,500 men, and it also published two weekly newspapers. In November 1963 Chau Dara was captured by Vietnamese government forces, and this weakened the movement.

11. The background on this movement is derived from a KKK document that was given to me by Khmer Krom leaders in Phnom Penh in August 1970. This document, written in French, had no title, author, or publisher.

12. Pu Kombo, founder of the Dap Lanh cult in the 1880s, and Huynh Phu So, who began the Hoa Hao sect in the 1940s, also spent much time in the Seven Mountains.

A South Vietnamese source reports that in 1960 a movement called the Front for the Liberation of Northern Cambodia was founded by Khmer Krom.[13] At the same time a Front for the Liberation of Champa was begun. There are indications that a figure active in the establishment of both movements was Lt. Col. Les Kosem, a Cambodian Cham (also a Muslim) officer in the Royal Khmer Army security forces. The latter movement was intended for the Cham populations in the coastal provinces of central Vietnam and in the Chau Doc and Tay Ninh areas. In 1962 the Front for the Liberation of Northern Cambodia and the Front for the Liberation of Champa were, according to the South Vietnamese source noted above, fused into the United Front for the Struggle of the Cham. Finally, in 1963, the movement was renamed the Front for the Liberation of the South Vietnamese Highlands, also sometimes known as the Front for the Liberation of the Champa Highlands.

OUTBREAKS OF INSURGENCY

The activities of the Bajaraka Movement do not appear to have had any effect on the implementation of the Land Development Program. By 1960 over 60,000 settlers, most of them Vietnamese, had been relocated in the highlands. It was noted above that in 1959 there were 37 Land Development Centers, and by 1962 the number had increased to 117 with a total population well over 100,000. The increase in the Vietnamese population of Darlac was considerable; in 1954 there were 35,000 Vietnamese, most of them around Ban Me Thuot and on plantations. By 1963 this figure had risen to 84,291, of which 24,867 were in Land Development Centers. Also, it was estimated that by 1963 the Vietnamese accounted for 40 percent of the total populations of Kontum, Pleiku, Phu Bon, Tuyen Duc, Lam Dong, and Quang Duc provinces.[14]

The influx of Vietnamese into the highlands during this period was

13. Nguyễn Trắc Dĩ, "Nhật-ký các phong-trào tranh-đấu của đồng bào Thượng" (Chronicle of the Highland Compatriots' Struggle Movements), *Thượng-Vụ* (Highland Affairs), no. 17 (1969): 19–20.

14. Minh Túy, "Kết-Quả của quốc sách dinh-điền," (Results of the Resettlement Policy), *Sáng Dội Miền Nam* (Southern Brightness) 4, no. 10 (1962): 28–29; Foreign Area Studies Division, Special Operations Research Office, American University, U.S. Army Area Handbook for Vietnam (Washington: Government Printing Office, 1967), p. 322; Việt Nam Công Hòa (Republic of Vietnam), *Tỉnh Darlac 1963* (Darlac Province, 1963) (Ban Mê Thuột: Tòa Hành Chánh Darlac, 1963), pp. 36–40.

made easier by improved communications. As the result of a Vietnamese-American agreement in 1954 to make the vast network of roads throughout the country usable again, routes 21 and 19 were completely rebuilt. By 1960 the 151 kilometers of Route 21 between Ninh Hoa and Ban Me Thuot had been refurbished by an American construction company. Whereas in 1957 there were only an estimated 10 vehicles passing daily over this road, by 1960 there were 400.[15]

The Highlander Resettlement Program also continued, and by 1961 there were 102 centers containing 65,259 people. By the end of 1963 there were 137 centers with a total population of 90,000.[16] This figure, however, includes many of the refugees being generated at this time by the mounting insurgency effort of the Viet Cong.

It was noted previously that during my field trips to the highlands in 1956 and 1957, certain areas were still considered "insecure" due to "Viet Minh" (i.e., Viet Cong) presence. The Viet Cong's activities, for the most part, were restricted to recruitment and spreading of propaganda among the villagers in Darlac, Kontum, and Pleiku. Subsequently, in November 1957, I made another field trip into the Katu country of Quang Nam province, accompanied by Rev. Gordon Smith (who was interested in expanding his missionary activities among the Katu) and Philip Hodgeson from the British Embassy. Boarding sampans in a village inland from Hoi An (Faifoo), we moved into the tidal current of the Thu Bon river, going westward into the valley where the ruins of My Son, the ancient Cham capital and religious center (see map 4), were located. Proceeding into the Cai river, we suddenly were in very hilly, heavily forested country, with only a few very small Vietnamese settlements along the banks. For three days the husky boatwomen, standing in the back of their boats using one large oar, rowed the sampans against the strong current. At the small village of Ben Giang we obtained Vietnamese bearers and a wood vendor who spoke Katu. After a full day's walk in the stifling heat of the inland valleys we finally arrived at a Katu village.

The village had a stockade wall, the gate was closed, and there were some freshly made bamboo symbols by the path, raising the question of whether or not they were taboo signs. The wood vendor went to the gate where a young man informed him that the village was indeed taboo. The inter-

15. "New Highway Turns Forests into Farms," *Times of Vietnam Magazine* 2, no. 23 (1960): 14–22.
16. Republic of Vietnam, *Seven Years of the Ngo Dinh Diem Administration* (Saigon, 1969), p. 115; Minh Túy, "Kết quả," p. 29.

preter talked to the headman, who relented and said that we could enter the village for a very short time. We would have to proceed directly to the men's houses. Inside the village no one was to be seen and there was a strange quietness. Doors were closed, but we could see eyes peering at us through the cracks of the bamboo walls. In the semidarkness of the men's house, with its smell of smoke, and walls covered with heads of buffalo that had been sacrificed, the headman sat on a mat. Around him was a group of young men with long hair. They were garbed in very brief loincloths and clutched long Katu spears made of hardwood with flat, very sharp blades—the kind used in human sacrifices. They all appeared to be somewhat tense.

The headman expressed dissatisfaction at having "Frenchmen" in the village, saying that the "Viet Minh" would not like it. When asked if there were any Viet Minh in the area, he replied that they were "back in the forest," adding that his brother who had "gone to the north" had returned and was with the Viet Minh. The headman complained that the village was short of food. Gordon Smith said that if his men went down to the river in a few days they could get rice from a boat. (He had arranged earlier for a larger sampan to transport some relief rice to the more remote villages along the river.) The headman, however, shook his head, saying that he could not do that because "the Viet Minh would be angry if we took food from the French." We left the village and went to a neighboring settlement where we remained a week before returning to Danang.

By the end of 1959 the Viet Cong agents were involved in an insurgency throughout the rural areas in Vietnam.[17] In the highlands, this created a new situation that seriously affected the government programs in the region. It also brought about the first deep American involvement in the highlanders' struggle to retain their ethnic identity.

Warner points out that the Vietnamese army that had been formed during the 1955–1960 period was geared to cope with conventional warfare but not with insurgency.[18] He notes that Diem grasped the lessons of the Indochina War and "struggled to persuade the State Department and the Pentagon that Mao Tse-tung had laid down his rigid rules for instigating a peasant revolt and that in South Vietnam all the indications were that the first phase was soon to be followed by a more violent

17. During the 1958–1959 period I was engaged in a long field study in the Vietnamese village of Khanh Hau in Long An province. During 1959 the activities of the Viet Cong increased, with propaganda-recruitment teams visiting hamlets, and by the end of the year there were reports of minor officials being assassinated in more remote areas.

18. Denis Warner, *The Last Confucian* (New York: Macmillan Co., 1963), pp. 106–08.

second." Warner adds that the responsibility for the type of Vietnamese army that had emerged rested with Lt. General Samuel T. ("Hanging Sam") Williams (head of MAAG) and his successor, Lt. General Lionel C. McGarr. Warner cites Lucien Conein, an American observer of the Indochina War, as saying that General Williams knew about conventional warfare but not insurgency. Conein reported that "the French officer handling the intelligence organization embracing all the Montagnard tribes in the High Plateau and the Annamite Chaine offered to turn it all over to Williams. He was not interested. He didn't even look through the files. When things got tough on the High Plateau, we didn't even know where to begin. We had to start all over again, right from the beginning."

Pike calls attention to the fact that, of all the ethnic minorities in South Vietnam, the highlanders were "wooed most strongly" by the Viet Cong.[19] In the mountain areas, the Viet Cong cadres were Vietnamese and highlanders who had remained in the south, and as of 1959 they were being joined by highlanders who had gone north in 1954. Fall reports that by 1959 the Minorities School in Hanoi was graduating some 120 highlanders every nine months, after which they were returned to the south.[20] Pike noted that these "infiltrating teams" into the south generally were led by Vietnamese.[21] He adds that the bulk of infiltration by highlanders appears to have taken place in 1959 and 1960.

Pike also reports that the most common method employed by the Viet Cong in the highlands was to send in a "penetration agent," usually a member of the ethnic group concerned. After this agent had laid the groundwork, the "agit-prop" (agitation-propaganda) teams would arrive. If things went well and the villagers were receptive, a team of cadremen would move into the village to begin directing such activities as organizing porters or guerrilla bands. At the same time, they would recruit highlanders to be sent to North Vietnam or to some training area in the south.

Radio Hanoi broadcasts in Rhadé, Jarai, Bahnar, and the Koho languages continued through this period. The main propaganda themes were that the Saigon government did not care about the highlanders while the Viet Cong did, and there was the oft-repeated promise of autonomy. At the Third Congress of the Lao Dong Party in September 1960, the policy

19. Douglas Pike, *Viet Cong: The Organization and Techniques of the National Liberation Front of South Vietnam* (Cambridge, Mass.: M.I.T. Press, 1966), pp. 204–05.

20. Bernard Fall, "Commentary: Fall on Wickert," in *Viet Nam: The First Five Years*, ed. Richard Lindholm (East Lansing: Michigan State University Press, 1959), p. 137.

21. Pike, *Viet Cong*, pp. 204–05.

of overthrowing the Diem government by force and of "liberating" the
south received "quasi-formal endorsement."[22] Subsequently, on 20
December 1960, "somewhere in the south," one hundred delegates from a
dozen or more political parties and religious groups formed the National
Front for the Liberation of the South (usually called the National
Liberation Front or NLF). Point VII of the NLF's program stated that the
movement desired to:

> ... ensure the right to autonomy of the national minorities. To set up, within
> the framework of the great family of the Vietnamese people, autonomous
> regions in areas inhabited by minority peoples. To ensure equal rights among
> minority nationalities. All nationalities have the right to use and develop their
> own spoken and written languages and to preserve or change their customs
> and habits. To abolish the U.S.-Diem clique's present policy of ill-treatment
> and forced assimilation of the minority nationalities.[23]

Fall reports that at this time one of the highlanders serving as a leader of
the southern highland minorities was Y Ngong Nie Kdam, a Rhadé
medical technician who had joined the Viet Minh in 1945. Y Ngong, who
had been trained in Russia and spoke fluent Russian, was serving in the
National Assembly in Hanoi.[24]

In the central highlands, Viet Cong recruitment lured several others
who had been working in the administration. According to Y Thih Eban,
early in 1961 Y Bih Aleo, who had been active in the Bajaraka Movement,
suddenly departed from his village, where he had been serving as headman.
It was learned later that he had joined the Viet Cong. Not long after,
Banahria Ya Don (4.6), a Chru from the Danhim valley who had been in
the Viet Minh in 1945 but had returned to work in the administration,
joined the Viet Cong. (Touneh Han Tho contends that he had been
sympathetic to their cause while working with the government.)

Soon after Y Bih Aleo joined the Viet Cong, he was named vice
chairman of the NLF Central Committee Presidium. On 19 May 1961 a
congress of twenty-three highlanders in the NLF met to form the
Committee for Autonomy of the People of the Western Plateau (Ủy Ban
Tộc Tự Trị Tây Nguyên), more commonly known as the Central
Highlands Autonomy Movement. Y Bih Aleo was elected chairman. The

22. Joseph Buttinger, *Vietnam: A Dragon Embattled*, 2 vols. (New York: Frederick A. Praeger, 1967),
2: 980–81.
23. George McT. Kahin and John M. Lewis, *The United States in Vietnam* (New York: Dial Press,
1967), pp. 393–94.
24. Fall, "Commentary," p. 138.

secretary general was Rcom Briu (2.20), a Jarai teacher of the elite Rcom clan who later became a general in the North Vietnamese army.[25]

In January 1962 the existence of the People's Revolutionary Party (PRP) was made known. This was the southern branch of the Communist Labor Party (Lao Động) in North Vietnam, although the PRP claimed to be independent of the northern party. The PRP described itself as "the vanguard of the NLF." As the southern branch of the Labor Party, however, the PRP received direction from Hanoi through the Central Office for South Vietnam (COSVN). The NLF and its military wing, the Liberation Army, were in effect branches of the PRP. The entire structure of the movement was organized from the national level to the hamlet level. Attempts at mobilizing segments of the population were carried on through liberation associations that functioned locally. The most important were the Farmers' Liberation Association and the Youth Liberation Association. In addition the NLF had two political parties, the Radical Socialist Party and the Democratic Party. There also were special interest groups, including the Patriotic and Democratic Journalists' Association (intended for professionals), the Hoa Hao Morality Improvement Association, and the Highland Autonomy Movement.[26]

At the First Congress of the NLF, held between 16 February and 3 March 1962, Y Bih Aleo was elected chairman of the minorities committee. Burchett notes that at this gathering there were decisions "to safeguard the interests of minority peoples, with guarantees of complete equality in all fields and the creation of autonomous zones."[27] He adds that, since most of the ethnic minorities already were living in "liberated zones," these new policies could be put into practice immediately.

Since its inception, the Diem government had carried on an anti-Communist effort that intensified in the late 1950s. In May 1955 the People's Directive Committee for the Campaign of Denunciation of Communist Subversive Activities organized the First National Congress of Anti-Communist Denunciation in Saigon, with speeches decrying not only communism but the Geneva Agreements as well. A second congress

25. Pike, *Viet Cong*, p. 204; Commission des relations extérieures du Front National de Libération du Sud Vietnam, *Personnalités du Mouvement de Libération du Sud Vietnam* (Sud Vietnam: Imprimerie Tran Phu, 1965), pp. 4, 30.

26. Pike, *Viet Cong*, pp. 136–55; United States Mission in Vietnam, *A Study of the Communist Party of South Vietnam* (Saigon, 1966), pp. 1–23.

27. Wilfred Burchett, *The Furtive War: The United States in Vietnam and Laos* (New York: International Publishers, Inc., 1963), pp. 29, 103–04.

was held the following year, and the report issued afterward claimed that in the highland provinces of Dong Nai Thuong, Pleiku, and Kontum, and in the city of Dalat, a total of 741 interfamily groups had been formed, resulting in 60 Communists denounced and 149 defecting to the government. One upland hideout was reported to have contained 91 grenades, 17 mortars, and 12,500 rounds of ammunition.[28]

The Communist denunciation drive resulted in the arrest of some highlanders who had followed the Viet Minh during the period following the Japanese capitulation. One of those detained was Touprong Hiou (4.4). He was not only accused of being sympathetic to the Communists but also charged with the murder of a Vietnamese at the Quinquina plantation during the Viet Minh occupation. Hiou was imprisoned at Chi Hoa, near Saigon, and subsequently at Vung Tau and Dalat before he was released in 1961.

There also was, at this time, an increase in the police and paramilitary programs in the highlands. In 1957 a police training school (advised by MSUG staff members) was established in Dalat. About the same time the Directorate of Self-Defense in the Ministry of the Interior established a training center in Ban Me Thuot for preparing village self-defense cadres. This center also had a program for providing some self-defense training for civil servants.[29]

A 1961 U.S. State Department report indicated that as of that year the Viet Cong had 8,000 to 9,000 organized troops in some 30 battalions operating in South Vietnam.[30] There were an additional 8,000 or more troops operating under the leadership of regular Viet Cong officers at the provincial and district levels. These figures, however, did not include the "many thousands of village guards, political cadres, special agents, bearers, and the like." This report also noted that, with recent Pathet Lao victories enabling them to control much of the Laotian highlands, infiltration from North Vietnam into the south had increased considerably. Cases of such infiltration were cited. One example described how a Vietnamese army operation at Calu in northern Quang Tri resulted in captured documents indicating that some 1,840 Viet Cong had infiltrated through the local trail between October 1960 and March 1961.

28. The People's Directive Committee for the C.D.C.S.A., *Achievements of the Campaign of Denunciation of Communist Subversive Activities* (Saigon: Second National Congress of Anti-Communist Denunciation, 1956), p. 115.

29. Republic of Vietnam, *Seven Years*, pp. 187–98.

30. Department of State, *A Threat to the Peace*, part I, pp. 9–10, 27–29.

This report also cited an October 1960 attack by a force of 1,000 Viet Cong against a series of South Vietnamese military outposts along the Laotian border in Kontum province. One Viet Cong unit, Company 3 of the 20th Battalion, was made up largely of highlanders who had been trained in North Vietnam (they were led by Vietnamese officers). This unit concentrated its efforts on the outpost at Dak Dru in northwestern Kontum. After several assaults on the post failed, the unit moved back across the border. Another Viet Cong unit attacked the village of Dak Rotah, and during the fighting four highland soldiers of the Communist force were captured. One of them was Y Lon, who was mentioned above in the discussion about the Viet Minh cadre moving north after the Geneva Agreements. When questioned, Y Lon related that he was taken from the minorities' school on 1 May 1959 to be given special training in propaganda methods. Three weeks later he was sent by automobile to Vinh Linh, where after three days of rest he and thirty colleagues set out on foot to cross the Ben Hai river in the demilitarized zone. Moving southward through the mountains, Y Lon and his group reached Mang Hon in northern Kontum around August. He remained there, visiting surrounding villages to spread Communist propaganda, until he was assigned to a reconnaissance mission at Dak Dru and Dak Rotah where he was captured on 23 October 1960.

Also in October 1960 a company of Viet Cong attacked Tra Bong, the center for the cinnamon trade in the Cua country of upland Quang Ngai. In the savage fighting that ensued, 34 of the Viet Cong were killed (seven of the dead had photographs of themselves in North Vietnamese army uniforms).

A South Vietnamese intelligence source documents the case of a highlander named Nei (probably Nay) Phuong who was among the infiltrators from North Vietnam.[31] He had been born in 1936 in the highlands of Binh Dinh province (his name would identify him as Jarai). In 1954 he joined the Viet Minh and went to North Vietnam where he was assigned to the 120th Independent West Highlands Regiment. He was given military training and courses in techniques of political indoctrination (during which he met Y Ngong Nie Kdam, the Rhadé who had been a leader of the southern highlanders regrouped in the north). In June 1961 he and thirty colleagues were detached from the regiment and organized as

31. Central Intelligence Organization, "National Interrogation Center Case No. 324/4, 9 December 1965" (Saigon, 1965), pp. 1–4.

Infiltration Group 2. Entering South Vietnam on 10 October 1961, Phuong was assigned to "production work" in Ban Me Thuot district. On 2 May 1965 he was caught in an ambush laid by the South Vietnamese army and was taken prisoner. Phuong outlined some of the Viet Cong appeals to the highlanders. One of the main points was that the minorities in North Vietnam had attained "autonomy," and this status would be extended to the southern highland people when they were "liberated." Each year, leaders from the central highlands were sent to North Vietnam to visit the "autonomous zones."

By the beginning of 1961, the insurgency was intensifying. Roads in the highlands were again becoming insecure as the Viet Cong blew up bridges and laid ambushes. The highlanders found themselves a people in between, as they had been during the Indochina War.

Early in 1961 while visiting a village outside of Ban Me Thuot, a small convoy in which Y Ut Nie Buon Rit, the noted Rhadé leader and member of the National Assembly, and former assemblyman R'mah Pok were riding was attacked. Both leaders were killed. During 1961 there also were attacks on highland villages by the Vietnamese Air Force (VNAF) during military operations against the Viet Cong. One such incident occurred in September 1961, when VNAF fighter-bombers struck the Mnong Rlam villages of Buon Plum, Buon Krong, and Buon Jar in Lac Thien district in southern Darlac. According to Y Char Hmok (a Mnong Rlam leader who received an A.B. degree in the U.S.), there was heavy destruction in all three villages. Twenty-five in Buon Jar and twenty in Buon Plum were killed. In all three villages there were many wounded. In an effort to obtain aid from the provincial authorities, leaders from the villages went to Ban Me Thuot where they sat outside the province chief's office for a week before they received any attention. Meanwhile, in the three villages, more of the wounded were dying. Sister Benedict, one of the Benedictine nuns who ran a school for highland girls in Ban Me Thuot, heard of their plight and rushed to the villages with two jeeps loaded with food and medicine. When Y Char was told about the bombing, he wrote to Ngo Dinh Nhu, younger brother of and also political adviser to President Diem. Nhu visited the villages and arranged to have some rice delivered to the victims.

Boulbet reports that early in 1962 VNAF aircraft also attacked some Maa villages with napalm.[32] The village of Bordee was struck, and as the

32. Jean Boulbet, *Pays des Maa domaine de génies Nggar Maa, Nggar Yaang* (Paris: Ecole Française d'Extrême-Orient, 1967), pp. 117–20.

aircraft approached the villagers began to flee. Some, however, such as the mother of Maa leader K'Bruih, remained to guard their lineage altars and were killed.

The situation at this time was generating an increasing number of highland refugees, which brought to an end the government's Highlander Resettlement Program. In 1961 the government had authorized 128 million piasters for the Commissariate for Land Development to implement a "three-ring project" that would involve resettlement of 150,000 highlanders living within certain radii of the existing Land Development Centers. No sooner had the funds been allocated than suddenly an estimated 4,000 highlanders in Kontum province began fleeing their villages. These refugees either fled to other villages or constructed shacks along the main routes. They lived as best they could, with many of the males becoming laborers in nearby Vietnamese settlements for very low wages.[33]

Despite an effort to organize a Highland Village Youth Defense program in many upland areas, the flood of refugees continued as security began to worsen.[34] In Quang Ngai, for example, Hre villagers abandoned their traditional territories in the mountains to descend on valley towns such as Ba To, the district headquarters, where, overnight, some five hundred refugees converged.[35] As of August 1962, when the government launched a drive to aid the highland refugees (Catholic Relief Service and CARE were already lending aid), there were reported to be 111,464 highlanders who had left their villages. (Refugee figures on the highlanders were invariably low because, as was indicated above, many went to other villages rather than to refugee areas.) The highest numbers were in the provinces of Kontum (13,012), Pleiku (24,192), Quang Ngai (16,000), Tuyen Duc (10,686), Quang Tri (15,485), and Phuoc Long (7,250). The relatively low figure of 3,623 refugees for Darlac more than likely was due to the Village Defense System being implemented by the Americans around Ban Me Thuot at this time (see below).[36]

33. Directorate General of Information, "The Highland Refugees" (Saigon, 1963), pp. 13–15.

34. "Thanh niên thượng bảo vệ buôn ấp" (Highland Village Youth Defense), *Hình Ảnh Việt Nam* (Vietnam Images), no. 49, 1961, p. 12.

35. Hoàng Ngọc Minh, "Đồng bào Thượng di cư ở Quảng Ngãi" (Highlander Refugees in Quang Ngai), *Sáng Dội Miền Nam* (Southern Brightness) 1, no. 10 (1962): 24–25.

36. "Trên một trăm ngàn đồng bào thượng di cư lánh nạn cộng sản" (Over One Hundred Thousand Highlanders Flee the Communists), *Hình Ảnh Việt Nam* (Vietnam Images), no. 58, 1962, pp. 1–12; Nguyễn Cao, "The Commissioner Reports on the Migration of Highlanders," *Times of Vietnam Magazine* 4, no. 33 (1962): 16–18.

In spite of the increased insurgency in the highlands during the late 1950s and early 1960s, the activities of the Catholic and Protestant missions not only continued but expanded. Father Darricau relates that when he first began to visit the Danhim valley, in the Chru country, there were only three Vietnamese Christians living there. When some young Chru expressed interest in the Catholic religion, Father Darricau obtained permission from the administration to begin proselytizing in the valley. The priest soon found himself with an ever-increasing number of Chru catechumens. After the children of Touneh Han Dang (4.1) converted, the number of Chru Christians swelled. Finally, in February 1962, Han Dang himself became a Catholic, and practically all of the Chru followed his example.[37]

In 1959 Dr. Patricia (Pat) Smith arrived in the highlands with the goal of establishing a hospital for charity patients. She began to practice medicine in the leprosarium that had been established near Kontum by Sister Marie Louise of the Sisters of Charity order. Within a few years Pat Smith had opened her own hospital on the edge of Kontum, and it attracted highland patients from the whole province.

Another significant development for the highlanders during this period was the establishment of the Summer Institute of Linguistics (SIL) with its staff of Wycliffe Bible translators. In February 1956, SIL linguist Dr. Richard Pittman met with President Diem to explain his program of linguistic studies, preparation of literacy material in vernacular languages, and Bible translation. Diem granted permission for the SIL to begin its project in South Vietnam. The following December Dr. Pittman and David Thomas arrived to organize the project, which was to be sponsored by the University of Saigon. Soon after, Milton and Muriel Barker arrived to begin working on the language of the Mnong refugees living near Ban Me Thuot. David and Dorothy Thomas took up residence in Xuan Loc to begin their study of the Chrau language.

In 1959 additional members of the SIL arrived to begin linguistic research. (Everyone studied Vietnamese first.) David and Doris Blood moved to Phan Rang to begin their work on the Cham language while, in Darlac, Jean Donaldson worked on White Tai. At Kontum, John and Betty Barker studied Bahnar and, at Lac Thien, Henry and Evangeline Blood concentrated on Mnong Rlam. Ernest and Lois Lee did research on

37. F. Darricau, "Semailles," *Bulletin de la Société des Missions Etrangères de Paris*, 2ᵉ série, no. 126, 1959, pp. 586–94.

Roglai, and Ralph and Lorraine Haupers moved to Song Be to begin working on Stieng. Wherever possible, the SIL researchers lived in villages so they could immerse themselves in the languages and cultures.[38]

More researchers arrived during the next few years, and by the end of 1963 the SIL was studying sixteen languages. In isolated Khe Sanh in upland Quang Tri, John and Carolyn Miller studied Bru. At Kontum, Mr. and Mrs. James Cooper worked on Halang, Mr. and Mrs. Kenneth Smith studied Sedang, and research on Jeh was being done by Dwight Gradin, Maxwell Cobbey, and Patrick Cohen. At An Diem, where the U.S. Special Forces had a post, Judy Wallace, Nancy Costello, and Eva Burton worked on the Katu language. (Subsequently, Eva Burton and Jacqueline Maier collaborated in a study of Katu.) In Hue, Mr. and Mrs. Richard Watson conducted research on Pacoh. Among the northern highland refugees near Dalat, Mr. and Mrs. Colin Day focused on Tho (Tay) while Janice Saul and Nancy Freiberger worked on Nung.

In 1962, however, the first move against any of the American civilians took place at the Christian and Missionary Alliance leprosarium, located some twenty kilometers from Ban Me Thuot. A night raid on this installation resulted in Dr. Ardel Vietti, Dan Gerber, and Archie Mitchell being captured. They were never heard from again.

Another development during this period was the 1958 opening of the University of Dalat, established under Catholic sponsorship. It was the first private university in Vietnam and the first university in the highlands. Initially, it offered only secondary level courses given by French instructors from the Lycée Yersin. By 1961 there were faculties in Letters and Science and student enrollment had exceeded four hundred—all Vietnamese.[39]

AMERICAN INVOLVEMENT AND THE BAJARAKA REVIVAL

By mid-1961 the deteriorating situation in the highlands was a cause for serious concern in Saigon, prompting the Vietnamese government and the American mission to devise new strategies for maintaining control of the region. One result was a deepening American involvement in the high-

38. Information on the early SIL activities was provided by Dr. Richard Pittman in personal correspondence dated 3 October 1975.

39. Nguyen Dinh Hoa, "Higher Education in the Republic of Viet Nam," *Times of Viet Nam Magazine* 3, no. 9 (1961): 19.

lands, both militarily and politically, with the CIA-sponsored Village Defense and Mountain Scout programs. Another consequence was the government's launching of the ill-fated Strategic Hamlet Program.

Concomitant with the intensification of insurgency was an expansion of the U.S. aid program and the U.S. military advisory effort. The actual strength of the U.S. military staff in Vietnam during the late 1950s was treated confidentially. Fall claims that as of 1958 the American military personnel numbered "well over a thousand officers and men."[40] Duncanson, however, reports that when the French military mission withdrew in 1956 there were reported to be 685 foreign military personnel in Vietnam, half of them French and half American.[41] He contends that the number of Americans remained more or less the same until 1960, when 1,000 additional advisers were added to the roster. He also points out that after John F. Kennedy took office in January 1961 the number of advisers "quietly tripled," and by the end of 1961 it had risen to 1,346. By late 1962 the number of advisers had increased to 9,965.

The first American military advisory program in the highlands began in 1955, when MAAG personnel were sent to the Combined Arms School (Ecole Militaire Inter-Armes) at Dalat. As was indicated before, by early 1957 there were MAAG detachments at Ban Me Thuot, Pleiku, and Kontum. On 29 July 1959 Diem signed a decree establishing the Vietnamese National Military Academy in Dalat, and construction of the new installation began the following year.[42]

Both the Village Defense and Mountain Scout programs came about by a series of circumstances rather than as a result of any overall strategy devised by the U.S. Mission in Saigon. In an interview in Washington on 17 January 1977, Gilbert Layton, a retired U.S. Army colonel who had been assigned to the CIA in Vietnam, pointed out that the Village Defense Program in the highlands "just happened." In the late 1950s, the U.S. State Department requested the Combined Studies Group (the CIA's designation in Vietnam) to obtain intelligence—particularly case studies and photographs—proving that there was infiltration of Communist agents from North Vietnam. As a consequence, the CIA and its Vietnamese

40. Bernard Fall, *Viet-Nam Witness 1953–66* (New York: Frederick A. Praeger, 1966), p. 162.

41. Dennis J. Duncanson, *Government and Revolution* (New York and London: Oxford University Press, 1968), p. 404.

42. MACV, Viet-Nam, VNMA Detachment, "The National Military Academy of Vietnam" (Dalat, 1969), p. 2.

counterpart organization, the Presidential Survey Office (under control of Ngo Dinh Nhu), carried out intelligence-gathering activities in the highland border area.

According to Layton, as the situation worsened in the highlands, the upland experience of the CIA led to discussions concerning the possibility of using highlanders to gather intelligence on Viet Cong movements. This, however, did not lead to the formulation of any plan to do so. During this period, Layton and his wife had been entertaining some of the young IVS volunteers in their Saigon home. Among these guests was David Nuttle, who was involved in agricultural programs for Darlac province. He had plans for a "seed farm" but needed the funds to get it started, so Layton obtained the money for him. In July 1961, when the farm was in its initial phase, Layton went to Ban Me Thuot to visit the project. This stirred up interest in meeting some of the needs of the Rhadé, and Layton also met with some of the Vietnamese intelligence officers in Ban Me Thuot to talk about possible ways of gaining more support for the government among the highlanders. This, in turn, led to similar discussions with Col. Le Quang Tung, head of the Presidential Survey Office and counterpart of the CIA station chief, John Richardson. Tung had left the seminary at Ngo Dinh Diem's behest and was given an army commission. He proved a loyal follower to Diem and Nhu and therefore was entrusted with the Presidential Survey Office, reporting directly to Nhu. Meanwhile Layton went ahead with a small medical program for Rhadé in the vicinity of Ban Me Thuot, obtaining the services of a Special Forces sergeant who had been trained as a medic and was available.

These events led to a plan to launch a Village Defense Program at Buon Enao, a Rhadé village of about four hundred inhabitants close to Ban Me Thuot in the vicinity of Nuttle's seed farm. Approval for the project had to be obtained from the palace in Saigon, and this was the responsibility of Le Quang Tung. According to former Vice President Nguyen Ngoc Tho, by 1961 both Diem and Nhu were becoming increasingly suspicious of American intentions in Vietnam. There was little rapport between these two leaders and any of the high-ranking American officials. Moreover, given the French strategy of using the highlands as a political pawn, Diem was particularly sensitive about any foreign involvement in that region. Tung assured Diem and Nhu that the Americans working on the Village Defense Program would coordinate everything with his office. The Vietnamese, he said, would maintain control. Layton noted that he was taken by CIA official William Colby to talk about the project with President Diem.

The palace approved the program, so for several weeks in October 1961 Layton and Nuttle met daily with the leaders of Buon Enao to explain that they needed their cooperation. Such cooperation involved having the villagers denounce the Viet Cong and declare their support for the government. In return, the villagers would receive arms and training in defense methods. The village leaders agreed, and by late October the program was begun.

On 1 November 1961 the first volunteers appeared at Buon Enao. None were from Buon Enao itself. Most were from a nearby village that had been attacked and occupied by the Viet Cong several weeks before. Buon Enao villagers built an enclosure around the settlement (this was supposed to symbolize their rejection of the Viet Cong) and they dug bunkers and constructed buildings for the training center and a dispensary. The trainees were taught to use weapons, to form an intelligence system in order to control movement into the village, and to provide an early warning system in case of an impending attack. On 15 December there was a ceremony at Buon Enao to mark the end of the first training course. The trainees (who were carrying spears) were presented with carbines, which they readily accepted. According to Y Thih Eban, it was the understanding of Rhadé involved in this Village Defense Program that they were given the weapons to keep.

Nuttle began to devote all of his time to the program, and some highlanders who spoke English became associated with it. One of them was Rcom H'un, daughter of the Cheo Jarai leader Nay Moul (2.17), who later married the young Rhadé leader Y Kdruin Mlo (2.24), who called himself Philippe Drouin. Another English-speaking highlander who assisted informally was Y Klong Adrong (5.9), a member of the Protestant congregation.

With Buon Enao now considered secure, the Village Defense Program was extended to neighboring villages. In addition to training village defenders, the program was expanded to provide training for a Strike Force of volunteers who would remain in Buon Enao as a reserve that could be rushed to a village being attacked. According to Layton, the volunteers flooded into Buon Enao. The problem of possible Viet Cong infiltration was coped with by having the chiefs of the villages from which the volunteers came vouch for their loyalty to the government.

Layton noted that up to this point there had been no overall plan. Decisions were made as situations unfolded. There was no rigid organizational structure for the project. Layton himself "scrounged" much of the needed equipment and vehicles from Vietnamese army dumps. As the expansion of the defense network began to take place late in December 1961, however, things began to change gradually. Half of the U.S. Special Forces Detachment A-35 (six men) arrived from Laos to assist in the training, serving as advisers to counterparts from the Vietnamese Special Forces (most of them highlanders).[43] This quiet development had great significance. It marked not only the beginning of the Special Forces' presence in the highlands but also another step in a deepening American military involvement in Vietnam.

During this period, the CIA also was engaged in another highland project farther north. According to a retired CIA official (who preferred to be unnamed) interviewed in January 1977 in Washington, he had been sent to central Vietnam in September 1961 to assess the deteriorating situation there. In Hue, he contacted Ngo Van Hung, the Vietnamese major in charge of the Bureau for Highland Affairs. They discussed what might be done to cope with the crumbling security, particularly in the highlands where there was increasing infiltration from North Vietnam. Since the Vietnamese major had been dealing with the highlanders at the bureau, he suggested some kind of program to muster their support for the government. He also raised the possibility of highlanders being trained to gather intelligence and spread progovernment propaganda.

The CIA official and Major Hung settled on a scheme to recruit and train highlanders in intelligence gathering and in ways of spreading progovernment propaganda. Major Hung was close to Ngo Dinh Can, brother of Diem and Nhu, who functioned as the most powerful political figure in central Vietnam, so he sought his approval for the project. He assured Can that the Americans would be involved minimally, and Can gave his approval.

This was the beginning of the Mountain Scout program (often called the Commando program). In November 1961 the first buildings for the training center were constructed in Hue, and the CIA obtained 6,000 Springfield rifles from Taiwan. The province chiefs in Quang Tri, Quang Nan, Quang Ngai, Kontum, and Pleiku were instructed to select "re-

---

43. Francis J. Kelly, *U.S. Army Special Forces, 1961–1971* (Washington: Department of the Army, 1973), pp. 24–25.

liable" highlanders in each district to be sent to Hue. Thirty-five men, all known by their district chiefs and most of them veterans of the French army, arrived in Hue for training. All were given polygraph tests (Touneh Han Tho, who was serving in the administration at Quang Tri at this time, reported that the highlanders were mystified by the polygraph, thinking it some strange American magic) to ascertain that they were not Viet Cong agents. The training included intelligence gathering techniques (including use of radios and map reading), infiltration methods, some psychological warfare principles, civic action ("helping villagers"), and use of weapons.

The first group of 350 "Mountain Scouts" completed their training in January 1962. The CIA official noted that he invited General Tran Van Don (who later was involved in the overthrow of Diem) to the ceremony celebrating this event, and Don shook his head as he expressed some doubt about arming highlanders. The trainees were grouped in teams of fifteen men divided into three five-man units, and each team selected its own leaders. As the teams dispersed to their own districts, they were given "gifts" (things like bolts of cloth) to be distributed to villagers in the areas where they would be operating. The CIA official claimed that within a short time captured Viet Cong documents indicated that the Mountain Scouts were effectively harassing Viet Cong operations. It was reported that as a result the number of Viet Cong in Kontum province dwindled from 5,000 at the beginning of 1962 to 500 in March.

In December 1961 half of U.S. Special Forces Detachment A-35 (the other half was at Buon Enao) arrived at the Hoa Cam Training Center near Danang to begin advising on training for "special programs," one of which involved using highlanders in paramilitary operations in remote areas. Eventually, this program was merged with the Mountain Scout program (see below).

The year 1962 proved a crucial year for the CIA efforts in the highlands. In addition, it was the time when the course of the American involvement in this region—and subsequently throughout Vietnam—would be defined. Finally, during 1962 and most of 1963, the perceptions of the Americans (particularly the CIA and the military mission), the Vietnamese, and the highlanders regarding this involvement were most clearly manifest. These varying, and often disparate, perceptions contributed a great deal to the dire events of the decade that followed.

The expansion of the Village Defense Program in early 1962 resulted in

40 additional Rhadé villages becoming part of the network. Between December 1961 and March 1962 it involved an estimated village population of 14,000 with 975 men in the Village Defense units and 300 in the Strike Force.[44] Layton noted that early in 1962 the British Advisory Group (see below) brought in some Australian army officers to participate in the Village Defense Program.

By April 1962 the Village Defense Program in Darlac was adjudged a success. Roads and villages in the network area had become very secure and, as was noted previously, the number of highland refugees in the province was considerably lower than in the neighboring provinces. It was decided, therefore, to enlarge the defense network. This, in turn, necessitated an expansion of the U.S. Special Forces involved in the program. In February 1962 there was one full Special Forces A Detachment (twelve men) deployed in Darlac. As new training centers similar to Buon Enao opened at Buon Ho, Buon Krong, Buon Tah, Ea Ana, and Lac Thien, 200 new villages became part of the program. By August there were five A Detachments operating in the province.

During this period there were related developments that would have a profound effect on the future of the CIA's operations in the highlands. One such development occurred in February 1962 when the U.S. Military Assistance Command Vietnam (MACV) was established to replace MAAG. MACV was put under the command of General Paul D. Harkins, and it clearly was geared for an expanded U.S. military presence in Vietnam.

Another development was the growing hostility of the Vietnamese leaders toward the Village Defense Program. In an interview held in Washington in January 1977, former CIA official Lucien Conein pointed out that General Ton That Dinh, commander of the II Corps (with its headquarters in Pleiku), was becoming increasingly uneasy over the expansion of the Village Defense Program. General Le Quang Tung, head of the Presidential Survey Office, functioned as liaison between the CIA and the palace, so it was he, rather than Dinh, who had control over the program. According to Conein, Tung invited Ngo Dinh Nhu and Ton That Dinh to a "highlander celebration" at Buon Enao. The villagers gathered in their traditional clothes, buffalos were sacrificed, and everyone drank from the jars as gongs played in the background. Conein described

---

44. Ibid., p. 29.

how, at one point in the festivities, Dinh took Nhu aside and told him that "the Americans have put an army at my back." He then informed Nhu that the Americans had armed 18,000 highlanders. (Conein said that this figure was accurate and it also had been a deep secret.) Nhu turned his face back to the crowd and wore a "coldly impassive" expression. Clearly the news had come as a shock.

This event led to an attempt by Nhu to gain more control over the Village Defense Program (see below). It also was an important consideration in the decision of the CIA to "get out of the program," as Conein put it. In discussing this period with William Colby, who had been station chief and then head of the pacification program in Vietnam and later director of the CIA, it was pointed out that the Bay of Pigs disaster that had taken place in April 1961 was another reason for the CIA leaving the Village Defense Program. Since that event, Washington had been very sensitive about the CIA becoming involved in any military or paramilitary operations that might become "another Bay of Pigs." As the Village Defense Program began to expand, it fell into that category. This resulted in Washington meetings between the CIA (represented by Desmond Fitz-Gerald) and the Department of Defense (represented by Paul Nitze), and in May 1962 it was agreed that complete control of the Village Defense Program and other CIA highland operations would be turned over to MACV in Operation Switchback, to be completed by 1 July 1963. Initially the CIA retained responsibility for both the logistical and operational aspects of the program. The CIA and MACV would coordinate everything with the newly formed Vietnamese Special Forces, which had grown out of the Presidential Survey Office and was commanded by General Le Quang Tung. The Village Defense Program now became the Civilian Irregular Defense Group (CIDG). In July 1962 the U.S. Department of Defense decided to transfer complete responsibility for U.S. Special Forces operations to MACV, thus making the army responsible for American support of the CIDG.[45]

July 1963 marked the end of the CIA involvement in the Village Defense Program and the Mountain Scout program farther north. The former CIA officials interviewed expressed considerable bitterness at the military takeover of their programs. (Conein refers to Operation Switchback as "Operation Switchblade.") They emphasized that the CIA

45. Ibid., pp. 29–30.

A Jarai strategic hamlet near Pleiku (1964)

concept of these programs was that they would be "defensive" in character. Intelligence gathering would be involved, but no offensive operations
would be mounted. The programs also were political in that they involved
winning more support for the Saigon government. These officials noted
that the American involvement in the programs was minimal, and one
reason the programs were effective was that the Americans participating in
them were not bound by bureaucratic restraints.

Layton pointed out that the MACV officers who came to take over the
Village Defense Program immediately asked for the "TO" (the Table of
Organization found in all military units), so he had to devise one for them.
They also had many questions about logistical procedures where no procedures resembling those of the army existed. For these CIA officials, the
worst effects were that the takeover resulted in the programs becoming
"military" rather than "political" and "offensive" rather than "defensive"
as they had been. As one CIA official put it, "they turned them into 'kill
operations'."

As was indicated above, the CIA operations in the highlands, as perceived by Vietnamese leaders such as Ngo Dinh Nhu and Ton That Dinh,
were fraught with danger in that they involved arming large numbers of
highlanders. The Vietnamese still retained fresh memories of the recent

Bajaraka affair and, furthermore, these were programs over which they had little control—as was witnessed by the fact that they were not supposed to know how many arms had been distributed. It is apparent from the fact that Operation Switchback provided for the integration of the CIDG camps and the pacified villages into the Strategic Hamlet Program (which by early 1962 was being widely implemented in the lowlands) that this was the means by which Saigon would restore its control in the highlands.

The Strategic Hamlet Program was another result of the effort in 1961 to cope with the crumbling security in rural South Vietnam. In June 1961 President Kennedy had sent a large commission headed by Stanford University professor Eugene Staley to Vietnam to review the military situation and American aid. According to Buttinger, Staley's recommendations concerning rural pacification stirred interest in village defense. At the same time, "the Staley mission was largely responsible for the misguided zeal with which the strategic-hamlet program was tackled."[46] In September 1961 President Diem invited Robert Thompson of the British Advisory Mission (composed of former British officials who had been involved in the effort against Communist insurgents in Malaya) to contribute his opinion on the situation. The British Advisory Mission proposed a strategic plan that drew on the Malaya experience. A result of these reports and the interest they stimulated with Ngo Dinh Nhu was the Strategic Hamlet Program, which involved, among other things, defense enclosures for hamlets and organized self-defense groups within the community.

As the program began to be widely implemented early in 1962, the results were more apparent than real, due to the desire to have impressive figures. The Vietnamese had long since become aware that numbers were important to Washington. Often a strategic hamlet was created by placing a sign at the village entrance announcing that it was a "strategic hamlet."[47] In the highlands, all of the land development centers and highland refugee camps became "strategic hamlets."[48]

---

46. Buttinger, *Vietnam: A Dragon Embattled*, 2:991.

47. Early in 1962 John Donnell and I conducted a study of some of the first strategic hamlets implemented in the vicinity of Saigon and in the Mekong river delta. We found that there was a tendency to create the strategic hamlets too rapidly and at too great a cost to the villagers. The findings were summarized in John C. Donnell and Gerald C. Hickey, "The Vietnamese 'Strategic Hamlets': A Preliminary Report" (Santa Monica, California: The Rand Corporation, 1962).

48. Directorate General of Information, "The Highland Refugees," pp. 21–27.

The highlanders' perception of the American involvement in the highlands differed considerably from the perception of the CIA, the American military, or Vietnamese leaders. The highland leaders who had been involved in the Bajaraka Movement saw the American presence as a buffer between themselves and the Vietnamese government. The Americans would provide a shield of protection behind which the highlanders could carry on their ethnonationalist activities.

Although most of the Bajaraka leaders had been arrested or dispersed in the lowlands in 1958, one who remained in Buon Ale-A—probably because he was affiliated with the Protestant Mission and was not a civil servant—was Y Preh Buon Krong. According to Layton, when implementation of the Buon Enao project began late in 1961, Y Preh began to "hang around." He appeared to have good relations with the villagers, and he proved to be a help in dealing with them. Meanwhile, Y Thih Eban (5.2), who still was imprisoned in Hue, wrote on 1 May 1962 a letter in English to Frederick Nolting, the American ambassador in Saigon, asking his intervention with President Diem in obtaining the release of the jailed Bajaraka leaders. The letter also was signed by fellow prisoners Nay Luett (2.26), Touneh Yoh (4.10), Siu Sipp, and Y Ju Eban. Y Thih's brother-in-law, a medical technician in Hue, took the letter to Ban Me Thuot, where he gave it to David Nuttle. Nuttle, in turn, delivered it to Nolting, who brought it to the attention of President Diem. Y Thih reported that Diem at first disclaimed any knowledge of the highlanders' imprisonment but finally agreed to have them released in three months. On 18 August 1962, as promised, the group that had signed the letter was let free.

Y Thih and Y Ju returned to Ban Me Thuot. Y Thih's friend Y Preh secured a position for him as an interpreter at Buon Enao. Y Ju Eban found a job as interpreter in the newly opened USOM office in Ban Me Thuot. Nay Luett went to Danang where he was accepted as an interpreter for the U.S. Special Forces and was assigned to "special operations" in the camp at Kham Duc in the remote interior of Quang Nam province.[49] Siu Sipp returned to Pleiku, and Touneh Yoh found a position in the Tuyen Duc provincial administration.

According to Y Thih there were many Bajaraka sympathizers among the highlanders in the Village Defense Program. He lost no time reorganiz-

49. I visited this camp in 1964 and was told that Ngo Dinh Diem had the excellent airstrip built in 1962 so he could visit Kham Duc. He also had a statue of the Blessed Virgin placed on a nearby hill where he would go and spend days in prayer.

ing the Bajaraka committee, which included himself, Y Preh Buon Krong, Y Dhon Adrong, Y Nam Nie Hrah, Y Kong Eban, and Y Du Nie—all of them Rhadé from the vicinity of Ban Me Thuot. Y Thih and Y Preh already had had considerable experience with the American missionaries, and they felt that all Americans would be as sympathetic and helpful as the missionaries.

In October 1962 Y Thih requested the Americans at Buon Enao to intercede with the Vietnamese government for the release of the other jailed Bajaraka leaders. He stated that the movement would declare its support of the government and drop its demand for autonomy. Nothing came of this.

During this period of diminishing CIA control of the highland projects, the U.S. Special Forces operations in the CIDG program increased in other parts of the mountains and in some lowland areas as well. By September 1962 the CIDG program in Darlac included 200 villages with a total population of around 60,000. There were 1,500 trained Strike Force personnel and 10,600 village defense militia. As of the end of 1962 the CIDG program had 24 U.S. Special Forces detachments scattered throughout Vietnam. Of these, there were 20 A Detachments on temporary duty from 1st Special Forces Group in Okinawa and from the 5th and 7th Special Forces Group at Fort Bragg, North Carolina. Each A Detachment had twelve men, and they advised a counterpart team of twelve men from the Vietnamese Special Forces. Both teams collaborated in recruiting and training a Strike Force and hamlet militia (as the village defenders were now called).[50]

Curiously, a number of the A Detachments in the highlands were located in sites that historically had been occupied by French military installations (see maps 3 and 4). In December 1962, one A Detachment was established in an old French fort above the small town of Khe Sanh in the Bru country of Quang Tri province. Another detachment was at Tra Bong, the cinnamon trading center in the Cua country, and there was one at Ba To in the Hre area of Quang Ngai, where, in the nineteenth century, the Vietnamese had a Son Phong fort that was taken over by the French. A CIDG camp was located at Dak Pek, where the French had had a political prison in the 1930s, and another detachment was established at Ban Don, Khunjanob's elephant trading center, which also was the location of the

---

50. Kelly, *U.S. Army Special Forces*, pp. 30–32.

first French military-administrative post at the turn of the century. Cheo
Reo was another location for an A Detachment.

Later, A Detachments were established at the old Son Phong fort sites at
Gia Vuc and Son Ha in the Hre country, as well as at Dak To, Plateau Gi,
and Kannak, where the Viet Minh had attacked in 1954 just before the
Mobile Group 100 debacle. Finally, detachments were sent to Bu Dop and
Bu Gia Map, both locations of old French forts built in the 1930s during
the effort to pacify the Stieng and Mnong areas.

In September 1962 the Darlac province chief agreed to accept responsibility for 32 of the 214 villages in the Buon Enao complex. This was in
keeping with the plan to integrate CIDG-controlled villages into the
Strategic Hamlet Program. According to Kelly, the Vietnamese government had arranged a very strict schedule for the turnover in Darlac, but the
American Special Forces commander at Buon Enao was not shown the
plan in advance.[51] There was some apprehension on the part of the
Americans involved that a sudden change would stir up resentment and
discontent among the highlanders. At the end of 1962, however, the 32
villages were under the province chief in name only. He was unable to
support them, and so the U.S. Special Forces continued to be responsible
for logistical support of the villages and the pay of the Strike Force.

Vietnamese concern over the large number of weapons in the hands of
the highlanders resulted in efforts late in 1962 to repossess the rifles. Kelly
points out that there was great difficulty in achieving this goal because the
highlanders had been given the weapons with no explanation. From their
point of view, they had received the guns to defend their villages, so they
could keep them indefinitely. Duncanson reports that various schemes
were devised to get back the weapons, such as "exchanging" them for farm
tools. He contends that these methods only realized about 2,000 of the
guns.[52]

Kelly points out that during Operation Switchback the Viet Cong
mounted an increased number of attacks against the CIDG camps and
villages.[53] The worst attack came on 3 January 1963 at Plei Mrong, located
in the Jarai Tobuan country west of Pleiku. Two reinforced Viet Cong
companies, with the assistance of an estimated thirty-three "penetration
agents" in the Strike Force, attacked and overran the camp.

51. Ibid., pp. 41–44.
52. Duncanson, *Government*, p. 408.
53. Kelly, *U.S. Army Special Forces*, p. 40.

By the end of 1962 there was considerable tension among the high-landers in the Buon Enao program over the turnover of the villages and attempts to retrieve the weapons. In January 1963 reports reached Layton and the Americans at Buon Enao and also General Nguyen Khanh, commander of the Second Corps Area (there were now four corps areas in South Vietnam), that the Darlac and Pleiku Bajaraka committees had decided to join with the Viet Cong after rising in rebellion. Layton and other CIA members met with Y Thih and Y Preh, both of whom disclaimed any knowledge of an impending revolt. They explained that it was possible, however, that Y Bham (who still was jailed in Ban Me Thuot) may have ordered an uprising without their being informed. Layton, Y Thih, and Y Preh flew to Pleiku to meet with General Khanh. The two highlanders were afraid that they would be punished but were pleasantly surprised to find that Khanh had arranged to bring Y Bham and Paul Nur (1.13) to the meeting at the general's house. Y Bham assured Khanh that the reports of a Bajaraka uprising were false. Siu Sipp joined the meeting, and afterward he called a meeting of the Pleiku Bajaraka committee to denounce the Viet Cong. Three weeks later he was killed by the Viet Cong.

According to Y Thih, on 1 February 1963 he received word from Y Bih Aleo that he would be willing to meet with Vietnamese officials if Y Bham were released. Y Thih, Y Preh, Layton, and some of the Vietnamese associated with the Buon Enao project made arrangements to have Y Bham and some of the Vietnamese meet Y Bih at the Yang Prong, the Cham tower in western Darlac. Before the meeting, however, Colonel Le Quang Trong, commander of the 23rd Division at Ban Me Thuot, learned of it and ordered VNAF aircraft to bomb the locale of the tower. (It is not known whether the tower was hit.) Y Bih was unharmed, and he sent a message to Ban Me Thuot accusing the government of bad faith. Layton also received a letter from Y Bham containing the same accusation. Through his "contacts" with the Viet Cong he sent a letter to Y Bih denying that he and the others who had made the arrangements had had any knowledge of the attack until after it took place.

During the first half of 1963, Operation Switchback continued, with more villages being turned over to the Darlac province chief. In spite of his not being able to support the first 32 villages, a second group of 107 villages were put under his control by 20 March 1963. The following month 604 of the 900-man Buon Enao Strike Force were designated by the province chief as "border surveillance" troops and moved to Ban Me Thuot for "indoctrination." Another company of Buon Enao Strike Force was set to open the new camp at Bu Prang, on the Cambodian border southwest of Ban Me Thuot in the Mnong country. Kelly reports that these moves were decided upon unilaterally by the Vietnamese with no "psychological preparation" of the Strike Force.[54] In addition, the removal of the troops left the Buon Enao complex without a Strike Force during the hours of darkness. To make matters worse, on 30 April 1963 the province chief had assumed the responsibility for paying the Strike Force, but as of 26 July they still had not received any money. The health workers at Buon Enao also were without pay. A serious situation was narrowly avoided when the American Special Forces provided back pay for both groups. In describing these events, Kelly notes that "the problems encountered in turning over the Buon Enao project to the Vietnamese proved to be the same problems which arose every time turnover was attempted in the CIDG program."

Farther north, Operation Switchback also was being carried out in the Mountain Scout program. By mid-1963 the CIA had turned over complete control of the program to the Special Forces. The CIA, however, continued to support cadre programs in the highlands. In 1962 some of the CIA personnel from Hue had gone to Pleiku and organized a new Mountain Scout training center. According to Touneh Han Tho (4.2), his brother Touneh Han Tin (4.13), an army captain, was assigned to this center and had a staff of highland military personnel. (In 1964 Touneh Han Tin died of fever.) The CIA provided financial support and advisers. Recruits came from all over the highlands, and after their training they were sent back to their native areas where they were under the direction of Vietnamese and highlander military officers, who were representatives of the Bureau for Highland Affairs in each province.

With the Americans out of the Buon Enao project in June 1963, Y Thih and the other Bajaraka leaders departed. Y Thih found a position at Buon Sar Pa, a new Special Forces camp that had just opened in the Mnong country close to the Cambodian border. At Buon Sar Pa there were other Bajaraka members, so in the evening they would gather to discuss further moves and ways of getting Y Bham released. One scheme was to raid the Ban Me Thuot jail, free Y Bham, and flee into Cambodia. Also, at Buon Sar Pa, Y Thih became friendly with a Mnong-Lao from Ban Don with

54. Ibid., pp. 41–44.

the Rhadéized name Y Klong Nie who was a distant kinsman of Y Keo, the nephew of Khunjanob. Y Klong joined the evening discussions, which now began to center on the possibility of the Bajaraka people establishing some kind of contact with the Cambodians. The time might come when the Bajaraka members would have to seek refuge, and Cambodia would be the ideal place for it. There were many Mnong and Cham in Cambodia who would welcome highlanders from Vietnam. Also, Cambodia was a neutral country that had given refuge to other people fleeing Vietnam, such as Nguyen Chanh Thi after his abortive 1960 mutiny.

At Buon Sar Pa, Y Thih organized a Bajaraka committee, and as if to reflect their mood it had a military cast. Y Nam Eban was selected to be camp commander, Y Mut Hwing became battalion commander, while Y Krong Eban and Y Em Nie were intelligence agents. In addition, there were two supply men and a radio operator. Y Klong Nie was named liaison agent with the Cambodian government.

Meanwhile, events in the lowlands were creating a situation that would drastically affect the future American involvement in Vietnam. By early 1963 it was clear that the Diem regime was headed for trouble. On 2 January there was the military debacle at Ap Bac in the Mekong river delta where a well-equipped government force of 2,500, supported by helicopters and bombers, failed to defeat a band of 200 Viet Cong. In May there was a clash between Buddhists and police in Hue during which nine of the demonstrators were killed. Buddhist leader Thich Tam Chau demanded compensation for the families of the victims and punishment for those responsible for the deaths. The government, however, rejected these demands. Another monk, Thich Tri Quang, emerged as leader of a new Buddhist movement to confront the government, and on 30 May 1963 a large group of Buddhist faithful marched in a Saigon demonstration. The situation became more tense on 11 June when an elderly monk burned himself in the center of Saigon to protest the government's treatment of his confreres.[55]

At the same time there was a widening gap between Saigon and Washington. In a 1972 interview, former Vice President Nguyen Ngoc Tho expressed the view that no one in the American mission understood Diem and Nhu, and by the same token neither Diem nor Nhu understood or trusted the Americans. Fearing that the U.S. was on the road to

55. Buttinger, *Vietnam: A Political History*, pp. 461–67.

expanding the war in Vietnam, Diem and Nhu had begun to make overtures to the Viet Cong. By early 1963 they were in the process of working out some kind of accommodation with the Viet Cong that would lead to a coalition government and end the conflict. According to Tho, the Americans became aware of this, and it was one of the primary reasons they began to look for some means of toppling the Diem government.

In mid-August Ambassador Nolting was replaced by Henry Cabot Lodge. On 21 August units of the Vietnamese Special Forces commanded by General Le Quang Tung raided Buddhist pagodas in many cities, jailing thousands of monks and killing some. Three days later a series of student demonstrations began at Saigon University and within days over 4,800 demonstrators were arrested.[56]

These events precipitated a series of planned coups and countercoups that involved Ngo Dinh Nhu, various Vietnamese generals, and some American officials. The coup d'état that brought down the Diem government on 1 November 1963 was led by generals Duong Van Minh; Tran Van Don; Le Van Kim, who had been chief of staff of the French army's 4th Infantry Division, the so-called "Montagnard Division," during the Indochina War and also director of the Highland Land Development Program; Tran Thien Khiem; and Ton That Dinh, who had served as commander of the Second Corps Area. The coup also involved Ambassador Lodge and the CIA's Lucien Conein. As a result of the coup, Ngo Dinh Diem, Ngo Dinh Nhu, and Le Quang Tung were executed.[57]

56. Ibid., pp. 468–69.
57. Robert Shaplen, "Nine Years After a Fateful Assassination: The Cult of Diem," *New York Times Magazine*, 14 May 1972, pp. 16–17, 40–56.

3 THE FULRO MOVEMENT

The coup d'état that toppled the Ngo Dinh Diem government on 1 November 1963 was a blow to South Vietnamese nationalism in that it brought to power military officers, all of whom had supported continued French rule before 1954. In the highlands, however, this event prompted an upsurge in ethnonationalism as more Bajaraka leaders were freed from jail and sought to revive their movement. This effort unfortunately was blunted by the intervention of Cambodians—of Cham and Khmer Krom origin—who, in league with militant Bajaraka activists, formed a new movement, the Front Unifié de Lutte des Races Opprimées (United Struggle Front for the Oppressed Races). This movement, better known by the acronym FULRO, made its abrupt appearance in September 1964 with a revolt that burst forth in five Special Forces camps. The revolt brought to the highlands a new era of armed dissidence and at the same time made highlander ethnonationalism a force to be reckoned with. It also led to the emergence of new, more militant leaders within FULRO and within the Vietnamese government who were prepared to assert their rights and preserve their ways. Another phase in the growing identity of being "Sons of the Mountains" had begun.

ORIGINS OF THE FULRO MOVEMENT

Following the coup d'état, General Duong Van Minh signed a proclamation abolishing the presidency, the 1956 constitution, and the recently elected National Assembly. A Revolutionary Military Council took over the reins of government, and generals Duong Van Minh, Ton That Dinh, Tran Van Don, and Le Van Kim became the leaders of the new junta. On 4 November Diem's vice president, Nguyen Ngoc Tho, declared himself prime minister in an effort to maintain the structure of government and avoid excessive disruption. Political prisoners were released and nationalists who had left Vietnam returned. The junta invited most of them to join a newly formed Council of Notables in an effort to weld some political unity among the disparate political groups.[1]

According to Nguyen Ngoc Tho, there was some concern in the new government about the problems that had plagued the highlands since 1958. An effort to cope with the situation took place late in November 1963 when General Do Mau, Political Commissioner of the Armed Forces Revolutionary Council, drafted a series of proposals for programs to better the lot of the highlanders and generate more cooperation between them and the central government. One scheme involved setting up a Committee on Highland Affairs, which would be composed of representatives of all highland ethnic groups. None of these proposals, however, was acted upon.

At the same time there were initiatives by some highland leaders. Just after the coup d'état, the Darlac Committee of Bajaraka commissioned Y Thih Eban to send a message of congratulations to General Minh. Soon the committee dispatched another message, requesting the new government to release Y Bham Enuol and Paul Nur from jail.[2] As a result, Nur was set free and subsequently became Deputy Province Chief for Highland Affairs in Kontum. According to Y Thih Eban, General Minh was very distrustful of Y Bham and refused to grant him freedom.

It was noted earlier that in mid-1963 the revived Bajaraka committee at Buon Sar Pa Special Forces camp had decided to establish contact with the Cambodian government. According to Y Thih Eban, General Nguyen Khanh, commander of the II Corps (the country now was divided into four corps), had become aware of this and early in January 1964 sent Y Sen Nie Kdam (3.18), a young Rhadé officer in his security forces, to Phnom Penh to ascertain what contact had been made between the Cambodians and Bajaraka. Born in 1943, Y Sen had been educated in Ban Me Thuot and had converted to Catholicism. His sister was married to R'mah Blui, son of the Jarai leader Rcom Rock (3.11). At Phnom Penh, Y Sen met with Lt. Col. Les Kosem, a Cambodian Cham security officer in the Royal

1. Dennis J. Duncanson, *Government and Revolution in Vietnam* (New York: Frederick A. Praeger, 1966), pp. 342–46.
2. Y Bham Enuol, "Extraits de l'histoire des hauts-plateaux du centre Viet-Nam (Pays Montagnards du Sud-Indochinois)," mimeographed (Zone d'Organisation, 1965), p. 12.

Khmer Army who, according to Y Thih, had been involved in the formation of the earlier Front for the Liberation of Northern Cambodia and the Front for the Liberation of Champa. Les Kosem and Y Sen discussed the Bajaraka movement, which Kosem had been following with great interest, and he encouraged the young Rhadé to become an active member in it. Shortly after Y Sen returned to Ban Me Thuot, the Vietnamese police went to Y Thih's house in Buon Ale-A to arrest him, but his parents informed them that Y Thih was at the Special Forces camp. Y Thih noted that the police were reluctant to go there, so he remained free.

In April and August 1970, I interviewed Les Kosem in Phnom Penh. A tall gangling man with a long face and expressive, large hands, he admitted that for a long time he had been active in dissident movements among the Cham and Khmer Krom and that in 1964 he had become involved with the highlanders. He was candid in his dislike for the Vietnamese, whom he viewed as invaders of Cham and Khmer lands. Les Kosem was particularly close to Lon Non, brother of Lon Nol (who led the March 1970 move that deposed Sihanouk), and to Khmer Krom leaders as well. All of them had studied at the Lycée Sisowath in Phnom Penh, which had become a fountainhead for anti-Vietnamese sentiment. Those from the lycée shared the vision of the Cham kingdom and Khmer empire being restored some day. This, they felt, could only be realized through the extinction of the Vietnamese, so they considered the war in Vietnam a blessing. Formation of dissident movements in Vietnam among the Khmer Krom, Cham, and highlanders (to whom he kept referring as "nos petits frères, les Montagnards") were an essential part of the plan.

In January 1964 one of the first sizable meetings of highland leaders organized by Vietnamese authorities was held. According to Touneh Han Tho, Lt. Nguyen Van Nghiem, a psychological warfare officer assigned to the 23d Division headquarters in Ban Me Thuot, had obtained permission in December 1963 from his superior, Col. Vo Van Trong, who was in charge of highlander resettlement in Darlac, to convene a meeting of highland leaders. Prior to the meeting, Tuyen Duc province leaders, including Touneh Han Tho (4.2), Touneh Han Din (4.3), Touneh Han Tin (4.13), K'Kre (4.5), K'Biang (a Lat judge and uncle of K'Kre), and Ya Yu Sahau, prepared a letter addressed to General Minh requesting the government to restore the highlander law courts, legitimize highlander land claims, allow highland languages to be taught, and to free all highland political prisoners. Everyone present signed the letter, and K'Kre, the delegate for the Ban Me Thuot meeting, carried it with him. Before the meeting, K'Kre had showed the letter to the Darlac delegation, which included Y Dun Ksor (5.8), Y Dhuat Nie Kdam, Y Blu Nie Buon Drieng, Y Blieng Hmok, and Y Dhe Adrong (5.10). All of them signed it. At the meeting, on 8 January, K'Kre read the letter to Col. Trong, who promised to take up the matter with his superiors.

Meanwhile, during the first week of January 1964 Y Bih Aleo and other highlanders in the Highland Autonomy Movement were among the 150 representatives attending the Second Congress of the NLF in Tay Ninh province. Among other things, Chairman Nguyen Huu Tho called for a negotiated settlement following the withdrawal of American military forces.[3]

On 29 January 1964 the ruling junta in Saigon was overthrown in a coup d'état headed by General Nguyen Khanh. According to Nguyen Ngoc Tho, General Minh, who like Diem and Nhu became uneasy at the deepening American involvement in Vietnam and the intensification of the fighting, had by late 1963 made contact with kinsmen and friends in the NLF. The objective was to make arrangements for a political accommodation leading to a coalition government, thereby avoiding any expansion of the war. But, Tho explained, the Americans found out and were angry. He added, "They (particularly Mr. McNamara) wanted a military solution."

Khanh was supported by General Tran Thien Khiem, who had been involved in the overthrow of Diem and was now commander of the III Corps, and Col. Nguyen Chanh Thi, a leader of a 1960 mutiny attempt and recently returned from exile in Cambodia. They moved quickly, sending generals Ton That Dinh, Tran Van Don, and Le Van Kim into house arrest in Dalat. Nguyen Khanh became prime minister, General Duong Van Minh was appointed head of state, and Southern Dai Viet leader Dr. Nguyen Ton Hoan returned to Vietnam to become vice-premier.[4]

On 11 February 1964 General Khanh ordered the immediate release of Y Bham Enuol. In a discussion concerning these events while Khanh was visiting Cornell University on 6 December 1973, he explained that he felt

3. Douglas Pike, *Viet Cong: The Organization and Techniques of the National Liberation Front of South Vietnam* (Cambridge, Mass.: M.I.T. Press, 1966), pp. 356–57.
4. Ibid., pp. 347–48.

that he understood the highland problems better than most Saigon leaders because of his background. He had been commander of Mobile Group II which had been involved in highland operations in 1954. Also, as commander of the II Corps he had met with Y Bham and other Bajaraka leaders. After he became prime minister, Khanh said, he thought it was time to give the highlanders an opportunity to assume some responsibility in the administration.

Following his release, Y Bham was named Deputy Province Chief for Highland Affairs in Darlac. Although he was closely watched by the province security police, Y Bham began to meet with Nay Luett (2.26), who now was working as an interpreter for the USOM representative in Cheo Reo, to discuss the future of the Bajaraka movement. Meanwhile, at Buon Sar Pa, Y Thih Eban was moving ahead with plans to contact the Cambodians. According to him, in March 1964 he sent Y Klong Nie to meet Col. Les Kosem on the bank of the Dam river, a dividing line between Vietnam and Cambodia. Y Klong carried with him a request for Cambodian help should the Vietnamese police move against any of the Bajaraka leaders. Les Kosem replied in a letter to Y Bham that his government would respond if such a need arose.

During this period the Khanh government was making attempts to formulate programs that would meet the highlanders' needs. Some staff officers of the II Corps commander General Do Cao Tri produced a booklet entitled *The Highlander Issue in Vietnam* which became the basis for new highland policies. Essentially, it advocated programs for improving the highland people's standard of living and called for a new organization to deal with highland affairs, i.e., to replace the Bureau for Highland Affairs, which did little but monitor cadre programs supported by the Americans. As a result of this booklet, on 28 April 1964 Premier Khanh issued an order inviting fifty-nine highland representatives to Saigon to discuss the needs and desires of their people. Among them were Bajaraka activists, including Y Bham Enuol, Paul Nur (1.13), Y Dhe Adrong (5.10), Nay Luett (2.26), and Touprong Ya Ba (4.9). Other leaders included Touneh Han Tho (4.2), Touneh Han Tin (4.13), and Y Chon Mlo Duon Du.

There also were some leaders from more remote ethnic groups in central Vietnam. One of these was Anha, a Bru from Khe Sanh in upland Quang Tri province. He had been born in 1930 at Ta Cong, a village near Khe Sanh. When he was interviewed at Ta Cong in May 1964, he related that the French wife of Felix Polin, one of the local coffee planters, left her husband (he also had two other "wives," one Vietnamese and one Bru) and took up with Anha's father, a Bru leader. Madame Polin sent Anha to be educated in Hue at the same school her son Philippe was attending. Around the age of twenty, Anha joined the French army and after the French departed found a position in the administration. Following the anti–Diem coup d'état, however, he was jailed as a "Diemist." Released early in 1964, he became Deputy District Chief for Highland Affairs.

Other representatives from central Vietnam were Dinh Roi (who later would be elected to the National Assembly) and Major Dinh Ngo, both Hre from the Re river valley of interior Quang Ngai province. Dinh Ngo was born around 1920 in Son Ha, inland from Quang Ngai city, where his father was a well-to-do local leader who owned "many slaves." When he was interviewed in Quang Ngai in June 1964, he admitted that he had owned twenty slaves himself. He also related that in 1954 he was involved in a Hre uprising against the Viet Minh who were occupying the Re river valley. He claimed that as many as 6,000 Viet Minh were killed. In 1964 Major Dinh Ngo was in charge of the Regional and Popular Forces among the Hre, and he was considered a leader in the Re valley. While we were talking, a Hre and his three sons from a village near Gia Vuc appeared at the door, explaining that the Viet Cong had attacked his village and his three sons were injured. One had an arm missing, the other two had bandaged feet. The American Special Forces had arranged for their treatment at the hospital at Danang, and now they were trying to return to their village. Dinh Ngo took them in, giving them food and cold drinks. The boys had never seen ice and registered strong dislike of it.

On 5 May 1964, five days before the meeting of highland leaders, Khanh signed a decree upgrading the Bureau of Highland Affairs to a Directorate of Highland Affairs under the Ministry of Defense. He named Lt. Col. Nguyen Phi Phung of the Central Intelligence Organization as head, and the headquarters was moved from Hue to Saigon. On 9 May the highland representatives met with Premier Khanh. According to Touneh Han Tho, they presented him with a request for a revival of the *statut particulier* that had been promulgated by Bao Dai on 21 May 1951. This document stressed the need for a "free evolution" of the highlanders with the government aiding them through socioeconomic development programs. It called for greater participation of highlanders in the administration. It also guaranteed the continuance of the highlander law courts and the right of highland people to own land. The representatives also asked that they be allowed to organize a "special force" of their own to provide security for the mountain region.

This was the first time that highland leaders had had the opportunity to communicate directly to the head of state their desire to maintain their own ethnic identity. It also signaled the willingness of an ever-growing number of highland leaders who were not Bajaraka activists to voice the same views as those in the movement had. In addition, this gathering served as a means of spreading ethnonationalist sentiments among leaders from more remote parts of the highlands. Both Anha and Major Dinh Ngo expressed their contentment at meeting the leaders from Ban Me Thuot, Kontum, Pleiku, Cheo Reo, and Dalat. Both said that they agreed with the things these men demanded of the government, and they had carried news of these events back to their own provinces.

I had returned to Vietnam in January 1964 with the intention of conducting additional research on the highlanders for the RAND Corporation. Until approval of the project could be obtained from the Advanced Research Projects Agency of the Department of Defense, I agreed to do a study of cross-cultural communication between American military advisers and their Vietnamese counterparts.[5] This research took me to many parts of rural South Vietnam, and I took the opportunity to gather information on the highland leaders.

In May 1964 I visited Khe Sanh in the Bru country of upland Quang Tri just below the demilitarized zone (see map 4). I stayed in the Special Forces post, located in an old French fort above the town, which was set in a beautiful green valley. Khe Sanh was very small, but the stone bridge and small shops gave it the look of rural France. Close by were several French coffee estates (the coffee from Khe Sanh was reputed to be the best in Indochina), one of which was run by Philippe Polin, whose father had recently been killed on Route 9 by the Viet Cong. Philippe explained that his father had begun the plantation in 1904, building his stone house and also planting the avocado tree, still heavy with fruit, that stood next to the entrance.

There must have been a time when the beauty of Khe Sanh was enhanced by tranquillity, but that time was long gone. By early 1964, fighting around the town in the green forests had prompted Philippe to

5. The results of this research were summarized in G. C. Hickey (with W. Davison), "The American Military Advisor and His Foreign Counterpart: The Case of Vietnam" (Santa Monica, California: The Rand Corporation, 1965).

send his wife and children to live in coastal Hue. The Bru had been fleeing their villages in the mountains, settling along Route 9 as best they could. Receiving some help from the government, they were now building new houses, and some were farming in the nearby hills. To the west of Khe Sanh was the Lao Bao pass, the historic invasion route, and there the ruins of the notorious Lao Bao French political prison were obscured by the tall, waving elephant grass. The Lao village nearby looked exactly like those I had seen in the Mekong river valley.

After leaving Khe Sanh, I visited other remote Special Forces camps located in the highlands of central Vietnam. At Ashau there was a small settlement of Pacoh, and at An Diem (where the French had had a post) there was a village of Katu refugees. There also were Katu refugees in the northern end of the Ta Rau valley, inland from the Hai Van pass, between Hue and Danang. I stayed at Nam Dong, the small Special Forces camp located on a rise surrounded by thick forest. On the morning of 6 July 1964 a reinforced battalion of Viet Cong, newly arrived from North Vietnam, attacked the post, leaving two Americans and a large number of Vietnamese dead. In the vicious fighting, the entire post was destroyed. (The field notes I carried with me were burned.) The American team leader, Captain Roger Donlon (who was badly wounded leading the defense of the camp), was the first American in Vietnam to receive the Congressional Medal of Honor.

Traveling farther south in July 1964, I found the town of Cheo Reo (now the capital of Phu Bon province) had grown considerably since 1957 due to the influx of Vietnamese civil servants and military personnel with their families. Also, there were land development centers in the vicinity of Cheo Reo, increasing the market functions of the town. A main street had developed and was lined with shops, most of which were owned by Chinese and Indians. At the Special Forces camp, located in the Jarai village of Bon Beng four kilometers from the town, there was strong Bajaraka influence among the Strike Force, which was composed of Jarai and Bahnar. Two of the leaders were the interpreters, a Rhadé named Y Kdruin Mlo (2.24) and Kpa Doh, a Jarai. Both were handsome young men, born in 1937, and educated in Ban Me Thuot. Y Kdruin Mlo always called himself Philippe Drouin, and in the camp the Americans called him "Cowboy" because he favored tight-fitting clothes, a belt with a large brass buckle, and a sizable hat. Kpa Doh's name became "Pardo" for the Americans. Philippe was married to Rcom H'un, daughter of the Jarai

leader Nay Moul (2.17), making him the brother-in-law of Bajaraka
activist Nay Luett (2.26) who was working as an interpreter for USOM in
Cheo Reo. Nay Luett reported that Philippe treated the girl badly, often
beating her, and they soon separated. Subsequently, the girl had severe
mental problems.

In July 1964 some drastic changes began to take place in the Bajaraka
movement that were to bring a new and militant phase in highland
ethnonationalism. Y Thih Eban was ordered to leave Buon Sar Pa and
become Deputy Province Chief for Highland Affairs at Bao Loc (Blao),
capital of Lam Dong province. He left Y Dhon Adrong in charge of the
Bajaraka committee at Buon Sar Pa. Soon after, a Bajaraka delegation
consisting of Y Dhon, Y Nuin Hmok (who later was killed in Cambodia),
and Lt. Y Nham Eban met with Col. Les Kosem and Col. Um Savuth of
the Royal Khmer Army at a post in the forest of the Cambodian province
of Mondolkiri. According to a South Vietnamese source, Les Kosem
succeeded in convincing Y Dhon that he should merge the Bajaraka
Movement with the Front for the Liberation of Champa and the Struggle
Front of the Khmer of Lower Cambodia (the KKK).[6] Les Kosem and Y
Dhon then designed a new flag with three horizontal stripes of green, red,
and blue and three stars representing the Cham, Khmer Krom, and the
highlanders.

According to Ksor Kok (5.11), who spent a long time in Cambodia with
the highland dissidents, a French "adviser" (whose name he did not know)
to Les Kosem in Phnom Penh was responsible for these developments. This
adviser told Kosem that the only plausible strategy for the Cham and
Khmer Krom was to merge their ethnonationalist movements with the
Bajaraka in order to make one concerted effort to achieve their similar
goals.

Meanwhile the Vietnamese government was continuing its efforts to
gain more support among highland leaders. On 25 August 1964 a
government-sponsored conference for highland representatives was held
in Dalat. Each province of the II Corps sent a delegation that submitted a
list of what they wanted of the government. These lists included a wide
range of health programs (additional hospitals, dispensaries, and village
medical services) and an education program. They also requested that more
highlanders be appointed to the administration.

6. Nguyễn Trắc Dĩ, "Nhật Ký các phong-trào tranh-đấu của đồng bào Thượng" (Journal of the
Highland Compatriots Struggle Movements), *Thượng-Vụ* (Highland Affairs), no. 17, 1969, p. 22.

That same month, General Nguyen Huu Co, commander of the II Corps, formed a committee consisting of Lt. Nguyen Van Nghiem, Captain Touprong Ya Ba (4.9), Captain Y Pem Knuol, Y Chon Mlo Duon Du, and Siu Plung (1.23) to organize a gathering of highland leaders with the goal of expressing their "aspirations." The meeting was held at the new ARVN Officers' Club (called the Phuong Hoang or "Phoenix") in Pleiku. The Rhadé delegation included Y Bham Enuol, Y Dhe Adrong (5.10), Y Soay Kbuor (1.11), Y Chon Mlo Duon Du, and Y Blu Nie Buon-Drieng. The Bahnar were Pierre Yuk (1.12), Paul Nur (1.13), and his maternal uncle, Hiar (1.7). Siu Plung (1.23) was the only Jarai, and the Chru leaders were Touneh Han Tho (4.2), Touprong Hiou (4.4), and Touneh Han Tin (4.13). K'Biang, the Lat judge, also attended.

According to Touneh Han Tho, the representatives again presented their request that the *statut particulier* of Bao Dai be reinstated. Y Bham was the spokesman for the group, and he particularly emphasized the right of the highland people to have titles for the land they claimed and the right to their own courts. He also asked that a special secondary school (like the Collège Sabatier) be established for highland students.

On 20 September 1964 Saigon was jolted by news of revolts that had broken out in highland Special Forces camps. Violence struck at Buon Sar Pa and Bu Prang, both close to the Cambodian border southwest of Ban Me Thuot, and also at Ban Don, the old elephant trading center. There was trouble too at Buon Mi Ga, southeast of Ban Me Thuot (see map 4). At Buon Brieng, northeast of Ban Me Thuot, a revolt was averted by the quick thinking of the American captain (see below). According to Kpa Doh, who was interviewed at Phnom Penh in July 1970, the revolts had been planned by Col. Les Kosem and Col. Um Savuth with the aid of Y Dhon Adrong and Ksor Dhuat, a Jarai from Cheo Reo who had many contacts in the camps affected.

In a later discussion of these events, Tracy Atwood, who had been an IVS volunteer, described how he had been caught in the Buon Sar Pa revolt. At the time he had been running an agricultural training center at Duc Lap district town, and on the evening of 19 September 1964, while visiting the Special Forces camp at Buon Sar Pa, he decided to spend the night. Around 10:00 in the evening a Rhadé battalion commander came into the American quarters and said, somewhat incoherently, that there would be "trouble" that night but that the Americans would not be harmed. Captain Charles Darnell, head of the Special Forces team (it was a

"split" team of six men with the other six at nearby Bu Prang) gave
Atwood a carbine and told him that if anything happened he should go to a
bunker. At 1:00 A.M. on the morning of 20 September Atwood was
awakened by shouting, screaming, and shooting. He reached for the carbine but it was gone (the dissidents had taken it). When he reached the
front door of the hut, he found himself face-to-face with several highlanders. One shouted in English, "This is our night! We're going to kill
Vietnamese!"

They took Atwood to the "team house" (where the American team had
their office and mess), which was built on piling. Just as they were going up
the stairs, Atwood was startled by angry shouts accompanied by bursts and
flashes from an automatic weapon. One of the highlanders was emptying a
clip of ammunition into the back of a Vietnamese interpreter under the
veranda. The rebels pushed Atwood into the main room where the six
members of the American team were gathered. Shortly afterward, Y Dhon
Adrong came in and sat down, placing a flag over his knees. He explained
that the camp had been taken over by the United Struggle Front for the
Oppressed Races—FULRO—and he pointed to the three stars, noting
what they represented. Then he read a "FULRO manifesto" stating that
the aim of the revolt was to retake the territory that the Vietnamese had
"stolen" from the highlanders, the Cham, and Khmer Krom. Atwood
noticed that there were some references in the text to "American imperialists," but Y Dhon carefully skipped them. The manifesto was signed by Y
Bham Enuol (for the highlanders), Chau Dara (for the Khmer Krom), and
Ponagar (for the Cham). Y Dhon informed the Americans that the
FULRO troops were going to attack Ban Me Thuot, and if they tuned
into Radio Ban Me Thuot at 7:00 A.M. they would find it in the hands of
the rebels. Y Dhon then departed.

Outside there was continued shooting as the Vietnamese Special Forces
team defended itself in its quarters. The cook brought the Americans some
coffee, and Captain Darnell reached the Bu Prang camp team on the radio.
Lt. Webb, commander of the Bu Prang team, reported that the Americans
still had control of the camp but that most of the Strike Force had gone to
Trois Frontières to meet FULRO troops coming from Cambodia. He
speculated that they might be planning to attack Gia Nghia, capital of
Quang Duc province. By 6:00 A.M. the shooting had ended. The
Vietnamese camp commander was tied to the flagpole, but all of the
Vietnamese Special Forces team had been killed and their bodies thrown

into the latrine. With the camp under their control, the FULRO agents led most of the Strike Force in the direction of Ban Me Thuot. At 7:00 A.M. VNAF aircraft (T-28 and A1E fighters) began to buzz the camp, but they did not open fire.

At Buon Brieng a different situation unfolded. In his account of it journalist Howard Sochurek described how on the morning of 20 September 1964 Captain Vernon Gillespie was informed of the events taking place at Buon Sar Pa and Bu Prang.[7] Without hesitation he summoned Y Jhon Nie, a Rhadé battalion commander, and his four company commanders. When they arrived at the mess hall, Gillespie was firm. He informed them that a revolt had begun, quickly adding that he was in charge of the camp. He told Y Jhon not to move against any of the Vietnamese, saying, "To kill them, you'll have to kill me first." If there was any disturbance in the camp, he pointed out to Y Jhon, it would jeopardize all of their lives. "The Viet Cong have infiltrated this camp," he noted. "You and I both know it."

Y Jhon pondered the situation and then suggested to Gillespie that since he and the American already were "brothers" because they had performed an alliance ceremony, they might have another ritual to ally themselves with Captain Truong, the Vietnamese camp commander. Gillespie agreed and Y Jhon obtained the services of a shaman from a nearby village. Dressed in Rhadé loincloths and shirts, Y Jhon, Gillespie, and Truong participated in the alliance ritual, which involved the slaughter of a pig and some chickens and ceremonial drinking from seven jars of alcohol while the shaman placed brass bracelets around their wrists. The strategy had its desired effect, and a revolt was averted at Buon Brieng.

By midmorning of 20 September a total of around 3,000 Strike Force members were in revolt. They had moved on Ban Me Thuot from Buon Sar Pa, Ban Don (where the Vietnamese were held prisoner), and Buon Mi Ga (where most of the Vietnamese had been killed). They captured the radio station south of the town and occupied some villages, such as Buon Enao. According to Atwood, at about 10:00 A.M. some of the camp leaders still at Buon Sar Pa asked for an American to go with them to Ban Me Thuot. Captain Darnell volunteered, and they departed in a jeep. In Ban Me Thuot they picked up Y Ju Eban, who had been working as an interpreter for USOM, after which they went to the house of Y Bham

7. Howard Sochurek, "American Special Forces in Action in Vietnam," *National Geographic* 127, no. 1 (1965): 38–65.

Enuol, who got in the jeep. They returned to Buon Sar Pa, and Y Bham went into the team hut to have coffee. Soon a jeep full of rebel soldiers arrived and took Y Bham down a road in the direction of Cambodia.

In midmorning of the first day of the revolt (20 September), a jeep sped through the center of Ban Me Thuot as someone threw out leaflets. The leaflet, written in French, was a "declaration" by the "High Committee of the United Struggle Front for the Oppressed Races" stating that the highlands had been overrun by "expansionist Vietnamese" who were pursuing a "systematic genocidal policy." It cited "ten years of suffering," specifying that "our leaders have been shot, our historical monuments and temples have been bombed, and our schools have been closed." Because of these things, the leaflet declared, the highlanders, Cham, and Khmer Krom joined in the United Struggle Front for the Oppressed Races so that they might "cope with the Vietnamese imperialists who are supported by the American imperialists who seek to drag all Southeast Asian countries into their block of war." The document was signed by Y Bham, Ponagar, and Chau Dara.

I was in Danang when news of the revolt reached me late on 20 September 1964. George Tanham of the RAND Corporation was meeting with Ambassador Maxwell Taylor and General William Westmoreland in Saigon. They asked me to go to Ban Me Thuot. The following morning I flew to Ban Me Thuot in a Caribou cargo aircraft. The airstrip near town was empty and the streets of Ban Me Thuot were quiet. At the Grand Bungalow the American senior military adviser informed me that the revolt was continuing, although the radio station had been reoccupied by the Vietnamese security police. Col. John Freund, deputy senior adviser of the II Corps, had been sent to Buon Sar Pa to deal with the situation. The rebels still threatened to attack Ban Me Thuot, and their first ultimatum was that all Vietnamese must leave the highlands.

Atwood was still at Buon Sar Pa on 21 September 1964 when Freund arrived by helicopter. Freund and Darnell, the team leader, met and later told the Americans that "we are going to act like we are in charge here." Freund mounted the veranda where some of the rebel leaders in the camp had gathered. Speaking loudly in French, he shook his finger in the face of Y Tlur, a Rhadé interpreter and revolt leader. Atwood and some Americans who had come that morning from Ban Me Thuot decided to depart. As they were driving along Route 14 they passed some of the Buon Sar Pa troops en route back to the camp. Not long after Atwood and the others left, the rebels suddenly decided to hold Freund, the American Special Forces team, and some Vietnamese civilians hostage.

This created a new and tense situation. Vietnamese leaders in Saigon already were rankled at having the FULRO flag flying over the camps. There were reports that, upon hearing of the revolts, Premier Khanh blamed the Americans for the trouble, because it was they who had armed the highlanders. General Westmoreland dispatched General Ben Sternberg to Ban Me Thuot to make sure everything was coordinated through General Nguyen Huu Co, II Corps' commander, and General Hoang Xuan Lam, commander of the 23d Division.

On Tuesday 22 September Sochurek and I were on our way to find Y Blieng Hmok at Buon Pan Lam near the airstrip when we encountered Captain Barry Peterson, a young Australian officer who had been working with the Village Defense Program and now was organizing young Rhadé into a CIA-sponsored village cadre that had its training center in Pleiku. He was accompanied by one of his young Rhadé leaders, Y Jut Buon To (1.19), son of Y Soay Kbuor (1.11), who had been one of the Darlac representatives at various meetings with government officials. Y Jut was married to H'rec Eban, sister of H'met Eban, who had married the Bahnar leader Hiup (1.20). Hiup's uncle, Phem (1.17), had taken another sister, H'bum Eban, as his third wife. Peterson and Y Jut led us to Buon Enao, where FULRO troops from Buon Brieng and Buon Mi Ba had set up a local headquarters. They were in the process of improving the defenses, digging new bunkers and trenches. The leader of the camp outlined FULRO demands. They wanted one leader for all of the highlanders to represent them in Saigon. They also wanted foreign military and economic aid directly channeled to the highlands. Finally, they desired a special highland military force, trained by the Americans, to provide security in the region.

Concerning the events at Buon Mi Ba, the leader said that the Vietnamese there were slain because of the great hostility that had built up against them. He was aware that Premier Khanh had met with highland leaders, but he was not impressed by the many promises made by the government. FULRO, he added, felt that the government had to be goaded into action. "We had to wake the sleeping dog," he concluded.

That afternoon William Beachner, the regional director for the Political Section of the U.S. Embassy, and I met with General Sternberg to discuss the situation. Afterward we flew to Saigon. First we went to MACV to meet with generals William Westmoreland, Richard Stillwell, and Richard Depuy and report to them what was taking place in the troubled camps. Following this, we went to the American embassy to join a gathering that included Ambassador Maxwell Taylor, Deputy Ambassador U. Alexis Johnson, Barry Zorthian, head of the Joint U.S Public Affairs Office, and officials from the Political Section and from the CIA. We discussed the American position in the affair and possible suggestions that might be made to the Vietnamese government. After Beachner and I outlined the current demands of the FULRO, U. Alexis Johnson said that in his view " all of the points were negotiable." There was some specu- lation that the uprising might have been the work of the Viet Cong. Generally, however, the tone of the meeting was that, while this distur- bance was of concern, it was more or less something minor.

We returned to Ban Me Thuot the following day. The town was quiet in a dismal rain under low-flying clouds. There was some tension due to reports that the FULRO and Viet Cong were going to attack the town. ARVN troops were very much in evidence and the townspeople had retreated into their shuttered houses.

Annoyance with American involvement in the whole affair was ap- parent with the Vietnamese leaders in Ban Me Thuot. General Nguyen Huu Co openly criticized the American stand of negotiating with FULRO rather than attacking the occupied camps. Other Vietnamese military officers implied that there would not have been any trouble if the Americans had not armed the highlanders. One Vietnamese general ex- pressed the view that the highlanders considered the Americans, like the French, to be superior to the Vietnamese. He stated, "The white man has a certain mystique for the highland people that the Vietnamese do not have."

General Co ordered ARVN troops deployed in the vicinity of the camps (at Duc Lap, for example, near both Buon Sar Pa and Bu Prang), although they had orders not to attack. At Ban Me Thuot, with the approval of the province chief, some two hundred highlanders gathered to organize a Provisional Liaison Committee to serve as an intermediary agency between FULRO and the government. Y Char Hdok, a Mnong Rlam and director of a primary school, was elected president. The vice- president was Ksor Dun (5.8), and others included civil servants Y Blum Buon Ya, Y Dhuat Nie Kdam, and Y Blu Nie Buon Drieng.

On 23 September General Richard Depuy (who had been involved in Operation Switchback) was sent to Ban Me Thuot to cope with the continuing crisis. At the Grand Bungalow he formed an ad hoc committee that included Beachner and me. Word had come in that Y Bham was willing to meet with government representatives and a favorable reply was sent by General Co. Meanwhile, the hostages at Buon Sar Pa were still being held, although Freund was allowed to have radio contact with the Americans at Ban Me Thuot and a messenger was allowed to go back and forth by helicopter. The following day Premier Khanh arrived in Ban Me Thuot as an indication of his growing impatience. After he departed in the afternoon, generals Le Van Kim and Ton That Dinh were released from house arrest in Dalat to go to Ban Me Thuot as Khanh's representatives.

That evening, at their request, General Depuy and I went to meet with them and General Hoang Xuan Lam, commander of the 23d Division. Le Van Kim recalled how he and I had met in the highlands in 1957, and he asked how I thought the uprising could be resolved. Fortunately, I had prepared a written plan, but before I presented it I reviewed briefly some of the background (Diem policies and so forth) that had led to the development of ethnonationalist movements among the highlanders. Then I outlined what I would do to cope with the situation. First, to avoid further violence, I would continue negotiating with FULRO. Second, I would announce a series of programs that could be implemented immediately to meet some of the outstanding needs and desires that already had been expressed by highland leaders. They would include such things as restoring the highlander law courts, allowing indigenous languages to be taught, reestablishing courses for highlanders at the National Institute of Administration, and naming qualified highland civil servants to more responsible positions in the province and district administrations.

I also expressed my opinion that it would be better to deal with a wide spectrum of highland leaders. This could be done by calling a congress of representatives from every ethnic group and FULRO once the revolt had subsided. It would be held in Pleiku. I passed Le Van Kim the written plan. The two Vietnamese generals expressed approval and telephoned Premier Khanh in Dalat to read him the plan. General Depuy and the Vietnamese officers shifted to a discussion of how to cope with the continuing revolt. It was agreed that a show of force was necessary, accompanied by a cutoff of supplies.

On 26 September a letter written in French arrived from Y Bham saying that he regretted not having communicated further about his proposed meeting, but, he stipulated, such a meeting could only take place if the Vietnamese were removed from Ban Me Thuot. The American messenger bringing the letter noted that at Buon Sar Pa the rebel who seemed to be in charge was a "bearded Cham." While discussing these events with me at Phnom Penh in 1970, Col. Les Kosem admitted that he was the bearded Cham. He had gone to the camp to direct the FULRO operations, and he had dealt with Freund. He laughed as he recalled the situation, saying, "Please give my regards to Col. Freund."

Le Van Kim was called back to Dalat, and Khanh arrived in Ban Me Thuot to confer with Ton That Dinh. Unknown to the Americans, they decided that military action would have to be taken. No congress or any other concessions to the highlanders could be made until the revolt was completely resolved with the Vietnamese hostages freed unharmed. Shortly after midnight on 27 September 1964, Freund sent word to Depuy that he had just been told that Khanh had secretly given the order to attack Buon Sar Pa at 9:00 A.M. Depuy gathered his ad hoc committee in his quarters. He was angered at what he considered to be a "double cross" by the Vietnamese, who had agreed that no military action would take place. I expressed the view that perhaps it was a ploy by Khanh to goad the Americans into action. The "secret" was leaked to Freund so that Depuy would have to get the hostages released and end the dissidence.

Depuy formulated two schemes to get the hostages freed before 9:00. The first called for Freund to get Y Tlur to gather everyone at 8:00. Freund would then announce that he was going to free the Vietnamese hostages, after which he would take a crowbar and spring the lock on the prison compound. Meanwhile helicopters dispatched from Ban Me Thuot would arrive just as the prisoners were released (if the rebels had not restrained Freund or, worse, killed him) to pick them up. The second strategy called for sixty-eight U.S. Special Forces men to attack the camp (which was defended by over three hundred well-armed highlanders). Depuy then consulted with generals Lam and Dinh, asking that they refrain from any attack on the camp until all of the hostages were freed. They telephoned Khanh in Dalat and he agreed.

At daybreak, it appeared that ground fog might delay the departure of the helicopters, but by 7:45 they were able to leave. Meanwhile, at Buon

The 1964 FULRO revolt: released Buon Sar Pa hostages arrive in Ban Me Thuot

Sar Pa, Y Tlur had gathered everyone in the center of the camp, and Freund made his declaration. In the tense atmosphere, he wrenched the lock, opening the prison compound just as the helicopters appeared. Y Tlur and the FULRO troops were immobile as the Vietnamese hostages ran for the helicopters. Arrangements had been made for Major Touprong Ya Ba (4.9) to go to Buon Sar Pa with General Depuy. They arrived as ARVN units at Duc Lap began moving in the direction of the camp. Ya Ba explained to the FULRO leaders that the ARVN troops were coming and that the highlanders should not open fire on them or it would set off a bloodbath. All of the Americans boarded the waiting helicopters and, unwittingly, left Ya Ba behind. Ya Ba explained afterward that he pleaded with the FULRO troops to remain calm and had very anxious moments when the ARVN commander entered the camp. The FULRO leaders agreed to have their men stack their arms around the flagpole. After they had done so, Premier Khanh entered and, assisted by Y Tlur, lowered the FULRO flag. He announced that amnesty would be granted Y Tlur and other agitators and that the FULRO troops would be sent to Ban Me Thuot for reassignment.

At the other dissident camps, the situations were resolved as ARVN units moved in to assume control. With the revolts now ended, the Vietnamese government announced that new highland province and district chiefs would be appointed and a congress of highland leaders would be convened in Pleiku. Major Touprong Ya Ba was promoted to Lt. Colonel.[8]

Y Bham Enuol and his followers, including many of the Strike Force personnel from the camps that had been in dissidence (estimates ran from 500 to 2,000), were reported to have moved to the old French military post at Camp Le Rolland in the neighboring Cambodian province of Mondulkiri. Y Bham's group of assistants included Y Dhon Adrong, Y Bhan Kpuor, Y Ju Eban, and Ksor Dhuat. In addition, his leadership attracted some young, educated highlanders who subsequently went to join FULRO in Cambodia. Typical of these were Kpa Doh, the Jarai interpreter from the Special Forces camp at Bon Beng, and Ksor Kok (5.11), nephew of Ksor Dun (5.8), who was a leader in Ban Me Thuot. Ksor Kok was staying with his uncle while attending secondary school in Ban Me Thuot, but he abandoned his studies to join FULRO.

A FULRO document dated 17 October 1964 outlined the Provisional Government of the "High Plateaus of Champa."[9] Discussing the various FULRO designations, such as the High Plateaus of Champa, Les Kosem pointed out that at one time the central highlands had been part of Champa. This hegemony ended with the southward expansion of the Vietnamese and the defeat of the Cham in 1471. According to the FULRO document, the president of the Council of Ministers was Y Bham Enuol and the first vice-president was Y Dhon Adrong. Y Ju Eban, one of the founders of the Bajaraka movement, was first vice minister of foreign affairs. The first vice minister of agriculture was Y Dhe Adrong (5.10), owner of a coffee estate near Ban Me Thuot; Y Wick Buon Ya, who later served in the Lower House of the National Assembly, was the vice minister of health. There also was a Ministry of Finance, a Ministry of Information and Psychological Action, and a Ministry of Youth, Cults, and Social

8. In M. A. Jaspan, "Recent Developments among the Cham of Indo-China: The Revival of Champa," *Asian Affairs* 87, part 2 (1970): 170–76, a curious version of the emergence of the FULRO movement is presented. Considering the highlanders "Cham minorities," Jaspan sees the appearance of FULRO as a revival of Champa, which greatly exaggerates the role of the Cham in these events. An equally inaccurate account of the FULRO revolt is found in Wilfred Burchett, *Vietnam Will Win*, 2d ed., rev. and enl. (New York: Monthly Review Press, A Guardian Book, 1970), pp. 132–34.

9. Le Haut-Comité du Front Unifié de Lutte de la Race Opprimée, "Gouvernement Provisoire des Hauts Plateaux du Champa," Zone Libre, 17 October 1964, pp. 1–2. Similar information was contained in Front de Liberation des Hauts Plateaux du Champa, *Historique* (Phnom Penh: 1965), pp. 2–21.

Action. Most of the other positions in the provisional government were held by Cham (Cambodian Cham for the most part) or Khmer Krom.

THE PLEIKU CONFERENCE

The FULRO revolt took place at a time when the government of Nguyen Khanh was beset with problems due to growing opposition, mostly from Buddhists. After the coup d'état by Khanh in January 1964, the Buddhist leaders had organized the United Buddhist Church, with monks occupying most of the high positions. Thich Tri Quang, who had been a leader in opposing Diem, was secretary general of the Clerical Council, responsible for matters of faith and doctrine. Thich Tam Chau became director of the Dharma Institute, charged with secular affairs. The Khanh government gave the Buddhists some land in Saigon for their Dharma Institute and the administration also increased the number of Buddhist chaplains in the army. Nonetheless, the Buddhists were becoming increasingly critical of Khanh.

There also was trouble brewing between the Buddhists and Catholics, who had been strengthening their militant wing. Early in 1964, there were Catholic marches and countermarches on feast days, political anniversaries, and Sundays. To make matters worse, Khanh began to have trouble with his Southern Dai Viet supporters. Thinking that American support of his government was unqualified, in August 1964 Khanh produced a "Provisional Charter" which would, in effect, have given him absolute powers. This set off demonstrations and riots in Hue, Danang, Qui Nhon, Nhatrang, and Saigon. By September there was open conflict between the Buddhists and Catholics.[10]

The FULRO revolt was disquieting for the Americans in Saigon and in Washington as well. Not only did it come at a time of internal turmoil in Vietnam but also at a moment when American military involvement was deepening. The Tonkin Gulf bombings had taken place on 5 August, and there was a steady increase in American military personnel in Vietnam. (By the end of 1964 there were 23,000—an increase of 7,500 during the year.)[11] The situation was rendered even more complicated due to an

10. Duncanson, *Government*, pp. 348–51.
11. Ibid., p. 404.

American strategy that related the Tonkin Gulf bombing and projected future bombing of North Vietnam to attainment of political stability in South Vietnam. In this context, the FULRO uprising and dissidence took on added significance.

According to the Pentagon Papers, on 18 August 1964 Ambassador Taylor cabled Washington recommending that "a carefully orchestrated bombing attack" on North Vietnam be undertaken on 1 January 1965 in relation to two courses of action. The first would be to use the attacks as an inducement "to persuade the regime of Gen. Nguyen Khanh to achieve some political stability." The second would be to bomb the north regardless of whatever progress Khanh had made in order to prevent a "collapse of national morale in Saigon."[12]

A secret memorandum dated 5 October 1964 from Undersecretary of State George W. Ball to Secretary of State Dean Rusk, Secretary of Defense Robert McNamara, and President Johnson's Special Assistant for National Security Affairs McGeorge Bundy raised many questions about the premises of a policy of military action against North Vietnam.[13] One was "Would action against North Viet-Nam increase political cohesiveness and improve morale in South Viet-Nam so as to strengthen the government base?" Expressing doubt that such action would have that desired effect, Ball cited the FULRO revolt in September as one of the disrupting political events that took place *after* the American bombing of North Vietnamese installations following the Tonkin Gulf incidents in August. Events early in 1965 (see below) prove that Ball's argument was rejected.

On 2 October 1964 Premier Khanh and a group of high-ranking Vietnamese officers held a large news conference at the Joint General Staff in Saigon, which I attended. In reviewing the events that had led to the FULRO uprising, Khanh stressed the role of the Americans in building the CIDG program from the Buon Enao project, pointing out that by the end of 1963 there were 20,000 CIDG troops, all armed by the U.S. Special Forces. Now, he added, there was the recent revolt and "capture" of Y Bham Enuol. Going over the late September period day by day, Khanh said that there were "foreigners and Communists involved in the trouble,"

12. Neil Sheehan et al., *The Pentagon Papers: As Published by the New York Times* (Toronto, New York, and London: Bantam Books), pp. 311–15.

13. George W. Ball, "Top Secret: The Prophecy the President Rejected," *Atlantic Monthly* 230, no. 1 (1972): 36–50.

and he emphasized the important role of the Vietnamese army and air force in bringing the revolt to an end.

On 15 October 1964 the conference of highland leaders that the government had promised opened in Pleiku at the Phoenix Officers' Club, located under the pine trees where Jarai longhouses had stood in 1957. Along the road, banners in Vietnamese and Rhadé warned that "Vietnamese and highlanders must oppose the dark plots of the neutralists, Communists, and foreign elements." The schedule of the conference called for eighty highland delegates to meet with General Nguyen Huu Co and Major Ngo Van Hung, chief of the Directorate for Highland Affairs, on the afternoon of the 15th. The following morning General Co would meet with "selected Americans," including all of the USOM representatives from the highland provinces, to discuss United States support for programs in the highlands. That afternoon the highland delegates would meet with Premier Khanh.

As if to remind those in Pleiku of their presence, on the morning of the 15th the Viet Cong attacked the CIDG camp at Plei D'lim, south of the town. Beginning with a shelling attack, they assaulted seven villages in the vicinity, causing some 2,000 Jarai to flee into the surrounding countryside.

Highland delegates included Bajaraka and FULRO sympathizers as well as politically innocuous civil servants. The Pleiku delegation included Rahlan Beo (2.14), who had married Nay Nui's daughter Rcom H'but, the former wife of Viet Minh leader Nay Der; Siu Plung (1.23); Ksor Glai (3.10), who later became a judge; Nay Blim (2.25), a future member of the National Assembly; and Ksor Kham (3.19), a FULRO supporter. Another Jarai group represented Phu Bon province. It included Nay Luett (2.26), his father-in-law Nay Moul (2.17), Captain Nay Honh (2.23), Rcom Perr (3.13), and Rcom Kek (3.16). The Kontum delegation had Bahnar leaders Paul Nur (1.13), his brother-in-law Hiup (1.20), and Pierre Yuk (1.12). The delegates from Darlac included Ksor Dun (5.8), Philippe Drouin (Y Kdruin Mlo, 2.24), Y Dhuat Nie Kdam, Y Blieng Hmok, and Y Char Hdok (a Mnong Rlam school teacher). Representatives from Tuyen Duc province were Touprong Hiou (4.4), his brother Lt. Col. Touprong Ya Ba (4.9), Touneh Han Tho (4.2), his half-brother Touneh Han Din (4.3), and Ya Yu Sahau. Anha was the only Bru delegate, and the Hre were represented by Major Dinh Ngo and Dinh Roi.

Most of these delegates were dressed in natty dark suits with white shirts and dark ties, but other ethnic group representatives were garbed in a combination of traditional clothes (usually shirts) and western dress (usu-

ally trousers). The first morning they met with General Co and each group
presented its "aspirations." The lists were somewhat long, so that evening
many of them met and agreed that the list of needs and desires expressed by
the Darlac delegation would be presented to Premier Khanh. Essentially,
the Darlac delegation asked for a government policy that would respect the
customs and traditions of the highland people and for programs that would
raise the standard of living. It specified that these goals were embodied in
the *statut particulier* that had been promulgated by Bao Dai and should be
adopted by the present government. It also outlined the need for more
highlanders in the provincial and district administrations and the right of
highlanders to own land and have their own law courts. Indigenous languages would be taught in the primary schools. The Darlac delegation also
requested that more highlanders in the military services be promoted to
officers and noncomissioned officers and that a 25,000 to 50,000 highland
military force with its own flag (the French text used the word *fanion*—a
guidon or pennant) be formed. It also asked for special consideration for
highland students applying for entrance into secondary schools and uni-
versities. Finally, the delegation wanted foreign aid destined for the
highlands to be administered by highlanders directly rather than being
channeled through Saigon.

On the afternoon of the second day, 16 October 1964, all of the
delegates gathered while Premier Khanh addressed them, calling for unity
between highland and lowland people and warning them to be on guard
against Communists and colonialists. He also promised that the government would respect the highlanders' customs and traditions. Khanh then
reviewed all of the requests, stating that the government would act on all of
them except those concerning foreign aid and the formation of a highland
military force. He also announced that prior to coming to Pleiku, he had
signed an order placing the Directorate of Highland Affairs under the
prime minister, thus satisfying the desire for representation at the high
levels of government. Lt. Col. Touprong Ya Ba would be the new chief of
this directorate.

Standing apart from all of these events, Y Thih Eban left his post at Bao
Loc late in November 1964 to take another position at Gia Nghia. Upset
by the violence of the FULRO revolt, Y Thih wrote to Y Bham to express
his feelings. He urged Y Bham to return to Vietnam and begin a new
ethnonationalist movement called the Mouvement d'Union de la Nation
Indépendente, using the acronym MUNI. Nothing came of this. As of the

end of 1964, highlander ethnonationalism was identified with the FULRO (heavily influenced by Les Kosem and the Cambodians) and the Highland Autonomy Movement (a vehicle of the Communists).

INTENSIFICATION OF THE CONFLICT

During this period the opposition to Khanh increased as Buddhists and Catholics continued to mount demonstrations. Late in October 1964 Khanh was forced to turn over the reigns of government to Phan Khac Suu, who became head of state, and Tran Van Huong, who assumed the role of prime minister and minister of the armed forces. Buddhist and student groups in Hue and Danang, however, refused to accept the leadership of Huong and Khanh's Provisional Charter, so they continued to agitate. On 20 December Khanh moved again, arresting the members of the High National Council which had been provided for in the Provisional Charter. He quickly formed a new Armed Forces Council. This did not bring about any stability, and in mid-February 1965 Khanh stepped down and, soon after, departed for Paris. He was replaced by Air Force General Nguyen Cao Ky, chairman of the Armed Forces Council. A new cabinet was formed by Dr. Phan Huy Quat, who became the new prime minister.[14]

In his discussion of these events while visiting Cornell University in December 1973, Khanh attributed his diminishing support by the Americans late in 1964 to his opposition to an expansion of the war and a continuing buildup of U.S. forces. He noted that on the occasion of the lunar new year early in 1965 he had publicly predicted that the war would be over by the end of the year. This, he said, was based on the fact that he already had made contact "with the other side" in preparation for making an accommodation with them.

Khanh related that on 7 February 1965, after being informed of the Viet Cong attack on American military installations in Pleiku, he flew to that city to find General Westmoreland and McGeorge Bundy already there. Khanh claims that they informed him of their decision to recommend bombing of North Vietnam to President Johnson. Khanh stressed that he had been *informed*; his opinion had not been solicited. On 9 February

14. Duncanson, *Government*, pp. 349–51.

President Johnson ordered reprisal attacks on North Vietnam. Soon after, according to Khanh, Ambassador Taylor telephoned him and told him to leave the country. Khanh said he realized that he had either to resign and leave or to "submit to Washington's decision." On 15 February the Armed Forces Council announced that Khanh's government had ended, and on the 21st he resigned and left the country. On 13 February President Johnson had given the order for the sustained bombing of North Vietnam, an operation code-named Rolling Thunder.

During this period, the first use of American jet fighters in military operations began. According to Westmoreland, in mid-February 1965, "after necessary clearance had been obtained from South Vietnamese officials," twenty-four B-57 Canberra bombers attacked Viet Cong positions in Phuoc Tuy province.[15] Not long after, on 24 February, twenty-four F-100s, B-57s, and helicopters were called in by Westmoreland to relieve an entrapped Special Forces unit at the Mang Yang pass (where Mobile Group 100 had been ambushed in 1954). It is interesting and perhaps significant that the first American bombings authorized by the South Vietnamese government were in areas inhabited by highlanders—Chrau-speaking people in the first instance and Jarai in the second. As a matter of fact, throughout the Vietnam War, American advisers pointed out that in the highlands approval of the province chiefs was readily given for bombing of highland villages but rarely for assaults on Vietnamese villages.

According to Y Thih Eban, early in 1965 a faction within FULRO led by Y Dhon Adrong began to take a stand against what it considered to be the too moderate posture of Y Bham Enuol. Y Dhon was supported by younger, more militant men, including Kpa Doh, Y Bhan Kpuor (who had been an ARVN lieutenant), and Y Nham Eban (also a former lieutenant). In spite of this, the movement was making great gains in winning support among the highland people, particularly among those in the various military and paramilitary organizations. Some were even going to Cambodia to join the FULRO forces, which at this time were said to number around 2,000. The reputation of the movement and of Y Bham as a notable highland leader was spreading among all segments of highland societies, and, as was indicated before, leaders from the smaller ethnic

15. W. C. Westmoreland, "Report on Operations in South Vietnam: January 1964–June 1968," in U.S. G. Sharp and W. C. Westmoreland, *Report on the War in Vietnam: As of 30 June 1968*, 2 sections (Washington: U.S. Government Printing Office, 1969), section 2, p. 107.

Y Bham in dress uniform at his forest headquarters (1965)

groups were carrying news of FULRO to the more remote areas. These developments served to spread an awareness of the highlander ethnic identity.

At this time FULRO began to receive open support from the government in Cambodia, and according to Meyer this was due to General Lon Nol's "grandes idées politiques," one of which was for Cambodia to lead all Mon Khmer people in a struggle against the Vietnamese.[16] This support was most graphically demonstrated late in February 1965 when the Cambodian government convened a Conference of Indochinese Peoples at Phnom Penh. In addition to inviting the North Vietnamese and Viet Cong (one of the delegates was Y Bih Aleo), a group of FULRO representatives led by Y Bham also attended. Y Bham addressed the conference, beginning his speech by identifying the FULRO group as one of the "Austrien"

16. Charles Meyer, Derrière le sourire Khmer (Paris: Plon, 1971), pp. 269–71.

delegation. The term Austrien had begun to appear in some of the FULRO communications to the Vietnamese government, and its meaning was not clear. Meyer claims that Lon Nol devised it from the word Austroasiatic, the designation for the stock to which the Mon Khmer languages (Cambodian and some highland dialects) belong. Meyer sees it as a reflection of Lon Nol's notion of himself as the "occult chief of all the 'Austriens.'" In 1970, however, Les Kosem contended that he had devised the term from Austroasiatic and Austronesian (another designation for Malayopolynesian, the stock to which some highland languages belong).

The main part of Y Bham's address was a review of the history of the Austrien people, emphasizing the friendly relations among the highlanders, Cham, and Khmer. There was a reference to the King of Water and the King of Fire, and Y Bham noted that the latter was guardian of a sacred saber, the hilt of which was held by the Cham while the Khmer had the sheath. Then Y Bham declared that the Austriens were now struggling with the "American imperialists" and "South Vietnamese colonialists" to attain their freedom. His speech ended with lavish praise for "Samdech Preah Norodom Sihanouk Varman."[17]

A photograph taken during the conference—and shown to me in Ban Me Thuot by Y Dhe Adrong—recorded the presence of a group that included Sihanouk, Les Kosem, Y Bham, and Y Nuin Hmok. According to Y Dhe, the Viet Cong and North Vietnamese were careful to keep Y Bih Aleo (around whom they always had guards) from meeting Y Bham.

Meyer reports that by this time FULRO leaders were well installed at Sen Monorom, the capital of Mondulkiri, where they were receiving material and financial aid from the Cambodian government.[18] In an interview held in 1970 at Phnom Penh, Les Kosem and Col. Um Savuth described how Viet Cong representatives Y Bih Aleo and Rcom Briu (2.20) approached Y Bham in March 1965 with a proposal to make FULRO part of the Central Highlands Autonomy Movement. They explained that the highlanders would have autonomy when they were "liberated" just as the northern highland people had autonomy. They had this in a written document which they were willing to sign at that time. Y Bham and the FULRO leaders declined, but during 1965 they were approached again several times by Viet Cong agents.

17. "Discours de S. E. Y Bham Enuol, Chef de la Délégation du FULRO," *Agence Khmer de Presse* (Phnom Penh), no. 5, 15 March 1965.

18. Meyer, *Derrière le sourire Khmer*, p. 270.

Y Bham at flag-raising ceremony at the forest headquarters (1965)

According to Ksor Kok (5.11), who, it was noted above, joined FULRO just after the revolt and now lives in the United States, the Viet Cong avoided contact with FULRO in Cambodia because, if there had been any conflict between the two, the Cambodians would have stopped supplying food to the Communists. Inside the borders of Vietnam, however, FULRO and the Viet Cong often clashed. Kok carried messages from the FULRO headquarters to Ban Me Thuot and was attacked by the Viet Cong several times in Vietnam. According to Kok, FULRO had at this time between 5,000 and 6,000 troops in Cambodia (all of them either Rhadé or Mnong) and around 15,000 dependents.

Kok also reported that once the highlanders became organized in Cambodia there was some conflict between Y Bham and his primary contacts with the Cambodian government, Les Kosem and Um Savuth. They insisted on having the three stars on the FULRO flag represent the Front for the Liberation of Lower Cambodia, the Front for the Liberation of Champa, and the Front for the Liberation of Northern Cambodia (Kampuchea Nord). Y Bham resented having the central highlands considered "Northern Cambodia." Later, Les Kosem and Um Savuth changed the designation to the High Plateaus of Champa (Hauts Plateaux du Champa). This did not satisfy Y Bham, who wanted the highlands referred to as the Hauts Plateaux Montagnards. They eventually resolved their differences by settling on the Front for the Liberation of the Dega-Cham High Plateaus (*Dega* is a shortened form of Anak Ede Ga which in this context means "sons of the mountains"). This became the FULRO term for all the highland people.

On 29 April 1965 Premier Nguyen Cao Ky sent a letter to Y Bham and on the same day U. Alexis Johnson, Deputy American Ambassador, sent a companion letter. In his communique Ky invited Y Bham and his followers to "join in the common struggle against the Communist aggressors," promising them "appropriate positions in Government institutions at both the central and local levels to enable them to serve the country." The American letter expressed the hope that Y Bham and FULRO would elect to cooperate with the Vietnamese government. Since the U.S. Embassy had been receiving communications from Y Bham, the letter ended with the reminder that the American government "cannot formulate any suggestions concerning the requests made by Mr. Y Bham, because this is regarded as an internal matter between the Vietnamese government and Mr. Y Bham."[19]

If it had been seriously believed in Washington that the bombing of North Vietnam and the ouster of Khanh would bring about internal stability in South Vietnam, the situation in the first half of 1965 did not bear this out. The government of Dr. Quat and General Ky fared no better at dealing with Buddhist discontents than had the Khanh administration. To make matters worse, security in the rural areas, particularly in the central highlands, was fast deteriorating in spite of the increased American effort at organizing "pacification" programs.

19. U. Alexis Johnson, "Communiqué of the United States Government" (Saigon, 2 August 1965).

Part of the American effort at creating stability in the highlands was to assist the Vietnamese government in implementing the programs that had been promised the highlanders at Pleiku. In order to do this, USOM created the Office of Montagnard Affairs, the head of which was Lamar Prosser, who had been USOM representative in Pleiku. (The highlanders normally were called Montagnards by the Americans, who pronounced it "Mountain Yards" and often shortened it to "the Yards.") Prosser immediately began a survey of the various ministries to determine what was being done on programs for the highlands. After his research, he related to me in March 1964 that at the Ministry of Education he had been informed that highland students were now exempt from all fees and that new boarding schools (there already were 35 in 9 provinces) were being planned. Highland languages would be taught in primary schools when primers were available (the SIL had already begun preparing some), and the Normal School in Ban Me Thuot was being expanded. He found that the matter of highland land titles was given to the Directorate of Agriculture and Land Development in the Ministry of Agriculture. Prosser was told that the problem was that the highlanders were "semi-nomadic," all of them practicing swidden farming. Nonetheless, there was a plan to give families five to eight hectares. Prosser was also told that the highlander law courts were going to be revived and reorganized.

Prosser reported that the Directorate of Highland Affairs, now under the prime minister's office, had not changed appreciably from when it was under the Ministry of Social Welfare or the Ministry of Defense. It still had no functions other than operating boarding schools and the Technical Training Center in Hue, both financed by the CIA. It had offices in twenty-two provinces, but the personnel were attached to ARVN, and in many of the offices there were no highlanders.

The year 1965 brought the full impact of the war to the highlands. By the beginning of 1965, according to Westmoreland, an estimated 1,000 a month were infiltrating from North Vietnam.[20] They included elements of the People's Army of Vietnam (PAVN), the North Vietnamese army. (The North Vietnamese never admitted they had troops in South Vietnam until their victory in 1975.) In July 1965 there were the "first tentative reports" of some type of participation by PAVN in Viet Cong operations. In December 1964 the PAVN 95th Regiment arrived in Kontum and by

---

20. Westmoreland, "Report on Operations," pp. 93, 95, 107.

the end of February 1965 it had been joined by the 32d and 101st regiments.

Among the infiltrators were highlander regroupées who had been trained in North Vietnam. One of them was Nay Wen, whose movement north was described earlier. Nay Wen had been trained in medical care and was working at the Bach Mai hospital near Hanoi. Early in 1965 he and nineteen other highlanders who had received varied training in political propaganda, photography, and engineering were put on a special "Cadre Delegation Truck" that looked like a large jeep and driven southward for two days and nights, reaching a place in the mountains. From there, they walked on forest paths into the mountains for three months and twenty-five days. Nay Wen entered the south somewhere in Kontum province, walking southeasterly through Pleiku province into Phu Tuc district of Phu Bon province. Finally reaching the Mount Ju area where he was born, he organized a small dispensary in a thatched hut hidden by trees. In 1966 he married a local girl. In 1967 the Americans bombed the dispensary. He then returned to his natal village, but the Viet Cong came and persuaded him to go with them again.

Communist propaganda had greatly intensified. A favorite technique among the Stieng was to sing propaganda songs, one of which urged the villagers to make bamboo stakes to place in paths and to dig traps—as the Stieng had done to harass the French in the 1930s. It went:

> Comrade Stieng, strive to strike the invaders
> As we catch spies, we smash, we strike!
> We diligently make stakes, make traps,
> Dig trenches, dig ditches
> Everyone, from old men to young children.[21]

Early in 1965 I began research on the highlanders for the RAND Corporation. One of the goals of the project was to determine the socioeconomic needs of the highland people so as to formulate programs to meet these needs. I began an ethnographic survey, visiting all parts of the highlands that were accessible, to gather the wide range of data necessary for understanding the context in which these socioeconomic programs would function. Also, much time was spent with highland leaders getting their views on the subject. This led to an additional study of highland

---

21. This sample was translated by Neil Jamieson.

leadership above the village level and resulted in the genealogies summarized in charts 1 to 5.

In February 1965 I went to Kontum and spent considerable time with
Paul Nur (1.13), the Assistant Province Chief for Highland Affairs. Kontum
had changed somewhat since 1957. The town now had its own airport.
(Previously they had used the airstrip at the Catecka tea estate.) It had paved
streets and the main part of the town had new shops and a modern marketplace. Nur described the situation in the provinces as "serious," noting that
Communist activity had increased considerably. He blamed it on the influx
of Vietnamese settlers, saying, "Where you have Vietnamese, you have
Viet Cong." I accompanied him on visits to villages north of Kontum
town in the vicinity of Route 14, where Nur had been organizing a Force
de la Jeunesse Montagnarde (Highlander Youth Force) among the villagers. (The word "youth" was used rather loosely, since some recruits
were in their forties and fifties.) The function of this force was not only to
provide village defense but also to mount operations against any Viet
Cong units that might come into the area.

On Route 14, ten kilometers north of Kontum, the bridge had been
blown up by the Viet Cong the previous week. We continued to the large
Rengao village of Kon Trang Moné where we were greeted by a group of
village chiefs who had gathered there to meet with Nur. Sitting on small
carved rattan and bamboo stools, we drank from the jars and ate roasted
chicken and fish while Nur talked to the chiefs. Several of the chiefs said
that the Viet Cong had recently come into their villages. With them were
Vietnamese with northern accents and they were dressed in uniforms. One
chief told how some of them had said that they were "army regulars"
(*chính quy*). Two of the chiefs noted that the Viet Cong were accompanied
by several big, light-skinned orientals who had "large feet."

Nur talked with the chiefs about the Youth Force and we departed. On
the way back to Kontum, the sun began to set. The forest turned beautiful
nuances of green and gold. It seemed peaceful, but as the light faded the
darkness brought with it the menacing chill that is the curse of a place in the
throes of guerrilla warfare.

Nur was planning an operation south of Kon Trang Moné on 6 March
1965, and he sought assistance from the MACV contingent in Kontum
(located in a large compound where the first MAAG adviser tents had been
in 1957). The American advisers, however, were not interested. On
7 March the senior adviser and the district chief were en route to Dak To

on Route 14 when not far from Kon Trang Moné they were ambushed by the Viet Cong. The same day news reached Kontum that Communist forces had attacked the district headquarters at Dak Sut, north of Dak To. Some 400 Jeh refugees had converged on Dak Sut.

Nur felt strongly that it was necessary for highland leaders to keep pressing for the programs that had been promised at the Pleiku meeting. He and other leaders had been invited to Saigon in January 1965 to discuss with some of the officials at various ministries some of these programs. At the Ministry of Justice they had talked about reestablishing the highlander law courts, and at the Ministry of Rural Affairs they discussed land titles. (Some of the delegates from Darlac had brought copies of Sabatier's 1925 land tenure report.) They also had met with Lt. Col. Touprong Ya Ba, but Nur noted that the highlanders regarded him as a spokesman, not a leader. There was a joke among the Rhadé that Ya Ba, a Chru, had only received his promotion because they, the Rhadé, revolted.

On 15 March 1965 there was a Convention for Administrative and Military Affairs in Saigon sponsored by the Directorate of Highland Affairs. Many of the highland leaders who had been at Pleiku were flown to Saigon on CIA-financed Air America aircraft. They met again with officials from various ministries to discuss programs that had been promised at Pleiku.

Ever since the CIA had become involved in the Bureau of Highland Affairs in 1961 to organize the Mountain Scout Program, its continued financing of the bureau's activities gave CIA staff members an increasing degree of influence. In April 1965 the Pleiku Training Center (which had been enlarged in 1962) was expanded and renamed the Truong Son Training Center. Lt. Col. Touprong Ya Ba officiated at the opening ceremony. Men from highland villages who had been selected by their district chiefs were sent to the center to be trained in gathering intelligence and spreading progovernment propaganda as well as organizing community development projects in agriculture and village health. The establishment of the Truong Son Center also brought out some of the latent conflicts in the Directorate of Highland Affairs and planted some of the seeds of corruption that would plague the highlanders' representation in Saigon for a long time to come.

According to Touneh Han Tho, when Ya Ba had been named head of the directorate in October 1964, his appointment had been welcomed by Major Ngo Van Hung, who had been the original head of the Bureau for

Highland Affairs before his demotion to deputy when Nguyen Phi Phung became chief of the Directorate for Highland Affairs in May 1964. Hung was one of a group of Vietnamese who had become involved in highland affairs because they saw it as a means of attaining upward mobility. They regarded themselves as superior to the highlanders associated with the bureau and the directorate and saw the highlanders as people they could manipulate. Hung, therefore, felt that he could easily influence Ya Ba. Soon after he assumed office, however, Ya Ba replaced him as deputy with Capt. Nguyen Van Nghiem (another ambitious Vietnamese). Nghiem was a close friend of Vietnamese ethnologist Nghiem Tham and of Nguyen Dang Thuc, a professor in the Faculty of Letters. They had plans for organizing a highland students association and had supported Khanh's naming Ya Ba as director.

Chagrined at being replaced, Hung accused Nghiem of stealing 150,000 piasters of Asia Foundation funds intended for highland students' scholarships. Hung also accused Nghiem of being a Communist sympathizer. Nghiem was jailed for two months and transferred to Mytho. Hung regained his position as deputy of Ya Ba and became involved in the organization of the Truong Son Center. Conflict between Hung and Ya Ba arose, however, when Hung secured the services of Ngoc Dieu, a Vietnamese contractor (and close friend of General Co) to build the new center at Pleiku. Ya Ba had wanted the construction done by a friend of his brother, Touprong Hiou. This ultimately led to Hung's resignation in November 1965.

One graphic sign of the deteriorating security situation in the highlands was the crumbling of the Land Development Program. In discussing the failure of this program, Bui Van Luong, who had been in charge of it between 1956 and 1960, voiced the opinion that one of the main reasons the program had faltered was that Diem was in too great a hurry to implement it and realize results. Luong favored establishing the land development centers in accessible areas so that they could receive the necessary support in their early phases. Luong, for example, wanted the centers to be built along Route 19 just west of Pleiku first and then gradually extended farther west as the initial centers became self-supporting. Diem insisted, however, on locating the first centers at Duc Co, close to the Cambodian border, and then built the subsequent centers closer to Pleiku. The isolated Duc Co centers became targets of the Viet Cong, and by mid-1965 most of the settlers had fled.

A Bru village (1965)

An August 1965 report of the Ad Hoc Committee on Land Development Centers—it included representatives from the USOM Provincial Operations Office, the MACV Pacification Planning Office, and the Vietnamese Directorate for Land Development—presented a very dim picture of the state of this program.[22] Following the toppling of the Diem government, people began leaving the land development centers in large numbers. Of the peak population of 274,954 in 225 centers throughout Vietnam, 35,000 immediately quit the centers. During 1964 their populations diminished by 25–30 percent. As of August 1965, out of the 23 centers in Pleiku, only 5 were under government control. In Phu Bon, 6 of the 7 were "relatively secure," while in Darlac only 7 of the 30 were controlled by the government. In Quang Duc, 4 of the 9 centers were secure, and in Phuoc Long, 4 of the 26 centers were under government control.

In the highlands, those leaving the land development centers usually went to the nearest towns. Ban Me Thuot, Pleiku, and Cheo Reo ex-

22. Ad Hoc Committee on Land Development Centers, "Joint Report on Land Development Centers" (Saigon, August 1965).

perienced an influx of these refugees, who built ramshackle settlements with poor sanitation facilities. The intensification of the war also generated larger numbers of highland refugees, although they tended to avoid the towns. Many went to other highland villages—where they usually had kin. In May 1965 at Khe Sanh the district chief reported that there were 4,000 Bru refugees along Route 9 outside the town. He also pointed out that, of the estimated 14,000 Bru who had lived in villages in the Khe Sanh area, some 6,000 had either moved into Laos or gone into the Viet Cong-controlled areas. In the refugee villages of Lang Troai (380 families) and Lang Van Chuoi (45 families) on the Laotian border, some of the Bru explained that one advantage of going to the Viet Cong-controlled zones was that there was more land for their swidden farming. They added that 200 villagers had departed for the Viet Cong zone the previous week.

At Danang the province chief admitted that he had declared most of highland Quang Nam a "free strike zone for VNAF" and added, "That will take care of our Katu problem."[23] Moving farther south, it was apparent that the refugee problem was universal in the highlands. In remote Gia Vuc in the Re river valley, there were 3,000 Hre who had come down from the hills. At Plateau Gi, the small Monom ethnic group found it necessary to move its villages closer together. In the southern part of the highlands, the Mnong, Stieng, and Chrau-speaking people were moving as refugees.

The worst situation, however, was in Kontum province, where by late June security had crumbled, giving rise to conjecture in Saigon and Washington that the Communists were going to "cut the country in half"—as the Viet Minh had tried to do in 1954. All of the roads in the

23. At this time Nancy Costello, the SIL staff member working on the Katu language, and I had been obtaining ethnographic information on that group from a Katu boy about 16 years old who had been wounded during a skirmish between Viet Cong and Special Forces troops. He was a High Katu, from a remote area near the Lao border. Nancy had been conducting research with the goal of devising a Katu alphabet, and the boy had been giving us information about Katu society. He had surprised us by describing terraced paddy fields (a relatively sophisticated type of farming), when anyone who had visited the Katu area had found only swidden cultivation. When we asked if his people had always farmed that way, he just smiled and turned away. Later in a discussion about the men's house, he astonished us by taking the pen and writing a sentence which read, "Where is my older brother and sister?" He used the same diacritical marks as the Vietnamese to indicate vowel differences. He beamed and noted that I had written similar terms for "older brother" and "older sister" the day before (using Nancy's orthography). It turned out that he had a complete alphabet, which Nancy judged to be well done. When we asked where he had learned to write, he just smiled and looked away. It would appear that these innovations had been introduced among the Katu by the Vietnamese Communists, the only outsiders who had been in the High Katu area in 25 years.

highlands were subject to roadblocks and ambushes. In Kontum, Pierre
Yuk (1.12), Paul Nur (1.13), Hiup (1.20), and Hiu (1.16) all lamented that
it was very reminiscent of 1954 when the Viet Minh were menacing the
town from the north. As then, the Vietnamese civil servants were evacuating their families. Prices were rising by the day, and essentials, such as rice
and gasoline, had to be brought in by air. Tickets for Air Vietnam flights
were selling on the black market at inflated prices. The highland leaders
noted that refugees were flooding into the Toumarong valley and into Dak
To and that Viet Cong were appearing in villages just outside of Kontum.
They and their families were making plans to flee across the Bla river if
necessary, as they had in 1954.

The SIL had just opened a new linguistic research center in Kontum for
their Bible translation work. Located on the northern edge of the town, it
was a collection of small, simple houses around a central building that
served as a meeting place and library. Staff members and their families who

A Cua refugee in
Tra Bong (1966)

had been living in remote places such as Dak To, Dak Pek, and Dak Sut had evacuated to Kontum, where they continued their research with informants. Like everyone else in Kontum, they dug deep bunkers.

At the Minh Quy Hospital, Dr. Pat Smith worked long hours to treat the increased flood of sick and wounded. A tall woman with a strong face and short hair, she explained during a coffee break that when she first began to practice in 1959 she had encountered many problems. The most serious was the hostility of the shamans, who spread the word that she had "bad medicine" that would cause harm to any who used it. This had a deadly effect, because the villagers still were dubious of anything alien, such as a western hospital. As a result, she would get only patients who had tried all of the traditional means to be healed, and consequently many of them were ready to die when they got to her hospital. She persisted, and slowly more and more sick highlanders began coming to the hospital. As most of them returned to their villages cured, it became known that the "big grandmother" had "powerful medicine." She clearly was in harmony with the spirits. Initially most of her patients were from the Catholic Bahnar villages near Kontum, but in time patients, many of them carried by their kinfolks, began to make their way to Minh Quy from very remote parts of the province.

Fortunately, when the influx of patients began, Pat had moved to her new installation on the edge of Kontum not far from the Dak Bla. It had two wards, each with 100 beds, built around a surgical suite. Pat was assisted by several Bahnar nuns and laboratory technicians she had trained as well as by a young Jarai named "Scotty" who had been trained by the American Special Forces. Scotty had adopted their slang and expletives too, e.g., at a birth he once said in front of some prim visitors, "Doc, that's a f___ good lookin' baby.")

Now that Pat's hospital was successful, a new problem arose. Well-to-do Vietnamese such as the wives of the province chief and the ARVN commander sought medical treatment and demanded preference. Pat explained that hers was a charity hospital and that if they insisted on being seen they would have to wait like the others. They were outraged at this and claimed she was anti-Vietnamese.

By late June the wards had been filled and patients were being put on mats laid on the floor, which in any case many of the highlanders preferred since they were unaccustomed to the high beds and were afraid of falling out of them at night. It was curious to see some of the elderly male patients, wearing their loincloths, smoking their hand-carved pipes, and surrounded in bed by their familiar objects—water gourds, woven rattan backpacks, knives, sometimes crossbows, and food wrapped in banana leaves. The patients' kinfolks camped around the hospital. Pat provided some large army tents for them and they turned the area into a village scene with cooking fires, wash hanging on lines, and naked children scampering about.

South of Kontum, near Route 14, Sister Marie Louise of the Sisters of Charity was also experiencing an influx of patients at her leprosarium. A small, wiry woman who spoke very rapid French, Marie Louise had begun her leprosarium in the mid-1950s and there now were around 400 patients. She pointed out that before it existed, lepers in the Kontum area were expelled from their villages to live alone in the forest. With help from Bishop Seitz, Marie Louise built wards on piling in the highland fashion. Each ethnic group had its own ward. The central buildings were for therapy, and, since there were a great many dependents, Marie Louise constructed a special pavilion where the children studied and played. It was a light and airy structure with an interesting winding stairway that Marie Louise had copied from a magazine photo of a stairway at Orly Airport in Paris. She was completing a chapel that had decorative ironwork with motifs borrowed from Sedang and Bahnar weaving. It also had impressive murals depicting highlanders which had been painted by Sister Boniface, a talented Benedictine nun who had been trained in art and architecture in Paris and Vienna and who was the great-granddaughter of Emperor Franz Josef. The leprosarium was self-sufficient in food except for bread, which they baked with USOM flour, and this was reflected in the excellent lunch Marie Louise served—steak, french fried potatoes, bamboo shoot salad, and a dessert of avocado with a sweet syrup from a tree in the nearby forest.

The Communists' strategy in the highlands had changed considerably from the 1957 days when their guerrillas were successfully blending with the local population, never resorting to violence. Pike expresses the view that, following the appearance of the American programs (particularly the CIDG program) in 1962, the government side attracted more highlanders than did the Communists.[24] The result was a "harsher approach that in turn not only further alienated the montagnards but also drove an es-

24. Pike, *Viet Cong,* p. 205.

timated 100,000 of them out of the highlands." With the introduction of
PAVN units, the harshness of the Communist tactics increased. This,
combined with the equal harshness of ARVN methods and the all-too-
often indiscriminate bombing by VNAF and the American air force,
produced havoc in areas of the highlands caught in military operations.

On 1 July 1965 PAVN and Viet Cong units attacked and captured
Toumarong district town in the beautiful valley north of Kontum. They
also launched assaults on Dak Sut and Dak To. Air strikes were called in
against Toumarong because the Communists captured two howitzers.
Within days, refugees from the area began to pour into Kontum. Buses and
trucks filled with refugees and their belongings crowded Route 14, and
many others hurried along on foot. Michael Benge, a former IVS agricultural worker now with USOM, quickly organized a relief program for
them, and Paul Nur flew to Dak To to organize aid for the highlanders
converging on the town.

Refugees from Toumarong who brought their wounded to Pat Smith's
hospital related that the Communist attack began with heavy shelling of
the town and nearby villages. The highlanders fled in the night, grabbing
blankets, a few cooking pots, and some rice. They ran through the thick
forest so fast that many tore their flesh on the tree branches and brush.
Some had sprains and broken ankles. One old man with a strange ailment
that was affecting his flesh had carried his grandson while his own son
clutched his arm, pulling him as they fled. The child and the son had held
the old man so tightly that their blue handprints remained on his arm.
Treatment of this new flood of patients was rendered difficult by a lack of
many basic medicines and other necessities. A Bahnar couple stood by with
anguished looks while their little boy, who had had typhoid and then
developed pneumonia, breathed the last of the oxygen in the hospital and
quietly died.

In Kontum the townspeople were being organized into self-defense
units, sandbags were piled around houses, bunkers were being dug, and
windows were taped. Gasoline was available only to officials, and some city
generators had ceased to operate. One quiet afternoon Mike Benge and I
were having lunch in a small Vietnamese restaurant on the main street,
now empty of vehicles, when two trucks belonging to a Chinese transport
firm in Saigon rolled to a stop in front of a Chinese general foods shop.
Since all of the roads to the highlands were cut by the Communists, we

were astonished and went to see what they were delivering. They were unloading deluxe foods, such as cans of imported French peas, lichees in syrup, French wine, and Cholon brandy. The drivers smilingly told us that they had come from Saigon via Dalat, Nhatrang, Ban Me Thuot, and Pleiku. What they did not say—and what everyone knew—is that they had paid the Communists to get through the roadblocks.

At the SIL center, language research continued, and I worked with several of the staff and their informants, collecting ethnographic data. I also met with some of the staff to discuss some anthropological concepts and field methods, although our sessions were disrupted by artillery fire from the 22d Division headquarters and the din of helicopters at the nearby MACV compound. On 4 July 1965 the SIL staff organized a modest celebration of Independence Day, serving lemonade, cake, and sandwiches. Mike Benge and I attended and, as we ate, American jet fighters swooped over to begin air strikes against reported Communist positions around ten kilometers north of Kontum. They were the first American bombers in operation that any of us had seen.

The appearance of American jets over Kontum was a reminder of the U.S. military buildup that was taking place. On 8 March the 9th Marine Expeditionary Brigade had arrived in Danang from Okinawa to provide security for the large airbase. The U.S. Army's 716th Military Police Battalion had arrived in Saigon on 21 March to guard some American installations in the face of increased Communist terrorism. (On 30 March a car full of plastic explosives was detonated at the U.S. Embassy in Saigon.) In May the U.S. Army's 173d Airborne Brigade had landed at Bien Hoa, where they pitched their tents in a nearby rubber plantation. Soon after, additional Marines and Seabees landed at Chu Lai to develop a major base. By the end of May the U.S. forces in South Vietnam surpassed 50,000— 22,500 Army; 16,000 Marines; 10,000 Air Force; 3,000 Navy.

Early in June the 1st Battalion of the Royal Australian Regiment arrived in Vung Tau, while the U.S. Seventh Fleet Task Force 77, composed of aircraft carriers, destroyers, and cruisers, took up battle stations in the South China Sea to provide air and naval gunfire support for American and allied ground forces. In response to a request from General Westmoreland, B-52 bombers from the Strategic Air Command's Third Air Division on Guam appeared in the skies over South Vietnam for the first time on 18 June 1965 to bomb Communist positions in War Zone D, a heavily forested area northeast of Saigon in the terrace region. On 28 June

the 173d Brigade launched its first major operation against the
Communists in Zone D. The following month the 2d Brigade of the 1st
Infantry Division arrived and established a base camp at Di An, just outside
of Saigon. On 29 July the 1st Brigade of the 101st Airborne Division
landed at Cam Ranh Bay. The day before, President Johnson had ordered
the U.S. forces in South Vietnam to be increased to 125,000 and stipulated
that additional troops would be sent if necessary.[25]

25. Westmoreland, "Report on Operations," pp. 108–09.

4 INCURSION OF THE VIETNAM WAR

The strange and, in many respects, unique character of the Vietnam War is illustrated by the fact that, unlike most wars in history, it had no starting date. There was the insurgency of the early 1960s, which, during the 1965–66 period when American forces became actively involved, became "the war in Vietnam." Soon, however, at some indeterminate time when the effects of the war began to be felt in the United States, everyone began calling it "the Vietnam War." It was to become the most controversial and the longest conflict in American history.

For the highlanders, the Vietnam War was the latest phase of the conflicts that had been visited upon them since 1945 by the "civilized" people from beyond the mountains—the Japanese, French, Vietnamese, and now the Americans. With only a brief respite in between (1954–60), the Indochina War and the Vietnam War came like huge thunderheads of the rainy season, emitting frightening flashes and sounds as they swept everything in their paths. But of the two, the Vietnam War, with its modern, sophisticated weaponry, proved a storm of greater fury. Moreover, it was a fury centered in the highlands (the Indochina War was fought mostly in the northern highlands) as the American forces and the Army of the Republic of Vietnam (ARVN) clashed with the Viet Cong and the People's Army of Vietnam (PAVN).

FULRO–GOVERNMENT NEGOTIATIONS

In the midst of this intensification of the war, Dr. Quat resigned as head of the government on 8 June 1965, turning over his mandate to the Armed

Forces Council. On 19 June (the day after the first B-52 mission), Air Force General Nguyen Cao Ky took over the government. He formed a directorate under the authority of the Armed Forces Council and organized a military Committee of National Leadership. Ky appointed General Nguyen Van Thieu titular head of state and General Nguyen Huu Co the minister of defense.[1]

Just before the end of the Quat administration, formal contacts between the government and FULRO had been established. In May, a letter from Y Bham to the Darlac province chief, Col. Le Van Thanh, had proposed that a meeting between FULRO and government representatives be arranged. It was agreed upon and on 6 June, Thanh, Beachner (the highland reporter for the embassy), and an American major met at Ban Don with FULRO representatives Y Dhun Nie (a middle aged Rhadé who had been in the Darlac administration) and Y Sen Nie Kdam (3.18, who had left the army to join the movement). A letter from Y Bham outlined three demands: a flag (*fanion*) to represent all highlanders, a highland army of 50,000, and a conference in the Philippines or Thailand to bring together FULRO and government delegations. Thanh accepted the letter and promised to pass it on to his superiors. Nothing was concluded at the meeting, but it opened negotiations between the dissidents and the government.

In spite of the fact that Americans were involved in this meeting, there continued to be suspicion of American motives by the Vietnamese leaders. This suspicion was heightened by an incident that occurred in mid-July and was described in a booklet that appeared later in 1965 under the authorship of General Vinh Loc, the II Corps commander.[2] On 16 July General Lam, commander of the 23d Division, was informed that FULRO members Y Sen Nie Kdam, Y Ngo Buon Ya, and Y Preh Buon Krong (from the Protestant Mission) were meeting with Dorsey Anderson, a CIA official and adviser to the Directorate of Highland Affairs; Capt. Barry Peterson, an Australian army officer and adviser to the Truong Son Program; and Beachner at his house. Also present was Nay Luett, of the Directorate of Highland Affairs. Lam telephoned the house and asked to speak to Nay Luett, his way of letting the group know that he was aware of the meeting.

1. Dennis J. Duncanson, *Government and Revolution in Vietnam* (New York: Frederick A. Praeger, 1966), p. 351.
2. Vinh Loc, *The So-Called Movement for Autonomy, FULRO* (Saigon: Le Trang An Quan, 1965), pp. 40–50.

Vietnamese resentment of this gathering led to a meeting in Ban Me Thuot on 30 July of General Co with General Westmoreland and Philip Manfull, Political Counselor for the embassy. Co accused the Americans of becoming too involved in the FULRO affair. He demanded that Beachner and Peterson be removed from the highlands and that Anderson's activities be severely restricted. The next day the two were transferred to Saigon.

In July 1965 the Political Section of the American Embassy decided to form a Montagnard Committee made up of representatives from the Political Section, MACV, CIA, USOM, and the U.S. Information Service. I was invited to be the only nongovernment member. The purpose of the committee was to exchange information on events in the highlands and formulate recommendations for the American Mission concerning ways of improving relations between the highlanders and the Vietnamese government.

On 23 July 1965 an armed clash between FULRO and ARVN very nearly occurred at the Buon Brieng Special Forces Camp (where, during 1964, Capt. Gillespie had averted an uprising). According to Y Dhe Adrong, some FULRO troops were in the Ban Don-Buong Brieng area to provide security for another FULRO-government meeting. As they came close to the camp, the Vietnamese commander called in an air strike. Angered by this, some of the Rhadé in the camp tied up the camp commander, disarmed the Vietnamese and Americans, and let the FULRO troops into the post. Some of the FULRO went to Ban Me Thuot, where they contacted Carolyn Griswold, a Christian and Missionary Alliance youth worker who was regarded as a close friend of the highlanders. She arranged for them to meet with General Lam. They agreed to let some ARVN troops into Buon Brieng as part of a truce. Once in the camp, however, the ARVN commander had the FULRO troops arrested. Meanwhile, the American senior adviser to the 23d Division had elements of the U.S. 173d Airborne Division brought to the Ban Me Thuot airport to stand by in case they were needed at Buon Brieng. The captured FULRO troops were reported by General Vinh Loc to have "rallied" and were sent to Duc My for training in the ARVN.[3]

General Vinh Loc, a tall portly man with an imperious air (he liked to point out that he was a member of the royal family), was disliked by the highland leaders, who considered his attitude toward them condescending.

3. Ibid., pp. 43–44.

At public ceremonies, Vinh Loc liked to wear a Rhadé shirt. When I asked Y Chon Mlo Duon Du what he thought of it, he replied, "It is like the tiger that eats the sheep and then wears its pelt as a shirt." Chagrined at the FULRO demands, Vinh Loc let it be known that he favored a "hard line" with the dissidents. Meanwhile, negotiations between FULRO and the government led to an agreement to have a FULRO delegation installed at Ban Me Thuot where it could pass communications from Y Bham to Col. Thanh, who would act as government representative. Soon after, Y Bham sent General Vinh Loc two letters in which he demanded a "pays libre Dega-Cham." It was noted previously that the term *Dega* means "sons of the mountains," Y Bham's designation for the highland people.[4] This infuriated Vinh Loc, and on 25 August he called a press conference at Pleiku to denounce the FULRO demand for an independent state for the highlanders.

The FULRO delegation set up its headquarters at Buon Ale-A, just south of Ban Me Thuot, in a large frame house with a wide balcony in front that gave it the appearance of buildings in the American west during the nineteenth century. The delegation was led by Y Dhe Adrong (5.10), a tall man with white hair who owned a coffee estate of ten hectares; Y Tang Phok, a Mnong Rlam who used a Rhadé version of his name; Y Ngo Buon Ya; Y Preh Buon Krong; and Y Sen Nie Kdam (3.18).

On 13 September the FULRO delegation met with Col. Thanh, who outlined some of the achievements since the Pleiku conference. The Junior Military School, for sons of military personnel, had opened in Pleiku and 38 highlanders had graduated from the Thu Duc Officers Training Center. The 1958 and 1959 decrees inhibiting highlanders from owning land had been abolished, and a decree dated 22 July 1965 provided for reestablishment of the highlander law courts. A new normal school, financed by American aid, was being constructed near Ban Me Thuot and the new Y Ut Technical Training School (named for Rhadé leader Y Ut Nie Buon Rit) had opened in the town. Y Dhe then presented Thanh with FULRO requests. They included the flag, the military force, and the *statut particulier*. In addition, he asked for a General Commission for Highlanders to be located at Ban Me Thuot and participation by highland leaders in any future international conference concerning the fate of South Vietnam—

---

4. Norman C. La Brie, "FULRO: The History of Political Tension in the South Vietnamese Highlands," M. A. thesis (University of Massachusetts, 1971), p. 84. La Brie was the U.S. Embassy political reporting officer for the highlands between April 1968 and September 1969.

this latter reflecting the resentment often expressed by highland leaders that they were not represented at the Geneva Conference in 1954. Thanh promised to relay these demands to Saigon.[5]

In spite of the FULRO-government negotiations, tensions were increasing in the highlands. Early in September there was a clash between highlanders in a Regional Force unit and Vietnamese Rangers in Pleiku. Not long after, a 480-man FULRO unit appeared in the vicinity of the Special Forces camp at Buon Ea Yong in search of food and medicine. Two battalions of Vietnamese marines were sent to the area, surrounding the FULRO troops who surrendered. At the same time, a rumor spread that 200 highlanders had been poisoned by Vietnamese at a celebration in Dalat.

Considerable concern over worsening relations between the highlanders and Vietnamese was expressed at the embassy Montagnard Committee meetings at this time. As a result, some committee members and I worked out a scheme for programs to meet the needs and desires that had been expressed by highland leaders at the various meetings. We emphasized the importance of some kind of highlander political representation in Saigon. A high commission under the premier seemed to be the answer. This would give the commissioner flexibility in dealing with the numerous ministries involved in programs for the highlands. It also would give the commissioner direct access to the head of the government. The plan was presented to the embassy committee and it was agreed that it would be given to Ambassador Lodge, who could take up the matter with General Ky. Weeks later the committee was notified that Lodge did not consider the matter important enough to discuss with General Ky.

Early in October 1965 Paul Nur led a group of leaders from the Bahnar, Sedang, Jarai, Jeh, Rengao, and Halang ethnic groups in Kontum province to meet with the province chief and express what they wanted of the administration. Prior to this meeting Nur had explained that, while not a member of FULRO, he was sympathetic to their goals, which he felt were the goals of most highland people. At the meeting, therefore, they outlined many of the same requests that had been voiced by the FULRO leaders. They did, however, emphasize the land question, noting that some of the newly built military and administrative compounds were on land claimed

5. Republic of Vietnam, Administrative Office of Darlac Province, "Minutes on the Meeting between Government Agencies and FULRO Representatives on 13 September 1965" (Ban Me Thuot, 1965).

by some of the highlanders. The province chief replied that the government was concerned about the land question and titles were being given out in some areas. I had just witnessed a land title distribution ceremony at Dalat. After speeches by Premier Ky and Vinh Loc, the former gave out titles to fifteen villagers, ten of whom were Vietnamese. Also, the titles were for squatters, allowing the government to expropriate the land at any time. Similar titles were given out in villages near Ban Me Thuot.

During the last half of 1965 the war worsened in the highlands and American troops became involved in operations there for the first time. As Westmoreland put it, "the tactical picture in the central Highlands during this period was not encouraging."[6] On 18 August the Communists overran a Special Forces camp in Dak Sut district in northern Kontum. Of the 250 CIDG troops there, only 50 escaped with 8 of their American advisers. On 14 September the 1st Cavalry Division (Airmobile) arrived in An Khe, the first American combat unit to be assigned to the highlands. Its arrival was protected by the 1st Brigade of the 101st Airborne Division in Operation Gibraltar, which involved clearing Route 19 from Qui Nhon to An Khe, the first large-scale American military operation in the highlands.

In October 1965 the PAVN launched a major operation in the highlands. It had assembled three regiments—the 32d, the 33d, and the 66th—in western Pleiku and in adjacent Cambodian territory. On 19 October they attacked Plei Me Special Forces camp, 45 kilometers from Pleiku. Air strikes were called in by the defending Americans while ARVN units arrived to counterattack. The 1st Cavalry Division provided support for the ARVN. On Westmoreland's orders, the 1st Cavalry launched a "search and destroy" operation against the PAVN units in western Pleiku. This resulted in a month-long campaign known as the "battle of the Ia Drang Valley." The peak of the fighting took place between 14 and 19 November at the base of Mount Pong. In Pleiku, we watched helicopters bring back bodies of American soldiers, and some of the highland leaders there shook their heads, saying that it reminded them of the Indochina War. By the end of November 1965 American military strength in South Vietnam had reached a total of 148,300.

By November it was clear that the FULRO-government negotiations

6. W. C. Westmoreland, "Report on Operations in South Vietnam: January 1964–June 1968," in U.S. G. Sharp and W. C. Westmoreland, *Report on the War in Vietnam: As of 30 June 1968*, 2 sections (Washington: U.S. Government Printing Office, 1969), section 2, pp. 109–10.

were reaching an impasse, and at the Montagnard Committee meeting at the embassy it was reported that both Vinh Loc and General Co were advocating military action against FULRO. There were also growing complaints among highland leaders that the Directorate of Highland Affairs, which should have been playing an important role, was not doing anything. In addition there also was some speculation that the government really was not interested in having strong leadership at the directorate. Lt. Col. Touprong Ya Ba was an amiable man but an ineffectual leader. Nay Luett was capable and intelligent, but he had been sent to Ban Me Thuot, where he opened a small office for the directorate. According to Touneh Han Tho, the situation at the directorate was made worse by Major Ngo Van Hung, who was trying to undermine Ya Ba. Hung advocated replacing Ya Ba with Major Nay Lo, a Jarai Hung he knew he could manipulate. Han Tho noted that Nay Lo was not regarded as a strong leader and he would not have made a good director because he did not speak Vietnamese very well. Han Tho illustrated this with an amusing story about how Nay Lo visited a highland school in Dalat where the children had been very well trained in Vietnamese. Nay Lo addressed them, intending to say, "I am the representative in charge of highland affairs," but he used the wrong tones for "highland affairs" (*thượng vụ*), saying instead, "I am the representative in charge of loving female breasts" (*thương vú*). The children began to giggle. Then Nay Lo lamented that there was a lack of funds for better food. He intended adding, "Nonetheless, I hope that you are enjoying the sparse fare," but again he used the wrong words for "sparse fare" (*cực khổ*), saying instead, "Nonetheless, I hope that you are enjoying the dried manure" (*cứt khô*). The children were reduced to uncontrollable fits of laughter.

Early in November 1965 the Directorate of Highland Affairs was moved from a barren military compound outside Saigon to a neglected building on Nguyen Du Street, just behind the Independence Palace. The building, which still retained traces of former elegance, had been the principal Masonic temple in Saigon during the French period. Subsequently it had served as headquarters of Dr. Tran Kim Tuyen, who had been in charge of Ngo Dinh Nhu's secret service. Shortly after the move, Ya Ba was informed that Hung had been passing information about FULRO to Vietnamese Student Movement newspapers, so Hung was dismissed. According to Touneh Han Tho, this ended some of the conflict within the directorate, but new troubles arose. The Vietnamese staff at the directorate launched a protest because they disliked the new headquarters, claiming that the building was haunted. At the same time, Ya Ba began to experience problems with his new house, located near the directorate on a main street facing the end of Huyen Tran Cong Chua Street. The Vietnamese quickly pointed out that the main door of the house faced the trifurcation of the streets, thus enabling evil spirits to enter. Ya Ba became very upset and had the main entrance moved to a side of the house but the problems persisted. Finally he moved to an apartment.

As FULRO-government relations deteriorated, there was an increased flood of communications and letters from Y Bham to American officials in Saigon and Washington. Most of them explained the goals of the movement and the "aspirations" of the highland people. Typical was his letter of 8 November 1965 to President Johnson that reviewed the "autonomous" status that had been accorded the highlanders by the French and the loss of this autonomy under Ngo Dinh Diem.[7] Y Bham noted that the people of Dega-Cham belonged to the "free world" and therefore deserved the support of the United States in realizing the goals that had been made public. Letters to President Johnson followed on 9, 10, 11, 25, and 27 November. There also were letters to the American ambassador in Saigon and to the Secretary General of the United Nations.

On 15 December I met with Y Dhe Adrong and Y Preh Buon Krong at the FULRO delegation's house in Buon Ale-A. They were very discouraged and angry. They pointed out that the intensification of the war had made life difficult for the highland people. Villages were being bombed by the Americans and VNAF or were getting caught in the military operations that were increasing. The Communists entered villages to exact their "taxes" and force young men to go with them and ARVN came into the villages to steal. The government made many promises but did little for the highlanders. Then they informed me that talks between them and the government had broken off. Col. Thanh and Vinh Loc claimed they were too "busy" to see the FULRO representatives. Y Dhe warned that the present situation could lead to serious trouble. I returned to Saigon the following day to notify some members of the Montagnard Committee that there was a chance that trouble might erupt in the highlands. On the morning of 17 December the second FULRO revolt began.

The first indication that another uprising was in the offing was on 16

7. Y Bham Enuol, le Président du Front de Libération Dega-Cham à son excellence, Monsieur le Président des Etats-Unis d'Amérique (Zone Libérée, le 8 November 1965).

December, when a group of then FULRO cadremen who were arrested at Pleiku revealed that on 17 December there would be attacks by FULRO forces against the town and Special Forces camps. According to Y Thih Eban, who at this time was working in the Gia Nghia administration, the order to revolt came from Y Bham. It was the result of anger and frustration over what the FULRO leaders considered Vietnamese duplicity in not keeping the promises made at Pleiku in 1964. They felt that the Vietnamese government was indifferent to the highlanders' needs. Y Bham had sent word to his followers in ARVN, the CIDG, and the Regional and Popular Forces, and he explicitly instructed them to avoid bloodshed.

At Gia Nghia, Y Thih led the FULRO forces numbering 60 men (all from the Regional Forces) and moved on the town, defended by four ARVN battalions. When the province chief realized that FULRO was ready to attack, he ordered his forces to withdraw from Gia Nghia. Y Thih said that he and his men were astonished, and they asked George Gaspard, the USOM representative, if they could use his radio to contact the delegation in Ban Me Thuot. Y Thih also contacted the province chief, who promised not to arrest any of the FULRO contingent if he and his troops were allowed to reoccupy the town. Y Thih agreed and it was arranged that ARVN would "capture" Gia Nghia. After a staged "shelling," the FULRO forces let the army take the province headquarters. Not keeping his word, the province chief ordered Y Thih and his men arrested. Gaspard was expelled from the province.

At the Plei Joring Special Forces camp in Pleiku province, the Strike Force was reported to be in a position to take over the camp, but when expected orders from Y Bham failed to arrive, the situation returned to normal. A similar situation occurred at the Plei Mrong Special Forces camp. At Lac Thien, in Darlac, FULRO forces approached the Special Forces post and tried but failed to enlist the aid of the Strike Force for a move on Ban Me Thuot. The worst incident took place the following day when FULRO elements in the Regional Forces attacked the headquarters of Phu Thien district, north of Cheo Reo. In the fighting, 35 Vietnamese, including civilians, were killed. Some of the rebels went to the Mai Linh Special Forces camp, expecting to receive support, but were arrested. Nay Moul (2.17) and Rcom Pioi (2.21) were sent to the camp to deal with the rebels.

On the morning of 17 December, Premier Ky, Vinh Loc, General Co, and Lt. Col. Ya Ba joined American officials at Pleiku for the opening of the new Truong Son Training Center. Just as the ceremony ended, news of the revolt was received. Ya Ba reported that Ky became very angry because he had been discontent with the way Vinh Loc had been handling the highland situation. Vinh Loc, for his part, blamed the Americans for the uprising. As they were returning to Saigon, General Co told Ya Ba that the Americans had done a "secret survey" of minerals in the highlands and found many valuable things such as plutonium. Co added that the Americans, like the French, wanted control of the highlands.

Vinh Loc ordered swift justice for the rebels. A military tribunal was organized in Pleiku, and late in December four of the rebels were condemned to death. They died in public executions. Fifteen others, including Ksor Kham (3.19), were given jail sentences.

The morning of the revolt I received a telephone call in Saigon from Philip Habib, Political Counselor for the American Embassy, asking me to meet him. He was concerned over the events in the highlands, particularly since American combat units were now operating in that region. He emphasized that it was essential that the FULRO matter be resolved and asked for my views. I had brought the paper that Montagnard Committee members and I had prepared months before, and I gave it to him. We discussed the points in it and I departed.

The effects of the revolt were felt for several months after the executions. Among these, a rumor that the ghosts of those executed had appeared to Y Bham demanding revenge spread through parts of the highlands. Vinh Loc implicated the Communists and the Cambodians, accusing the latter of supplying FULRO with arms.[8] This accusation was the result of a news release from Phnom Penh dated 19 November 1965 that listed those in the new Administrative Committee of the Association of the Austrien People.[9] It included Ung Hong Sath, president of the National Assembly, and two deputy prime ministers, General Lon Nol and Son Sann. Another prominent Cambodian leader on the list was Im Tam. The vice-president of the committee was Y Bham Enuol. In a speech at Phnom Penh on 27 December Sihanouk denied that the Cambodians had given arms to FULRO, claiming that his government was "too poor" to arm the rebels.

Not long after the revolt, there was a crisis in the FULRO leadership.

8. Vinh Loc, *The So-Called*, p. 40.
9. "Comité Administratif de l'Amicale des Peuples Austriens," *Agence Khmere de Presse*, 19 November 1965.

According to Ksor Kok (5.11), two young FULRO leaders, Y Sen Nie Kdam (3.18) and Y Ngo Buon Ya, had gained the confidence of Y Bham Enuol. They began talking against Y Dhon Adrong. They claimed that the violence of the revolt was due to Y Dhon, and they convinced Y Bham that Y Dhon was going to destroy the FULRO movement. Enraged, Y Bham ordered Y Dhon executed. He was buried up to his waist and then killed. His body was thrown into a river to be devoured by the fish. Some of the FULRO leaders had been somewhat wary of Y Sen, remembering that he had been an intelligence officer in the ARVN and in 1964 had gone to Cambodia to gather information on Bajaraka for General Nguyen Khanh. It was not long before all of the FULRO leaders began to realize that both Y Sen and Y Ngo were spies for the Vietnamese government.

In spite of the criticism that had been leveled against him, Vinh Loc's position at the beginning of 1966 was stronger than it had been previously. He was given control over the Directorate of Highland Affairs and immediately ordered its headquarters moved to Pleiku, leaving a small staff in the Saigon office. Vinh Loc then moved against some highland leaders he suspected of having been involved in planning the December revolt. Siu Plung (1.23) and R'mah Liu (an early Bajaraka leader) were arrested, as was Y Thih Eban, who was sentenced to five years of labor. (He served two and was released.)

Most of the Ban Me Thuot delegation hurriedly left for Cambodia. Early in January 1966 I met with a group of pro-FULRO leaders, including Y Char Hdok and Y Chon Mlo Duon Du, at the house of Protestant pastor Y Ngue Buon Dap in Buon Ale-A. Word had just reached Ban Me Thuot that the village of Buon Ea Mur, northwest of the town, had been bombed by American jet fighters. They had made two passes at the village, destroying nine longhouses and badly damaging six others. There were at least three dead and many wounded. American aircraft also had just bombed Buon Kram, some 15 kilometers southeast of Ban Me Thuot, destroying ten longhouses and the school. The leaders pointed out that the loss of life was bad enough, but the families also lost their houses and possessions, including their valuable gongs and jars. The news saddened them and they said that the Vietnamese were invading the territory of the highland people with the aid of the Americans. "Why are the Americans betraying us?" one of them asked. They said that the U.S. Special Forces were hiring capable young men who should remain in school to be educated. They added that the Americans would turn on the FULRO just as they had at Buon Brieng in September and at Mai Linh during the December revolt. One of them said that the French had been forced by the United States to give the Vietnamese independence. "France gave birth to the baby, Vietnam," he added, and then inquired, "Why does a powerful nation like the United States let the Vietnamese baby push it around?"

After returning to Saigon, I had a meeting with General Westmoreland to discuss ways in which the worsening conflict between FULRO and the government might be resolved. I pointed out that, despite the disruptions of the war, there were programs that had been promised the highlanders that could be implemented. These would include such things as instruction in indigenous languages, revival of the law courts, and distribution of land titles. Westmoreland asked if I would meet with General Co and I agreed.

General Co, at our meeting in his office the following day, lamented that the approach to the highland problem taken thus far had not been success-ful and asked what I thought could be done. I expressed the view that there was need for the government to demonstrate good faith so as to improve its image in the highlands and that this could be done by implementing some of the promised programs. I outlined some of them as I had done for General Westmoreland. Co agreed, and said that he would allow each ethnic group to have its own flag. The highlanders are like "big children," Co observed, adding that he could not be harsh with them. Still, he concluded, one must be firm with them or they would take advantage. According to Charles Mohr of the *New York Times*, following the December revolt, generals Co and Nguyen Chanh Thi were highly critical of the "blundering" by Vinh Loc.[10] Co met with Westmoreland to ask his opinion on how to deal with the FULRO problem, and Westmoreland suggested he talk with me. After our meeting the U.S. Mission prepared a memorandum suggesting a series of programs dealing with the highland law courts, languages, and land titles. The purpose was to present this to the Vietnamese government.

Mohr also reported that General Co privately asked Philip Habib, the embassy's political counselor, to intercede with Premier Ky to have the Directorate of Highland Affairs turned over to Co, but Habib declined. The State Department, which had been following the situation closely, asked Ambassador Lodge to take a strong stand with the Vietnamese government, urging it to make good the promises made to the highland-

---

10. Charles Mohr, "Vietnamese Fear a Tribal Uprising," *New York Times*, 13 April 1966.

ers. The State Department felt this would be justified by the involvement of American combat troops in the central highlands. Lodge refused to heed these instructions on the grounds that American-Vietnamese relations were already very strained. At the end of January, however, Secretary of State Dean Rusk, who was visiting Saigon, had a twenty-minute chat with General Ky on the subject. Also, according to Mohr, "Premier Ky and other South Vietnamese officials were again pressed on the subject by Americans at the Honolulu conference early in February." This was the meeting of Ky, Thieu, and Co with President Johnson, Dean Rusk, and Robert McNamara.

As a result of these developments, on 21 February 1966 Premier Ky announced that a new war cabinet had been formed and that one of the newly created positions was to be a Commissioner for Highland Affairs who would serve as head of a Special Commission for Highland Affairs. Paul Nur (1.13) was named commissioner. One of the principal goals of the new commission was to aid in the government's implementation of the programs that had been promised the highlanders.

Lt. Col. Touprong Ya Ba was made assistant in charge of the Truong Son cadre program, and Nur appointed a Vietnamese named Ton That Cu as special assistant. According to Touneh Han Tho, Ton That Cu was a kinsman of the wife of Lt. Nguyen Van Phien, who had been in the directorate and was about to become chief of cabinet in the new commission. A native of Hue, Ton That Cu was a close friend of General Vinh Loc. His appointment came about because of Phien's advice that if Cu got this post it would ingratiate Nur with the general. Major Nay Lo was named head of the Truong Son Training Center in Pleiku, and Capt. Ton That Tu, cousin of Ton That Cu, was appointed his assistant. Han Tho noted that, since Capt. Tu had control of the ample funds provided the center by the CIA, he held the real power. A manifestation of this was the fact that Nay Lo had a modest office, while Ton That Tu had an office Han Tho described as "fit for a general." It was here that high-ranking Vietnamese and American visitors were received.

In Saigon, Nur moved into the apartment occupied by Ya Ba and his family. (When Nur's dependents arrived, there was a total of 25 people in the apartment.) The first evening he called a meeting. Earliest to arrive were a group of highland leaders—Ya Ba (4.9), his brother Touprong Hiou (4.4), Touneh Han Tho (4.2), Ksor Dun (5.8), Ksor Rot (3.20), and a Cham leader named Chau Van Mo. Speaking a mixture of French and, among the highlanders, Rhadé, they began discussing appointments for the new commission. Soon they were joined by Lt. Nguyen Van Phien and Ton That Cu. Vietnamese became the language of discussion, although the highlanders continued to speak Rhadé among themselves and the three Chru (Ya Ba, Hiou, and Han Tho) made comments among themselves in Chru. Ya Ba proposed that Capt. Nguyen Van Nghiem (who, it was noted previously, had been in the directorate and was jailed when Major Hung accused him of stealing student funds) be named director of operations (under Ya Ba). Ya Ba also favored having Nay Luett (2.26) and Y Chon Mlo Duon Du assume roles in Ban Me Thuot as liaisons with FULRO. Ton That Cu opposed all of these appointments because, according to Han Tho, he disliked all three men. Nonetheless, everyone agreed that they should be appointed. There also was agreement that Ngo Dinh Bao, a stout Vietnamese who had worked in the directorate as an interpreter, be named liaison with the American Mission.

The establishment of the commission marked a new phase in the development of ethnonationalism among the highlanders. It involved the formation of a small group of highland leaders that would come to represent the highland people in Saigon. Unlike the expression of ethnonationalism in Bajaraka and FULRO, this would not entail the emergence of any organized movement. Rather, it would take the form of what Barnes and others call a social network.[11] While all of those at the meeting had previously known one another and had attended meetings together, social links had been more or less restricted to those from the same elite group (such as Ya Ba, Hiou, and Han Tho, all of whom are Chru and kinsmen). The formation of this new social network within the context of the commission, and centered on Paul Nur, resulted in new social links being formed. The network also was to be affected very much by the presence of the Vietnamese officials, whose influence was to prove generally baleful.

This new phase of ethnonationalism also brought with it the first meaningful highlander presence in Saigon. Previously, Ya Ba was the only highland leader residing in the capital city, but now more leaders began to spend time in Saigon. At first most of them preferred leaving their families in the highlands. The result was that they shared common quarters and

11. J. A. Barnes, "Social Networks," Addison-Wesley Modular Publications, Module 26, 1972, pp. 1–29.

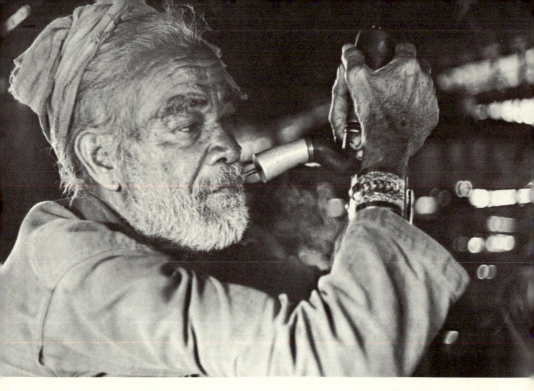

Oi Anhot, the King of Fire, at his village (1966)

those from different ethnic groups began to develop closer social relations.
They also were the first highland leaders to become sophisticated in the
ways of Saigon politics. In the corrupt wartime world of Saigon, this had a
damaging effect on some of these leaders.

THE KING OF FIRE IN 1966

In March 1966 I encountered the King of Fire for the first time and had the
good fortune to be able to witness the ritual he performs annually during
the dry season to bring prosperity and good health to Jarai villages. Since
beginning intensive research on the highlanders in February 1965, I had
collected information on the King of Fire, the King of Water, and the King
of the Wind from a variety of sources, notably Ksor Wol (3.5), husband
of Rcom H'nher (3.4), who was a member of the elite Rcom clan of Cheo
Reo. Ksor Wol was an "assistant" of the King of Fire and functioned as his
representative in the Cheo Reo area along with Siu Banh (2.15), husband
of Rcom H'blon. Whenever the King of Fire visited Cheo Reo, it was the

Ksor Wol, assistant of the King of Fire (1966)

duty of his assistants to prepare special shelter for him outside of the settlement and make arrangements for any rituals, i.e., provide sacrificial animals and jars of alcohol. The role of assistant to the King of Fire requires long years of apprenticeship with older assistants. The renowned Jarai chief Nay Nui (2.11) had held this position for a long time. When he was quite aged, he turned over his responsibilities to Ksor Seng, husband of Rcom H'areng (3.3). Ksor Wol eventually succeeded Ksor Seng after being his apprentice for many years.

Information obtained from Ksor Wol corroborated some of the information about the kings contained in French accounts. The King of Fire and King of Wind must be of the Siu clan, while the King of Water is from the Rcom clan. In 1966 the King of Fire was known teknonymously as Oi Anhot (grandfather of Anhot). His confreres Oi Bo, the King of Water, and Oi Co Ba, the King of Wind, had died in 1964. There was some reluctance to discuss whether the king is killed when he is on the brink of death as was reported by some French investigators. Subsequently, however, some younger Jarai indicated that this was the case, although they noted that no one would admit it because a murder charge might be brought by the Vietnamese authorities. When a king dies, his body is burned on a pyre. The teeth, some bones, and the heart (thought to be the abode of the spirit through which the king derives his power) are collected and placed in a bamboo tube or a jar sealed with leaves. The container is then placed in a Jarai-style tomb graced with carved figures and symbols. When a new king has been selected, the tomb of the old king is abandoned, an event marked with a buffalo sacrifice and several days of drinking and celebrating.

As Ksor Wol and others describe it, the selection process for a new king is not in conformity with methods described in some of the French accounts. All of the assistants in the region of the Ayun and Apa rivers constitute the elders who make the selection. Ksor Wol noted that elders of the Ksor clan are particularly influential in the choice of the new kings and in the selection of their wives as well.

Since the new king must be of the proper clan, the most likely candidates for succession are sons of the king's sister. Following the matrilineal descent of the Jarai, they will belong to their mother's clan and therefore of the same clan as her brother. In the case of Oi Bo, the King of Water, the likely candidate was his sister's son, Rcom Ho, who was in fact later selected. Although the King of Fire was still living, the favored candidates were his sister's four sons, Siu Choi, Siu Lung, Siu Punh (with the CIDG in Kontum), and Siu Jonh. Ksor Wol pointed out that Siu Choi had a beard like his uncle, the King of Fire, and since beards are a sign of *kdruh*, i.e., the favor of the spirits, this would give him an advantage over the others. Wol added, however, that Siu Jonh was literate in Jarai and Vietnamese, and this would be a factor to consider in the selection. But, he concluded, in the final analysis, the determining factor was some manifestation of the will of the spirits. This would be some sign, interpreted by the elders according to traditional Jarai religious beliefs. If, for example, one of the candidates should be struck by a sudden malady just after the death of the old king, it would likely be interpreted as a sign from the spirits that he was the favored one. Normally the official selection of the new kings is not made until the former king has been dead for seven years (which for the new King of Wind would have been 1971) but in September 1969 Ksor Wol announced that because there had been unusually heavy rains that caused floods the time was propitious for the elders to select a new King of Wind to replace

Oi Co Ba. They selected his sister's son, Oi Bom. Recalling the succession of Kings of Wind, Wol recited the names Oi Co Ba, Oi Jom, and Oi Kteo. Before Oi Bo, the last King of Water, there had been Oi Dang and Oi Anuach.

The Jarai often pointed out that women are reluctant to be married to any of the kings because the spirits associated with them are too powerful. If a new king is not married (or his wife has died), the elders, particularly the Ksor clan elders, select one for him. Oi Co Ba, the King of Wind, had been married to a woman of the Nay clan, but when he became King of Wind he took a second wife from the R'mah clan because it had been traditional for the kings to be married to R'mah women. When Oi Anhot became King of Fire, the Ksor elders had to pay a woman from the R'mah clan to marry him.

Ksor Wol related that the King of Fire had the blade of a sacred saber associated with a host of spirits, and his power was derived from his role as guardian of the saber. He added that the Cambodians have the hilt and the Vietnamese have the sheath. The King of Fire is forbidden the flesh of white cows, frogs, and rats or the intestines of any animal. Wol repeated the legend about a previous King of Fire who was visiting a village. An animal was slaughtered for a feast. At a nearby stream, one of his hosts was washing the intestines when suddenly a large fish devoured them. The man became frightened, so he substituted large earthworms. The king ate the dish, but that night the spirits informed him that he had eaten foul food and he must never again consume intestines or there would be earth tremors. The King of Fire's assistants share his taboos, and they also have the privilege of smoking his pipe (which is fashioned out of a large bamboo root). When the assistants visit the King of Fire's house, they are permitted to drink water from his special gourd, eat from his rice pot, and drink from the jar with his tube.

On 9 March 1966 Robert Reed of the Christian and Missionary Alliance in Cheo Reo and I were in the village of Buon So Ama Biong, some ten kilometers northwest of the town. We were in the process of discussing marriage and residence patterns with a group of villagers. It was late in the afternoon. Suddenly some of the group became agitated when they observed some men moving along Route 7 in front of the village. One woman remarked, "I hope he does not come into my house. It would bring us sickness." Bob Reed inquired and found that they were referring to the King of Fire. We went out to find the King of Fire standing in the road with four men and a boy. The king was an elderly man with white hair and a trimmed white beard. His face was bronzed and wrinkled and he had curious eyes that had a somewhat mischievous glint. He, like the four men, was dressed in a loincloth and traditional Jarai ceremonial shirt— black cloth with the front decorated with embroidered slim horizontal red stripes and two vertical rows of round brass buttons with the back dominated by a large embroidered red square trimmed with white. All wore tightly wound black cloth turbans. All but the King of Fire carried bundles containing clothes, cooking utensils, and some food.

At their request (the King of Fire had met Bob before), we drove them to Plei Malel farther east, where the Mai Linh Special Forces camp was located. There the King of Fire intended to perform rituals for the villages in the vicinity to bring them rain for the new planting season and good health. The Special Forces camp commander was Jarai, and he asked the King of Fire to perform a ritual to bring good fortune to his post. The King of Fire and his group installed themselves outside the village in a thick bamboo grove just above a sandy flood plain by the Ayun river. As we were departing, the King of Fire invited us to return in the morning to witness his ritual.

In the still heat of the dry season dawn, we returned to the river bank. The King of Fire's assistant and some of the villagers had spread out rubber army ponchos on the floor of the grove. They also had hung some ponchos on the bamboo branches to keep out the rays of the white sun that was rising in a pale blue sky. A large woven reed mat was spread out for the King of Fire. He squatted on it, smoking his pipe, and motioned for us to share the mat with him. This brought comments of approval from a group of men sitting on the slope because it was considered a great honor. I had brought some gifts to present to the king. My sister Catherine had sent a box of old costume jewelry that she had gathered from kin and friends for me to give highlanders as gifts. I gave the king a glittering pin and a bronze pendant on a chain, which he immediately put on.[12]

The King of Fire's "first and second assistants" sat with him on the mat. The first assistant was a man of the Ksor clan and the second assistant was of the Ro-o clan but was married to the king's wife's sister's daughter. The

---

12. In Jacques Dournes, *La culture Jörai* (Paris: Musée de l'Homme, 1972), p. 29, there is a photograph of the King of Fire wearing the pendant.

king referred to them as his "soldiers." The first assistant related that Oi Anhot had been the King of Fire since 1945. He pointed out that the Cambodian sovereigns used to present each king with an elephant. As he talked, men from surrounding villages began to gather in or near the bamboo grove. Women appeared, but they stayed a good distance away. It was explained that they feared the powerful spirits associated with the king. One group of men entered the grove carrying a large drum and some gongs. One of them identified himself as Ksor Na, a resident of Plei Bahrong (also called Plei Potao), the king's village (see map 4). Another gong bearer also was from the village. The others were from the Special Forces camp. They explained that the largest gong was the "mother gong," the middle-sized one was the "sister gong," and the smallest, the "child gong."

Another group of men approached and bowed in the direction of the King of Fire. One stepped forward and presented the first assistant with a polyethylene bag of tobacco. Another put a brass bracelet on the first assistant's wrist. The assistant passed the tobacco to the King of Fire, who did not speak but produced his pipe, filling it with tobacco which he then lit. Another group of villagers brought a live chicken and jars of alcohol. Hacking down some bamboo, they staked the jars in place and then built a fire to cook the chicken. A large cooking pot of river water was placed before the King of Fire, who reached over and took a shirt from his bundle of clothes. Dipping a sleeve of it in the water, he passed it to the men who had been preparing the jars. They wiped their faces and hands with it. Another man passed the king a glass which he filled with the water. The man washed his face, elbows, and knees with it.

Around ten o'clock the gongs and drum began to sound. A new visitor approached the King of Fire, giving him some money. The second assistant explained that this was an offering from the man's village. The second assistant and the boy busied themselves building a fire on the sandy flood plain to cook some rice and chopped green vegetables. When the food was ready, they placed it on a large banana leaf and put it near the jars, where the first assistant had placed some uncooked rice, buffalo flesh, and cooked chicken. He lit a candle and placed bamboo tubes in the jars. The King of Fire came forward and, squatting, took a handful of the uncooked rice and cast it over the chicken and the candle. Then he held a rice bowl of water in his right hand over the jar while he chanted. Setting the bowl down, he continued to chant while he tore some flesh from the chicken, a gesture he repeated twice. The first assistant pointed out that each gesture was for a village that had made contributions to the ritual.

These ritual acts done, the King of Fire began drinking from a jar while the second assistant broke up the chicken to distribute morsels to the villagers. As the king continued to drink, the drum and gongs played faster and the two assistants squatted before the jar, clapping their hands in rhythm. The first assistant began to grunt and slowly move his body as his arms spiraled upward in a gesture similar to that seen in a Thai or Lao dance. Swaying, he rose, and, putting his head back, uttered low squeals and trills. Continuing to sway, he assumed the squatting position and began to clap to the music. The second assistant occupied himself replenishing the water in the jar as the king drank.

When the King of Fire had finished his libations, the first and second assistants drank from the jar. Additional chickens were brought in, along with more jars of alcohol and bottles of Vietnamese beer, brandy, and soft drinks. I was invited to drink from the jars and the villagers also began to drink. Men and women approached the bamboo grove to hand in cups to obtain some of the water, with which they bathed their face, arms, and legs. The first assistant explained that when the King of Fire prayed over the water and touched it with an article of his clothing it became lustral water that would protect anyone who washed with it from evil spirits.

As the atmosphere became more festive, Bob and I made some inquiries about the King of Fire. We spoke to the first assistant because it would not have been proper to address the king himself (although he listened to our conversation while he smoked his pipe). The assistant could name nine kings who had preceded Oi Anhot. In reverse chronology they were Oi Tu, Oi At (who is remembered in French literature as the King of Fire responsible for Odend'hal's death in 1904), Oi Y, Oi Yi, Oi Nong, Oi Bom, Oi Blech, Oi Song Bang, and Oi Anur. The assistant repeated the information about food taboos that had been related by Ksor Wol. When asked about the sacred saber, he became very guarded, simply answering that it existed but it was forbidden for anyone to gaze upon it. The King of Fire listened and, without changing expression, continued to smoke his pipe.

At 4:00 P.M., men from other villages arrived, carrying large jars, chickens, and a sack of rice. They bowed before the King of Fire and presented these offerings. The jars were staked to the ground while the chickens were cooked. The ritual by the King of Fire and his assistants was repeated. At one point the king, who had drunk quite a bit, forgot the name of a village and had to be reminded. As the festivities continued, we talked with some of the villagers and the men from the Special Forces camp. They all knew about Y Bham and the FULRO movement and expressed strong sympathy with the goals of the movement. Then some of them began complaining about the "American airplanes" that prevented them from fishing in the river. They explained that Jarai villagers out fishing in the river had been strafed by American aircraft, so many were reluctant to venture beyond the tree-lined shore.

NEW FULRO–GOVERNMENT NEGOTIATIONS

On 7 May 1966 Paul Nur, accompanied by Lt. Col. Touprong Ya Ba and Ton That Cu (a crafty Vietnamese who, because of Vinh Loc's insistence, was named assistant to Nur at the Commission for Highland Affairs), went to Ban Me Thuot where they met with Nay Luett, Major Y Pem Knuol, Y Dhuat Nie Kdam, and Y Blu Nie Buon Drieng. It had been arranged for all of these leaders to meet with the FULRO representatives, led by Y Dhe Adrong. After three days of discussions FULRO had scaled down its demands of the government to four points. It wanted the *statut particulier* promulgated, a highland flag (described as having three sections: the top dominated by a white crescent and white star on a green background, below which is a middle section of alternating blue and white vertical stripes, and then a solid red section), a highland military force (no size specified), and an expansion of the commission to include more ethnic groups' leaders. Then the delegations left to report to their respective authorities. A second meeting was held on 6 June at which they agreed to form a joint liaison office in Ban Me Thuot. General Vinh Loc was reported to have agreed with the demands, and they were sent on to Premier Ky's office. On 8 August, in a letter to Vinh Loc, Ky agreed *in principle* with the demands.

The law signed by Ky on 22 July 1966 provided for a Constitutional Assembly and authorized FULRO members "who had rallied to the government prior to 15 August 1966" to run as candidates in the election, set for 11 September. Before the August deadline, four FULRO members submitted their applications for candidacy. They were Y Wik Buon Ya, a

Rhadé from Ban Me Thuot; Y Tang Phok, a Mnong Rlam from Lac Thien; Jean Jem, a Bahnar from Kontum; and Ksor Rot (3.20), a Jarai from Cheo Reo. Ksor Rot had been born in 1937 and had graduated from a junior military academy established by the French. He joined FULRO in 1965 and now was a regimental commander along with his cousin Ksor Kham (3.19), who had been arrested following the December 1965 revolt and soon would be released. At one point in 1965 Rot had been captured by the Viet Cong, but he managed to escape.

The highlanders were allotted nine seats of the total 117. Two of the FULRO candidates—Ksor Rot and Y Wik Buon Ya—were elected, as was Nay Blim (2.25), a Jarai from Cheo Reo who was married to the granddaughter of the famous chief Nay Nui; Peang, a Sedang from Dak To; Pang Ting K'Te, a Lat from the Dalat area, where he worked in a hospital; and Dinh Van Roi, a Hre from the Re valley in Quang Ngai province.

The combination of FULRO and non-FULRO highlanders in the Constitutional Assembly symbolized the fusing of viewpoints that had now come to characterize the highland leaders. In terms of what they wanted of the central government, there was no distinction between the two. In the new assembly, the highland delegates cooperated to try to get a Highlander Bill of Rights (based on the *statut particulier*) incorporated into the proposed constitution. They were not successful, but nonetheless their action reflected the extent to which ethnonationalism had swept the highlands by mid-1966.

In mid-October 1966 Vinh Loc organized a large Highland-Lowland Solidarity Conference in Pleiku to celebrate the second anniversary of the Pleiku Conference and also to "welcome" eight hundred FULRO troops who were going to swear loyalty to the government. On a large field below the hill where the II Corps headquarters were located, a number of tents (supplied by the U.S. Army) and a reviewing stand, flanked by shelters fashioned out of colored parachutes, were put in place. On 15 October, the eight hundred "FULRO troops" arrived on Air America, an arrangement made by USAID (as USOM was now called), and were housed in the tents. A large collection of highland leaders also arrived. These included the FULRO delegation from Ban Me Thuot, the members of the Constitutional Assembly, the staff of the Commission for Highland Affairs, all of the deputy province chiefs for highland affairs, and highlanders from the Army and People's Council (a short-lived effort at having some kind of representative advisory body to the government).

Vietnamese officials and American guests began arriving on the afternoon of 15 October. Riding into Pleiku from the new jet airstrip built by the Americans, they passed under signs that proclaimed "Highland-Lowland Solidarity," and one sign (in English and Vietnamese) announced that "Big Brother Vinh Loc is most eager about the future of the highland people." Someone must have explained to Vinh Loc the implication of "big brother" in English, for later in the day that portion of the sign was painted over. Late in the afternoon VNAF planes began landing with a bevy of "hostesses" who had been recruited in Saigon nightclubs to brighten up the occasion. Their heavy makeup and gaudy miniskirts were reminders of the new cabaret world the war was bringing to Saigon.

That evening a large dinner was held at the Phoenix Officers' Club. Vinh Loc sipped champagne at the head table with a Vietnamese singer who was popular in Saigon (and was described as "his latest girl"). She was garbed in a modish gown cut from highland cloth. The hostesses from Saigon were seated at other tables with high-ranking Vietnamese officers and American officials from MACV, USAID, CIA, and other agencies. Of all the highland leaders assembled in Pleiku, only Nur and Ya Ba were invited to the dinner. The entertainment began with a "highlander fashion show" that consisted of Vietnamese girls in vinyl versions of highland clothes, a parody that amused everyone. Suddenly Ksor Dun appeared in a loincloth, leaping around the dance floor, grimacing at the audience (particularly at Vinh Loc and Nur) and generally behaving in a simian manner. At this point I left the party. Outside I encountered Touneh Han Tho, Nay Luett, and some other leaders. They were insulted at not having been invited. At their quarters they explained that the whole celebration was a fraud as far as they were concerned. Of the eight hundred "FULRO" troops, only around two hundred were actually members of the movement; the remainder were young villagers who had been offered a free trip to Pleiku. There was a good deal of unrest among them because their quarters had no water, they were not given blankets, and their food consisted of rice and watery soup. No highlanders were involved in the planning of the affair, which Vinh Loc put in the hands of Ton That Cu. Ksor Dun appeared and, laughing bitterly, announced, "I played the savage for them."

The following morning Premier Ky and General Nguyen Van Thieu arrived (they were served a champagne breakfast en route) as did Ambassador Lodge. Everyone gathered on the field before the II Corps headquarters, where Vinh Loc brought some American officials' attention to the "highlander motifs" on the decorations. None bore any resemblance to anything in the highlands and looked like a Hollywood version of African designs. There was a parade of highlanders dressed in traditional clothes, after which the "FULRO troops" pledged loyalty to the government. Then a buffalo was slaughtered by Jarai with their spears. Lodge visibly blanched as he turned his head away from the gory scene and almost fainted dead-away when they smeared some of the blood on his shoes. Vinh Loc addressed the gathering, exclaiming how much the government had done for the highland people. Afterward, Nur spoke (in Vietnamese), also outlining the government's achievements. He was followed by Y Dhe Adrong, whose talk (in Rhadé, which was not translated) was a plea for the *statut particulier*, which he emphasized the highlanders should be granted "in exchange for the blood we have shed." That evening the Vietnamese generals repaired to the Phoenix Club with the hostesses to celebrate. By that time most of the highland leaders had departed for their homes.

The year 1966 brought a vastly enlarged American presence in the highlands and a concomitant widening of the war in that region. In 1966 the military use of herbicides, which had begun in 1962 and slowly increased between that year and 1965, reached a peak. Some 4,880,000 gallons of herbicide were used throughout Vietnam, many of them in the central highlands (see chap. 7 and app. C).[13]

During the first half of January 1966 the 1st Brigade, 1st Cavalry Division, conducted Operation Matador in Pleiku and Kontum provinces. That same month the 3d Brigade of the 25th Infantry Division moved into Pleiku on operations, after which it went to the Ban Me Thuot area. Some residents of Buon Ko Tam complained that they were shelled while they were preparing their fields for planting. In April the 1st Air Cavalry engaged in Operation Lincoln in western Pleiku. In March the 3d Brigade, 25th Infantry moved up Route 14, repairing bridges and road bed, opening the Ban Me Thuot-Pleiku link for the first time in many months. On 2 June the 1st Brigade of the 101st Airborne Division and some

---

13. Committee on the Effects of Herbicides in Vietnam, Division of Biological Sciences, Assembly of Life Sciences, National Council, *The Effects of Herbicides in South Vietnam: Part A—Summary and Conclusions* (Washington, National Academy of Sciences, 1974), pp. S-3, II-3.

ARVN units launched Operation Hawthorne in the Toumarong valley north of Kontum (claiming to have killed 531 PAVN troops). In August the 2d Brigade of the U.S. 4th Infantry Division arrived in Pleiku to establish a headquarters, and by mid-October the whole division was operating in the highlands.

During this period the U.S. Special Forces increased its "border defense and surveillance" by establishing twenty-two new camps along the Laotian and Cambodian borders in the highlands. In addition, the Mobile Guerrilla Force was transformed into the Mobile Strike (MIKE) Force to be used in guerrilla operations. Company-sized groups of 150 to 200 men were taken by helicopters into Communist-controlled areas to conduct operations, after which they were extracted by the same means. By October 1966 the total CIDG was 34,800 (in October 1964 it had been 19,000) with 3,200 in the MIKE Force. At least half the personnel in these forces were highlanders.[14] In Cheo Reo there was at this time a Jarai girl who had the reputation of being particularly adept at improvising songs (a favorite pastime of the Jarai) which usually told of current events. She sang sadly of highland boys going off in helicopters to distant places (she mentioned Cambodia when operations there were very secret) and never returning.

Young highlanders also were being recruited by the Viet Cong. In July 1972 Ksor Yap, who had been born in the Jarai village of Bon Dla-Ya in 1950, related that in 1966 the Viet Cong forced him to go with them to the Mount Boh-Mih area in southern Phu Bon province. The Viet Cong unit there was a company, whose commander was a southern Vietnamese while all the troops were Jarai. Some had received military training and some were trained in propaganda methods. Yap was put to work farming swiddens in which they grew upland dry rice, maize, and potatoes. He was given little food and slept in a hammock under a tree. The Jarai troops had no jars of alcohol nor did they perform any traditional rituals. In 1968 Yap was sent with the unit to attack Buon Blech, the capital of Thuan Man district, as part of the Tet offensive. During the operation he was captured and spent two years in a Pleiku prison camp before being released to join the Kit Carson Scouts, an American-sponsored paramilitary effort.

The American-sponsored pacification program continued and in November 1966 the Office of Civil Operations was created with Deputy

14. Westmoreland, "Report on Operations," pp. 118–19, 123–29; Kelly, *U.S. Army*, pp. 78–95.

Ambassador William Porter as head. It brought together personnel from USAID and the Foreign Service of the State Department and resulted in an increased number of American civilians in the highlands.

The activities of the CIA in the highlands also increased. In 1965 the CIA launched the Counter Terror program, resulting in the appearance of the Provincial Reconnaissance Units (PRUs). In the highlands, the CIA recruited young highlanders (some of whom had been in the Truong Son Program, which was separate) for the PRUs. Marchetti and Marks quote a former Foreign Service officer who described the PRU as a "unilateral American program, never recognized by the South Vietnamese government. CIA representatives recruited, organized, supplied, and directly paid CT (counter terror) teams, whose function was to use Viet Cong techniques of terror—assassination, abuses, kidnappings, and intimidation— against the Viet Cong leadership."[15] By 1966 the CIA had also become involved in the Provincial Interrogation Centers, a program under the direction of the National Police. The first centers had been started in 1965, and when they were deemed successful they were extended to the highland provinces. According to Marchetti and Marks, the centers were constructed with CIA funds. They also note that a CIA operator or contract employee directed each center's operation, "much of which consisted of torture tactics against suspected Vietcong, such torture usually carried out by Vietnamese nationals." The CIA personnel in the highlands were invariably housed in expensive villas or compounds, which they immediately surrounded with high fences, spotlights, and special guards.

The vast influx of American troops in the highlands brought changes to many of the towns, particularly Pleiku. For the huge construction projects (military installations, air bases, and roads) private American construction firms brought in Korean, Filipino, and Vietnamese workers. The Vietnamese usually brought their families with them and, combined with the large number of ARVN personnel and their dependents, the result was huge population increases in highland towns. No census had been conducted, but by 1966 Pleiku's population was estimated to be in the vicinity of 50,000 (official figures were much lower, but they were considered conservative—see app. A). A whole new large section called "New Pleiku," a dismal collection of Vietnamese shacks and flimsy shops, had

---

15. V. Marchetti and J. D. Marks, *The CIA and the Cult of Intelligence* (New York: Dell, 1975), pp. 236–37.

spread over a hillside and was continuing to grow by the day. The main part of Pleiku had been transformed into a "G.I. town" with endless bars, snack shops, and steam baths (another designation for brothels). The Christian and Missionary Alliance compound, which in 1957 had been outside the town, was now engulfed by a group of gaudy "Soul Brother" bars that catered to black American soldiers. The streets were jammed with jeeps, military trucks, bulldozers, and seemingly endless convoys. It was curious to see files of Jarai men in their loincloths, clutching machetes, followed by women with backbaskets and children, walking along the edge of the sidewalks filled with American soldiers, prostitutes, pimps, vendors, shoeshine boys, and petty thieves. The Jarai kept their eyes straight ahead as if to ignore the squalid scene around them.

Outside the town, the undulating green plateau now became filled with American and Vietnamese military cantonments, fire bases (artillery), airstrips, helipads, and truck parks. On some hills, large antennas swung about like strange windmills. The 4th Infantry built its headquarters on the slope of the Hodrung Mountain, revered as sacred to the Jarai. The Americans called it "Dragon Mountain" because of its twin rounded peaks (a shape that earned it the name "titty mountain" for most of the American soldiers). Close to the headquarters, Vietnamese entrepreneurs established a small collection of bars and steam baths, and the soldiers dubbed this little settlement "Plei Poontang" (*poontang* is a southern American slang word for sexual intercourse). The American presence around Pleiku also brought another novelty to the highland villagers—huge piles of garbage. Streams of dump trucks went daily from the bases to unload the garbage, through which bands of highlanders picked, carrying off what they could use in their backbaskets.[16]

General Vinh Loc and some of his high-ranking officers announced at this time that they were building a special "amusement area" outside Pleiku where American soldiers could enjoy such things as horseback riding and other sports. With American aid cement, they built a collection of buildings with shops around a fountain. The shops were leased and all of them turned out to be either bars (with names like The Gold Bar, The Liz

16. Since I was concerned, as many were, by the expansion of the war, I devised at this time a scheme to resolve the conflict (which I felt was basically political) through a process of political accommodation leading to a coalition government with the NLF. After briefings on this subject in Washington, the ideas were published in two Rand Corporation reports: G. C. Hickey, "Accommodation in South Vietnam: The Key to Sociopolitical Solidarity" (Santa Monica, California: The Rand Corporation, September 1969).

Bar, London Bar, OK Bar, The Apollo, and the Kiss Me Bar) or steam baths. The American military authorities in Pleiku, however, put the "amusement area" off limits, and so it stood like a ghost town, crumbling in the rain and the heat of the dry season.

On 1 April 1967, after meeting for six months, the Constitutional Assembly promulgated the new constitution. Article 66 stated that the vice president would serve as chairman of the Ethnic Minorities Council, which article 97 defined as a body to advise the government on matters affecting ethnic minorities and also to brief the National Assembly on matters concerning the minorities. Article 98 specified that one-third of the council would be appointed by the president, that the remainder would be designated by the ethnic minorities, and that members would serve four years. Just after the new constitution was promulgated, Major Nay Lo was named chief of Pleiku province, the first highlander to attain that level in the administration.

These developments generated the feeling in the American Mission that the government was making headway in its relations with the highlanders. But conversations with highland leaders revealed that they still were discontent because too many promises went unfulfilled and they felt that the Commission for Highland Affairs was not functioning as it should. There were too many Vietnamese in high positions (some said it should be called the "Commission for Vietnamese Affairs"), a reference to Ton That Cu, Capt. Ton That Tu, Lt. Nguyen Van Phien, and Major Nguyen Van Nghiem. Also, the commission's areas of responsibility were too limited and too ill-defined. They also were unhappy that negotiations with FULRO were at a standstill.

Based on what the highlanders had already declared they wanted of the government, I wrote a report for the Rand Corporation drawing together social and economic programs into a comprehensive "blueprint."[17] This report took the position that, while assuming a place in the state of South Vietnam wherein they would contribute socially and economically, the highlanders would retain their ethnic identity. It would be important, therefore, that they preserve certain cultural institutions, such as their own languages (which would be taught in the first years of primary school), their own law courts, and special land tenure laws that would accom-

17. G. C. Hickey, "The Highland People of South Vietnam: Social and Economic Development" (Santa Monica, California: The Rand Corporation, September 1967).

modate to their varied forms of agriculture (particularly to swidden farming). The report also advocated special education programs geared to further economic development (which was taking place in some areas) in the highlands. Copies of this report were distributed to the Vietnamese government, to highland leaders, and to American agencies.

This report also contained population estimates of highland ethnic groups from three different sources (see app. A). Since beginning this research project on the highlanders early in 1965, I had been gathering data on the populations of the many ethnic groups. Since no complete census has ever been conducted in the upland regions (the 1943 "census" was really an estimate), I gathered estimates from missionaries and from SIL staff members who had arrived at estimates in the course of their field work. Estimates also were obtained from local authorities and highland leaders. These figures totaled 877,000 highlanders. The Special Commission for Highland Affairs in 1966 estimated 610,314. FULRO leader Y Dhe Adrong had estimates that totaled 792,635.

In 1967 the NLF announced its political program, declaring in article 10 its intention to "implement the agrarian policy with regard to peasants of national minorities. To encourage and help them settle down to sedentary life, improve their lands, develop economy and culture."[18] It also granted the minorities the right to use their own spoken and written languages and "maintain or change their customs and habits." Finally, it stated that "in the areas where national minorities live concentrated and where the required conditions prevail, autonomous zones will be established within independent and free Viet Nam."

On 15 April 1967 a meeting was to take place between Y Bham and Paul Nur, who was accompanied by two Americans from the U.S. Embassy and by Leslie Smith, son of Laura and Gordon Smith. Leslie Smith had been a professional hunter and consequently was close to many of the Rhadé leaders, including Y Bham. The FULRO leader failed to appear, but he did send letters to Smith and Ambassador Lodge. Another meeting was arranged for 2 May between General Vinh Loc and Y Bham. Beforehand, Y Bham inquired how many stars Vinh Loc had and was told that the general had one star. When he stepped off the helicopter at Bao Dai's elegant hunting lodge, Y Bham was wearing three large stars on his

---

18. South Vietnam National Front for Liberation, *Political Programme of The South Viet Nam National Front for Liberation* (South Vietnam: Giai Phong Publishing House, 1967): pp. 29–30.

shoulders. Following the meeting, Vinh Loc issued a communiqué which said, in effect, that all FULRO forces would rally to the government once a *statut particulier* had been made official. On 12 May, however, Y Bham denied that he had made such an arrangement.

On 25 June 1967 Vinh Loc convened a congress of highland leaders to demonstrate "solidarity" between them and the government. While it was of no consequence, it did reveal some changes that were taking place in the FULRO movement. The FULRO delegation was led by Y Dhe Adrong and included three young leaders—Y Ngo Buon Ya, Y Tang Phok, and Philippe Drouin. The three represented a group of "young Turks" in the movement who were growing impatient at the moderate posture of the older leaders, such as Y Bham and Y Dhe. Nay Luett was very wary of this group. He related that earlier in the year Y Ngo Buon Ya had brandished a pistol at him and Y Dhe, threatening to kill them. Mike Benge, who at this time was involved in agricultural programs for USAID and was close to many highland leaders (he spoke Rhadé), was told by some of them that Y Ngo Buon Ya was a "spy" for the Vietnamese. They pointed out that he was seen visiting Col. Thanh, the province chief, every morning. This was in keeping with the FULRO view noted previously that Y Ngo (and Y Sen Nie Kdam) were paid agents of the government.

Philippe Drouin was the flamboyant figure of this younger group. According to Y Klong Adrong, Philippe's father (it was said that his real father was one of the Javanese brought in by the Japanese for road construction) had been a chauffeur for Emperor Bao Dai, and he indulged his son. "He was a spoiled kid," Y Klong observed, relating that when they were at school together Philippe had a motorbike, a great luxury at the time. He also was very aggressive, often getting into fights with the other boys in the school. Against his father's wishes, Philippe had joined the French army and was sent to Cambodia. His father appealed to Ton That Hoi to intervene with the French officials to have the boy returned home. It was noted previously that Philippe had married Rcom H'un, daughter of Jarai leader Nay Moul (2.17), but he treated the girl badly, often beating her.

Philippe had developed a certain mystique among young highlanders, particularly those in the CIDG and MIKE Force. He was considered a fearless fighter (who was said to have killed fifteen Viet Cong), and they came to believe him to be indestructible. According to Benge and Nay Luett, Philippe was in charge of collecting FULRO "taxes" levied on every highlander in the CIDG and MIKE Force. (This later was corroborated by FULRO leaders.) As a member of the FULRO delegation in Buon Ale-A, Philippe lived in a masonry house (considered very expensive for one in his status), and when I visited him he proudly displayed an expensive hi-fi set on which he played rock music. He also had sets of American army fatigues on which Spanish names such as Sanchez and Gonzales had been sewn. On the shoulders were American Special Forces patches. He explained that from time to time he would go to Saigon and pose as an American of Spanish origin (he spoke English with only a slight accent). Philippe also drove around Ban Me Thuot either on a Honda motorcycle (these and other Japanese products, including transistor radios, were very much in evidence in highland towns at this time) or in his new pickup truck (robin egg blue in color). Almost every evening he went to the Darlac II nightclub, frequented by American and Vietnamese military personnel, where he drank Scotch whiskey and danced with the Vietnamese hostesses.

Elections for a president and vice president of South Vietnam and for the Upper House of the National Assembly were set for 3 September 1967, with a subsequent election for a Lower House fixed for 22 October. In order to rally votes among the highlanders, presidential candidate Nguyen Van Thieu and his running mate, Nguyen Cao Ky, flew to Ban Me Thuot on 29 August 1967 to attend a gathering of highland leaders. As chairman of the National Directory, Thieu signed Decree No. 003/67, which covered a wide range of programs for the highlanders. One article stated that a "statute stipulating special rights for the minorities" was now enacted. Another article created the Ethnic Minorities Council provided for in the constitution, and another concerned land rights, declaring that title to lands which the highlanders "farm in rotation" would be distributed.

FULRO reaction to this proclamation came in a letter dated 11 October 1967. Y Bham took exception to the term "special rights," insisting on the expression *statut particulier*. He also reiterated the demand for a highlander flag, the right to have relations with foreign nations, and to have direct foreign aid to the highlands. He also wanted a guarantee of participation by highland leaders in any international conference concerning the future of Vietnam.

In the September election the Thieu-Ky ticket won. One of the senate slates elected was Tran Van Don's Nông Công Binh (Farmers, Workers,

Soldiers) bloc, and it included Ksor Rot (3.20), a member of FULRO who had been in the Constitutional Assembly. At age thirty, he was the youngest member of the senate (and the only one to list his religious affiliation as animism). A stocky man with a pleasant manner, Ksor Rot declared when he arrived in Saigon, "I know nothing of driving or dancing, and I would like to learn about both."

In October, six highlanders were elected to the Lower House. Four were from the Constitutional Assembly: Y Wik Buon Ya, Peang, Nay Blim (2.25), and Dinh Van Roi. The other winners were Rcom Anhot (3.12) from Cheo Reo, a graduate of the National Institute of Administration, and Lieng Hot Ngeo, a Lat from Dalat. One candidate who was not elected was Nay Blim's wife's sister, Rcom H'ueh (2.28), the first highland woman to run for office.

When in November 1967 the new government was formed, a cabinet post was created for the Minister of Development of Ethnic Minorities. An order dated 16 December outlined the function and organization of the new Ministry for Development of Ethnic Minorities (MDEM). The ethnic minorities represented were the highlanders, northern highland refugees, and the Cham (the Khmer Krom were not included).

While these events were taking place, the Vietnam War continued to rage in the highlands. In February 1967 the U.S. 3d Marine Division launched Operation Prairie Fire III along the Demilitarized Zone in the Bru country around Khe Sanh. On 6 April two brigades of the 4th Infantry Division and elements of the 25th Division launched Operation Francis Marion along the Cambodian border in Pleiku province, bringing them in contact with the PAVN 1st Division. PAVN infiltration from Laos increased in May, and their forces occupied hills dominating the airfield and Special Forces post at Khe Sanh. The U.S. Marines dispatched two battalions, and there was heavy fighting in the area. Also in May, the entire American pacification effort was placed under MACV control, and an agency called the Civil Operations and Revolutionary Development Support (CORDS) was formed to direct civil affairs.

As of mid-June 1967 the American military strength in South Vietnam reached 450,000. Intelligence estimates placed the Communist forces at 260,000 including over 50,000 North Vietnamese. Late in June, reconnaissance revealed the presence of four PAVN regiments in the vicinity of Dak To. Special Forces elements accompanied by units of the 4th Infantry Division and a South Vietnamese battalion went into the area. They soon were joined by units of the U.S. 1st Cavalry, the 173d Airborne Brigade, and six South Vietnamese battalions in Operation Paul Revere IV. Massive air strikes were provided by jet fighters and B-52 bombers.[19]

At this time a project in the highlands related to the American pacification effort that caused considerable disruption in western Pleiku (and angered many highland leaders) was the Edap Enang Resettlement Program. When the 3d Brigade of the U.S. 25th Division arrived in Pleiku in January 1966, its commander and General Vinh Loc envisaged a scheme for resettling almost all of the Jarai villages (with an estimated total population of 10,000) west of Pleiku city in order to provide a vast "free strike zone" for shelling and bombing. The program was discussed through 1966, and early in 1967 the U. S. 4th Infantry Division, commanded by General William Peers, began implementation in conjunction with General Vinh Loc and ARVN. The plan called for relocating some 8,000 highlanders from eighteen villages to a large settlement called Edap Enang (which in Rhadé means "peace and prosperity" but the planners thought it was a Jarai term).

I gained information on Edap Enang from visits to the center as well as from Americans familiar with the project. One of the most critical reports on Edap Enang was prepared by a U.S. Army Civil Affairs officer.[20] The project was a masterpiece of bad planning. It was decided to move the villagers in April, just after they had planted their new crops. ARVN was supposed to have informed the villagers involved, but most had not been told about it when the Chinook cargo helicopters landed to take them away. Nonetheless, they were forced to go, leaving most of their belongings (including their precious jars and gongs), their cattle, and their newly sown fields. The villages were burned, and one American civilian was furious, reporting that an American officer had boasted, "We set the houses on fire before the villagers were taken away to show them we meant business."

A Vietnamese contractor was hired to build frames and roofs (the settlers would provide their own walls). He obtained poor wood from a nearby forest and tin roofing from USAID. The wily contractor, in effect, only had to purchase nails. Nonetheless, the settlers were charged a large portion of their 5,000 piaster resettlement compensation for house construction

---

19. Westmoreland, "Report on Operations," pp. 152–56.
20. "Edap Enang Resettlement Center," Team 9, 41st Civil Affairs Company, July 1968.

materials. The houses, built on the ground Vietnamese style, were a far cry from the sturdy Jarai houses built on piling with thickly thatched roofs. In May 1967, 7,200 people were moved into the bleak Edap Enang center. By August the situation was becoming dire. Food rations were delayed (for two weeks at one point), forcing the inhabitants to subsist on bamboo shoots and leaves. Pigs were shipped from Saigon for the settlers, but they were very small, and the Jarai had nothing to feed them. Many of the pigs were eaten by the hungry villagers or, since the pigs were not used to highland conditions, died. Banana trees had been planted in the dry season and soon withered. The wells dried up, and when the rains began both the spillways and fish ponds overflowed. Security was very poor and Viet Cong propaganda teams entered the settlement at will during the night. Finally, it was deemed necessary to allow the villagers to return to their old fields and harvest what was left of the crops that had been planted before the resettlement. This precipitated an exodus, and by the end of 1967 only about 2,700 remained in Edap Enang. The others had gone back to the "free strike zone."

Touneh Han Tho related that at the end of 1967 a helicopter landed at the Chru village of Proh Tom Lan, dropping off a group of twelve American Special Forces men accompanied by some Vietnamese officers and Rhadé soldiers. They forced the residents to come out of their houses with their hands behind their heads. Among them was Yolong Ma, elderly widow of Chru leader Banahria Ya Hau (4.8), who was pushed to the ground by one of the Rhadé. When her grandson Ya Loan objected, telling the intruders that there were no Viet Cong in the village, an American threw him to the ground and put an M-16 to his head. Then, while the villagers huddled under the hot afternoon sun, the soldiers killed pigs and chickens and ransacked all of the houses. Madame Ya Hau lost ivory and an ancient saber. Photographs of her family were torn up. The villagers protested to the district chief, but nothing came of it.

In other parts of the highlands, villagers were suffering as a result of a PAVN strategy that involved attacking villages. Beginning in June 1967 there was a rash of such attacks in the vicinity of Kontum. The pattern was for the PAVN units to attack during the night and penetrate the defenses to enter the village, killing as many defenders as possible. The PAVN attackers threw grenades into the bunkers where the elderly, the women, and children huddled. I visited the village of Kon Sitiu, close to Kontum, after one such attack, and villagers described what had happened. Also, infor-

mation on similar attacks was gotten from victims who had been taken to
Pat Smith's hospital. The worst PAVN attack occurred on 5 December
1967 at Dak Son, a Stieng refugee village near Song Be. According to
Ralph Haupers, the SIL staff member working on the Stieng language, the
Communists had been sending warning notes to the camp, ordering the
villagers to join them in the forest on the Cambodian border with the
threat of "punishment" if they did not adhere. Undoubtedly the Stieng
were to be used as bearers in the movement of arms and supplies through
the area. Few villagers obeyed, so the PAVN assaulted the camp. The men
rallied to the defense with their spears, crossbows, and the few rifles that
some possessed while the women and children hurried to the bunkers. The
Stieng defenders were no match for the Communists with their sophisticated Russian weapons. Once inside, the attackers used grenades and flame
throwers against the Stieng, killing over two hundred of them. Haupers
visited the village the following day to find charred bodies of adults,
children, and tiny infants in the scorched earth of the bunkers. Their metal
wrist and ankle decorations were melted into grotesque shapes. Survivors,
most of them wounded and burned, picked through the ruins and ashes in
the hope of finding some of their missing family members still alive.

5 THE TET OFFENSIVE AND CHANGING GOVERNMENT POLICIES

As is the case with many wars, the Vietnam War took several years to reach its full fury. Following the arrival of the American combat units in the highlands late in 1965, and the increase in PAVN forces at the same time, the war steadily intensified. The effects were noted in the previous chapter which documented the death and destruction wrought by both sides as well as the folly of American and Vietnamese military commanders who, in a war with no front lines, sought to create them with "free fire zones." But it was not until 1968 that the war reached its first real peak of violence with the Communist Tet Offensive. This event, which had such widespread repercussions, only touched the highland villages indirectly, however, for it was the urban centers of Ban Me Thuot, Pleiku, Kontum, and Dalat that were attacked by the Communists. The war, which until 1968 had been restricted to the rural areas, now encompassed the cities. Everyone realized that suddenly the war had enveloped all of Vietnamese society.

Still, despite the increasingly wide disruptions due to the war, people carried on their daily lives, and in parts of the highlands there even were encouraging examples of economic development being conducted by villagers. This development included such things as Rhadé starting their own small coffee estates (by 1970 there were 326 registered highland coffee planters in Darlac), villagers doubling their yields by adopting new farming methods, and highlanders' kitchen gardens being expanded into truck gardens. There also was that strange, gossamer web of modernity that the war brought to some places in the highlands. In towns like Cheo Reo or

Kontum, one might see a young highlander wearing a loincloth fly by on a Japanese motorcycle, and it was not unusual to see highland soldiers with transistor radios pressed to their ears.

For the highland leaders, the 1968–1971 period was a new phase in their struggle to assert highlander ethnic identity. By early 1969 FULRO had faded as an ethnonationalist force, leaving the Ministry for Development of Ethnic Minorities the only organization making any effort to try to realize implementation of governmental promises made at the October 1964 Pleiku Conference. The ministry, however, was weak, and the Thieu government was indifferent to highland problems. Also, as the Americans began to withdraw their military forces, the Vietnamese assumed responsibility for the defense of the highlands. This meant more destructive relocations and it also meant a deteriorating security situation in the highlands following the chilling defeat of ARVN early in 1971 in Operation Lam Son 719 (involving an invasion of Laos to cut the Ho Chi Minh trail).

There was a glint of hope in June 1971 when Nay Luett, an intelligent and dedicated highland leader, became Minister for Development of Ethnic Minorities, bringing about sweeping changes in the staff. He and his able colleagues set about coping with the host of problems that were increasing as the situation in the highlands worsened. The deadly effects of the war were compounded by continued forced relocations and land-grabbing by Vietnamese. It was becoming rapidly clear to the highland leaders that their primary task would be to assure the sheer survival of their own people.

THE EXECUTION OF PHILIPPE DROUIN

The year 1968 began on a note of violence, caused by a crisis in the FULRO leadership that led to the execution of Philippe Drouin. It was indicated previously that Philippe (whose real name was Y Kdruin Mlo, 2.24) was one of a group of FULRO "young Turks" who favored a militant posture in dealing with the government. As a member of the FULRO delegation in Ban Me Thuot (he held the rank of colonel in the Dam Y Division of the movement), Philippe collected the FULRO "taxes" from the highlanders in the CIDG and Strike Force. He also was accused of extorting money from CIDG personnel and demanding a payoff from young men seeking to join the MIKE Force. According to Michael Benge, Philippe played the role of paid agent for the Vietnamese Intelligence Agency, for Colonel Le Van Thanh, the Darlac province chief, for the Viet Cong, for the American CIA, and for the U.S. Military Intelligence.

The U.S. Military Intelligence (which was under the Defense Intelligence Agency) had been active in the highlands under the name Field Sociological Survey (I protested this in Saigon but to no avail). They recently had established a compound in Buon Ale-A on Route 14, complete with high fence, guard posts, and spotlights. Their agents could be seen often in civilian clothes dining at La Souris Blanche, a small Ban Me Thuot restaurant run by a Madagascan and catering to French planters who gathered there to sip drinks and exchange news. Since Vietnamese intelligence agents (usually wearing sunglasses) also frequented La Souris Blanche, and it was known that some of the "planters" were members of the French Deuxième Bureau, the restaurant had the reputation of being the spies' hangout. In addition to paying Philippe for information, some of the military intelligence agents were giving him M-16 rifles in exchange for Communist AK-47 rifles, highly prized "war souvenirs" among the Americans in Vietnam.

On the night of 8 December 1967 Philippe had a fight with a Vietnamese sergeant on the glass dance floor of the Darlac II nightclub over one of the hostesses, a Vietnamese girl named Thu who was known to be Philippe's current mistress. In the heat of anger, Philippe killed the sergeant and fled south on Route 14 to the FULRO base in the vicinity of "Bridge 14," some fourteen kilometers from Ban Me Thuot.

According to a FULRO indictment dated 26 January 1968, leaders of the movement had been informed by its agents that following this incident Philippe had talked with Colonel Le Van Thanh, who had arranged a meeting between Philippe and government officials in Saigon.[1] (I had seen Philippe in Saigon at this time, and he claimed to have had a discussion with Nguyen Cao Ky.) The FULRO indictment alleged that Philippe returned to Ban Me Thuot with the intention of killing the FULRO leaders, for which he would receive a large sum of money and be elevated to the role of president of the movement.

---

1. Y Bham Enuol, "Relevé des fautes très graves et des crimes commis par Y Kdruin Mlo selon les renseignements receuillis" (P. C. FULRO, 26 January 1968).

Benge relates that soon after Philippe returned to Ban Me Thuot he and another "young Turk" named Y Sen Nie Kdam (3.18), accompanied by several Rhadé girls from one of the dance teams organized by the Psychological Warfare branch of the ARVN, went to the International Bar. Some Vietnamese soldiers came into the bar, and when one of them asked a Rhadé girl to dance a fight broke out between the Vietnamese and the two FULRO leaders. Several of the Vietnamese were wounded, the bar was wrecked, and Philippe again fled the town. He went to the Special Forces MIKE Force post next to the East Field outside of Ban Me Thuot, where most of the highland personnel were loyal FULRO members. Led by a young Rhadé named Johnny, the FULRO members smuggled weapons (two 30-caliber machine guns from helicopter gun ships, a bazooka, grenades, and M-16 rifles) to Philippe and some of his followers.

Early in January 1968 Philippe called a meeting of his followers (one of whom was Johnny's brother) in a longhouse at Buon Kosier, a village near the Ban Me Thuot City Airport. Also in attendance were two Americans from Military Intelligence. In the course of outlining his plan to assassinate the FULRO leaders Philippe got into a heated argument with Johnny's brother and in a fit of temper took out his 38-caliber pistol and shot him. Everyone fled—so hastily that the two Americans left their jeep. Philippe went to the MIKE Force post near the East Field and recruited some of the FULRO members. Taking three of the Special Forces' trucks, they drove to the Dam San camp (operated by the CIA's Truong Son Program) near Buon Ea Kmat, where they had little success getting more followers. From there they proceeded farther east to the village of Ea Pur.

Told of the events by a FULRO friend, Benge immediately headed for the Bridge 14 post where he found Johnny, Y Sen Nie Kdam, and others of the "young Turk" group. They had taken Johnny's brother to the province hospital and were planning to move against Philippe. They were angry at the interference of the Americans in FULRO politics and told Benge that the Military Intelligence people should leave Darlac province. Mounting an assortment of motorbikes, Vespas, Lambrettas, and Honda motorcycles, they sped off in the direction of Buon Ea Pur. Benge went to inform the American Senior Military Adviser at the Grand Bungalow and also to meet with Colonel Thanh. The Senior Adviser ordered one of his Forward Air Control L-19 pilots to monitor the movements around Buon Ea Pur.

The following morning the pilot reported that trucks full of men had left Buon Ea Pur and had gone to Buon Kram, near Route 21, the road leading south from Ban Me Thuot to Lac Thien (Dak Lak). Benge went to Buon Kram where his adoptive father Y Bham Nie informed him that the FULRO troops had Philippe in a house near the village. Benge then proceeded back into town and down to the FULRO post at Bridge 14. Johnny and some of his colleagues were there with several American Special Forces officers who were trying to retrieve their stolen trucks. Johnny had been informed that his brother had died. Colonel Thanh had alerted the local ARVN units to secure the roads into Ban Me Thuot and ordered the American Military Intelligence out of the province.

The L-19 pilot reported that a truck full of men left Buon Kram and headed south on Route 21 to Buon Aleo (natal village of Y Bih Aleo, the Communist leader in the highlands). The pilot kept watching and radioed that they had gone into the village where they assumed a military formation, after which they stacked their arms. With nightfall there was no further information. The following day, however, Benge was told by a FULRO friend that they had taken Philippe to Buon Ale-A and then southward to Bridge 14. He claimed that they had been ambushed by the Viet Cong and Philippe was "shot between the eyes." He held up his hand to reveal Philippe's prized cat-eye sapphire ring on his finger. Vietnamese intelligence sources reported that Philippe had been taken to the FULRO post at Bridge 14 and executed.

The FULRO indictment called Philippe "un garçon mal élevé de son bas âge" and charged him with "crimes of treachery and thievery." It claimed that he had squandered FULRO funds amounting to 5,812,000 piasters on "ses plaisirs personnels (dancer, manger, et boire, etc.)." It also noted that he had given his girlfriend Thu a gift of 260,000 piasters. The indictment described his contacts with Vietnamese officials, and his intent to commit murder, concluding that because of these violations of his position as a colonel in FULRO he was condemned to death.

THE SIEGE AT KHE SANH AND THE TET OFFENSIVE

In mid-January 1968 the smoldering situation that had been building up since May 1967 at Khe Sanh, just south of the Demilitarized Zone, exploded into one of the major battles of the Vietnam War and brought devastation to the Bru people in that area. The PAVN 304th Division had infiltrated across the Laotian border to join the 325C Division in the vicinity of Khe Sanh, while the 320th Division appeared to be getting into position along the Demilitarized Zone to attack Route 9 east of Khe Sanh in the vicinity of Camp Carroll, where U.S. Army 175-mm guns provided artillery support for Khe Sanh. At Khe Sanh itself, two battalions of the 26th U.S. Marine Regiment held the position and on 16 January a third battalion was flown into the area as part of Operation Niagara II.[2]

As it became apparent that a major battle was in the offing, the Americans ordered all of the Vietnamese population (around 1,500) in Khe Sanh to evacuate to the base where they would be airlifted to Danang. John Miller, an SIL staff member working on the Bru language, described how his Vietnamese neighbors in the town quickly packed their belongings and boarded up their houses. At the same time, Anha, the Bru leader, led a large group of Bru villagers inside the defense perimeter of the base. Busy packing his linguistic materials, Miller was the last one to leave the town. No sooner had he departed than PAVN troops began to infiltrate the abandoned buildings. This prompted the Marines to call in massive air bombardment on 21 January that completely leveled Khe Sanh. The Bru at the base were airlifted to Cam Lo, on the coastal plain. Miller reported that some 3,000 Bru villagers began to make their way down the Bao Long valley on foot to Cam Lo, where large numbers of Vietnamese from the Demilitarized Zone were converging. Also, on 21 January the Marine positions on Hill 861 came under heavy attack. The Marine battalion and a reinforced company that occupied that hill, and hills 558, 881 South, and 950, faced two PAVN divisions numbering between 15,000 and 20,000 men with one more division within striking distance. These events marked the beginning of the Khe Sanh siege that lasted seventy-seven days.

Attention was focused on Khe Sanh, which was beginning to be described as a possible "Dien Bien Phu of the Vietnam War." Suddenly, however, Saigon and Washington were shaken by a massive Communist assault on many urban centers throughout South Vietnam. This was the "Tet Offensive" that began the first days of the Tet Nguyen Dan, the lunar new year, marking the beginning of the Year of the Monkey.

On 27 January 1968 I went to Ban Me Thuot on an aircraft crowded with Vietnamese going to Danang, Hue, and other central Vietnamese

2. W. C. Westmoreland, "Report on Operations in South Vietnam: January 1964–June 1968," in U.S. G. Sharp and W. C. Westmoreland, *Report on the War in Vietnam: As of 30 June 1968*, 2 sections, (Washington: U.S. Government Printing Office, 1969), section 2, pp. 163, 182.

The eve of the Tet Offensive: A group of Rhadé girls in traditional dress

cities to spend the Tet holiday, which began at midnight 29 January. Mike Benge, as usual, offered hospitality at the USAID house, located near the center of the town, across the street from the Catholic church known locally as the "cathedral" (see map 6). There was a report that a Communist sapper squad was going to penetrate the town that evening. At the USAID house, the Rhadé guards were piling sandbags around the balcony and in front of the house. Other than that, Ban Me Thuot seemed normal and bustling.

One of my objectives on this field trip was to determine if Route 21B that ran southeast from Ban Me Thuot to Lac Thien would lend itself to an experiment combining aerial photography and a ground survey for obtaining cadastral data needed in the program to grant land titles for highlanders practicing permanent cultivation and swidden farming. On Sunday, 28 January Mike and I went to Buon Kram, a Rhadé village some twenty kilometers from Ban Me Thuot on Route 21B. Mike was well known in the village, having been adopted by the village chief Y Bham Nie. We were warmly welcomed. January is in the dry season, the harvest is ended, and clearing of new fields has not yet begun. The atmosphere in highland villages at this time is relaxed, almost drowsy. At Buon Kram, celebrations were going on in several longhouses, with groups gathered around jars drinking while the gongs played. We were invited to these longhouses and as we drank from the jars we discussed the situation in the area and the possibility of doing the survey of fields along the road. The general consensus was that security farther south was not very good. Mike and I returned to Ban Me Thuot.

The following day was hot and still as we drove back to Buon Kram. It was immediately apparent that the atmosphere in the village had changed. Villagers wore anxious looks as we made our way to Y Bham Nie's longhouse. He informed us that the Communists had savagely attacked the post at Lac Thien the night before, leaving many of the defenders and villagers dead. Among them were some Buon Kram men, and Y Bham was organizing a dog sacrifice. "Don't go farther south on Route 21B," he said, adding, "All of the villages are filled with North Vietnamese troops, and they are taking the villagers' rice and killing all of their animals for food." He explained that everyone was fleeing into the forest because the Communist troops were massing for an attack on Ban Me Thuot.

Periodically during the war there were rumors of impending attacks that never materialized, but Y Bham's news was obviously based on good information. Mike and I immediately decided to return to Ban Me Thuot. He wanted to stop at Buon Ale-A, and when we arrived it was clear that the news of the Lac Thien attack and a Communist assault on the town had not reached there. A group of pretty Rhadé girls dressed in traditional clothes were going from longhouse to longhouse inviting everyone to a celebration at the house of Y Wik Buon Ya, a member of the Lower House in the National Assembly. We had just arrived at the longhouse of some FULRO people when a young man came with news of the impending attack. They quickly dispersed to alert their own armed groups. Mike and I went over to the Grand Bungalow, where in a calm atmosphere some of the American military officers said that they felt the Communists would honor the truce. We encountered a group of American missionaries coming out of the mess hall. Among them were Bob and Marie Ziemer, whom I had not seen since the 1950s, and Carolyn Griswold (smartly dressed in a white gown and wearing red pumps), who was accompanied by her father Leon, a genial man. He was retired and had come to Vietnam to assist the mission in any way he could. Bob Ziemer and Mr. Griswold expressed their concern over the deteriorating security situation in the area, and we told them what the Rhadé had said about a possible attack.

At the Special Forces B Team, behind the Grand Bungalow, there was feverish activity. The CIDG troops were digging trenches and bunkers and filling sandbags. Men were sitting about cleaning weapons. An American sergeant invited us into the bar, informing us that their intelligence was that Ban Me Thuot would be attacked that night. He suggested that we evacuate the USAID house and move into the Special Forces Compound. We thanked him and departed.

Driving through the streets of Ban Me Thuot, I had a sinking feeling as I looked at the shops displaying the festive Tet decorations. Crowds of smiling people, many of them clutching the hands of small children, milled along the streets and filled the central market buying new clothes (a lunar new year requirement) and Tet food specialties, all wrapped gaily in red and gold paper. Music blared from loudspeakers. The restaurants were jammed. At a small sidewalk café, some highlanders we knew were drinking beer and they waved for us to stop. When Mike told them the news, their smiles vanished, and they quickly paid their bill to leave.

At the USAID house, Mike gathered the other Americans and the Rhadé guards to work out a defense of the compound. Weapons were distributed. More sandbags were piled up on the balcony and in front of the main entrance. Cans were filled with water, and we checked food supplies, candles, and other essentials. We prepared some dinner while everyone became curiously silent. We could hear the tanks and armored personnel carriers from the ARVN 8th Armored detachment rumble by in front of the house, the first sign that there might be trouble.

As the sun went down and darkness fell, the town became very quiet. Only military vehicles sped through the streets. At midnight, in spite of the province chief's order not to fire weapons to celebrate the arrival of the new year (and chase away evil spirits) there was a great deal of shooting of weapons mixed with firecracker explosions. By 12:30 the noise began to subside quickly and within a half hour the noise tapered off. The night was warm and still.

Suddenly, around 1:30, the Tet attack on Ban Me Thuot began. A rapid succession of explosions broke the silence as mortar rounds and rockets began to rain down on the military installations and the center of the town, jarring us out of bed. Quickly there was the sound of small arms fire and then machine guns beginning to clatter from every direction. The explosions spread and came closer to the house. The staccato of automatic weapons burst from the Darlac Hotel (where U.S. Air Force personnel were billeted) and from the CIA compound nearby. Flames shot up from burning buildings in downtown Ban Me Thuot and in the crowded Vietnamese sections. We huddled behind the sandbags on the balcony as the house shook from explosions. ARVN tanks positioned themselves in front of the gate, and we could hear the high-pitched voices of the soldiers shouting on their radios. From the nearby airstrip, American helicopter gunships began swirling into the air, their machine guns blazing from the side doors.

From the balcony, we could see that there was heavy fighting taking place in the direction of Buon Ale-A to the southeast and at Buon Kosier near the airstrip. Mike and I worried aloud for our friends in these villages. Flares threw an eerie orange light on the trees and roofs of the shuttered houses around us that seemed to have withdrawn into themselves.

The experience was very reminiscent of the attack I had witnessed in the Special Forces camp at Nam Dong on 6 July 1964. There were the same sounds of unrestrained violence that is war at its worst. The clatter and staccato of the weapons mixed with the explosions in a strange counter-point steadily mounting to a staggering crescendo that fell and then rose again. To the west of Ban Me Thuot, an enormous explosion sent shock waves over the rooftops as a fuel dump blew up. Then, around 3:30, there was an unusually resounding blast from the direction of Buon Ale-A (see below).

Suddenly the house was engulfed in the violence (we found out later that a Communist unit was coming up the road behind us). There were loud explosions all around, and the tanks began to spray gunfire in every direction. Tracer bullets flew everywhere. In an instant, helicopter gunships began swooping low over the roof, firing rockets that spewed sparks. Flares descended directly overhead with their bright orange light that caused shadows to distend. Windows shattered, and the crash of bullets hitting the walls could be heard. The garden, filled with acrid smoke and lit by flares and explosions, seemed unbelievably tranquil.

Finally there came the reassuring first signs of dawn, and, as at Nam Dong, the morning light seemed to have a soothing effect, bringing the fighting to a halt. Calm, broken by occasional bursts of gunfire and the thud of mortars, descended as the sky began to brighten on what normally would have been a still, sultry day.

The tanks began to move away, still sporadically firing their guns. We began to take stock of the house and to locate everyone. Fortunately, no one was injured. As the sun rose, there was a stirring on the street as military vehicles, some of them ambulances, passed the house. Several young Vietnamese sped by on motorcycles. People began to open their shutters and gingerly peer out and some women held handkerchiefs to their eyes. There were several bodies on the square in front of the cathedral and the carcasses of dead cattle could be seen on a main street. Great clouds of black smoke rose from several parts of the town. As more people appeared on the street, some of the American civilians converged on the house. Jane Ford, a hardy woman who was the education adviser for the Highland Normal School, walked over from her apartment and reported that the market area was quiet. As we stood in front of the house, Mike Benge suddenly roared out of the front gate in a vehicle, obviously on his way to Buon Ale-A to assess the situation there. I walked back down the road behind the house. People stood in their doorways looking dazed. At the beautiful chapel that the Benedictine nuns had built (Sister Boniface had designed it along the lines of a Rhadé longhouse) as part of a highland girls' school, the priest was looking at the damaged roof while the nuns swept broken glass. The priest told me that during the night the Communist troops had come down the road and the tanks had been firing at them.

Around 10:00 A.M., Vietnamese refugees from the sections of the city that were burning began to appear on the streets, making their way to the cathedral (they were northern Vietnamese who had been in Land Development Centers which they had abandoned, moving to Ban Me Thuot). They hurried along the edge of the roads, clutching what belongings they could salvage. The bewildered children were wearing their new Tet clothes. The refugees reported that the fires were getting worse and that the Communist troops were still in the southern part of the city. At noon, American fighter-bombers began to dive on the Buon Ale-A area and the exploding bombs rocked the downtown. Some of the refugee women fell to the ground wailing and crying. The Italian owner of the Kinh Do Hotel and his Vietnamese wife said that they had had heard from her relatives that Communist troops were in the market area. They were trying to organize demonstrations and warned that there would be fighting again when darkness fell. It was becoming clear that the fighting was not over.

First afternoon of the Tet Offensive; reinforcements pour into Ban Me Thuot

By this time the cathedral was filling with people as they streamed down the streets from the south. I talked with some of them about organizing themselves so we could get some relief for them and then went to find the CORDS refugee adviser. The effort was hopeless, however, because the warehouse with refugee goods was in an area where fighting was breaking out again. By late afternoon the sounds of fighting in the southern part of Ban Me Thuot began to grow louder, the tanks began to fire down some of the streets, and the refugees continued to hurry to the cathedral. The bombing increased, and an American jet flew low over the USAID house, unloading a napalm bomb that burst with a huge mass of fire on the grotto behind the cathedral now jammed with refugees. (We learned later that the Communist troops were reported to be hiding in a church—the one in Buon Ale-A—but the pilot picked the cathedral by mistake.) Fortunately, no one was hurt. The Americans in the house decided to evacuate, so we made our way through the center of Ban Me Thuot, past the shuttered shops, through the sports field (where the oath ceremonies had been held in the past) to the Grand Bungalow. I went to the Special Forces B Detachment just as a French planter brought in a truck loaded with badly wounded Rhadé from Buon Kosier. Some of the villagers explained that the Viet Cong had forced them to march toward Ban Me Thuot for a demonstration. As they approached the police checkpoint, someone threw a grenade into the group. Two died while being lifted from the truck, but the Special Forces doctor, assisted by the CORDS public health nurses, saved the rest.

As darkness fell, the fighting began again, and during the night it reached the same peak of intensity that it had the previous night. There was an assault on the headquarters of the 23d Division nearby, and it brought heavy shelling all around the B Detachment. The following morning reports came in that the offensive had been launched against cities all over South Vietnam. Saigon was being attacked, with the American embassy, the Independence Palace, the airport, and ARVN compounds the major targets. There also was fighting going on in Pleiku and Kontum. Jane Ford appeared at the Grand Bungalow, relating that the Viet Cong soldiers had entered her apartment and, after pushing her around, had proceeded to smash everything. After they left, she pulled herself together and hurried to the MACV compound. We still had no idea where Mike Benge was.

Later we learned that Mike had been captured. His capture was described in Marie Ziemer's account of the terrible fate of the Christian and Missionary Alliance staff at their Buon Ale-A headquarters.[3] When the attack began at 1:30 A.M., Communist troops moved immediately into the Buon Ale-A area. The mission headquarters, including the three Italian villas built by Gordon Smith in 1950, was engulfed in the fighting. Viet Cong entered the villa occupied by Carolyn Griswold and her father and ordered them to their upstairs bedrooms. They then placed large amounts of explosives in the ground floor and at 3:30 detonated them. (It was the deafening explosion we had heard at the USAID house.) Leon Griswold was killed immediately and Carolyn was pinned in the wreckage of the house. Betty Olsen and Ruth Wilting, the mission nurses, did what they could for Carolyn after the Communist troops moved on, but she was gravely wounded. Bob Ziemer and Ed Thompson dug a bunker and tried to signal the American planes. They saw Mike Benge come along Route 14 and tried to warn him to turn back, but the Communist soldiers stopped him and led him away.

As the missionaries huddled in their bunker during the next few days, the fighting swirled around them and the remaining mission buildings were demolished. On Thursday morning (the attack had begun on

3. G. M. Cathey and R. Drummond, "The 'Tet Massacre' of Ban Me Thuot Missionaries," mimeographed (Saigon, 1968). This was an account obtained from Marie Ziemer on 3 February 1968 at the U.S. Army 8th Field Hospital in Nhatrang.

Monday morning), Bob Ziemer, in desperation, left the bunker to plead for mercy. Shots were heard, and he fell over the clothesline, dead. Ruth Wilting went out to get medicine for the dying Carolyn and she was shot dead. Soon after, an explosion ripped the bunker (probably a grenade), killing Ed Thompson and seriously wounding Marie Ziemer. Communist soldiers carried her into Buon Ale-A, and she saw that they had captured Betty Olsen and Hank Blood (a SIL staff researcher who worked on the Mnong Rlam language). The Communists had allowed Evangeline Blood and her children to walk back to Ban Me Thuot. Some of the Rhadé assisted Marie Ziemer to the MACV compound in Ban Me Thuot, where they arranged for her to be sent to Nhatrang. By Friday, 2 February, American combat troops reached Buon Ale-A and found Carolyn Griswold still alive. She was sent to Nhatrang where she died.

According to a FULRO report, thirty of their troops were stationed at the delegation headquarters in Buon Ale-A when the Tet attack began.[4] The Communist forces came from the southeast (from the villages south of Buon Kram), and for two days and two nights the FULRO fought back. The FULRO report claims that the movement suffered seven dead and four wounded, while they killed eighty-five Communists. The Communists captured some forty-five village residents, including Y Ngo Buon Ya, Y Wik Buon Ya (Benge reported that both were executed by the Communists), Y Blu Nie Buon-Drieng, and Y Ngue Buon Ya, a pastor and FULRO member. Y Blu related that when the PAVN troops got the group of Rhadé captives in the forest, they only had a few armed guards. Since the Vietnamese did not speak Rhadé, the captives all agreed that on a given signal they would run in different directions into the bush, and those with luck would escape. On the signal they scrambled, and both Y Blu and Y Ngue made good their escape. Mike Benge, who was held in the same Communist prison camp as Y Blu, disagrees with this and claims that Y Blu wrote a "confession" in the camp and informed on other prisoners, so he was released.

Benge related that on the second day of his captivity he was taken to the leprosarium (run by the Protestant mission) some twelve miles southwest of Ban Me Thuot. A group of between fifteen and twenty young FULRO members from Buon Ale-A were brought in, and the Communists or-

4. Y Dhe Adrong, "Engagements between the FULRO Dega-Cham Forces and the Communist Forces in Ban Me Thuot" (Ban Me Thuot, 14 March 1968).

ganized one of their "People's Courts." They rounded up the lepers to represent "the people." Communist cadre were placed amidst the lepers and a bizarre "trial" began. The Communist officer in charge listed the young men's "crimes against the people," and when he asked for a response from the people, the cadremen would shout and get the lepers excited so they would repeat the shout. The officer asked the people to denounce the prisoners, and the cadre responded, "Kill them, kill them!" They kept repeating it loudly and stirred up the lepers to join in the shouting. The lepers, clearly agitated, waved fingerless hands as they shouted, "Kill them!" The young FULRO men, their wrists bound with telephone wire, were taken to a nearby clearing and shot to death.

Y Dhe Adrong described how the FULRO troops fought for several days. But as the American bombing became more intense, they realized that they would have to evacuate. He and Y Tang Phok fled with their families across the fields to Buon Kosier. The offensive left one-third of Buon Ale-A in ruins. Y Preh Buon Krong wept as he told how he and his family tried to flee the first morning just as an American airstrike began. Several of his children were killed by a napalm bomb. Y Preh said, "My youngest son was hit by the bomb and we could not even find any remains." Among others killed was Y Say Mlo Duon Du, one of the founders of the Bajaraka Movement.

By the end of the week the fighting had subsided. Vietnamese refugees packed the cathedral and the center of the town. Some 4,000 Rhadé, whose rice and animals had been taken by the Communist forces in their villages, converged on the highlander boarding school seeking food. Ton That Hoi, the elderly mandarin, complained that his house, close to the Grand Bungalow, was burned and he had lost much of the equipment for his coffee estate south of Ban Me Thuot. Whole sections of the town that had been occupied by military dependents and people from Land Development Centers were in ashes. The administrative buildings built by the French on Route 14 at the entrance to the town were rubble, and Y Dhuat Nie Kdam, who lived in one building, lost his right arm. The Bao Dai hunting lodge across the road was badly damaged.

An ARVN source reported that 18,823 were rendered homeless in Ban Me Thuot because of the offensive.[5] This source also related that only 30 percent of the city's garrison had been kept on duty, the remainder having

    5. Pham Van Son, ed., *The Viet Cong "Tet" Offensive (1968)*, trans. J/JGS Translation Board (Saigon, Printing and Publications Center, A.G./Joint General Staff, RVNAF, 1968), pp. 327–38.

been granted Tet leave. The Communist forces numbered some 3,500 men from the 33d Regiment (composed of four battalions), the 401st and 301st Province Mobile Battalions, and Regional Guerrilla Companies H4, H5, H6, and H8. The first assault came from the southeast, followed by another thrust from the northwest. (The Benedictine nuns found toothbrushes and soap along the small stream near their plantation northwest of the town.)

At Kontum, the Communist attack began at 2:00 A.M. on 30 January, the first day of Tet, with heavy shelling of the ARVN 24th Special Zone Command headquarters, the airfield, and the provincial administrative section, which also was assaulted on the ground by infantry units. At the same time, sappers (who had infiltrated the city disguised as ordinary civilians) attacked several targets. The Communist forces included the 24th NLF Regiment, the 406th Battalion, and the X200 Mountain Light Artillery Battalion. Within hours the invading forces occupied the central market and downtown of Kontum as well as some residential areas.[6]

At the SIL center on the northern edge of Kontum, just above the MACV and Special Forces compounds, a Literacy Workshop was being held. It had attracted SIL staff members and other missionaries and their families. According to Doris Blood (who, with her husband David, brother of captured Hank Blood, was working on the Cham language), those staying at the center went to their bunkers when the attack began.[7] The following day there was sporadic fighting in the town, but the linguists thought that the main thrust of the assault was over. As they were sitting down for supper late in the afternoon, an American helicopter from the nearby MACV compound landed with instructions that they evacuate immediately. There was a scramble for suitcases (which Carolyn Miller wisely had suggested they pack earlier), books, and research materials. Suppers were left on stoves and tables as Carolyn and her children (John Miller who had been at Khe Sanh was now in Danang, see below), Pat Cohen, David and Doris Blood, Richard Phillips and his family (whose house in Ban Me Thuot was destroyed), Oliver Trebilco (who was with the World Evangelization Crusade in Danang), and their highland informants and Vietnamese helpers crowded on the helicopter. At the MACV compound they joined Ken and Marilyn Gregerson and their children in a deep bunker.

At her hospital Pat Smith continued to work, caring for the wounded

6. Ibid., pp. 310–14.
7. Doris Blood, "Deliverance from Kontum," mimeographed (Nhatrang, Vietnam, February 1968).

who were flooding in as the fighting continued. In town, John Banker and his family huddled with his informants in a makeshift bunker in their bedroom, and close by the families of Ernie Lee and Jim Cooper also took refuge in bunkers. Around them, Vietnamese neighbors were packing their belongings and attempting to flee the city. On noon of Wednesday, 1 February, Pat Smith was forced to leave her hospital (Communist troops came in afterward looking for her), and she stopped at the Coopers' on the way to the MACV compound. The Coopers, Bankers, and Lees packed their ten children into a Land Rover and Volkswagen and sped through the back streets to the MACV compound.

Meanwhile ARVN, supported by American airstrikes, was attempting to clear the Communist troops out of parts of Kontum. Just after the linguists had evacuated their center, Communist troops occupied the buildings, and helicopter gunships were called in to attack with rockets. On Wednesday afternoon a Special Forces team went into the center, putting demolition charges in the remaining structures (Pat Cohen went with them to retrieve more books from the library). On Thursday all of the civilians were taken in an armed convoy through heavily damaged parts of Kontum to the airport, where they were flown to Nhatrang. By 3 February the fighting in the town had died down, leaving much of Kontum in ruins.

The Tet attack on Pleiku began at 4:00 A.M. on 30 January. The Communist troops penetrated to the center of the town, the scene of several days of heavy fighting. On 1 February Communist troops attacked Dalat, a city that had been spared the violence of the war up to that time. After a shelling of the town, particularly the provincial headquarters, the NLF 186th Battalion launched an assault. They immediately occupied the central market and the center of Dalat. American helicopter gunships provided support as cadets from the Military Academy were rushed into battle, but this move failed to dislodge the Communist troops. Finally, tanks and Highlander Regional Forces were brought into the city. Fighting raged in the downtown market area and the Pasteur Institute for several days as the NLF 145th Battalion joined the fighting. On 6 February the Communists withdrew, leaving central Dalat a smoking ruin.[8]

Rhadé who had been captured in Buon Ale-A continued to escape from the Communists, and they told of seeing Mike Benge, Betty Olsen, and

8. Pham Van Son, *The Viet Cong "Tet"*, pp. 419–24.

Hank Blood in a jungle prison. When Benge was finally released in March 1973 in Hanoi, he told a harrowing story of watching fellow prisoners Betty Olsen and Hank Blood die after being denied food and medicine by their captors. He himself was forced to walk the 600 miles through the mountains to North Vietnam. Living mostly on rice, he lost a great deal of weight and suffered bouts of malaria, blindness, beriberi, dengue fever, rickets, and swellings. He was displayed to villagers en route as an example of "an American imperialist," and in the north he was incarcerated in a tiny dark cell full of rats and mosquitoes for one year and spent 27 months in solitary confinement.

While the Tet Offensive was going on, PAVN units along the Demilitarized Zone were moving into positions to surround the Marine base and airstrip at Khe Sanh. On 6 February a PAVN regiment assaulted the Lang Vei Special Forces camp southwest of Khe Sanh, using artillery, flamethrowers, and nine Soviet PT-76 tanks—the first time tanks were used by the Communists in the war. During an airstrike some bombs were dropped on Bru CIDG men by mistake, killing many of them. Lang Vei was abandoned. For the next eleven weeks the Khe Sanh base underwent heavy daily shelling (on 23 February, for example, some 1,307 rounds landed on the base and airstrip). Nonetheless cargo planes continued to resupply the garrison, although some were hit by shells and blew up.[9] One victim was Philippe Polin, the young French coffee planter, who was arriving in a C-130 that crash-landed.

During this period many Bru left their villages to go either into Laos or eastward to the coastal plain. Miller reported that the PAVN occupied some of the Bru villages south of Khe Sanh, forcing the residents to remain in order to deter any American bombing. Finally, in desperation, the Bru began to leave these villages. In one night, around two thousand men, women, and children left their villages to make their way to the coastal plain. Carrying belongings, wooden beds, chests, backbaskets filled with tools, pots, and food, they walked for at least ten days to reach the refugee camp at Cam Lo, already swollen with over 20,000 Vietnamese and Bru. An estimated 300 Bru died in their flight from the mountains, and at Cam Lo, on the hot barren plain, the Bru died at the rate of seventy-five per week. Some five hundred Bru refugees reaching Cam Lo later, reported that they had been forced by the PAVN to go into Laos, but they refused to

---

9. Westmoreland, "Report on Operations," pp. 164–65.

stay there when they discovered there was no housing and little rice for them.

At Khe Sanh, the conflict continued through March and April when the 1st Cavalry Division, the 1st Marine Regiment, and some ARVN airborne units combined to launch Operation Pegasus/Lam Son 207 to open Route 9 and allow ground communication with Khe Sanh. On 10 April they reached the base, and for the first time in forty-eight days no shells fell in the area. There were indications that the PAVN units were beginning to withdraw. Late in June MACV announced that the defenses at Khe Sanh would be dismantled, and during Operation Delaware, mounted at this time in the vicinity of the base, elements of the 1st Cavalry Division used up the supplies stockpiled, after which they destroyed the fortifications. Late in June the Bru refugees, numbering between 7,000 and 8,000, moved from Cam Lo to the Cua valley, a wide expanse of grass and trees between low hills. Although they were better off here than in Cam Lo, the Bru longed to return to green and cool Khe Sanh, which had now become a no-man's-land.

Following the Tet Offensive and the Khe Sanh siege, the war began to intensify. Westmoreland received approval for a manpower authorization of 549,500 military forces in South Vietnam. New units, such as the 27th Marine Regimental Landing Team and the 3d Brigade of the 82d Airborne Division, began to arrive. In the highlands, the Communists launched a series of shellings on bases and towns.[10] Outside of Vietnam, two important events occurred at this time. On 31 March 1968 President Johnson announced that he would not run as a presidential candidate in the November elections. He also called for a partial halt in the bombing of North Vietnam to induce the North Vietnamese to agree to negotiations. On 3 April, the North Vietnamese accepted President Johnson's invitation to establish direct negotiations. This led to the beginning of the Paris Peace Talks on 13 May 1968.

POST-TET GOVERNMENT–HIGHLANDER RELATIONS

The Tet attacks had jolted the highland leaders because they demonstrated the force of Communist military power throughout South Vietnam. In a

10. Ibid., pp. 165, 185, 188.

letter to Y Dhe Adrong in mid-March 1968, Y Bham repeated his desire to return to the highlands to lead his "liberation armed forces," and he wanted a guarantee for his personal safety.[11] In March an MDEM delegation composed of Paul Nur, Nay Luett, and Y Chon Mlo Duon Du met with General Lu Lan, the new II Corps commander, to present him with their scheme for the "highland force" to cope with the problem of defending the uplands in the face of increased Communist aggression. The general expressed interest and said he would give it further attention.

In Ban Me Thuot on 5 April, Y Dhe Adrong and Y Preh Buon Krong related that they had just received a communication from Y Bham that they had passed on to the province chief. In it, Y Bham expressed his desire to have the highlanders represented in these talks, specifying that, if North and South Vietnam unify, the highland people were to be given responsibility for their own affairs. He suggested that a federation, such as that in Malaysia, be formed. He added that now FULRO would be known as the "Liberation Front for the Highlander Lands of South Indochina," an organization explicitly independent of the Khmer Krom Liberation Front and the Liberation Front of Champa.

The FULRO leaders in Ban Me Thuot were concerned about reports that the government was considering moving large numbers of Vietnamese into the highlands. They also were upset at the forced relocation of highland villagers, explicitly mentioning the Edap Enang project. When I returned to Saigon, I brought these matters before the embassy Montagnard Committee, and I also wrote a memorandum reporting the views of the FULRO leaders.[12] I recommended that resettlement of highland villages be suspended. With government-FULRO relations strained, such unpopular projects would not improve the atmosphere for further talks. A copy of the memorandum was sent to General Westmoreland, who passed it on to William Colby, Assistant Chief of Staff for CORDS, and to Ambassador Bunker.

The Montagnard Committee prepared a recommendation that further forced movement of highlanders into Edap Enang be stopped, and it also called for an approval process for all future resettlement schemes in the highlands. Such a process would involve approval of the appropriate

---

11. Norman C. La Brie, "FULRO: The History of Political Tension in the South Vietnamese Highlands," M. A. thesis, University of Massachusetts, 1971, p. 96.

12. G. C. Hickey, "Memorandum on the Current Situation in the Highlands" (Saigon, The Rand Corporation, 3 May 1968).

government ministries and the Montagnard Committee. General William Peers, commander of the U.S. 4th Infantry Division, was furious at attempts to halt the relocations into Edap Enang. On 5 May 1968 there were reported to be 4,800 highlanders in Edap Enang, and a CORDS report indicated that around 1,200 highlanders had been "picked up and brought to the camp."[13] Most of these were elderly men and women along with some children. By 7 May around half of them had "drifted away from Edap Enang and possibly returned to their home areas."

Nonetheless, on 11 May 1968 General Peers called a meeting of his staff and II Corps MACV/CORDS personnel, and they agreed that a "proscribed area" southwest of Thanh An district in Pleiku province would be completely cleared of population. This plan would be implemented later in 1968 without consulting any Vietnamese government agencies (including the MDEM).

On 19 June 1968 Prime Minister Tran Van Huong signed a note guaranteeing safe passage for Y Bham and a FULRO delegation to the meeting to held 2 August at the Y Ut Technical Training School in Ban Me Thuot. Fifty highlanders and Vietnamese were invited. Accompanied by 500 FULRO troops, Y Bham led his delegation on foot through the forests of Mondulkiri province for seven days to reach the Special Forces camp on the Vietnamese border at Bu Prang. The FULRO delegation consisted of Y Dhe Adrong (5.10), Y Bling Buon Krong Pang (a former teacher, now a FULRO colonel), Kpa Doh (also a colonel), Thach Tham Apol (representative of the Khmer Krom), and Souleyman (representative of the Cham). The FULRO advisers included Y Sen Nie Kdam (3.18, a major), Y Preh Buon Krong (a colonel), Y Tang Phok, and Ya Duck (both majors). They were flown by Air America to Ban Me Thuot. The government delegation included Minister Paul Nur (1.13), Lt. Col. Touprong Ya Ba (4.9), and Chau Van Mo (the Cham representative). Government advisers were Y Chon Mlo Duon Du, Pierre Yuk (1.12), Y Thih Eban (5.2), and Nay Luett (2.26). Also in attendance were the highlanders from the National Assembly—Nay Blim (2.25), Ksor Rot (3.20), Rcom Anhot (3.12), Lieng Hot Ngheo, and Peang. The Vietnamese from the MDEM were Major Nguyen Van Nghiem, Major Nguyen Van Phien, and Ton

---

13. W. E. Colby, "To Report on the Current Status of the Edap Enang Resettlement Project," (Saigon, 8 May 1969).

That Cu. Also present were the ministers of Defense, Interior, and Chieu Hoi (a special ministry for Communist defectors), and the commander of the 23d Division.

According to Nay Luett, Nur was angry at Y Bham for bringing the Cham and Khmer Krom delegates with him and also for requesting an airlift of some one hundred FULRO Rhadé troops to Ban Me Thuot so they could visit their families. Y Bham arrived in an olive-drab uniform with the *galons* of a major general. He greeted Nur (who was drinking whiskey), and Nur remarked, "Here are the two Montagnard kings." The conference began on 3 August, and according to La Brie the FULRO delegates were "obviously confident of concessions" from the government.[14] They were not aware that the government officials had been informed that FULRO had worn out its welcome in Cambodia, so the government delegates expected Y Bham and his FULRO group to be the ones who would make the concessions.

Y Bham informed the gathering that FULRO was willing to withdraw its demands for direct foreign aid and participation in international conferences. He clung to demands for a highlander pennant to be flown under the national flag, a general commissariat with subdivisions for each ethnic group (as well as for the Cham and Khmer), and a highland military force. The Minister of the Interior remarked that FULRO should present its demands after the Council for Ethnic Minorities had been formed. To do it now, he said, "is like a child asking his parents for a kilo of diamonds."

The discussion continued for several days, and on 7 August Thach Tham Apol, the Khmer Krom, asked that an agency similar to the MDEM be established for the Khmer minority and that a meeting of Khmer Krom delegates and government representatives be convened in Ha Tien. The government delegation, however, would not consider this, pointing out that the conference was called to deal with FULRO exclusively. The meetings ended on 8 August with an agreement that Y Bham and his group go to Saigon with Nur to talk with Prime Minister Huong. In Saigon the points of difference narrowed to the matter of the military force, something the Vietnamese found difficult to accept. Nonetheless, when Y Bham returned to Cambodia, he carried a letter from the prime minister attesting to the government's agreeing "in principle" to a high-

14. La Brie, "FULRO," pp. 96–98.

lander pennant, a general commissariat headed by Y Bham, and a plan for incorporating FULRO troops that rally into Regional Force companies.

Through October and November 1968 there was an exchange of communications between FULRO and the government on numerous points that had been discussed at Ban Me Thuot. Major Nguyen Van Nghiem reported that the government was wary of any agreement that would allow the highlanders to have their own armed force. He noted that there were indications that Y Bham had become close to Sihanouk, which made the Saigon leaders uneasy. Moreover, FULRO had become too militant to give it control of a large armed force. The government, however, would agree to an integration of FULRO units into the Regional Forces.

Letters between the prime minister and Y Dhe Adrong (representing FULRO) resulted in an agreement on 19 December that the government would allow Y Bham and his followers to return "with honor and respect." Y Bham would be given a role "high in the national community" and his followers would be given positions suitable to their capabilities. According to La Brie, Y Dhe carried the letter to Ban Me Thuot, where arrangements were made to send it to Y Bham.[15] Beforehand, however, a Cham member of FULRO managed to make a copy of the letter, which he sent to Col. Les Kosem in Phnom Penh. Les Kosem and the younger group of FULRO militants led by Kpa Doh decided that they had to prevent Y Bham from going to Saigon. On 31 December two battalions of the Royal Khmer Army commanded by Captain Souleyman (the Cham representative at the August meeting) surrounded the FULRO headquarters at Post Command I north of Camp le Rolland in the forests of Mondulkiri province. Kpa Doh related during discussions in Phnom Penh in 1970 that he, Ksor Dhuat, Y Bhan Kpuor, and Y Nham Eban notified Y Bham that he should not resist, so as to "avoid bloodshed between brothers." The defenders, numbering around seven hundred, laid down their arms. Les Kosem took charge of the situation. Y Bham and thirteen members of his family were taken to Orang and then to Phnom Penh where they were kept in the villa of Colonel Um Savuth, located near Pochentong Airport on the edge of the city. Kpa Doh indicated that it was necessary to arrest Y Bham to avoid his "selling out" FULRO in Saigon.

15. Ibid., pp. 101–03.

The disarmed FULRO troops were told that they were free to return to Vietnam if they so desired. They and their dependents, numbering 1,337, walked to the Bu Prang Special Forces camp, and from there they were airlifted to Ban Me Thuot.

Consultations in Saigon involving Prime Minister Huong, Paul Nur, and some FULRO representatives from Ban Me Thuot resulted in an agreement by the government and FULRO to uphold the promises made by Huong in his letter of 19 December. They also agreed to organize a large gathering at Ban Me Thuot on 1 February 1969 to celebrate the return of FULRO troops to the government fold.

This celebration, held in the Ban Me Thuot stadium (where the oath ceremonies were held), drew large crowds. There were flags, banners, Rhadé dressed in their traditional clothes, and elephants. In attendance were President Thieu and high government officials (including six ministers) as well as high-ranking foreign diplomats (two Americans of ambassadorial rank, and the ambassadors of Australia, New Zealand, and Japan). Paul Nur, Y Dhe Adrong, and President Thieu addressed the gathering, after which Y Sut Buon Ya (brother of Y Ngo Buon Ya, the FULRO leader who had been captured in the Tet attack) presented his weapon to the president, who handed it back to him. The ceremony ended with 700 FULRO troops swearing loyalty to the nation. By the end of February 2,017 FULRO troops had rallied to the government and were organized into Regional Forces units.

A news release in Phnom Penh dated 21 February 1969 denied that the Cambodian government had Y Bham Enuol "under surveillance."[16] It also decried as "fantasies" any notions that the Royal Khmer Army officers and troops had anything to do with FULRO and its relations with the Vietnamese government.

While these events were taking place, there were some relevant developments beyond the highlands. On 10 June 1968 the Liberation Radio announced the formation of a Provisional Revolutionary Government (PRG) after a merging of the NLF and the Alliance of National, Democratic, and Peace Forces that had been formed on 20–21 April in a rubber plantation near Mimot in Cambodia. Huynh Tan Phat was named chairman of the PRG, and Mrs. Nguyen Thi Binh, one of the NLF

16. "Gazette du Pays Khmer," *Réalités Cambodgiennes*, no. 636 (21 February 1969), p. 17.

delegation at the Paris Peace Talks, was named foreign minister. In November 1968 Richard M. Nixon was elected president of the United States and took office in January 1969.

THE ISSUE OF FORCED RELOCATION

It was noted earlier that on 29 August 1967 General Thieu signed a decree containing several articles providing for land titles for highlanders. Article 1 stated that "ownership by the highlanders of land they have settled with intent to cultivate (*đất đai đã định canh*) is hereby confirmed." Article 2 declared that "the highlanders will be given ownership of lands they are farming in rotation (*đất hiện đang luân canh*)." Specifically, *luân canh* means rotation in the sense of crop rotation on the same field, thereby implying permanent cultivation. It purported to refer to swidden farming, which involved a rotation of fields, but the Vietnamese term for swidden farming, *rẫy*, did not appear in the law. Senator Ksor Rot called this a "jeu de mots Vietnamien."

In 1968 and 1969 the matter of highlanders' farming and living habits became an important issue again as the matter of resettling Vietnamese in the highlands and of forced relocation of highlander villages reemerged. According to Paul Nur, a letter dated 12 October 1968 from General Lu Lan, the II Corps commander, to the prime minister declared that it would be pointless to grant land titles to highland people because they were migratory. To implement the August 1967 law, Lu Lan pointed out, the highlanders would have to "change their custom of migrating" and settle in "permanent villages." Nur noted that on 4 December 1968 he had forwarded a letter to the prime minister concerning the land question. In it he pointed out that in the past the government had failed to protect the land rights of the highland people. Little had been done to implement the land law, and Nur requested the prime minister to give priority to a program for granting titles to highlanders.

To bring this situation to the attention of the American Mission, I prepared a memorandum pointing out that none of the highland groups was migratory; although many villagers practiced swidden farming, villages remained in place for years and, in many cases, for generations.[17] Also

17. Gerald C. Hickey, Memorandum on Land Titles for the Highlanders (Saigon, The Rand Corporation, 12 December 1968).

there was, in the highlands, a great deal of paddy farming where topography and water availability were amenable to it. But the myth of highland nomadism was very difficult to dispel among the Vietnamese and the Americans as well. The revised *Hamlet Evaluation System Handbook* published in November 1968, for example, stated that "in the central highlands, Montagnard settlements are often not fixed locations. These people practice slash-and-burn farming, moving to different locations within a tribal area every four or five years." [18] I sent a note pointing out that this statement was not accurate, and received the reply that it would be rectified.

Paul Nur and Nay Luett were particularly concerned at reports late in 1968 that the government planned to move between 4,000 and 7,000 Vietnamese from insecure areas along the coast to the Nam Phuong plantation (a Bao Dai property named for the empress), located in the Maa country in Lam Dong province. The plan called for 100 to 200 families to be moved on 15 February 1969 after the Regional Forces and the U.S. 1st Battalion, 173d Light Infantry Brigade, and the U.S. 116th Engineer Battalion had secured the area. One CORDS report stated the "the Province Chief plans to handle the political problems arising from the movement of Vietnamese coastal refugees into the Montagnard Highland Area by starting a vigorous land reform program for the existing Montagnards." [19] Another report, sent from the chief of New Life Development (the name of the CORDS pacification program in the provinces) for II Corps to the head of the Office for Ethnic Minorities Affairs (the former Montagnard Affairs Office) in Saigon, noted that there were highlanders living and farming a portion of the Nam Phuong plantation. [20] The author pointed out that the highlanders had been there a number of years and had no title to their land and that the government planned to remove them to make way for the Vietnamese refugees. He

18. Headquarters Military Assistance Command, Vietnam, Operations and Analysis Division, *Revised Hamlet Evaluation System Handbook* (Saigon, 1968), p. 5. The Hamlet Evaluation System was a computerized program for measuring development and security in rural areas. Using a standard form programmed for computers, American military district advisers in collaboration with their counterparts recorded accomplishments (e.g., how many hamlets had become secure) and incidents (e.g., ambushes). The monthly reports were compiled in Saigon and were supposed to reflect the situation in the rural areas throughout the country.

19. B. Reiff, "Field Trip Report, Lam Dong Province," MACCORDS (Saigon, 12 December 1968).

20. T. Stephens, "Memorandum on Movement of Refugees into Lam Dong Province" (Saigon, 10 December 1968).

recommended that government officials and their American counterparts meet to discuss this matter.

This resettlement project moved ahead, and according to Touneh Han Tho, who at this time was on the staff of the MDEM, some 6,000 Vietnamese were brought to the Nam Phuong plantation after the highland people who had been farming there had been removed. There had been active opposition to this project by Father Grison of the Kontum Mission and Father Quang, a local Vietnamese priest, but it was of no avail.

It was noted previously that General William Peers, commander of the U.S. 4th Infantry Division, and the MACV/CORDS staff had agreed in May 1968 on a scheme to relocate Jarai villages in southwestern Pleiku province for security reasons. Implementation of this plan began late in 1968 when 817 Jarai villagers were moved into the Plei Ring De center. Nay Luett reported that each family was given 7,000 piasters, but since there was no wood in the area for house construction a province official arranged with a local Vietnamese contractor (without consulting the villagers) to provide a standard package of building materials at a cost of 5,200 piasters per family. He provided bamboo and other flimsy materials that would only permit construction of a lean-to. During the month of February 1969 some 117 had departed.

There was growing anger among highland leaders at these relocation programs. At the Montagnard Committee meeting at the U.S. Embassy on 28 January 1969, several members (including myself) reported this, and it was decided that the committee would formulate a statement concerning the U.S. Mission policy regarding resettlement of highlanders. A subcommittee (of which I was a member) prepared a statement declaring that "no U.S. civilian agency or military command shall initiate or support any population relocation within or into the Central Highlands of South Vietnam until the project for such relocation has been thoroughly examined by the interested U.S. agencies and until final approval has been received by the Mission Council."[21] The statement also specified that, since there would be situations where immediate military necessity "dictates the rapid evacuation and relocation of small groups of civilians," the local military commander could initiate such relocation but would be responsible for providing logistical support to those relocated and return-

21. U.S. Embassy Committee on Montagnard Affairs, "Statement Concerning Resettlement of Highland Villages" (Saigon, 20 February 1969).

ing them to their homes as soon as it was practicable. We noted in the statement that this policy was in conformity with President Thieu's 1969 Pacification Plan which stated that "the object is to bring security to the people and not the people to security."

A copy of this statement was sent to General Creighton W. Abrams, Commander of MACV. Nicholas Thorne, chairman of the Montagnard Committee, delivered copies to Ambassador Bunker and William Colby, head of CORDS. The first reaction from Abrams and the military was negative. General Peers, now commander of the First Field Force in Nhatrang, saw a copy of the statement and immediately went to confer with Abrams for three hours. Peers clearly saw the statement as a criticism of his Edap Enang and Plei Ring De resettlement programs. The Montagnard Committee also learned that both the military and civilian personnel at CORDS felt that if the statement was accepted it would put undue restraints on their new pacification efforts. At CORDS there were ambitious young men who were determined "to make pacification work." They had set a goal of bringing 90 percent (Abrams is reported to have said, "Why not 100 percent?") of the population under government control by the end of 1969. As a result of the increasing pacification efforts, a conflict between CORDS and the Political Section of the U.S. Embassy had developed. Since the Political Section sponsored the Montagnard Committee, the statement was seen as an effort to assert the embassy's authority in the area of pacification.

To support acceptance of the statement, on 20 March 1969 I distributed copies of a report I had prepared concerning the negative effects of population relocation in the highlands.[22] In this report I reviewed the resettlement policies and programs since the Diem era, pointing out the disruptive effects on highland societies and the resentment they had generated among the highlanders. I concluded that the statement issued by the Montagnard Committee provided the best guidelines in the matter of population relocation. Ironically, at the same time, a comprehensive postwar plan for Vietnam compiled by a Vietnamese-American research group was gaining great attention.[23] Like other economic development

22. Gerald C. Hickey, "Population Relocation in the Highlands" (Saigon, The Rand Corporation, 20 March 1969).

23. Joint Development Group, *The Postwar Development of the Republic of Vietnam: Policies and Programs*, 4 vols. and summary (Saigon and New York: Postwar Planning Group, Development and Resources Corporation, 1969), 2: 465–90; Summary, pp. 61–66.

schemes in the past, it ignored the role of the highland people in developing their own area and recommended that Vietnamese be brought into the highlands to provide labor and skills for the new projects. On 22 March Thorne informed me that the Montagnard Committee's statement had been rejected. As it turned out, the Montagnard Committee was never to meet again.

NEW POLITICAL DEVELOPMENTS IN THE HIGHLANDS

On 22 March 1969 I met with Paul Nur, who lamented that the MDEM was not functioning as the highland leaders had hoped. It lacked definition, it had few prerogatives, and military mobilization had reduced the staff by 30 percent. The relocation programs that the Americans had initiated in the highlands should have been done in consultation with the MDEM, but this was not the case. Other highland leaders were upset at the continuing corruption in the ministry. Touneh Han Tho observed that when Ton That Cu had been relieved of his position as Director of Cabinet in 1968 because of corruption (his enemies, Y Chon Mlo, Secretary General, and Maj. Nguyen Van Nghiem, Inspector General, had uncovered evidence of it in Cu's files) he had hoped that things would improve. However, they did not. By 1969 the vast influx of American personnel and money had an erosive effect in Saigon, where corruption has always thrived. Chinese and Vietnamese entrepreneurs competed with one another for American contracts and they were prepared to cater to any tastes in order to get them. Vietnamese government salaries were modest, and with the constantly spiraling inflation a civil servant was hard put to remain honest while his family suffered. In the Vietnamese scale of values, it was less wicked to steal money than to allow one's family to sink into poverty. Nur was affected by this situation as the wily entrepreneurs provided him with gifts so they could get contracts for such things as provision of food for the highland boarding schools.

During this period, the social network within the ministry was centered on Paul Nur (1.13). Nur had close relations with Doan Chi Khoa, a Tho (Tay), who was Vice Minister for Northern Highland Refugees. Khoa remained apart from the other high-ranking officials. Nur also was friendly with Chao Van Mo, a Cham leader. Lt. Col. Touprong Ya Ba (4.9, who had become Pleiku province chief in late 1968) remained on friendly terms with Nur, but the minister's ties with other highlanders within the ministry were less strong. There was conflict between Nur and Y Chon Mlo Duon Du, who was ambitious to attain the role of minister. Y Chon, on the other hand, was close to Nay Luett (2.26) and Touneh Han Tho (4.2), both of whom were on friendly terms with Nur but were not in his in-group.

New political developments among the highland leaders occurred when, with the fading of FULRO early in 1969, the Vietnamese government quickly saw the possibility of organizing a new highland political party to fill the gap. This was the idea of Major Nguyen Van Nghiem (Inspector General at the MDEM) and his close friend Nghiem Tham, an ethnologist and University of Saigon professor. They presented their plan to Nguyen Van Huong, secretary general at the Presidency, and on 11 February 1969 he directed a group of former FULRO leaders, including Y Bling Buon Krong Pang, to begin organizing a new party. On 5 March, Y Dhe Adrong, Y Ju Eban (one of the founders of the Bajaraka movement), Y Du Nie, and Y Bling Buon Krong Pang met in Ban Me Thuot and formed the Movement for Southern Highlands Ethnic Minorities Solidarity. Y Bling was selected to be president, and other officers included Ya Duck (a Chru), Y Tang Phok (a Mnong Rlam with a Rhadé name), and Y Sen Nie Kdam (who still was suspected of being a government spy). On 29 March they issued a formal statement concerning the organization and goals of their movement.

On 9 April, Y Bling and Ya Duck met with President Thieu, who promised to certify their new party. According to Touneh Han Tho, Thieu also intimated that he was unhappy with the "situation" at the MDEM and would consider naming Y Bling as minister. Y Bling immediately approached the USAID liaison with the MDEM, asking for 4 million piasters so that the new party could construct its own building in Ban Me Thuot. When the funds were not forthcoming, Y Bling and his group moved into some wooden Buon Ale-A buildings that Christian and Missionary Alliance nurses had lived in before the Tet Offensive. Dedication ceremonies for the new party were held on 22 April.

Political events taking place in Saigon at this time were to have a profound effect on the highland political party. On 7 April (two days before he approved the new highland party), Thieu had addressed a joint session of the National Assembly, calling for an end to Communist

aggression and reunification of Vietnam through a "democratic process."
He stated that he would accept into the "friendly fold" all of those who
would give up their Communist affiliation. In addition he proposed a
"political merger" of all of those who agreed with him, at the same time
calling on those who did not agree to organize an opposition movement.
This, in effect, would bring about the bipartisan political system provided
for in the constitution. The active organizer of this new merger was
Nguyen Van Huong (who had been instrumental in forming the new
highland party). He invited a wide range of Vietnamese political parties—
such as the Hoa Hao Social Democratic party, the Revolutionary Dai
Viets, and the Catholic Greater Solidarity Forces—to join. The Southern
Highlands Ethnic Minority Solidarity party also was asked to become part
of it.

On 8 May 1969 Thieu announced that he would accept the chairman-
ship of the new political coalition, called the National Social Democratic
Front. Thieu and Nguyen Van Huong affiliated the highland party with
their People's Alliance for Social Revolution just before it joined the new
front. On 25 May some 2,000 delegates (including Y Bling Buon Krong
Pang and Ya Duck) from all over South Vietnam gathered in Saigon for
the first meeting of the new coalition.

Unfortunately, the first flush of solidarity that seized the new coalition did not last. Member groups of the newly formed National Social
Democratic Front were given no roles in the government nor any power.
It was a Thieu façade of democracy. On 1 September 1969 cabinet changes
resulted in Prime Minister Tran Van Huong's being replaced by General
Tran Thien Khiem, putting the three highest political positions in the
hands of the military. General Khiem retained his position as Minister of
the Interior. Most of the other cabinet posts went to technicians and
supporters of Thieu. Nur stayed on as Minister for Development of Ethnic
Minorities.

By the beginning of 1970 the National Social Democratic Front was a
thing of the past, and the Southern Highlands Ethnic Minorities Solidarity
party was losing its appeal. The most commonly heard complaint was that
the party "was not doing anything." There also were reports of discontent
because the party's cash assessment of 200 piasters for each adult villager
was too high. Members complained that they did not receive anything for
this payment. Finally, there was a scandal when millions of party piasters
were lost.

HIGHLAND LAW COURTS, EDUCATION, AND THE ETHNIC MINORITIES COUNCIL

Since the October 1964 conference, there had been slow progress made in reestablishing the highlander law courts. A decree dated 22 July 1965 provided for the "reorganization of the Highland Law Courts," which would have jurisdiction over civil cases, penal cases, and highland affairs in which both parties were Highlanders."[24] Criminal and other offenses committed by highland servicemen, or any crimes against the nation, would be brought before National Courts. This law provided for village, district, and province level courts. Cases not resolved by village authorities would be sent to the district court, the judge of which would be the district chief assisted by two highland assessors selected by the village notables within the district. Provincial courts would be organized within the National Courts to hear cases not resolved at the district level.

At the time the decree was promulgated, the only remaining highlander law court still functioning was in Ban Me Thuot. Y Keo Khue was the judge, coming in monthly from Ban Don as he had done in the past. Y Keo was reinstated officially as president (the new title of the judge) of the court, although he was not very active and eventually was replaced by Y Blieng Hmok. (Y Keo died in 1970.) Y Sok Eban, a Rhadé leader (who had joined the Garde Indigène in 1921) was named vice president. In April 1966 the provincial administration of Tuyen Duc province announced the names of all the highlanders who would serve in the courts. At the province court, located in Dalat, the president of the tribunal was Touprong Hiou (4.4), and among his eight staff members were K'Kre (4.5), Touneh Han Din (4.3, who not long after was killed in the crash of an American army helicopter), and Lieng Hot Ngeo (a Lat leader who had been elected to the National Assembly).

In August 1966 the Director of Cabinet of the Ministry of Justice asked for 5,598,000 piasters to establish law courts in Tuyen Duc, Darlac, Pleiku, and Kontum provinces. The following September the Minister of Justice issued a notice that the village level courts would have to be curtailed due to lack of security. It also was becoming clear that the proposed organization of the courts was too elaborate for the given needs. Justice at the village

24. Presidency, Republic of Vietnam, Decree No. 006/65, "Reorganizing the Highland Common Law Courts in the Cental Vietnam Highlands," 22 July 1965.

level among the highland people was a matter of tradition, and most difficulties were resolved within or among kin groups. Highlanders were very reluctant to air problems before a district chief, who more than likely would be a Vietnamese. As a result only very serious cases reached the province level and the case load did not require a court in each province. The Darlac court, therefore, heard cases from neighboring Quang Duc province, while the Dalat court adjudged cases from Lam Dong and Tuyen Duc provinces. In November 1967, Hiar (1.7), the elderly teacher from Kontum, was named president of the new court at Pleiku where cases from Kontum, Pleiku, and Phu Bon provinces were heard. Eventually he was replaced by Ksor Glai (3.10). By the end of 1968 only 50 of the proposed 366 village courts had been established whereas 10 of the 21 districts had functioning courts. Above the district level there were the courts at Ban Me Thuot, Pleiku, and Dalat.

In spite of the vast increase in American aid funds for education at this time, the war was having a deadly effect on education throughout the highlands. In 1967, just before the war intensified throughout much of the highlands, there had been some measurable progress.[25] The Commission for Highland Affairs reported that the total number of highlander primary school students was 14,494 (in 1949 there had been 3,486) and 425 teachers (in 1949 there had been 87). As of 1967, thanks to the work of the SIL and financial support from American aid, there were primers in Bahnar, Bru, Chrau, Pacoh, Northern Roglai, Sedang, and Stieng being used in schools. There had also been some gains for highlanders in higher education. Touneh Han Tho was the first highlander to be admitted to the three-year program at the National Institute of Administration. In addition, a special one-year program at that school was launched in 1965–1966 and included ten highlanders (eight Jarai and two Rhadé). The 1966–1967 course had four highlanders (two Jarai and two Rhadé). The Asia Foundation was sponsoring Y Gum Buon Ya, a Rhadé, in the Hue medical school.

There also were highlanders studying abroad for the first time. Three (Bal, Nay Bah, and Y Wer) were in Japan studying agriculture on Buddhist scholarships. Five highlanders were studying in the United States. Lieng Hot H'kin, a Lat, was at school in New York with financial support from a Christian organization. Walter Plunkett, who had been a

25. For more details on education programs in 1967 see Gerald C. Hickey, "The Highland People of South Vietnam: Social and Economic Development" (Santa Monica, California: The Rand Corporation, September 1967), pp. 49–62.

captain in the Special Forces at Cheo Reo, was supporting Kpa Dai, a Jarai, in his agricultural studies at the University of Hawaii, where a fellow student was Toplui K'Broi (4.12). K'Broi's brother, Toplui Pierre K'Briuh (4.11), was completing his degree in education at the University of Southern Illinois and in September 1968 would return to Vietnam to be assistant director at the new Normal School in Ban Me Thuot (housed in an attractive building that incorporated some Rhadé architectural features). Y Char Hdok, a Mnong Rlam (with a Rhadé name), also was working for his degree in education at Southern Illinois University.

After 1967, however, education in the highlands began to decline with the worsening of the war. In June 1969, Y Char Hdok returned for the summer vacation and, since he was sponsored by USAID, agreed to do an appraisal on highland education for that agency. He toured seven highland provinces and found education generally to be in a deplorable state. According to his report, in the more remote areas most of the hamlet schools either were in ruins because they had been hit by Communist rockets or had closed because the teachers had fled.[26] The district schools, all of which were for boarding students, varied. Y Char found that some were very rundown ("like pig pens") while others were in "fair condition." All of them, however, lacked sanitation facilities, potable water, and electricity. Provincial capital elementary schools were, for the most part, in bad physical condition with broken windows and leaking roofs. Since highland refugees had converged on many of the provincial capitals, the schools there were woefully inadequate with crowded classrooms and greatly diminished teaching schedules. Y Char adjudged most of the elementary teachers to be poorly trained and noted that teaching materials were lacking. He did have high praise for the SIL primers, however, although he thought that more of them could be in use. He also praised the efforts to provide quality education for highland children being made by some of the Catholic priests and nuns. He explicitly mentioned the schools being run by Fathers Bianchetti (in Darlac), Boutary (Dalat), and Morisseau (Quang Duc).

Y Char deplored the fact that many of the highland students (some of them only thirteen years of age) were abandoning their studies to join the CIDG and MIKE Force where they could earn money to buy transistor

---

26. Y Char Hdok, "The Present Situation of Education, Society, Economy, and Politics of the Montagnards in the Highlands of South Vietnam," Saigon, 1969.

radios and Japanese motorcycles. He observed that often U.S. military trucks would come to schools near a post to pick up students and pay them for helping to build fortifications, dig bunkers, and fill sandbags. Other highland students quit school to work for USAID or private American firms. In a conversation concerning these problems, Y Char expressed his view that this would deprive the highland people of the trained young men they would need in the future. He also felt that, when the war ended and the Americans departed, these young men would only be qualified to "work as coolies." Finally, Y Char, who had been away from Vietnam for several years, was shocked to see that many of the young highlanders had become "hippies," as he called them, because of their long hair and tight-fitting clothes (a mode they borrowed from young Vietnamese in the towns).

The Ethnic Minorities Council, when it finally was established, did not function as a political organization, but it did include some of the active highland leaders. It also brought some chiefs of the more remote ethnic groups into contact with these leaders (as some of the conferences in the past had done). Also, the council provided an opportunity for the highlanders and other minorities (its membership included refugee highlanders from northern Vietnam, particularly those of Tai-speaking groups and Muong, as well as Cham and Khmer Krom) to meet and discuss the things they wanted of the central government.

The 1967 constitution had provided for the council, but it was not until December 1968 that the Lower House approved the bill setting forth its structure and functions. The Senate got around to approving the bill on 1 April 1969. In October and November 1969 there were several decrees outlining the procedures for nominating candidates (this was done by a village nomination committee) and for holding elections (adult villagers were eligible to vote). The elections were held in mid–December 1969. An examining committee met on 10 March 1970 to review those elected to the thirty-two seats. The only rejection was Ksor Kham (3.19), a FULRO activist who had been jailed after the December 1965 revolt, and he was replaced by Siu Plung (1.23).

The representatives of the Jarai (there had been 34,211 Jarai votes) were Siu Plung and Rcom Po (3.22, son of leader Ksor Wol). One of the two Rhadé (16,988 votes) was Y Bling Buon Krong Pang, head of the Southern Highland Minorities Solidarity party. Other well-known leaders who won seats were Ya Yu Sahau, a Chru civil servant; Touprong Hiou

(4.4), who now managed his farms and business interests (see below); Touneh Ton (4.14); and Y Mo Eban (5.7). The Bru were represented by Anha, and the Sedang by Kek, a young leader from Kon Horing who had been a seminarian in Kontum and who had the 2d baccalaureate from Lycée Yersin. Other ethnic groups represented were the Bahnar, Hre, Halang, Jeh, Roglai, Stieng, Maa, Hroy (a Jarai subgroup that was treated as a separate group). Later, Vice President Nguyen Cao Ky announced additional members of the council, including Toplui Pierre K'Briuh (4.11), his brother-in-law Hiup (1.20), and Touneh Han Tho (4.2).

The Ethnic Minorities Council first convened on 4 November 1970 in a special session to discuss land titles for highlanders. As was indicated above, little had been done in granting titles since the August 1967 law was signed. A decree dated 15 July 1969, issued by the Ministry of Land Reform, provided a scheme for identifying lands being farmed by highlanders. It called for a Land Identification Team in each village and a Provincial Administrative Commission to supervise the village teams. Another ordinance dated 28 November 1969, issued by the same agency, fixed the land holding for each highland family practicing swidden agriculture at ten hectares. In March 1970 the MDEM had proposed legislation that would provide each highland village with title to a delimited territory (this had been one recommendation in my 1967 report).[27] This would be in addition to lands already claimed by individuals and families, and it would include grazing land and unused land that would serve as a reserve for future cultivation. Such communally owned land was traditional among some of the highland groups. According to Nay Luett, the only objection to this plan for village land was raised by the Assistant Minister for Land Reform, who held that a highland village was not a legal entity and could not claim any domain.

One reason the highland leaders at this time were anxious to have the land title program implemented was because of the increasing amount of land-grabbing by Vietnamese. The most blatant example of an attempt to grab land took place early in 1970, when Vice President Ky's wife applied for a concession of 1,500 hectares within the boundaries of Tu Tra village in the Danhim valley. According to Touneh Han Tho, she had flown over the area in Ky's special helicopter and had decided that the land would be good for a farm and ranch. When it was made public that she had bid for

27. Hickey, "The Highland People," pp. 91–93.

the land in the Chru village, the residents were outraged. They immediately wrote to Lieng Hot Ngeo, their deputy in the National Assembly, and the MDEM was informed. The newspapers printed articles about it. Touneh Han Tho and other Chru leaders marched to the district headquarters in protest. Finally, Mrs. Ky was forced to withdraw her bid.

At the Ethnic Minorities Council meeting, it was decided that every highland village would have a "main living area" (i.e., a village-owned territory), determined on the basis of ten hectares for each family. On 9 November 1970 the prime minister signed this into law. As of the end of November the MDEM reported that, in I Corps, Land Identification surveys for individual highlanders' claims had been completed on 168 hectares. In II Corps, surveys had been completed on 21,012 hectares, and, of these, individual claims for 8,471 hectares had been approved. In III Corps, 702 hectares had been surveyed. By the end of 1970 some 29,000 hectares of land had been surveyed, a figure considerably short of the announced goal of 40,000. Some USAID officials blamed this on the provincial authorities, whom they described as being "indifferent" to any program geared to giving land title to highland people.

The first session of the Ethnic Minorities Council presided over by Vice President Ky (this was provided for in the constitution) was held in February 1971. The highland delegates complained that the MDEM was having trouble coordinating programs with other ministries (such as Agriculture, Health, Education, Economy, and Social Welfare) that dealt with the mountain people. They suggested having an "Ethnic Minorities Development Coordinating Committee" to deal with this, a plan which the prime minister later rejected on the erroneous notion that the Central Coordinating Committee of Pacification and Development was doing that already. There also were suggestions concerning education (special consideration for minorities in higher education, increased technical training, and more instruction in indigenous languages). There was some additional discussion about land claims (only allowing Vietnamese concessions after highlander land claims had been resolved and compensation for lands seized during the Diem era).[28]

28. "Bốn quyết-nghị của Hội-Đồng Các Sắc-Tộc" (Four Decisions of the Ethnic Minority Council), Thượng-Vụ (Highland Affairs), no. 71 (Saigon, February 1971), pp. 45–49.

6 WARTIME INFLUENCES ON ETHNONATIONALISM

Despite the increasing disruptions caused by the Vietnam War, through the 1960s and early 1970s the highlander elite continued to expand, with its members gaining more positions in the provincial administration as well as in the Ministry for Development of Ethnic Minorities (MDEM) and the newly formed Council for Ethnic Minorities. It is interesting that, in spite of their being considered the least advanced of the South Vietnamese minorities, the highlanders played a dominant role in minority affairs, and their ethnonationalism eclipsed that of either the Khmer Krom or the Cham. With the appointment of Nay Luett as minister in June 1971, a new spirit of ethnonationalism swept the highlanders, who, as the war continued to intensify, realized that they were facing a struggle to survive as a people.

EXPANSION OF THE HIGHLANDER ELITE

Appendix B is a list of highlanders recognized as leaders. The list is not a random sample but rather a compilation of names of those that I and highlanders I know would consider leaders or, in the case of the younger ones, emerging leaders. They have moved beyond the village milieu (without abandoning it) into the world of politics. They are relatively well educated and most of them have been involved in ethnonationalist activities. They have all come to be known to one another. It is quite by chance that the list contains one hundred names.

As appendix B indicates, by the early 1970s fifty-four of the one hundred leaders listed (54 percent) were included in the four genealogies.

Intermarriages up to this time continued to take place among the highland elite, linking all of the genealogies, so that they formed a vast network that spread through the heartland of the mountain region, embracing members of the Bahnar, Bru, Chru, Jarai, Rhadé, Lat, and Sre. Because kinship for the highlanders is a very important institution, the nature of kin ties determines a wide range of social behavior. These genealogies, therefore, do not represent a network in the metaphorical sense but form a real social network. All of those in these genealogies were aware that there were kin ties among them, although they could only actually trace these ties to a limited number of consanguineal and affinal kin with whom they had frequent social contact. They also were aware that they constituted an elite, and in 1970 Nay Luett pointed out that they were arranging marriages among themselves—for example, the marriage of Binh (1.29), a young Bru leader, with the daughter of Hiu, a Bahnar leader, and the marriage of Toplui K'Broi (4.12), a promising Sre, with the daughter of Chru leader Touprong Hiou—so that they might develop an even more extensive elite with stronger interfamily ties.

It was noted previously that in the 1930s and 1940s marriages among local elite families, such as those in Kontum (chart 1), began to create an expanding elite that included some Bahnar, Sedang, Jarai, and Rengao. The continuation of this process was described and it also was pointed out that some marriages began to link elite groups in different ethnic groups located in widely separated areas. For example, the links between the Bahnar and Rhadé and also marriages created kin ties among the groups shown in charts 1 and 2 and those in 1 and 3. Marriages in the 1960s and early 1970s created even more links among the genealogies. A marriage was arranged between Toplui Pierre K'Briuh (4.11), the first highlander to receive a university degree, and Bui, daughter of Pher (1.22), whose father was Ber (1.10), the first highlander to achieve civil service status in the French colonial administration. This marriage, therefore, linked charts 1 and 4.

Hium, sister of K'Briuh's wife Bui, had married Paul Nur (1.13), the first Minister for Development of Ethnic Minorities, and Bui's brother Bih was Director of the Bok Kiom School in Kontum while another brother, Hiup (1.20), was a teacher and Bahnar leader. Hiup had married H'met Eban, of an elite Rhadé family from Buon Ko Tam on Route 21 east of Ban Me Thuot. (Since she married a Bahnar with a teaching position in Kontum, they did not live matrilocally as is Rhadé custom.) Also, Hiup's mother's brother Phem (1.17) had married H'met's sister H'bum Eban and had gone to live in the Buon Ko Tam longhouse. Since Hiup and Phem had studied in Ban Me Thuot, they both spoke Rhadé. Another sister, H'rec Eban, married Y Jut Buon To (1.19), son of Rhadé leader Y Soay Kbuor (1.11), who was killed in 1967, while a third sister, H'dam Eban (1.27), worked in the Ban Me Thuot highland law court and later married an Italian from one of the coffee estates. Their brother, Y Du Eban (3.21), wed Rcom H'blok, daughter of Ksor Wol (3.5), a Cheo Reo leader and assistant to the King of Fire, thus linking charts 1 and 3 again.

Another marriage during this period linked charts 1 and 5. Phem (1.17, son of Bahnar leader Ber) had taken a Rengao woman named Lap as his second wife—his first wife had been Rou (1.14), daughter of Bahnar chief Mohr—and they had a son, Buch (1.26), who married Rachel, daughter of Y Ham Nie Hrah (5.4), the first highlander to become a Protestant pastor. (He was the brother-in-law of Y Thih Eban, founder of the Bajaraka movement.) In chart 1 there also were other interesting marriages. Rou (1.14) took as her second husband Nhep, a Rengao, and their daughter Ter married Yup (1.28), an ARVN officer and son of Hlin, whose sister Gym was the wife of the Bahnar chief Ber (1.10).

In chart 2, Nay Honh (2.23), who had been in the French army and in 1970 had been Inspector for Regional Forces in Cheo Reo, married Rcom H'chem, daughter of Jarai chief Nay Moul (2.17). Nay Honh's brother, Nay Alep (2.29), a graduate of the National Institute of Administration and a rising Jarai leader, married Rcom H'jreo, sister of Rcom Perr (3.13). Perr and H'jreo were the children of the Jarai chief R'mah Dok (3.7) and Rcom H'kra. (R'mah Dok had married this woman and her sister H'dla.) As was indicated previously, Nay Moul's daughter Rcom H'om wed Nay Luett (2.26), a Jarai leader. Luett's brother Nay Re had been an instructor at the Truong Son Center in Pleiku and was killed in an ambush in July 1968. Luett's other brother, Nay Khuit, was a village chief. Luett's mother's brother, Nay Dai (2.27), had been in the French army and later was chief of Phu Tuc district in Phu Bon province. It also was noted before that Nay Moul's daughter Rcom H'un had married ill-fated Philippe Drouin. Moul's youngest son, Rcom Ri (2.30), married Nay H'tor, daughter of Rcom Brim (2.22), whose wife was the sister of Nay Phin (2.19), the Jarai teacher who had married Rcom H'trul, daughter of Jarai teacher Nay Der (2.12). Phin and his wife followed Der into the Viet Minh in 1945. Rcom Brim's other daughter, Nay H'loa, wed Ksor Hip (2.31), a young Jarai leader and noted musician.

Chart 3 is dominated by the descendants of Rcom H'areng (3.3) and her husband Ksor Seng. Rcom H'nher (3.4), the eldest daughter, had married Ksor Wol (3.5), assistant to the King of Fire. Their daughter Rcom H'kam married Siu Klir (3.23), a lieutenant in the police force in Cheo Reo, and H'kam's daughter Rcom H'lem became the wife of Y To Buon Ya (3.24), a Rhadé who was the first highlander to become a helicopter pilot in VNAF. Rcom H'kam's son Rcom Po (3.22) was elected to the Ethnic Minorities Council and was a rising leader. A daughter, H'lot, married Nay Wanh, a teacher. Another son, Rcom Nhut ("Ali," 3.25), was an active local leader and worked as assistant to Ed Sprague, CORDS representative in Cheo Reo. The youngest daughter, Rcom H'blok, married Y Du Eban (3.21), a young Rhadé leader from the Buon Ko Tam elite family in chart 1.

Rcom H'areng's daughter Rcom H'ca (3.15) was married to Ksor Broai, an army officer who had been chief of Lac Thien district in Darlac, and their son, Rcom Thun, worked for CORDS in the program to give land titles to highlanders. It was noted above that H'areng's daughter H'kra's son was Rcom Perr (3.13), and he wed Ksor H'piam, sister of FULRO activist Ksor Kham (3.19). Kham's mother's sister's son was Ksor Rot (3.20), who became a senator and noted Jarai leader. Rcom Rock (3.11), a Cheo Reo leader, was a son of H'areng, and his son, R'mah Wih (3.27), was an ARVN captain and popular figure, while another son, R'mah Blui, was a medic in Pleiku. Blui's wife was the sister of FULRO official Y Sen Nie Kdam (3.18). Other sons of H'areng were Kek (3.16) and Bek (3.17), both officials in the Phu Bon province administration, and Rcom Anhot (3.12), a graduate of the National Institute of Administration and member of the Lower House. His wife was Siu H'blec, daughter of Ksor Glai (3.10), judge in the Pleiku highlander law court. Another kinsman in this chart, Rcom Sut (3.26), also was a graduate of the National Institute of Administration.

It was noted above that a marriage had been arranged for Toplui K'Broi (4.12) and a daughter of Touprong Hiou (4.4), thus linking two elite families among the Sre and Chru. K'Broi had a degree in agriculture from the University of Hawaii and his brother K'Briuh (4.11) had a degree in education from the University of Southern Illinois. Their sister married

Yalong Ya Loan, son of Banahria Ya Don (4.6), son-in-law of the noted Chru chief Banahria Ya Hau. Ya Don had joined the Viet Cong in 1961, and his wife remarried, later having a son, Yolong Ya Thanh (4.15), who joined the Vietnamese navy. Touneh Han Tho's (4.2) sister, Touneh Han Dao, married Cil K'Se of an elite Lat family from a Dalat village. K'se's brother, Cil K'Din (4.16), had worked for the Americans in Dalat and Saigon and had received a scholarship to study in California. Their sister K'Det was married to Chru-Sre leader K'Kre (4.5). Touneh Han Tho's other sister was married to Nay Ri (4.17), a Jarai who worked for CORDS in Cheo Reo and is now living in the United States. Another relative, Touneh Ton's (4.14) brother Touneh Phin, was wed to a kinswoman of the famed Mnong-Lao chief Khunjanob.

In chart 5, Rhadé leader Y Thih Eban's (5.2) sister, H'suon Eban's daughter H'dim Eban, became the wife of the young Jarai army officer Ro-o Bleo (5.3). It was noted above that Rhadé pastor Y Ham Nie Hrah's (5.4) daughter Rachel married Buch, thus linking this chart with chart 1. Y Ham's sister H'chioh Nie Hrah married Ksor Dun (5.8, who remained in Buon Ale-A, using a Rhadé version of his name—Y Dun Ksor). Ksor Dun's sister's son Ksor Kok (5.11), a FULRO activist, wed another sister, H'li Nie Hrah, and both are now refugees in the United States. A third sister, H'kri Nie Hrah, became the wife of Y Siek Nie, whose brother Y Nhiam Nie was the husband of the daughter of FULRO leader Y Dhe Adrong (5.10). Also, Y Dhan Nie Hrah, son of Y Tuic Mlo Duon Du (5.6), wed the daughter of Rhadé leader Y Mo Eban (5.7).

Although in appendix B only one (Rcom H'ueh, 2.28) of the 100 leaders is female, it does not mean that the role of women in highland leadership is insignificant. It is interesting to note that 79 of the 100 listed come from ethnic groups with matrilineal descent—the Chru (10), Jarai (35), and Rhadé (34). There are other factors that are important, such as size of the ethnic group and development of education. The Jarai and Rhadé are the largest upland groups, and the French brought education to both groups at a relatively early period. While the Chru are a small group, Cham influence is undoubtedly an important thing to consider in assessing why this group has produced so many leaders. The Chru (who claim to be upland Cham) were located in a place accessible to Champa and the Chru traditionally used a Cham script, indicating that they had a literate elite for a long period. Still, it is interesting that so many leaders are found on charts 2 and 3 (a total of 25), both of which are dominated by the Rcom clan, i.e.,

Rcom women. It was indicated previously that well-known Jarai leaders such as Nay Nui (2.11) and Nay Moul (2.17) were able to attain their status through a combination of their having certain physical and personal characteristics that marked them as having the favor of the spirits—a "grand charisma" (*kdruh krin*)—and their marriages to women of the elite Rcom clan. Nay Nui's marriage set a pattern of Nay males marrying Rcom females, and on chart 2 eight Nay listed among the leaders are married to Rcom women. There also is significance in the fact that three leaders listed on chart 1 (Hiup, 1.20, Phem, 1.17, and Y Jut Buon To, 1.19) married sisters from an elite Rhadé family in Buon Ko Tam, and in chart 5 three leaders (Y Thih Eban, 5.2, Ksor Dun, 5.8, and Ksor Kok, 5.11) married sisters from the elite Rhadé Nie Hrah family of Buon Ale-A.

Appendix B also reveals that 44 of the leaders are Christians (30 Catholic and 14 Protestant), which is probably due to several factors. First, there was the establishment of the Catholic mission at Kontum in the mid-nineteenth century, which had considerable influence on the Bahnar (all of the Bahnar leaders listed are Catholics). Kontum was really the first non–Vietnamese settlement in the highlands, and it was one of the first centers of education. The Protestant mission at Ban Me Thuot had a similar influence and it introduced the English language among the highlanders. Both missions played an important part in the rise of ethnonationalism among the highland people. The French and American missionaries took personal interest in the highlanders and they sought to help them to preserve their ethnic identity. In the late 1950s it was apparent that by and large the missionaries championed highlander rights. Also, the Christian highland leaders were imbued with the Christian ideal of equality in the eyes of God and they interpreted this as meaning that they were equal to the Vietnamese and wanted to be treated as such.

Finally, the age groups of leaders presented in appendix B indicates that the bulk of the leaders (64) were born between 1920 and 1940. This is not surprising, since that was the period when ethnonationalism was on the rise in the highlands, education was expanding, and more highlanders were assuming roles in the administration and the army.

By 1971, with the MDEM and the Ethnic Minorities Council functioning, an increasing number of highland leaders went to Saigon for meetings and consultations concerning programs. They would stay at inexpensive (often somewhat squalid) hotels near the central market, not far from the MDEM, or in small rooms behind the MDEM. Many stayed with officials

Chru leader Touprong Hiou, at Diom (1970)

from the ministry, which raised some problems, since these officials had modest incomes and the expense of a never-ending parade of guests was a burden. By and large, highlanders did not like Saigon. They considered the city to be too crowded, noisy and dirty. With the thousands of Japanese motorcycles (brought in through American aid as part of a scheme to "soak up piasters" so as to avoid a runaway wartime inflation) the air was heavy with fumes and there was a constant roar of engines (many of them in bad repair). Also for some of the highland leaders, living in Saigon posed certain problems regarding their traditional religious beliefs. Han Tho described how he and other Chru leaders considered to have special charisma (*gonuh seri*) avoided going to a Chinese restaurant because they would have had to pass under clotheslines suspended from windows above, thereby violating a taboo.

The convergence of leaders in Saigon increased contact among many of them, giving rise to more awareness of their similarities (particularly their common ethnic identity) and their differences as well. Touneh Han Tho relates that when the Ethnic Minorities Council convened in November 1970, all of those who came to Saigon got together with the MDEM staff for a large dinner at a Chinese restaurant. As they ate and drank, the atmosphere became more festive (they spoke a mixture of French, Vietnamese, and Rhadé). Siu Plung began to chide Pierre Yuk and the other Bahnar about their not having surnames. "Why do you Bahnar have just one name when everyone else has a first name and a family name?" he asked. Touprong Hiou added, "Yes, why is that so? We Chru have surnames like the Jarai and Rhadé, so why don't you?" Everyone laughed and there were shouts that the Bahnar were "déraciné" ("uprooted"). Yuk was nonplussed, but Hiup (who was in his cups) became flushed and said that long ago the Bahnar had surnames, but when the French priests came to Kontum everything changed and they lost their names. The others scoffed goodnaturedly and said they did not believe it.

ECONOMIC INNOVATIONS AMONG THE HIGHLANDERS

In the course of traveling throughout the highlands during my research, I collected examples of economic innovations among the villagers. Much of this data was presented in a report in 1971 for the RAND Corporation with the objective of making the Vietnamese government and the American Mission more aware of the potential role of the highlanders in any future economic development.[1] Notwithstanding the disruptions caused by the war, there were some impressive examples of economic innovation among the highland people. Some were not really new, but they had been ignored by those concerned with economic development. When the French developed coffee estates in Darlac in the late 1920s and 1930s, they hired numerous Rhadé as laborers. Although it went unnoticed, in the course of time some of these laborers began to grow their own coffee trees in villages and eventually in small estates. By 1970 there were 326 registered highlanders with coffee estates. They totaled 531 hectares and the median holding was 1.0 hectare. These planters had their own association, and one of the officers was Y Dhe Adrong, the FULRO leader. They grew *robusta* and *arabica* trees, the harvests of which were purchased by Chinese entrepreneurs who transported the coffee to the Saigon market.

One of the first Rhadé planters was Y Sok Eban, a leader who had joined the Garde Indigène in 1921. After accumulating land in his village, Y Sok

---

1. Gerald C. Hickey, "Some Recommendations Affecting the Prospective Role of Vietnamese Highlanders in Economic Development" (Santa Monica, California: The Rand Corporation, 1971).

began a plantation and by 1948 had 4,000 trees bearing coffee berries. Another planter was Y Ju Nie Kdam, who in 1945 purchased five hectares of land in Buon Kosier from the Rhadé leader Y Ut Nie Buon Rit. Y Ju planted *robusta* seedlings he had obtained from a French planter for whom he had worked. While the seedlings were growing, Y Ju cultivated bananas, pineapples, and some vegetables as cash crops to supplement his income. By 1966 Y Ju had 5,000 mature trees producing berries all year around. In 1965 Y Yong Nie Ktuol cleared a half-hectare near Ban Me Thuot and planted 300 coffee trees. In 1969 he harvested 350 kilos of berries. Nearby there was a small depression drained by a stream, and in 1965 Y Yong cleared one hectare on the slope to plant dry upland rice. By his own estimate his first crop was around two metric tons of rice. In 1968 he cleared a half-hectare of the soggy bottom of the depression to plant paddy. The following year he cleared an additional half-hectare and planted "American rice" (IR-8 and IR-11), using some chemical fertilizer obtained from a Rhadé who had been trained at the International Rice Research Institute in the Philippines. Y Yong estimated that his 1969 crop yielded 6.8 metric tons of paddy.

In 1966 Y Bham Nie, chief of Buon Kram, obtained a new type of upland dry rice from his adoptive "son," Mike Benge. Y Bham planted some in a 10 by 15 meter plot and it thrived, yielding around 4.5 metric tons per hectare (his traditional rice produced only 3.25 tons). Farther south, in Buon Ea Khit, a seventy-year-old man named Y Bok Buon Dap decided in 1967 to expand the wet-rice fields his wife's family had farmed for generations. With the help of kinsmen, he dug a canal to tap water from a nearby stream for his new terraces. By 1969 he had doubled his crop and purchased an eight-horsepower tractor and a small roto-tiller (which got stuck in the mud and had to be pulled out by an elephant). Y Bok watched carefully when Lynn Cabbage, an IVS volunteer, planted some high-yield IR-5 rice nearby. Deciding that it was a worthy type of rice, Y Bok followed suit and realized an abundant harvest. Soon other farmers from the village were adopting the new rice and borrowing Y Bok's equipment.

In Kontum province, the Sedang traditionally were swidden farmers. After 1957, when there was an influx of Vietnamese who began farming paddy fields, some of the Sedang began to imitate them. As the war intensified in 1964, Sedang refugees began to move into the Kon Horing area (north of Kontum). Since there was not enough land for swidden farming, they began adopting paddy cultivation.

In many highland villages near towns, there was an increase in cash cropping. This was the case in the vicinity of Cheo Reo, where kitchen gardening was developing into truck gardening. According to Ksor Wol (3.5), this began to happen after 1962, when Phu Bon became a province with Cheo Reo (Hau Bon) its capital. There was an increase in the number of Vietnamese as civil servants and military personnel were sent there. The Jarai villagers saw Vietnamese planting gardens containing tomatoes, cabbage, onions, and chili peppers, all of which sold at the Cheo Reo market for high prices. Some of the Jarai, including Ksor Wol, began to plant more vegetables in their swiddens to sell in the market. By 1970 kitchen gardens in many swiddens had become sizable truck gardens and women were making daily trips at dawn to bring their produce to the Cheo Reo market. Dominating the open-air section of the market, these Jarai women were selling not only (the Vietnamese complained that they had a fixed price and refused to bargain) a wide range of fruits and vegetables but also tobacco and animals (chickens, ducks, pigs, and sometimes cattle). They even vended live river fish in polyethylene bags filled with water.

In the 1950s, when the Vietnamese began moving into the Danhim valley between Dalat and Phan Rang (the heart of the Chru country), they farmed, using their traditional method of transplanting paddy from seed beds into the fields. Many also used chemical fertilizers. According to Touneh Han Tho, his kinsman Touneh Ton (4.14) was one of the first Chru to imitate the Vietnamese in his farming. Others, including Touprong Hiou (4.4), followed suit. Hiou had the reputation of being an adept farmer, and over the years he had expanded his landholdings, cultivating a wide range of cash crops. In 1966 he and some Vietnamese farmers imported some seed potatoes from Holland and he began to farm potatoes for sale along with his other produce in Saigon, Nhatrang, Dalat, and Phan Rang, to which the produce was transported in rented trucks. Having accumulated considerable capital, Hiou joined two Chinese friends in December 1972 to open the first rural bank in the highlands. He insisted that the architecture he based on traditional Chru house lines "so the villagers would feel at home in the bank."

There also was an increase in the number of highlanders involved in nonfarming enterprises. Many were engaged in petty commerce, usually operating village shops. These shops, like those of the Vietnamese, were small and built of locally available materials, most often wood, bamboo, and thatching. The stock included a variety of manufactured goods likely to be in demand by villagers—laundry and face soap, toothpaste, rubber sandals, hairpins, matches, cigarettes, cut tobacco, beer, rum, rice wine, soft drinks, cookies, candy, soy sauce, fish sauce, dried fish, canned fish, sugar, kerosene, and some school supplies. A number of those running such shops had been in the CIDG program and had accumulated enough capital for the initial investment. Some of them pointed out that they had a problem with kinsmen and fellow villagers purchasing on credit. Since, among highlanders, it is more important to maintain good social relations than it is to make money, they could not force payment of these bills, and in most instances it was unlikely that they would ever receive the money.

In 1967 some Rhadé in the vicinity of Ban Me Thuot began to engage in the transport business, using tri-wheel Lambrettas. By early 1968 six men in Buon Ale-A were operating carriers. They made constant runs between villages and the Ban Me Thuot market. In January 1968, Y Hue Buon Krong, a resident of Buon Kram, purchased a Lambretta, paying cash he had saved while in the CIDG program. He operated his carrier between Ban Me Thuot and Buon Ea Khit (south of Buon Kram), making four round trips a day. The service was interrupted only during the planting season when Y Hue worked in his fields to clear, sow, and harvest. He explained that when he had accumulated cash he did not follow the usual Rhadé pattern of buying cattle. To begin with, the transport business had become very lucrative and, secondly, security in Darlac had gotten bad during 1967. Y Hue reasoned that if he and his family had to evacuate their village in a hurry—a contingency most highlanders considered very real—they would have to leave many things such as cattle behind. But with the Lambretta they could load all of the family and many of their personal belongings to flee into Ban Me Thuot. If they should need money, they could always sell the Lambretta. Ironically, I interviewed him in Buon Kram the day before the Tet Offensive began. While Buon Kram was untouched, large sections of Ban Me Thuot were scenes of fighting.

EXPANSION OF THE WAR FOLLOWING AMERICAN TROOP WITHDRAWALS

In 1969 the two large battles in the highlands were at Ben Het, a CIDG camp west of Dak To in Kontum province, and at Bu Prang CIDG camp southwest of Ban Me Thuot, where FULRO had been active since 1964.

In April the 101st Airborne Division launched Operation Massachusetts Striker in the A Shau valley of central Vietnam. On 6 May the PAVN 66th Regiment began a 56-day siege at the Ben Het camp with a heavy artillery and rocket barrage; some 6,000 rounds fell into the post during this period and it was assaulted several times. On 8 June 1969 Presidents Nixon and Thieu ended a one-day summit meeting on Midway Island and announced that by the end of August 25,000 American military forces would be withdrawn from South Vietnam. The Hamlet Evaluation System was reporting at this time that 86.5 percent of South Vietnam was pacified. By the end of August the 3d Brigade, 60th Infantry, 9th Infantry Division, had left for the United States.[2] As of the end of 1969 there were 321,600 American military personnel remaining in Vietnam, and by the end of 1970 this figure had dropped to 250,342.[3] Among the units that departed was the U.S. 4th Infantry Division, which closed its Pleiku headquarters in March and withdrew in November. Early in 1971 the U.S. Special Forces also left Vietnam.

Infiltration by some highlanders trained in North Vietnam continued. Typical was Nay Bam, a Hroy (Jarai), whose movement to North Vietnam in 1954 was described earlier. After being trained at the Southern Ethnic Minorities School near Hanoi, Bam studied at the Thai Nguyen Agricultural School (where some instructors were Tho—Tai-speaking highland people) from 1961 to 1963. Afterward he worked at the Agricultural Service in Lang Son in the Black Tai upland country. Between 1963 and 1968 Bam studied at the Agricultural University near Hanoi, graduating as an agricultural engineer. He reported that during that period he had heard of the FULRO movement, which initially the Communists praised but later began to condemn as "an American plot." In 1969 he was given some practical training in growing food for the troops in the south (priority crops were manioc, bananas, yams, and maize in that order). He also was given "political training," using a book written by Nguyen Duc Thuan (who had been jailed by Diem and released after the coup d'état of 1963). Bam related that he had witnessed some bombing in North Vietnam, noting that it was against military targets.

Early in 1969 he was given seven days of military training (firing weapons and practicing how to scatter if American jets appeared). On 4

2. "The New Look, 1969," *Tour 365* (*U.S. Army, Vietnam*), Winter 1969, pp. 42–48.

3. Office of the Deputy Chief of Staff for Personnel, *Strength of the Army*, 3 parts (Washington, Headquarters, Department of the Army, 1972), part 1, p. 24.

March he and others from the Agricultural University (two southerners and nine northerners) were sent southward. They walked fifteen to twenty kilometers per day in the mountains, sleeping at night by the trail. He described the Ho Chi Minh trail as "many trails" with a main route for trucks. He also witnessed some bombings: one was by B–52s (eight soldiers were killed), another was by fighter-bombers (killing four). Those moving south were given rice and they fished and hunted wild fruit and plants to supplement their diets. Along the way they encountered the "Lao Tin," whom he described as Laotian highland people, and in Quang Tri province he met some "Van Kieu" (a Vietnamese designation for the Bru and Pacoh). He also saw some Cua.

Between August and October 1969 Bam and his group moved from Quang Nam to Phu Yen, crossing the Ba river twice east of Cheo Reo. In Phu Yen he met Ksor Manh, Son, and Day, all of them Hroy who had been in the Southern Minorities School in Hanoi with him. From October 1969 until 5 December 1971, when he defected, Bam organized food production (the cadre he worked with were highlanders, but the troops were PAVN). Part of his training in Hanoi had been to prepare him to cope with the herbicides being used by the Americans. Bam was told to cover his face with wet cloth and to salvage the manioc that had been sprayed by quickly cutting the roots and washing them before cooking. In September 1969 planes sprayed the trail in the area, defoliating many trees. Viet Cong who drank water in a nearby stream after the spraying developed abdominal cramps and diarrhea. The second spraying was in March 1970, and it killed their entire crop, resulting in a food shortage that delayed military operations. Bam said that the settlement also was sprayed, causing most residents to become ill and a few to die. (For additional information on the perceived effects of herbicides, see below and appendix C).

On 29 October 1969 the PAVN 66th Regiment launched an assault on Bu Prang and nearby firebases after a series of shellings against posts along the Cambodian border in the vicinity. The allied commanders reasoned that the object of the Communist move was to gain control of Duc Lap (Dak Mil) and then march on Ban Me Thuot. Several weeks before this attack some of the FULRO leaders in Buon Ale-A had predicted that such a Communist effort would take place. They reported that the attack would start with shellings and assaults on the firebases, after which the Communists would concentrate on Bu Prang. Their "agents" were in the area (dressed in loincloths), and since they had been in the CIDG they could identify all of the Communist weapons. They had sent a full report to Buon Ale-A, even giving the coordinates for the PAVN artillery.

On 31 October Firebase Kate was evacuated and within days two more firebases had to be abandoned. Duc Lap also was attacked. Air strikes were called in daily, and additional American artillery was brought to the area as were MIKE Force and ARVN units. By late November the fighting had subsided with both Bu Prang and Duc Lap remaining in government hands.

In March 1970 Norodom Sihanouk was deposed as head of the Cambodian government by a military junta led by General Lon Nol. A month later I went to Phnom Penh to contact the FULRO leaders there and found the city much the same as it had been in May 1969 when I had visited it en route to Angkor Wat. Phnom Penh was one of the most attractive cities in Southeast Asia, with a French colonial charm that Saigon had lost during the Vietnam War. There were shaded streets, quiet squares, pastel colored buildings, beautiful wats (temples), and, by the river, a glittering royal palace. There was little street traffic, and between noon and three o'clock Phnom Penh closed its shutters and slept.

Everywhere there were posters denouncing Sihanouk as a dupe of the Communists, such as one depicting him dressed in a natty continental style suit with a herringbone twill pattern composed of conical hats, each containing the yellow Viet Cong star. Slogans called for support of the Salvation Government of Lon Nol. The word "royal" was deleted from buildings and names, e.g., the Royal Khmer Army became the National Khmer Army. Students and civil servants were rushing to join the army. Signs of the new war between the National Forces and the Communists were just beginning to appear. Sandbags were being placed in front of public buildings, and trenches were being dug along the Mekong river. Even at the serene Buddhist Institute the staff wore military shirts and trained in the dusty park during the afternoon.

I contacted Kpa Doh, Ksor Dhuat, Ksor Kok (5.11), and Y Bhan Kpuor, all of whom were FULRO leaders and now had commissions in the Khmer Army. They were living with their families in apartments on Boulevard Monivong across from a military compound where Lt. Col. Les Kosem had a house. Y Bham Enuol still was in the villa of Col. Um Savuth near Pochentong Airport.

Soon after he had been deposed, Sihanouk formed the Force Unifiée National Khmer in the rural areas to counter the Lon Nol government. It appeared that this new movement might cooperate with the Khmer Rouge, a name Sihanouk had given a rural dissident movement active in the Battambang area and in the remote northeastern provinces. There also was a question of when Sihanouk might rally the Pracheachon (Communist) party, thought to have some 30,000 members concentrated in the southeastern sector.

By April 1970 fighting was breaking out in parts of the rural areas, some of them close to Phnom Penh. Laughing soldiers rode from Phnom Penh in buses as well as in commercial trucks (beer and Pepsi Cola trucks) to battle areas south and east of the capital. Foreign journalists had flooded into Phnom Penh, and after the morning news briefing in the tea room (which had a large bar) above the Magasin d'Etat (which still was selling East European goods) they would scramble to their rented white air-conditioned Mercedes to go to the scenes of new fighting. Unlike Vietnam, Cambodia offered little protection for journalists near battles and a number of newsmen were killed or wounded.

The last groups of tourists from Angkor Wat were leaving Phnom Penh as were some dependents of the diplomatic community (including the Russians). French planters and their families were checking into the Hotel Le Royal. Rumors were rampant as foreigners gathered at Le Cyrene or La Taverne for lunch. The Cambodians were reporting dire signs, such as the appearance of a white crocodile in the Mekong river and the flash of a comet over Phnom Penh. François Sully (a French journalist who later was killed in Vietnam) and I went to have tea with Charles Meyer, a Frenchman who had been close to Sihanouk and who was then packing to leave for France. He confirmed a story that soon after Sihanouk had been deposed, the Queen Mother had the *baku* (the Brahmin priests who are the guardians of the royal treasure) bring her the Preah Khan, the sacred saber. She performed a ritual, partially removing the saber from its sheath (to remove it entirely would precipitate a great calamity for the kingdom). The blade was reported to have been rusted and dark in color, a sign of great trouble for Cambodia (at the end of the sixteenth century, a turbulent time, a similar ritual had revealed that the saber also was rusted).

On 30 April 1970 the American-South Vietnamese invasion of Cambodia began with the goal of destroying "Communist sanctuaries" to prevent further infiltration into the Saigon area and the Mekong river delta. When I returned to Phnom Penh in July, Kpa Doh informed me that the Communist forces had moved westward when the invasion began.

The Communists moved in trucks at night over the back roads. Kpa Doh also said that some 9,000 Khmer National Army troops and their dependents had evacuated Ratanakiri province, moving from Bokeo into Vietnam. He claimed that FULRO had two battalions of 550 men each in the Ratanakiri-Pleiku border area, and on 24 June they had mounted an operation against the Communists with American artillery and air support. He and the other FULRO leaders in Phnom Penh made trips on foot from Phnom Penh to Mondulkiri and Ratanakiri provinces to contact FULRO troops in both areas.

Bun Sur, a Mnong Rlam who had left Vietnam and had been studying in Paris, returned to Phnom Penh at this time, and we all met at Les Kosem's house. Bun Sur was given a commission in the Khmer Army and named chief of Mondulkiri province. He, Kpa Doh, and other FULRO leaders began to make frequent visits to Vietnam to recruit highlanders to go to Cambodia (some American military officers were involved in this effort). They had little success. Privately, Kpa Doh also began to complain about Les Kosem's treatment of the FULRO people in Phnom Penh, saying that the Cham leader was "too authoritarian."

By July the war had intensified in the Cambodian countryside and the government forces were concentrating on a defense of the population centers as the Communists took control of more rural areas. Southwest of Phnom Penh, the Khmer Krom were doing much of the fighting. I had a long discussion with Thach Chia, a Khmer Krom teacher in the Lycée Sisowath, who had been with the Khmer Krom delegation in the August 1968 Ban Me Thuot meeting. (He later was killed in a student demonstration.) He admitted that Khmer Strike Force CIDG personnel from Vietnam were doing much of the fighting. Thach Chia also outlined some of the Khmer Krom goals, expressing the hope that they might cooperate more with the highlanders in Vietnam. Another Khmer Krom leader was the flamboyant Kim Khet, who, sitting in the garden of the Hotel Le Royal drinking Bloody Marys, described how his "force" of sixty Khmer Krom had just warded off Communist attacks on Takeo. He claimed to have once been the bodyguard of Ba Cut, the Hoa Hao leader whom Diem had guillotined in 1956. Kim Khet related that he had fled to Phnom Penh, where he hoodwinked Sihanouk into thinking he was a hopeless playboy by frequenting nightclubs while he secretly was organizing the Khmer Krom.

By this time the effects of the war were beginning to be felt in Phnom

Penh. The rains had washed away the anti-Sihanouk posters from the walls, and bunkers were everywhere, as were coils of barbed wire. An artillery unit had been moved to the river bank close to the shuttered gambling casino and troops with their dependents had occupied the partially completed elegant Hotel Cambodiana (that Sihanouk had been building to lure the tourist trade). Civilian hospitals were now forced to accept wounded soldiers because the military hospitals were overcrowded. Newspapers carried many photos of Communist dead and the charred ruins of such towns as Kompong Speu and Skoun. On 2 August a bus, several taxis, and a beer truck were hit with B-40 rockets on the road from Kompong Som, leaving eleven dead. This was the first such ambush in the vicinity of Phnom Penh. River traffic on the Mekong had ceased, and the city was slowly being isolated. Early in August, in the quiet of early evening, there were the thumping sounds of mortars and explosions of artillery to be heard for the first time in Phnom Penh.[4]

With the American troops withdrawing and the Vietnamese assuming greater responsibility for the conduct of the war, in mid-1970 General Ngo Dzu, the new commander of II Corps, issued an order stating that by 31 October 1970 there would be no more "D or C hamlets" (in the Hamlet Evaluation System, D and C hamlets were not under government control) in the region. His method of attaining this goal was to launch a massive resettlement of highland villages in areas that were supposed to be "insecure." The first phase of this effort took place in the northwestern portion of Buon Ho district, north of Ban Me Thuot, where, General Dzu claimed, the Krung population was lending support to the Communists by supplying them with rice and recruits. The 23d Division made a "sweep" of the area, and Regional and Popular Forces were sent in to move the villagers. By early 1971 large numbers of Krung were being relocated in the vicinity of Buon Kli, north of Buon Ho on Route 14. At a conference in Nhatrang at this time, the American Senior Adviser in Darlac reported that "all of the villagers were happy to move." Kurt Sawatzky, a volunteer for the Vietnam Christian Service in Ban Me Thuot, however, informed me on 6 January 1971 that he had visited Buon Kli and found an appalling situation. Up to twenty villages were being moved, and the residents expressed great discontent at the way it was being done. They were forced to

4. I recorded observations of the situation in Cambodia during this period in "The War in Cambodia: Focus on Some of the Internal Forces Involved" (Santa Monica, California: The Rand Corporation, October 1970).

leave most of their possessions, including their valuable jars and gongs as well as cattle, pigs, and chickens. An ARVN unit burned one village to the ground and the soldiers looted all that they could find. At the Buon Kli resettlement center, there were not enough tents, the nearest water source was two kilometers away, and the relocated villagers were receiving little support.

On 5 February, Y Puk Buon Ya, a young Rhadé leader, and I went to Buon Kli. One group of villagers reported that in the vicinity of their former village there had been some Viet Cong activity since 1964 and they had asked the district authorities to "improve security," but nothing was done. They requested permission to move, but nothing was forthcoming. The Viet Cong entered their villages twice a month to engage in propaganda and "tax" each longhouse a 250-gram can of rice. This forced the villagers to purchase rice in Buon Ho town. Y Puk and I found that what Sawatzky had reported was accurate. The villagers had been given a three-day notice that they would be moved, and they left most of their possessions, which were then looted by the soldiers. Buon Ka and Buon Y Yung were burned. The new settlement was located on a barren, windy hill devoid of trees and water. The villagers were given only tin roofing, so they scoured the nearby forests for building materials. The result was an assortment of shabby structures of gnarled logs and weathered deadwood.

I wrote a memorandum concerning the situation at Buon Kli and managed to get a copy to Hoang Duc Nha, kinsman of Thieu and an eminence grise in the Independence Palace.[5] He in turn brought it to the attention of Thieu, who advised General Dzu to discuss it with me. The General and I did discuss it, but it was futile. Dzu went ahead with relocations, and by April 1971 an estimated 40,000 from 100 to 150 villages had been relocated. There also were reports of Vietnamese moving into some of the abandoned villages to begin farming some of the paddy fields. In the resettlement centers there was an increase in sickness and the number of deaths. Nay Luett visited a large group of Jarai who had been forced from their villages in Pleiku province and found them living in the open with no shelters and poor drinking water. Many were sick and dying. The doctors from the Vietnam Christian Service Hospital in Pleiku found a deplorable situation at Plei Degroi and Plei K'tu where 300 villagers had

---

5. Gerald, C. Hickey, "Memorandum on the Unlearned Lessons of History: Relocation of Montagnards" (Saigon, The Rand Corporation, 13 February 1971).

died since being moved. Those involved in Pat Smith's Village Health Worker program reported that between 1 and 5 May 1971 some 75 children died of a cholera-like ailment in the Bahnar relocated village of Mang Yang, east of Pleiku. To make matters worse, the Communists attacked the village on 19 May, prompting an ARVN reaction that resulted in 37 dead, many wounded, and 29 houses destroyed.[6]

Some American journalists investigated the relocation situation. My views were reported by *New York Times* writer Gloria Emerson and by *Washington Post* correspondent Peter Osnos.[7] Osnos also recorded the views of Irving Hamberger of CORDS, who was highly critical of the relocations. The Osnos article included some quotes from Americans who favored the moves. One was Lt. Col. Wayne R. Smith, the Senior Adviser in Darlac, who said that highlanders "are going to have to be assimilated into society, be modernized, go to school. A lot of them are basically lazy."

Early in April 1971 I had a long discussion about the relocations with William Colby, head of CORDS, and since he had been in Vietnam in the late 1950s I recalled the trouble that resulted from the relocations at that time. We were joined by John Paul Vann, a former army officer who had been an outstanding critic of American military strategy in Vietnam. I continued to outline the reasons why the resettlements would best be halted. En route back to Saigon, Vann told me that he soon would be named Senior Adviser in II Corps and he would do what he could for the highlanders. Upon assuming this position, he immediately organized an Office for Highland Affairs to deal with programs and problems for the highlanders. By May it was evident that Colby and Vann had decided to bring pressure to end the relocations. Early in June, General Dzu let it be known that he wanted to resettle 10,000 more highland villagers but that "American sensitivity prevented it."

NEW LEADERSHIP UNDER NAY LUETT

During this period Nay Luett (2.26) was rapidly emerging as the most dynamic and dedicated highland leader. He had had experience in various

6. T. G. Coles, "Montagnard 'Village Health Worker' Program, Minh-Quy Hospital" (Kontum, June 1971).

7. Gloria Emerson, "Anthropologist in Vietnam Seeks Montagnard Gain," *New York Times*, 25 April 1971; Peter Osnos, "Security a Disaster for Montagnards," *Washington Post*, 25 April 1971.

Nay Luett at Dalat (1971)

administrative positions and had received considerable formal training (Lycée Yersin, the National Institute of Administration, and the International Rice Research Institute in the Philippines). He spoke Jarai, Rhadé, Bahnar, Vietnamese, French, and English. He also had become adept at dealing with American and Vietnamese officials. At the same time Nay Luett had retained his ties with highland traditions, and whenever possible he returned to his wife's village near Cheo Reo to work in the fields and enjoy village life.

Nay Luett also was very concerned about preserving the ways of the highlanders while still organizing social and economic programs to raise their standard of living and prepare them to compete economically with the Vietnamese. Early in 1970 we visited Plei Bahrong (also known as Plei Potao), the home of the King of Fire, a figure Luett viewed as representative of Jarai tradition. First we stopped to pick up Siu Choi, the King of Fire's sister's son and likely successor to the king. (An elderly man in the village was excited to meet Nay Luett, about whom he had heard so much, but he was disappointed that the leader, a slight, wiry, dark-skinned man was not "big and light like an American.") Ksor Wol (3.5) and Tracy

Atwood (who now worked for USAID) also went along, and we spent the day with Oi Anhot, the King of Fire, who had been busy preparing his fields for planting. The village of Plei Bahrong was a very traditional Jarai village with none of the tin roofing that was becoming so popular. (Though tin roofing had the advantage of not requiring replacement so often and being inflammable, it had the disadvantage of being excessively hot under a brazen sun.) The village seemed very tranquil. It had fifteen longhouses in addition to that of the King of Fire. One small subsidiary building near the king's house was described as the "birth house," and Ksor Wol related that the sacred saber was hidden back in the wooded hills behind the village. Ksor Na, an assistant to the king, lived in the next longhouse, and the king's brother-in-law Siu Bla lived in the longhouse opposite. Next to him lived Nay Ngok, who was considered "close to Oi Anhot." Other residents of the village included Kpa Mot, a teacher, and a small house at the end of the village was occupied by a Bahnar refugee family. We discussed some of the traditional functions of the King of Fire, and Nay Luett emphasized the need to retain many highland customs so as to preserve the ethnic identity of the Jarai and other highland groups.

During 1970 and early 1971, Nay Luett formed a small group composed of Touneh Han Tho and Pierre K'Briuh, both of whom had been fellow students with Luett at the Lycée Yersin. They met frequently to discuss the fate of the highland people in the face of the continuing war and the disastrous relocation programs, such as the one taking place on orders from General Ngo Dzu. This group also, from time to time, had visitors from the highlands, such as Hiup (1.20), Ksor Rot (3.20), Rcom Anhot (3.12), Touprong Ya Ba (4.9), and Y Chon Mlo Duon Du.

On 15 June 1971 President Thieu announced changes in his cabinet, and Nay Luett was named the new Minister for Development of Ethnic Minorities. He brought about immediate reforms in the MDEM, appointing Touneh Han Tho as secretary general and Pierre K'Briuh as director general. One of those instrumental in Nay Luett's appointment was his friend Hoang Duc Nha, Thieu's kinsman, who had gone to the Lycée Yersin with Luett and the other highlanders and had played together with them on the soccer team. Nha wanted his colleague Pham Ngoc Kha to be liaison between Nha's office and the MDEM. Luett agreed, and soon there were references among the MDEM staff to the "Lycée Yersin mafia."

On 28 and 29 July 1971 the MDEM held a conference at the Hotel Majestic in Saigon for representatives of ministries with highland programs and all of the deputy province chiefs for highland affairs. Voluntary agencies with programs in the highlands were invited to send delegates. A wide range of programs were outlined by Nay Luett, and he called for the cooperation of those present in aiding the implementation of these programs. He specifically noted the importance of the land program, resettlement problems, and the refugee situation.

These three topics had been much discussed by the Luett-Han Tho-K'Briuh group, and they had agreed that they would give priority to the land question, since it was related to both the resettlement and refugee problems. Despite the fact that the government had agreed to give land titles to individuals and villages (the "main living area" concept) and USAID had several staff members working on it, relatively few titles had been distributed due to lack of action on the province level. Luett was very concerned over the increasing number of reports of Vietnamese taking land claimed by highlanders; in 1971 and 1972 the MDEM received 1,800 complaints from highland villagers of land-grabbing by Vietnamese. Most of the reports were from Darlac, where officers from the 23d Division and wealthy Vietnamese from Saigon (including some Vietnamese generals) were clearing land regardless of who claimed it. This land rush was prompted by the spiraling price of coffee on the Saigon market as well as by wealthy Vietnamese seeking plantations for their retirement. (The commander of the Vietnamese 25th Division told me he planned to get land in the highlands for a retirement plantation, and when I inquired whether he intended paying for the land he just laughed.) There also were instances of Rhadé civil servants selling Vietnamese land belonging to villages and clans. Two elderly women in Buon Kosier and Buon Pan Lam who were clan land guardians (*po lan*) pointed out that the nearby airstrip was on land belonging to their clans, as was the sprawling estate of the Société des Plantations Indochinoises. The owners of this estate were in the process of clearing a section of the estate near Route 21 to sell to Chinese and Vietnamese for commercial development. (They did, finally, agree to give the ladies back 300 of the 2,000 hectares.) There also were numerous reports of land-grabbing in other areas. Near Dalat, wounded Vietnamese army veterans moved onto land belonging to Touprong Hiou's daughter Rosette and her husband, but Hiou got the prime minister to order them removed. In Cheo Reo, the Vietnamese penchant for taking land earned them the name "the land eaters" among the local Jarai.

To cope with this situation, Luett organized the Committee to Resolve

Land Disputes, naming himself president while the Director General of Land Reform was selected as vice president, and K'Briuh became secretary. In each province the chief and the deputy chief for highland affairs were to deal with land-grabbing, but officials such as Ya Yu Sahau, Pierre Yuk, and K'Briuh complained that the province chiefs (all of whom were Vietnamese with the exception of Ya Ba in Pleiku) were not interested in taking any action concerning highlanders' lands. Finally, at the end of 1971, Luett managed to bring this question before the cabinet, resulting in an order by the prime minister that forbad any new Vietnamese concessions in the highlands. Nonetheless, the abuses continued. One elderly Bahnar said to Pat Smith, "We were here long before anyone else came. We now may be the first to disappear and, even then, the soil that covers our graves will be taken."

The second most important problem with which Luett and his colleagues had to cope was the rising number of refugees in the highlands. This was particularly the case in I Corps, where security was rapidly crumbling following the disastrous Lam Son 719 campaign mounted by ARVN early in 1971. Between January and mid-February the North Vietnamese moved 31,000 new soldiers southward along the Ho Chi Minh trail, and trucks were moving at the rate of 12,000 per month. While an estimated one-third were going into Cambodia, the remainder were heading into South Vietnam. This prompted Operation Lam Son 719, one of the largest ARVN efforts up to that time. Its goal was to invade Laos and cut the Ho Chi Minh trail with 16,000 troops (including the elite Ranger and Airborne elements) and heavy U.S. military support. The operation began on 8 February with troops and armored units moving along Route 9, using the abandoned Khe Sanh airstrip for planes and helicopters. The Vietnamese forces rolled through the Lao Bao pass and captured Tchepone, but they were savagely attacked by PAVN using Russian and Chinese rockets, 130-mm artillery, and effective antiaircraft weapons that took a heavy toll on Vietnamese and American helicopters. Although Thieu proclaimed it a great success, Lam Son 719 was generally conceded to have been a debacle for the government forces, which suffered very serious losses in men and equipment.[8] An American Army officer who was in Khe Sanh at the time later told me that he and other advisers had

8. Robert R. Shaplen, "Letter from Indochina," *New Yorker* (6 March 1971), pp. 87–91.

reported to their superiors that Lam Son 719 convinced them that the ARVN was no match for PAVN.

The leaders at the MDEM also were disturbed by a program in 1971 to move from 200,000 to 1 million Vietnamese refugees from the northern-most provinces (including the cities of Hue and Danang) to the south, raising the specter of the land development days. Nay Luett met with Dr. Phan Quang Dan, the head of the program, who asserted that there were no plans to move any of these refugees into the highlands.

In August 1971, as the situation in I Corps worsened, the leaders at the MDEM heard reports that the whole northern region was going to be abandoned because it could not be defended. Luett reasoned that, if this occurred, the Bru and Pacoh refugees at Cua would be caught in a "free fire zone" which would be heavily bombed by B-52s. He and his group decided that it would be necessary to resettle all of the highlanders in the region north of Danang in the southern portion of the highlands. They immediately drew up a plan for such a move and submitted it to the prime minister.

The plan was immediately opposed by General Ngo Dzu and the commander of the 23d Division, both of whom disliked the idea of increasing the highlander population in Darlac, which they saw as the most promising part of the uplands for future economic development. (This also was the province where most of the generals were getting their land concessions.) The plan also was opposed by Anha, the Bru leader, and province and district officials in Quang Tri. According to Touneh Han Tho, these officials knew that their loss of refugees would mean a loss of refugee funds and personnel for the Regional Forces, so they influenced Anha to oppose the plan. Opposition also developed in the prime minister's office in Saigon, thereby stalling the movement of the Bru and Pacoh refugees.

On 17 November 1971 I had a long discussion with Nay Luett in his office at the MDEM. He and his group had made efforts at fixing up the building, painting it and redecorating the somewhat cavernous offices. Luett had photographs of Oi Anhot, the King of Fire, Khunjanob the "Ivory King," and President Thieu signing the 31 August 1967 law. Luett was very disturbed by highlanders being forcibly relocated without suffi-cient reason. We estimated that since 1945 at least 65 percent of highland villages had been relocated for one reason or another. He linked these resettlements with the recurring schemes to move many Vietnamese into the highlands and feared the relocated highlanders would lose their land. He had had dinner with Dr. Dan, who had reiterated that no Vietnamese would be moved into the highlands, but recently, at Cheo Reo, General Dzu had announced that some of them would be settled in the vicinity.

Luett also was concerned about developing better leadership among the highlanders. The recent elections had brought Ksor Rot (3.20) back to the senate, and Y Bling Buon Krong Pang, the FULRO leader, also had won a senate seat. Y Dhe Adrong (5.10), Rcom Anhot (3.12), Touneh Ton (4.14), Nay Lo, Dinh Van Roi (a Hre), and Peang (a Sedang) all had been elected to the lower house. Luett noted, however, that Peang was a good example of a highlander in a position of responsibility to which he was ill-suited. Luett also was keenly aware that the MDEM needed more trained personnel. He then told how he recently had visited the Normal School at Ban Me Thuot to exhort the students to work and study hard. He warned that any of the male students with long hair and tight "cowboy" clothes would be expelled. Finally, Luett related that he had made several recent visits to see the King of Fire and had ordered a special new house built for the king in Plei Bahrong to lend greater prestige to his role.

Nay Luett had moved into the small villa located on a charming, quiet Saigon street that had been occupied by Paul Nur. There was a large garden in which he had arranged a fish pond, and, because of the large influx of visitors from the highlands, Luett had built a small dormitory in one corner of the garden. In addition to his own family and assorted kinfolk, Luett had two Bru refugee children who were staying with him while they studied. Meals in the small dining room had to be served in shifts and people slept everywhere. The flow of guests, as was noted previously, posed a problem for MDEM personnel, so Luett created a "social expense fund" to provide financial support for officials housing ministry visitors.

Nay Luett generally behaved differently from other ministers, who lived elegantly and rode through Saigon streets in large automobiles driven by chauffeurs. Luett's villa was modestly furnished and workers shared meals at the same table with him. He always insisted on driving the ministry jeep in spite of having a car and chauffeur assigned to him.

According to Touneh Han Tho, during the Nur administration there was little contact with other ministries. Luett and his colleagues tried to establish such relations but it was not easy. They began to invite various ministers to dine with them (usually using the house of an American official). They thus succeeded in forming better working relations with the ministries of Education, Health, and Social Welfare, but not with Agriculture. Nonetheless, by the end of 1971 the ministry was fast becoming a more viable political entity. It now was the center of highlander ethnonationalism.

7 NEW THREATS TO SURVIVAL

The new flush of enthusiasm that had accompanied the appointment of Nay Luett as the Minister for Development of Ethnic Minorities in June 1971 was unfortunately to be short-lived. Bolstered by their spirit of ethnonationalism, the minister and his dedicated group were able to cope with the mounting host of problems during the latter half of the year. Their courage was sorely tested, however, when suddenly, early in 1972, the Communists launched an offensive that soon proved to be more destructive than any previous event of the Vietnam War. PAVN forces equipped with Russian tanks threatened besieged Kontum, prompting massive B-52 bombings in the region north of the city. As the violence spread, large numbers of innocent villagers were trapped in the fighting and died. The flow of refugees became an inundation as whole ethnic groups were swept from their traditional territories. Soon, throughout vast areas of the highlands, villages stood either abandoned or in ruins.

To make matters worse, the offensive came at a time when the American military withdrawal from Vietnam was in full swing, leaving the defense of the uplands to the inadequate, badly trained Vietnamese units. As they watched the crumbling of their hard-won programs and progress, Nay Luett and his colleagues realized painfully that the very existence of the highland people was at stake. The struggle for ethnonationalism was now eclipsed by the struggle for survival.

THE 1972 COMMUNIST OFFENSIVE

On 6 January 1972 I accompanied Nay Luett, Han Tho, and Dorohim (the Cham Director for Highland Reconstruction) to Quang Tri to visit the Bru refugee camps. We also went to Hue, where there were two Bru and

Pacoh refugee settlements amidst the weathered tombs of mandarin families in the vicinity of the large, imperial-style tomb of Emperor Minh Mang. In both areas, the settlements seemed more dismal than usual in a misty, cold rain. According to Father Aimé Mauvais, the French priest living with the Bru and Pacoh at Cua, of the original 7,000 who had settled at Cua, some 6,000 remained.[1] Groups of young men had gone into the Regional Forces and families were moving to Cam Lo or to Hue. At Cua, the crumbling security prevented the Bru from gathering wood and farming in the nearby hills. Father Mauvais lamented the rise in theft among the refugees, a departure from their normal pattern. Nonetheless, in spite of the hardships, the Catholic mission had established a school with two Vietnamese nuns and two Bru giving instruction (and using SIL primers) to between 120 and 170 children. Seven Bru boys had been sent to the Ecole des Frères in Hue, while two girls were attending the Ecole des Religieuses de St. Paul de Chartres in Danang. At a dinner given by the Thua Thien province chief in an elegant nineteenth-century house in Hue, Nay Luett expressed his determination to move all of the Bru and Pacoh farther south to Darlac.

On 2 February 1972 I accompanied Nay Luett, Y Jut Buon To (1.19), Nay Alep (2.29), and Col. Y Pem Knuol to Kontum, where we found a great deal of tension at the approaching Tet holiday and rumors of a new Communist offensive. The airport was filled with civilians leaving the city and, as in 1965, the townspeople were piling sandbags in front of their houses and digging ditches and bunkers. Chinese merchants on the main street were closing their shops and taking their families to Saigon. Men and women of all ages were being armed. Pat Smith had moved her hospital to an old school in Kontum. It resembled a hospital in the American Civil War (her surgery was in a dank storeroom). There were more than the usual number of patients because, Pat explained, the Communists were attacking villages at night, burning the houses. They also had begun to fire on people working in their fields. She reported that Bishop Seitz (who obtained a great deal of information from his priests in the villages) was expecting an attack on Kontum.

On 31 March 1972 the Communists launched an offensive that was to have devastating effects in the highlands. It began with heavy shelling of

---

1. Aimé Mauvais, "Lettre aux bien chers Parents, Amis et Bienfaiteurs" (Dong-Ha, South Vietnam, 1 January 1972).

bases and towns along the Demilitarized Zone. The population in the area, including the Bru and Pacoh refugees, began to flee southward as PAVN units, using tanks, moved rapidly to capture the former American bases at Cam Lo and Gio Linh and the naval base at Cua Viet, north of the town of Dong Ha. By 3 April refugees were streaming out of Dong Ha and Quang Tri along Route 1 into the city of Hue. In Saigon, Nay Luett became furious at the news (his planned resettlement had been scheduled to end on 31 March) and immediately began formulating a new plan to move the Bru and Pacoh quickly. He dispatched Binh (1.29), the young Bru leader (who had married the daughter of Hiu, a Bahnar teacher), to Hue while Luett and a group from the ministry flew to Ban Me Thuot to arrange for settling the refugees in Darlac. He selected a site at Buon Jat, east of Ban Me Thuot, for them, but John Vann, the CORDS Senior Adviser for II Corps, objected to it, insisting that the refugees be resettled in more remote Quang Duc province. Luett refused to change his plan, and this precipitated a conflict between him and Vann. Han Tho and Luett went to Hue to find that around 1,100 highlanders, practically all of them Bru, had gathered. Most of those at Cua (including Anha's four wives and their children, who were reported to have been killed) had been caught in the PAVN sweep. Anha was with the Hue group and he had performed a divination ritual, using a chicken, eggs, and rice. Since the signs were unfavorable, he advised the refugees not to go south. Luett and Binh, however, convinced them it would be better, pointing out that the situation north of Hue was becoming very serious. The Bru finally agreed to leave and began to board the Air America cargo planes arranged by CORDS.

This was the first resettlement project sponsored by the MDEM, and everyone on the staff was concerned that it be successful. The cargo planes shuttled back and forth between Hue and Ban Me Thuot (John Miller of the SIL went with many of the flights). At Buon Jat, Rhadé Truong Son cadre built houses for the refugees (at first the Bru complained that the houses were not "Bru houses" because they were Rhadé-style structures), and Rhadé from surrounding villages received the first Bru refugees with food and drink. Eventually 2,300 Bru and a few Pacoh were settled in Buon Jat.[2]

No sooner had most of the Bru been airlifted from Hue than the defense

---

2. Nguyễn Trắc Dĩ, *Cuộc di dân sắc-tộc Bru từ Quảng Trị vào Darlac* (Bru Minority Resettlement from Quang Tri to Darlac) (Saigon: Bộ Phát-Triển Sắc-tộc Ấn-Hành [Ministry for Development of Ethnic Minorities Publication], 1972), pp. 1–50.

lines north of Quang Tri city collapsed, sending ARVN troops and civilians flooding down Route 1 in panic. Practically all of the population of Dong Ha fled. David Elliott was in the abandoned city and reported seeing some Bru wandering around the silent streets. As the mass of refugees reached Hue, the residents of the city also panicked and began pouring down Route 1 to seek refuge south of the Hai Van pass in Danang. Reserve troops were hurriedly sent from the Saigon area to the northern zone. On 6 April, however, PAVN units captured Loc Ninh and attacked An Loc, north of Saigon. What reserves still remained in the city (including the Ranger battalion guarding the Independence Palace) were rushed up Route 13 to meet this new threat. With these developments, the American Armed Forces Radio in Saigon announced that a squadron of bombers was being sent from Kansas to Vietnam.

When the attacks in the An Loc–Loc Ninh area began, many Stieng villagers were caught in the fighting and large numbers of them went south into An Loc to seek refuge. As the fighting continued, An Loc was surrounded by PAVN forces who subjected the city to constant shelling, assaulting it with tanks several times. The Stieng, like the An Loc residents, were unable to get out. Later, Huynh, a Stieng Protestant pastor, described how he and his kinfolk huddled in bunkers during the two-month siege, only going out to try to get some of the food that was being dropped from aircraft. The stench of decaying corpses lay heavy over the town which daily was being reduced to rubble. Huynh sadly told how many of his relatives died in the stricken city.

According to Ronald Ackerman, a Vietnam Christian Service volunteer who had an agricultural project among the refugees at Dak To north of Kontum, the situation had been calm during the month of March. The villagers had been busy preparing their fields in the valley for planting. On 2 April they paused in their labor when they heard explosions marking the beginning of rocket attacks by PAVN against the strategic ARVN firebases (Charlie, Yankee, and Delta) that had been established by the American army on the ridge dominating the valley and Route 14. As these attacks grew more intense by 7 April, the highlanders left their fields and retreated into their houses. It was as if their past experiences with war had prepared them to sense the beginning of a battle.

Meanwhile, farther south, PAVN forces captured some posts at An Khe, cutting Route 19 between Pleiku and the coast. On 17 April, a PAVN unit attacked what was now called "rocket ridge," overrunning Firebase Charlie and scattering its 500 defenders. Firebases Yankee and Delta were immediately abandoned. Two days later, on 19 April, PAVN units attacked the former CIDG Dak Pek camp. At a press conference held in Pleiku on 22 April, John Vann reported that the Communists had committed two divisions—the 2d and 320th—in addition to two independent regiments of infantrymen, an artillery regiment, and a sapper regiment to an offensive in the highlands that would focus on the towns of Kontum and Pleiku as well as on Binh Dinh province.[3]

Suddenly on the morning of 24 April PAVN tanks rolled into the compound of the forward headquarters of the ARVN 22d Division at Tan Canh as other units attacked nearby Dak To. The ARVN troops made no effort to defend the post and fled at the sight of the tanks. Not long after, American bombers began to swoop over the Dak To valley as helicopters attempted to evacuate the advisers. (One helicopter with six advisers was shot down.) Soldiers from the 22d Division, mixed with civilians, began heading southward on Route 14 in an attempt to reach Kontum. As they carried the news that Dak To and Tan Canh had fallen, people in villages along Route 14 began to join the exodus. When they reached Kontum, fear that the PAVN tanks would assault the city had already spread through

3. Peter Arnett, "Highlands Staggering Under NVA Assault," *Associated Press*, 26 April 1972; Peter Osnos, "Kontum Waits for Ax to Fall," *Washington Post*, 22 April 1972.

Dr. Pat Smith in her temporary hospital in Kontum

the town. People with automobiles began packing them to go south to Pleiku. As the PAVN units began to move down Route 14, B-52 bombings rocked the Dak To valley, sending highlanders either into the surrounding forests or down Route 14 with the swelling tide of refugees. In Kontum, more took to the road south, but the flow ceased abruptly when the PAVN 95 B Regiment occupied the Mount Pao pass, cutting the only means of escape south from the city on Route 14.

Busy trying to evacuate his seminarians, Bishop Seitz ordered Pat Smith to close her hospital. She objected, pointing out that most of the patients could not be moved. Dominic d'Antonio, the able CORDS representative, radioed Nhatrang for an aircraft to take some of the patients out. He called for a helicopter for Pat, her two adopted Bahnar sons (whose parents had been killed in a Communist attack on their village), and her American staff. It was decided to leave the hospital in the hands of the Bahnar nuns, Sister Gabrielle and Sister Vincent, and Pat's Jarai assistant Scotty, all of whom insisted on remaining. By this time the Communists had begun to shell Kontum and the airstrip from the surrounding hills. When Pat and her group arrived at the airstrip, the scene was chaotic. Civilians of all descriptions and soldiers were trying to force their way onto every aircraft

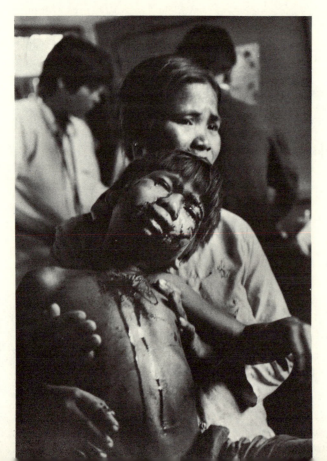

A Bahnar boy with fragment wounds at Pat Smith's hospital

landing. There were huge, lumbering C-130s and C-123s filled with troop replacements, ammunition, and other cargo, helicopters bringing troops, and even Air Vietnam DC-3s (the province chief's wife was selling tickets at vastly inflated prices). As they taxied to a halt, the mob rushed forward, pushing the elderly and children to the ground. The VNAF helicopter pilots were trying to charge those getting on board, and VNAF door gunners pushed soldiers to the tarmac so that they could haul their motor-cycles (probably stolen) on instead. Pat and her group scrambled on a helicopter along with some soldiers who forced their way on board—and sometime during the flight stole her bag containing the boys' adoption papers. Shells fell on the field, and two C-130s filled with ammunition were struck, killing many of the refugees (including some of Bishop Seitz's seminarians). The Air America C-47 sent to pick up Pat's patients quickly filled up, but when it arrived in Nhatrang the pilot found that most of his passengers were soldiers who had stripped off their uniforms.

As the B-52 raids increased north of Kontum, whole ethnic groups abandoned their traditional territories as Jeh, Sedang, Halang, Jarai Arap, Rengao, and Bahnar fled. Kek, a young Sedang leader from Kon Horing, a large village on Route 14 north of Kontum, related that most of the villagers packed what they could in their backbaskets and went into the forest as the B-52s began bombing in the vicinity. As he was leaving he encountered a large group of Vietnamese civilians from Dak To coming into the village. They told him that they had been on Route 14 going to Kontum but that PAVN tanks blocked the road and the soldiers told them to return to Dak To. They were frightened and tired, so they were going to remain in Kon Horing. Kek went into the forest as the Vietnamese men, women, and children moved into some of the abandoned houses. That evening the Sedang refugees heard ear-splitting explosions from B-52 bombs from the direction of Kon Horing. The following day Kek and some of the men went back into the village to find it completely de-molished, and everywhere there were mangled bodies of the Vietnamese refugees. No one appeared to have survived.

In Kontum, the confusion continued as evacuation helicopters began to land in a sports stadium near the center of the town. When it became apparent, however, that the PAVN forces were not going to attack the city at that time, the panic began to subside somewhat. Townspeople returned to their houses as great masses of refugees—most of them highlanders—continued to flood into Kontum. The schools and churches were now jammed with Jarai Arap, Bahnar, Sedang, Jeh, Rengao, and Halang refugees. The Kontum Mission was rapidly depleting its stores of rice to keep them fed.

At the beginning of May the situation worsened as shells and rockets began to rain down on the center of the town with a new intensity, immediately raising fears of a Communist assault on Kontum. Then, according to Dominic d'Antonio, when news spread that the American military advisers were evacuating the MACV compound on the northern edge of Kontum close to Route 14, panic again seized everyone. People bolted from their houses and headed for the airport and the sports stadium. At the province hospital, the few remaining staff fled, leaving the patients on their beds (their kinfolk tried to drag them to the airstrip). Again chaos reigned at the airstrip and in the sports stadium as both soldiers and civilians mobbed the few aircraft that landed. Clutching a few belongings, they looked frantically to the skies in the hope of escaping the besieged town. A Buddhist leader told d'Antonio that he was ready to lead a group of 10,000 desperate followers down Route 14 on foot carrying their religious flags.

Vietnamese soldiers burst into the MACV compound before the last Americans had boarded their helicopters. (They had to brandish their weapons to complete their evacuation.) The soldiers ran around the abandoned buildings looting hi-fi sets and other possessions left behind. They drank all of the alcohol in the abandoned clubs, then vomited everywhere and went on a rampage of destruction, smashing everything in sight. As the last of Kontum's officials and police left, soldiers began looting the downtown and shuttered houses. Later, Hiu (1.16) described how the soldiers came to Kon Rohai, as they did to all neighboring Bahnar villages, and pushed their way into his house, taking all of the family belongings and money. They killed fifteen head of cattle.

Later I found a handful of Kontum residents who had not left during those chaotic days. They explained that they were poor people with no money and they had no kinfolk or friends in places like Nhatrang, where most refugees went. "We are poor, and no one would take care of us," one elderly man said. He added, "Here in Kontum at least we have houses and small gardens." He and others described how they stayed in their bunkers, and when a semblance of order returned they sold some of their vegetables to the soldiers.

Meanwhile the panic had spread to Pleiku, sending an estimated 80 percent of the population down Route 19 to Qui Nhon or down Route 21 to Nhatrang. They moved out in every kind of vehicle, including many army trucks the drivers of which charged a high fee. Chinese merchants were hiring these trucks to carry all of their merchandise and household goods down to the coast. It was reported that 50 percent of the Vietnamese Regional Forces abandoned their weapons to flee with their families. Most of the civil servants and police left, and only one doctor remained at the province hospital.

In Saigon by early May there was a deepening gloom and sense of unease at the flow of bad news from Kontum, Quang Tri, and An Loc. In Quang Tri the ARVN 3d Infantry and the elite Ranger and Marine units had fled after burning the city when PAVN units with PT 76 tanks began to enter. Almost the entire population had fled to Hue and then to Danang, which was now jammed with refugees. But the attention of the Saigonese was focused more intently on An Loc, where new fighting was erupting along Route 13 within fifty kilometers of the capital. Saigon was swept with rumors that the Communist forces were preparing to attack the city or subject it to massive rocket and artillery barrages. Everyone was talking about a large force of U.S. Marines standing by on Seventh Fleet ships off the coast preparing to land in Vietnam. This was not true. In fact, the American military withdrawal was continuing at an unabated pace. (The 30 April figure of 44,748 remaining American military diminished to 37,129 by the end of May.)[4]

Thieu proclaimed martial law and asked the National Assembly for emergency powers. A stringent curfew was set for Saigon as the university and other institutions of higher learning closed. The draft age was changed to make men between the ages of seventeen and forty-three subject to call. Prices were rising, and there was a rush for basic foods. All bars, nightclubs, and other places of amusement were darkened. Nonetheless, the American Women's Association announced that it would hold a fashion show (with a "Far East" theme) in the Champs Elysée Room on the top of the Hotel Caravelle, and at the Saigon city hall there was an exhibition of Dada art.

At the MDEM, the staff worked feverishly on plans to remove the growing number (now estimated at around 15,000) of highlanders caught in the city of Kontum. Nay Alep (2.29) reported that he was unable to obtain any aircraft to take them out, prompting Nay Luett on 14 May to

---

4. Office of the Deputy Chief of Staff for Personnel, *Strength of the Army*, 3 parts (Washington, Headquarters, Department of the Army, 1972), part 1, p. 24.

Sedang and Bahnar refugees from Kontum arrive in Pleiku during the 1972 offensive

consult with John Vann. Vann informed him that he had already taken 20,000 Vietnamese out of Kontum and could do nothing for the high-landers because the American senior province adviser (a colonel) and the Vietnamese province chief claimed that the highlanders did not want to leave Kontum. The province chief was going to organize them to defend the city against an expected PAVN assault. Furious at this, Luett went to Kontum where he was greeted by Jeh, Halang, Sedang, Rengao, Bahnar, and Jarai Arap refugees who told him they were anxious to leave because of the heavy fighting and shelling. Luett returned to Pleiku for a confron-tation with Vann. Luett related to me that he had told Vann that he , Luett, was not afraid of Vann, Abrams, Bunker, or Nixon. He said to Vann, "I will praise you for the good you do and condemn you for the bad." Afterward Vann and General Nguyen Van Toan, the II Corps command-ing officer (whose role in a cinnamon scandal in Quang Ngai province had earned him the name "the Cinnamon General"), arranged for aircraft to take the highlanders to Pleiku. Unlike the Vietnamese (who stormed the planes and helicopters), the highlanders lined up in an orderly fashion, putting the elderly and children on the aircraft first. By 17 May some 8,000 highlanders had been airlifted from Kontum to Pleiku.

The following day I went to Pleiku with Nay Luett, K'Briuh, and some USAID officials. Chinook cargo helicopters were shuttling between Kontum and Pleiku and the streams of highlanders were being moved into old military compounds and schools. Since there was the possibility of a Communist assault on Pleiku, Luett told the CORDS officials that he wanted the refugees moved to Ban Me Thuot. The Americans responded that there were no aircraft available because the Communists had blown up the large ammunition dump near the airstrip and all of the planes were needed to fly in new supplies. We visited the refugee centers and it was clear that they soon would be inadequate. The buildings already were filled and there was not much space left for more tents. Firewood was lacking, and water was a problem because the rains had not yet begun. To make matters worse, the Pleiku city water trucks had gone to the coast with the exodus of the population. ARVN water trucks would only serve the army. Most of the refugees had fled their villages so rapidly that they were able to take very few personal possessions so that many lacked blankets, buckets, and sleeping mats. Fortunately the ethnic groups tended to remain together as did village groups, so there was cohesion and leadership, both of which made it easier to organize refugee relief.

At the first compound, a dilapidated former ammunitions dump, I met Kek, the Sedang leader (who related the story of the bombing of Kon Horing). Pat Cohen's Jeh linguistic informant also was there with his family. In the second center—a school—I encountered Hiu and his family. They had just arrived from Kontum with what few belongings they had left after the ARVN looting. They seemed dazed, and Hiu was very bitter. Tracy Atwood and Irv Hamberger were working with a group of young highland leaders, including Nay Alep and Y Du Eban (3.21), to provide rice for the refugees. The Jarai Son Thon Cadre (as the Truong Son was now called) also were assisting, pitching tents and distributing blankets.

Normally bustling Pleiku seemed strangely quiet. Most houses and shops were shuttered and locked. There were soldiers wandering around the center of town, which we were advised to avoid because of lack of order and rampant thievery. (Hamberger had had three watches pulled from his wrists while driving with the window open.) Atwood related that when panic struck Pleiku and the flight began, prices soared. In the market, a woman quoting a vastly inflated price for a sack of rice was shot in the head by an angry soldier. Soldiers and civilians who remained in Pleiku were breaking into houses to squat in them. Some of the remaining American military installations were locked and guarded after 2,300 of the 2,800 military personnel in Pleiku were evacuated as the situation in Kontum worsened.

Pat Smith had been given a new wing of the province hospital, where with the assistance of Ronald Ackerman and Bill Rose of the Vietnam Christian Service and Tom Coles, a former Special Forces medic who had been organizing a Village Health Program in Kontum, she was setting up her medical practice. Some of her patients were being airlifted from Kontum, and she already was treating some of the refugees.

At the urging of Atwood and Hamberger, I went to see Vann about trying to obtain some cargo planes to fly highland refugees south to Ban Me Thuot. In his wood-paneled office on the hill where the II Corps headquarters was located, Vann seemed agitated and defensive concerning his position regarding the highlanders in Kontum city. He claimed to have received fifteen reports from the Vietnamese province chief saying that the highland refugees preferred to remain in Kontum. Furthermore, because of an impending attack on Kontum, he could not be bothered with refugees. I replied that, as the senior adviser in II Corps, he was responsible for them. Besides, I added, many of them were refugees because of the B-52 bombings which he, Vann, had ordered. He replied that there were no available aircraft but that there was a convoy of trucks going to Ban Me Thuot in the morning and the refugees could go on the convoy.

Vann then went into an explanation of his use of the B-52s. The Communists, he said, had lost the war at Tet. Now they were resorting to conventional warfare using tanks, and the B-52s were the only means to deal with such a strategy. He stated that "Kontum will break the back of the North Vietnamese army," adding that "in six months there will be no more North Vietnamese army left." Vann asserted that he intended achieving his goal through the B-52s, and when I objected, noting that he had no intelligence on the ground north of Kontum, he retorted that he gained the information on Communist positions by sending helicopter gunships into the area. At night the gunships had spotlights to "draw fire" from the PAVN, thus revealing their positions. Vann would then quickly plot a "box" (a one-by-two-kilometer zone) that the B-52s would saturate with bombs. He claimed to have seen North Vietnamese troops dead and

Sedang and Bahnar refugees on a convoy from Pleiku to Ban Me Thuot during the 1972 offensive

wounded among the craters following some of the raids—so he called in napalm on them "to put them out of their misery." All of this was necessary, he continued, because the Vietnamese ground forces in the highlands were insufficient and inadequate to cope with the situation. I pointed out that, beginning with the FULRO revolt, the highland leaders had repeatedly asked for their own force to defend the uplands, because they were convinced that the lowland Vietnamese could never fight for what they considered an alien region. Vann, however, reflected the view common to the American leaders in Vietnam that it was hopeless to expect the Vietnamese government to ever agree to such a plan.

Since the refugees in the ammunition dump were living under the worst conditions, it was agreed that they would be the ones to leave on the convoy. The following morning, as we made preparations, it was clear that the major problem was the lack of water. (Pat pointed out that the highlanders dehydrate rapidly, causing death.) Atwood and I went to Lake Tenneung—in the waters of which, according to Jarai legend, a Cham army had once been drowned—north of Pleiku, but we found that the only city water pump was not working. Many of the highland refugees were there fetching water, but they were afraid to bathe in the sacred lake. We returned to the compound, where the refugees reluctantly were preparing to leave (they feared going farther from their villages) and some of the Catholics knelt to say their rosaries. Nay Luett came to assure them that when the situation improved the MDEM would transport them back to their villages. Meanwhile I went out on the road and stopped two ARVN water trucks, promising the drivers money if they would deliver water to the compound. Just as the convoy arrived, the two water trucks careened into the compound with plenty of water for all. (Kek had told the refugees to get out all their containers.)

Atwood went with the convoy, which would take eight hours on insecure Route 14 to reach Ban Me Thuot. Nay Alep and I took a helicopter (we flew over the convoy and the children waved at us) to Ban Me Thuot to make preparations. None of the panic in Kontum and Pleiku had affected Ban Me Thuot, which seemed almost surprisingly normal. We alerted the province chief; Y Jut Buon To, the MDEM representative; the Protestant Mission; and the Catholic sisters. The province chief ordered the Dam San (former Truong Son) camp just east of Ban Me Thuot (near a clear stream and a thick forest) to be prepared. When the convoy arrived, the hot, dusty, and sick (from the jiggling over the bad road bed) refugees got off the trucks to receive hot food, water, and relief goods from the province chief and his family, the Boy Scouts, the Catholic sisters, the Vietnam Christian Service, and Betty Mitchell of the Christian and Missionary Alliance (whose husband Archie had been captured at the leprosarium in 1962). Y Jut had rounded up some young highlanders who were there to help the refugees get settled in the buildings. Some of the refugees immediately went to bathe in the stream, while many of the women gathered wild greens and men began to chop wood for fires and fish traps. The different ethnic groups separated into the various buildings.

When Atwood and I returned very early the following morning, the refugees were busy getting settled. Some were roasting fish they had caught in the stream, and others were foraging in the nearby woods. Kek said that they were happy to be away from the bombs and shooting. There had been some grumbling, however, about having the Halang in the camp because they had the reputation of having powerful sorcery and witchcraft. Several Bahnar claimed that they had seen a disembodied head floating through the night. I suggested to Kek that he organize a ritual to cope with such a phenomenon because there was no possibility of moving the Halang out of the camp. As we walked through the camp, we came upon an elderly woman with sagging breasts, cataracts on both eyes, wearing a dusty skirt. She looked up and smiled as she churned the earth with a hoe to plant kernels of corn.

In Saigon, at the MDEM, Han Tho reported that fighting in other areas was generating additional highlander refugees. At Cheo Reo there were around 5,000, and a crowd of 3,000 Stieng had converged on the Long Thanh Orphanage close to the sprawling, empty Long Binh American military base outside of Saigon. Some 1,600 Chrau-speaking people had moved into Phuoc Le (Baria) east of Saigon. I got in touch with Mildred Colantonio and Marilyn Tank of the American Women's Association, and they immediately made plans for refugee relief for the highlanders. They were told by an official at the Ministry for Social Welfare that the minister would be happy to have them provide relief for the highlanders because he intended devoting the ministry's efforts to the Vietnamese in Danang and Hue. The two ladies efficiently collected clothes, mats, plastic buckets, canned milk, dried fish, and rice, booking Air America cargo planes to deliver all of it to the highlands. I accompanied most of the flights to see that the goods got to the refugees and were not delivered to the province warehouse (where they would have been sold out the back door). The first flight, on 24 May, went to Pleiku, where Atwood and Hamberger had arranged for a group of young (pro-FULRO) highlanders to organize distribution in the refugee centers. The task was made easier by the fact that those from the same village and ethnic group tended to remain together, so they had some group structure with leadership. They worked out an equitable distribution of the available goods (e.g., if a family did not receive a bucket, it got more sleeping mats). In typical highlander fashion, they also shared needed goods.

When the cargo plane arrived in Pleiku, Atwood informed us that Kontum was under attack by the PAVN. The defense of the city was in the hands of some elements of the 23d Division and some 2,000 highlanders who had been organized into a defense force. The attack had begun with heavy artillery shelling followed by sapper ground assaults on the western portion of the city where Pat Smith's hospital and the Kontum Mission headquarters were located. The highland refugees still in Kontum huddled in church compounds and schools while the fighting raged around them. Sister Gabrielle related later that some PAVN troops came into the hospital looking for Americans, but she told them that there were only poor, sick people in the wards and asked them to leave. They did leave, but soon thereafter the helicopter gunships began to swoop over the building firing rockets. Artillery shells burst nearby as the nuns and Scotty got all of the patients under their beds. Heavy fighting took place all around the hospital. Sister Gabrielle worked in the surgery, operating on wounded civilians and soldiers who were carried into the hospital. When the fighting reached its peak, she and the others remained on the floor. "We all prayed very hard," she said, "and God heard us." While every building in the vicinity was either badly damaged (as was the Mission headquarters) or totally demolished, the hospital was almost untouched.

On 27 May I went to Ban Me Thuot with Nay Luett and Touneh Han Tho. We were met by Y Dhuat Nie Kdam, Y Jut Buon To, and other Rhadé leaders. All of us went to Buon Pan Lam to pay our respects to Y Blieng Hmok, whose son had just been killed by some Vietnamese soldiers. That evening all of the highland leaders gathered in the village to discuss the organization of a highland military force. The highland leaders were very concerned about the failure of ARVN to mount an effective defense of the highlands, resulting in vast disruption and destruction because of the reliance on B-52s. Luett also was angry at the conversion of the CIDG camps into ARVN Ranger posts and what he considered the misuse of highland troops. Earlier in May the highland troops at Ben Het, northwest of Kontum, had revolted against their Vietnamese officers just as a PAVN assault on the post was about to begin. (They nonetheless fought well, withstanding two ground attacks and knocking out two tanks.) Also, as the siege of Kontum developed, General Nguyen Van Toan, the II Corps commander, ordered highlanders to be sent from some of the border (former CIDG) camps to open Route 14 between Pleiku and Kontum. The PAVN was well installed at the Mount Pao pass with artillery, and the highlanders were sent up the road without any armored protection or air support. Some of their units lost as many as 50 percent of the men, and many began to desert. One senior American adviser in Pleiku described it as a "meat-grinder operation." On 22 May, just before the PAVN attack on Kontum, Nay Luett had agreed with the prime minister to organize 2,000 highlanders in Kontum into a defense force, but ARVN would only give each of them a carbine and eighty rounds of ammunition.

On 1 June 1972 Vann met with the press in Pleiku and announced that the PAVN, which still held two military compounds on the northern edge of Kontum, had lost "phase one" of their campaign. He emphasized the importance of American air support in turning the tide of battle against PAVN. In addition to B-52s, there also were U.S. Navy planes that dropped "smart bombs" (with television nose cameras for accuracy). Vann was making daily trips from Pleiku to Kontum in his helicopter to direct operations. On 9 June the helicopter crashed, and everyone on board was killed. Soon after, the PAVN units withdrew from Kontum.

In early June the number of highlander refugees continued to increase. There were still an estimated 10,000 in Kontum, 10,000 in Pleiku, 7,000 in Ban Me Thuot, and 8,000 in Cheo Reo and Phu Tuc. Refugees were even converging on some of the small posts. At Ben Het, for example, it was reported that a French priest, Father Beysselance, led 136 Sedang villagers (many of them wounded) into the post after their village had been attacked by PAVN.[5] Nay Luett reported that there were 1,000 Jarai refugees outside the Duc Co post in Pleiku province. In addition, there were an unreported number of highlanders who had taken refuge in the forests and the more remote parts of the mountains.

Mrs. Tank and Mrs. Colantonio continued to provide refugee supplies. I accompanied the flights. In Pleiku, Atwood and Hamberger saw to the distribution of the goods and, at Cheo Reo, Ed Sprague and Rcom Ali made sure that the refugees in more outlying areas received some of the supplies. Nay Luett accompanied one shipment to Ban Me Thuot, helping with the distribution. Now with the Kontum airstrip open, we brought supplies to the shattered town (which was still being shelled), and Dominic d'Antonio provided trucks to carry goods to the crowded school yards and church compounds. One planeload was delivered to Pat Smith's hospital where food was badly needed. In the rain, Kontum had a dismal air. The whole northwestern portion of the town was in ruins, and buildings around the market were damaged from the shelling. There were gaping holes in the Kontum Mission headquarters, and the MACV compound, which once reflected military order, was now in shambles. The Communists had their cannons in the nearby hills, and they would fire volleys of shells into the town. Everyone could hear the guns fire and would wait to hear where the shells were landing before falling to the ground (if the explosions were close) or going about their business (if they were far away). At the Bach Dang restaurant, people paused in the midst of their

5. "Priest Leads 136 to Safety," *Associated Press*, 7 June 1972.

Young Bahnar, former
soldiers, in Kontum
(1972)

meal when a volley was heard. Pat Smith admitted that when she was in
surgery the sounds of the guns firing made her a bit nervous (many of the
shells fell in the vicinity of the hospital).

During the fighting in Kontum the 23d Division set up a command post
in Pat's hospital outside of town. It had been well maintained after she was
forced to move into the school in the city following the Tet Offensive. Pat
had proudly showed me her new kitchen and a thriving garden being
tended by highlanders. She also had a fine stock of cattle and pigs, and
masses of chickens. The hospital soon would be almost self-sufficient in
food. Claiming that Pat was anti-Vietnamese, the ARVN officers encouraged their troops to loot the hospital buildings and smash what they
could not take, such as the x-ray machines and surgical lamps. They killed
all of the animals and destroyed the gardens, after which they put mines in
them.

For most of the highlanders the refugee camps were a new and somewhat bewildering experience. In normal times the highlanders are self-
sufficient people who satisfy all of their own basic needs. With only a few
exceptions, in the camps they had no land to farm, no streams to fish, and
no forests to supply them with wood, bamboo, and rattan for artifacts.
They were forced to depend on outside agencies for almost everything
from rice to plastic mats for sleeping. Nonetheless, whenever possible they
planted small gardens among the barbed wire surrounding the camps.

They also walked long distances for firewood and wild fruits and vegetables. The Jarai Arap women had carried their shuttles in their backbaskets when they fled their homes, and they kept busy weaving. They wove particularly interesting cloth with a mixture of traditional and innovative motifs. The latter were based on the contemporary situation. As one woman put it, "We weave what we see around us." Their cloths, in effect, were chronicles, and in mid-1972 they were depicting various kinds of helicopters (Chinooks, Huey gunships, and the bubble-like Kayuse), jet fighters, army trucks, bombs, strange people the women identified as "Americans," and a scene that they said was "a group of Jarai waiting to get on helicopters" (they used a variation of the Vietnamese word for helicopter). One woman found a U.S. Navy mail order catalogue from which she reproduced a row of Japanese wrist watches. Another woman wove the names "Judy" and "U.S. Army" without having any idea what they meant, but she explained that she "likes the shape." [6]

During this time the siege at An Loc continued. Early in June word spread through the ruined town that Route 13 was open. Around 10,000 desperate Vietnamese and Stieng civilians emerged from their bunkers and, picking their way through the rubble and the burned vehicles, moved in a mass down the road. Some were elderly, and there were many women with small children and babies. Some young boys and girls whose parents had been killed carried their small siblings strapped to their backs. All of them were caked with red dirt. Ignoring the continuing fighting, they walked to Tan Khai, eleven kilometers to the south, where they were stopped temporarily by PAVN troops. Tired and hungry, they pushed on to Phu Cuong (Thudaumot) where there were refugee centers.

On 5 June I encountered a large group of Stieng fending their way through the tangle of motorcycles, pedicabs, and cars in central Saigon.

---

6. Dr. Mattiebelle Gittinger, Research Associate for Southeast Asian Textiles at the Textile Museum, Washington, D.C., did the following analysis of a piece of Jarai Arap cloth.

This is an all cotton textile length which has a tubular form created by continuous warp elements. Its warp-faced plain weave structure contains narrow warp stripes of commercially spun and brightly dyed yarns which alternate with broad bands of black, handspun yarns. Additional colored stripes concentrate about two decorative bands on one edge of the cloth. The commercial yarns of the warp are Z-spun 2-plied-S and the handspun are single Z-spun elements. Black Z-spun 2-plied-S yarns also make up the weft. The outermost decorative band shows a white on black diamond pattern that is created by white yarns interlacing in variable lengths in the manner of 2/2 diamond twill. A second decorative stripe shows multicolored figures on a white ground. These designs are paired supplementary wefts which are continuous through the width of the white band and laid in with the ground weft when not in use. 20 warp/cm. 9 weft/cm. 396 × 68 cm.

They had walked ninety kilometers from the vicinity of An Loc over the fields, avoiding embattled Route 13, to Saigon. They were tired and without money, but the men clutched their machetes. I guided them to the MDEM, where Touneh Han Tho quickly got them food and drink. They probably were the first highland refugees to enter Saigon on foot. Most of the Stieng refugees gathered at Long Thanh, where there now were an estimated 3,500. We organized a movement of trucks to transport goods gathered by Mrs. Colantonio and Mrs. Tank. Pastor Huynh (who had been in An Loc during the siege) directed the distribution. Martine Piat, the French professor of linguistics (Mon Khmer languages were her specialty), went to Long Thanh each day to help the Vietnamese Catholic sisters with a feeding program for the Stieng children.

NEW POLITICAL DEVELOPMENTS

The offensive provoked some new political developments that included the highlanders. Jolted by the unfavorable turn of military events, many of the existing parties and movements rallied to form new political blocs. Soon the blocs were consolidated into a new front whose purpose was "to oppose Communist aggression." On 17 May 1972 representatives of the central and northern highlands, along with Cham delegates, met at a conference in Nay Luett's Saigon residence. The highland leaders included Nay Luett, Senator Ksor Rot (3.20), and Lower House members Touneh Ton (4.14), Rcom Anhot (3.12), Peang, Nay Lo, and Dinh Van Roi (Hre). It also included Ethnic Minorities Council members Touprong Hiou (4.4), Toplui Pierre K'Briuh (4.11), Touneh Han Tho (4.2), Y Mo Eban (5.7), Hiup (1.20), and Ya Yu Sahau. Also included for the first time was a Katu. He was Kithem, who had been born around 1915 in the village of Pi Karong in Quang Nam province. His mother's father had been designated chief of the area by the Vietnamese, and when he died the mother's brother was given the same role by the French. After he too died, Kithem assumed the position. The Katu were forced to do fifteen days of corvée each year, much of it working on the construction of Route 14 through their area. Kithem was coerced into joining the French army, remaining in service for nine years. During that time the Japanese took over, and they used the Katu as guides and laborers. After the Japanese departed, the Viet Minh came to "talk against the French," but they fled into the more remote areas when the French returned. Kithem described how in recent years the area from An Diem to Ben Giang had been subject to heavy bombing. He lost several houses and his precious jars. There had been spraying also, making it impossible to farm in some places. As chief, Kithem resolved conflicts, organized hunting groups, restrained "blood raids" conducted to get victims for human sacrifices), and oversaw trade with the Vietnamese (the Katu trade chickens, ducks, rice, honey, betel leaves, and areca nuts for salt, metal, bush knives, axes, woven mats, cloth, crocks, and alcohol jars).

At this meeting, the minority leaders discussed the effects of the offensive. They all agreed it was important to evacuate all of the highland refugees from the "combat zone." The subject of the refugees was discussed at length, and the Nungs present promised that their organization would give aid to the highland refugees (they later sent a shipment of relief goods to Ban Me Thuot).

Early in June the highlanders, Cham, and northern highland leaders formed the Ethnic Minorities Bloc, which joined other political blocs in the People's Front to Oppose Communist Aggression. Ksor Rot was named chairman of the minorities' bloc, and other highlanders named above assumed various roles. The bloc obtained the use of a villa (that had been occupied by Daniel Ellsberg) near the Independence Palace as its headquarters. On 16 July the bloc held a conference and decided to send a delegation to President Thieu to inquire about the government's position regarding the Paris Peace talks, which had just been resumed on 13 July. The palace discouraged such a visit. As the effects of the offensive wore off, however, the activities of the minorities' bloc became infrequent and within several months the organization ceased to function.

Although this bloc, like the earlier political party for highlanders, was relatively short-lived, the experience of participating in national politics prompted some of the highland leaders to search for a common name for themselves. Although they often referred to themselves (even when speaking English) as the Montagnards, they did not want to use a French term. Y Bling Buon Krong Pang, for some unknown reason, suggested the term "Hinterlandois." The term "Dega" meaning "Sons of the Mountains" was considered but was adjudged too closely identified with FULRO. The Jarai expression "Ana Chu," also meaning "Sons of the Mountains," was more widely favored. Han Tho noted, however, that the leaders felt there was not sufficient agreement to settle on a name at this time.

Early in June 1972 Thieu succeeded in forcing the National Assembly to grant him "special powers," i.e., almost unlimited powers, for six months. On 8 July Thieu announced that the draft exemption for ethnic minorities was abolished. Nay Luett was furious, explaining that this had been done without any consultation with minority leaders. Thieu had used trickery to do this. According to Luett, at the palace there were two types of high-level meetings—the cabinet meetings, held in the presence of the prime minister, and the ministers' meeting, presided over by the president. At the cabinet meeting early in June the matter of drafting ethnic minorities was brought up, but it was decided that such a conscription was not necessary. Subsequently, at the minister's meeting (to which Nay Luett was not invited), it was agreed that the minorities would be subject to the draft. Thieu then called Luett to the palace and explained that, although this decision had been made, no minority men would be drafted. Luett pointed out when he related this that, at that very moment, ARVN and police were going into highland villages to round up young men for the army. Y Thih Eban reported that villages in the vicinity of Ban Me Thuot had organized a warning system so that when ARVN or the police approached a village all of the young men could flee into the forest. Nay Luett pointed out to the Minister of Defense at a cabinet meeting that a great many young highlanders already were serving in the armed forces, and young men were needed in the villages to help protect them and aid in economic development.

A great cloud of gloom descended at the MDEM. This development represented another manifestation of the government's indifference to the plight of the highland people. It raised more doubts in the minds of the highland leaders as to whether or not they would be able to survive and maintain their ethnic identity. In mid-August I had a long discussion with Nay Luett about the situation. He reported that there were estimated to be around 150,000 highlanders in refugee camps, and he figured that since 1965 some 200,000 highland people (both civilians and military personnel) had died because of the war. At least 85 percent of the highland villages had, for one reason or another, been displaced. (It was noted previously that, prior to the 1972 offensive, we had estimated 65 percent.) Whole ethnic groups, such as the Bru, Pacoh, Katu, Jeh, Halang, and Sedang, had been forced to abandon their traditional territories. The Bru well illustrated the effect of the war on one group; whereas in 1965 we had estimated around 40,000 Bru (see appendix A), only around 7,000 had been accounted for at Cua and Cam Lo, and half that number had been flown to Darlac. Where the others were was anybody's guess. Not one Bru village remained in place and not one Bru house remained intact; there were reports that Bru refugees in Laos were living in underground shelters.

Nay Luett pointed out that while the highland people were being decimated by the war, the number of Vietnamese in the highlands had been increasing. The ministry estimated that in Kontum, Pleiku, Phu Bon, Darlac, Tuyen Duc, Lam Dong, and Quang Duc provinces there were 448,349 Vietnamese—a figure vastly greater than the 30,000 Vietnamese population reported for that same territory in 1953.[7] Should the present situation continue, Luett added, the highland people will be pushed off their land. Ironically, soon after, while I was having lunch with Minister of the Economy Pham Kim Ngoc, he remarked concerning my interest in the highlanders, "You have bet on the wrong horse, because we Vietnamese are going to overwhelm those people."

Luett also noted that education in the highlands, which already was inadequate, was now suffering even more.[8] Many schools were destroyed and teachers had fled many areas, dealing primary education a severe blow. There also was too little progress in higher education. In 1967 there had been only two highland students with the second baccalaureate and by mid-1972 there were sixteen. Only two, however, had been admitted to the Faculty of Letters and two to the Faculty of Law. None was accepted in the Medical School; Y Thih Eban's son, Y Luinh Nie Hrah, was qualified, but he was rejected.

Nay Luett pointed out that another cause for concern was the withdrawal of American military forces. On 14 August, the 3d Battalion of the 21st Infantry Division, the last American maneuver battalion, departed.[9] He then outlined a scheme that he and his colleagues had devised to enable the remaining highlanders to survive. He planned to move all of the highland population into seven provinces (Kontum, Pleiku, Phu Bon, Darlac, Quang Duc, Lam Dong, and Tuyen Duc). This would, in effect,

7. *Annuaire des etats-associés: Cambodge, Laos, Vietnam, 1953* (Paris: Editions Diloutremer et Havas, 1953), p. 356.

8. Pre-offensive figures supplied by the MDEM indicated that in seven highland provinces (Kontum, Pleiku, Phu Bon, Darlac, Quang Duc, Lam Dong, and Tuyen Duc [excluding Dalat]) there was a primary school enrollment of 39,405 or an estimated 56.5 percent of the school-age population (figured at 16 percent of the total population), comparing favorably with the relatively poor lowland province of Quang Ngai, which had a percentage of 36.2, but not with the national percentage of 83.1.

9. "Last U.S. Maneuver Battalion in Vietnam Lowers Its Colors," *United Press International*, 14 August 1972.

Halang villagers running to an evacuation helicopter during the siege of Ben Het in August 1972

group all of the highlanders in a more restricted area for survival. An important part of the plan was that they would begin organizing their own military force of 50,000 men to protect this region. He stated, "This is the only way we can survive as a people." I agreed, but I had the feeling that there was something desperate about the plan.

PERCEIVED EFFECTS OF HERBICIDES USED IN THE HIGHLANDS

In October 1972 I offered to participate in a study being conducted by the National Academy of Sciences on the effects of herbicides used by the Americans in Vietnam (the details of my research are summarized in appendix C). During the chaotic movement of refugees as a result of the offensive, I had encountered some from areas that had been sprayed, and I was to collect information for the study. The method I selected was to locate villagers who had witnessed the spraying and have them relate their perceptions to me. Since they live close to nature, the highlanders readily detect any changes in the surrounding physical ecology. Normally, such changes are much discussed among the villagers in the light of their past experiences. The cause of a given change in the physical ecology may be defined as physical (they can identify numerous kinds of blights) or occult (such as the wrath of the spirits). In the latter case, the judgment is usually left to the older, wiser members of the group. The observations of these individuals normally become knowledge shared with all members of the community.

The characteristics of the highlanders interviewed are listed in appendix C, table 3. Most of the informants witnessed the herbicides being sprayed (agents white, blue, and orange [which contains highly toxic dioxin] were used) and they were able to give descriptions of the aircraft (either C-123s or helicopters). From the interviews it appeared that the forest or sometimes the swiddens were the targets, although spray also sometimes drifted into the settlements. There was a definite pattern in perceptions regarding the effect of the herbicides on humans in or near the sprayed area (see table 4). Most people reported abdominal pains and diarrhea, with vomiting, respiratory symptoms, and rashes also developing. A few said that they experienced dizziness. Some of the informants expressed the opinion that there was an unusually high number of deaths, particularly among children, following the spraying. They noted that small children developed skin rashes and died soon after.

Most respondents reported widespread deaths among their domestic animals, notably chickens and pigs. Villagers also found dead animals, such as wild boars, in the nearby forests. Near some sprayed areas, dead fish rose to the surface of streams. The fish were bloated and villagers who ate them suffered diarrhea. Over a period of weeks following the spraying, plants wilted and died. In the swiddens and the kitchen gardens, most of the crops died; rice plants that were growing lived, however, but did not produce any kernels. Fruit trees withered, died, or failed to bear edible fruit. Villagers who ate some of the partially sprayed fruit or vegetables suffered diarrhea.

The comprehensive report prepared by the Committee on the Effects of Herbicides in Vietnam was submitted to the President of the Senate, the Speaker of the House of Representatives, and the Secretary of Defense on 15 February 1974. In his introductory letter to the report, National Academy of Sciences President Philip Handler stated that

> the Committee was unable to gather any definitive indication of direct damage by herbicides to human health. However, to a greater extent than in other areas, there were consistent, albeit largely "secondhand" reports from

Montagnards of acute and occasionally fatal respiratory distress, particularly in children. The inability of the Committee to visit the Montagnards in their own locales so as to verify these tales is greatly regretted.[10]

There was not the slightest effort made by this committee or the National Academy of Sciences to visit the highlands to determine if there was any truth to the highlanders' "tales," as Dr. Handler calls them.

10. Committee on the Effects of Herbicides in Vietnam, *The Effects of Herbicides in South Vietnam: Part A Summary and Conclusions* (Washington, D.C., National Academy of Sciences), p. x.

8 BETWEEN ZERO AND INFINITY

It was February 1973, and the pale, dry-season sun shone through the French windows, illuminating the faded antique gold lettering on the books lining the shelves of the study in the Kontum Mission building. Bishop Paul Seitz leaned forward over his desk, bringing his hands together in a gesture of finality. "The future of the highland people, Monsieur, is dark." Then he added in an even tone, "They are between zero and infinity." The meaning was all too clear. We had been discussing the history that had swept the highlands since the relatively tranquil day in 1957 when I first saw the bishop coming down the stairs of the rambling building. It was just before a storm broke, a symbolic event in retrospect, for the storm of war in all its fury had ravaged the highlands since that day.

But the storm was not yet ended and no one, least of all Nay Luett and his colleagues at the ministry, dared even consider that worse might still be to come. With their unshakable faith in the future they labored to salvage the shattered socioeconomic programs. Doggedly they pursued their goal of regrouping all of the surviving highlanders in seven provinces. Nay Luett and his group were effective leaders, but, as had been the case so often in the past, the destiny of the highland people was not in the hands of their leaders. Their future was being determined by decision-makers in the world beyond the mountains. Already unfolding were events that would result in a more threatening situation than any the highlanders had faced thus far.

On 27 January 1973 the Agreement on Ending the War and Restoring Peace in Vietnam was signed in Paris by representatives of the United States, North Vietnam, the Saigon government, and the Viet Cong's Provisional Revolutionary Government. It called for a cessation of hostilities, exchange of prisoners of war, and withdrawal of American troops. The cease-fire went into effect the following day, but it only brought an upsurge of fighting in the highlands and further disruptions to the population. At the end of March the last American troops departed and, with this, American interest in the "Montagnards" waned. During the period that followed, the American desire to disengage from the war in Vietnam was manifest in a congressional ban on any further U.S. military intervention in Southeast Asia and continually diminishing military aid to Saigon. Now the dominant Communist force in the highlands, PAVN poured more men and arms down the Ho Chi Minh trail. During 1973 and 1974 there were sizable military conflicts in Kontum, Pleiku, and Quang Duc provinces.

By the end of 1974 the stage was set for a military showdown in Vietnam. It began on 10 March 1975 when PAVN launched an attack on Ban Me Thuot, which fell in a day. This led to the fateful decision to abandon Pleiku and Kontum, resulting in a disastrous rout of the government forces from the highlands. The ARVN collapsed as the Communist forces rolled ahead. Fifty-five days after the capture of Ban Me Thuot, the Communist armies entered Saigon, and the Vietnam War was ended.

The highlands now were under the rule of the Communists, but the autonomy that had long been promised for the region by them was never granted. Rather, in a pattern reminiscent of the Ngo Dinh Diem era, the new government began to move massive numbers of Vietnamese into highland provinces while at the same time ordering relocation of many highland villages. The rhetoric of Communist news releases concerning the latter program was like an echo of 1957 with their references to "highland nomads being settled in permanent villages." But, as in 1957, there was and continues to be resistance on the part of highlanders determined to preserve their ethnic identity. Members of the FULRO, along with former CIDG and military personnel, have gone into the remote forests to form a dissident movement against the Hanoi regime. Meanwhile the leaders, such as Nay Luett and Pierre K'Briuh, who were at the ministry in Saigon, were rounded up and incarcerated in reeducation camps. Since then there has been the sad news that Y Thih Eban and Ksor Rot were killed after the Communist takeover. In Cambodia, the FULRO leaders who remained in Phnom Penh, including Y Bham Enuol, Kpa Doh, Ksor Dhuat, and Bun Sur, were caught in the nightmarish events that followed the Khmer Rouge entry into the city. As a high-ranking officer in

Lon Nol's government, Bun Sur was probably executed, but the fate of the others is not known.

So, following the devastating events that have swept the highlands since 1945, the Sons of the Mountains have not only survived but have developed a new pride in their own identity. With the establishment of the Socialist Republic of Vietnam, however, that very identity is threatened, and the Sons of the Mountains may indeed be "between zero and infinity."

THE CEASE-FIRE

On Sunday morning 28 January 1973 at 8 o'clock the cease-fire agreed upon in Paris went into effect. In the highlands it was preceded by an outburst of fighting as the Communists and government forces attempted to capture or hold key positions—efforts that were quickly dubbed "land-grabbing." On the morning of 27 January, the day before the cease-fire, there was a Communist rocket attack on Pleiku during which Col. Y Pem Knuol was killed. At the same time, Communist forces moved into Buon Ho district town north of Ban Me Thuot on Route 14. When ARVN attempted to dislodge them with air support, the Rhadé villages in the vicinity were struck, leaving 7,000 homeless. There also was fighting at the Mount Pao pass (between Kontum and Pleiku) and west of Kontum, both attempts at "land-grabbing" by the Communists.

I was conducting the last of my interviews for the National Academy of Sciences' herbicide study at this time and was in Kontum after the cease-fire began. There were PAVN troops camped on Route 14 just north of the city (they could be seen washing their clothes in a stream), and the fighting at the pass and west of Kontum continued. On 9 February the PAVN forces moved into Polei Krong, where there had been a CIDG camp. The ensuing fighting and airstrikes forced the highlanders in the surrounding villages to flee into Kontum. ARVN was moving artillery into Kon Robang and an ARVN operation had been launched to retake the Mount Pao pass and open Route 14. Highland refugees also were swarming out of villages in that area. In the small Vietnamese settlement near the pass, my Bahnar assistant and I encountered Jarai Arap who had come through the mountains to escape the PAVN troops that had come into their villages the previous day. The Communists had tried to force the Jarai to go with them and, when the villagers refused, had shot a young man in the head. He still was alive, and the refugees were carrying him in a blanket. We sent him to Pat Smith's hospital, where he was treated immediately. A week later, in spite of having a bullet lodged in his skull, he was sitting up, smoking.

Kontum, which before the war had been a very charming town, now had a dispirited air. Sounds of the fighting to the south and west could be heard. Much of the city still was in ruins. Most of the shops in the market area were closed, but two restaurants were open and charging very high prices for indifferent Vietnamese food. There was no electricity and in the evening ARVN soldiers wandered around the main street, some of them eating roasted corn being sold by women near the market. Most of those who had fled had not returned, and many of those who did return were preparing to leave again. I found Nguyen Huu Phu in his small house, now empty of furniture. He explained that his family had gone to Saigon and he had returned to collect the last of his possessions. He shook his head sadly and said that they would stay in the south until the situation around Kontum improved.

Because of the renewed fighting following the cease-fire, Pat Smith's hospital was busier than usual. She was getting highlanders who had been forced to go with the PAVN during the offensive. They had been kept in a remote part of the mountains east of Dak To and many had malaria as well as being seriously undernourished. I accompanied Sister Gabrielle and Sister Vincent to the hospital that ARVN had looted. We were pleased to find the buildings battered but intact. The garden area was still mined, but nevertheless it was apparent that the place could be refurbished.

The cease-fire accords had provided for a four-part commission in Kontum. It would include representatives of the South Vietnamese, the American military (a group of four officers and one enlisted man), a team of Viet Cong delegates, and a representative of the North Vietnamese. It would oversee the cease-fire in Kontum province. The building that had housed the officers' club in the abandoned (and wrecked) MACV compound was being renovated as the meeting place for the truce team. The rest of the shattered buildings were serving as a temporary field hospital for the 22d Division, which was involved in the operations at the Mount Pao pass and west of the city. Many of the former bedrooms were filled with wounded soldiers lying on the filthy floors without mats to keep them from the dirt.

It was at this time that I went to see Bishop Seitz and discuss the situation in the highlands. We talked about the future prospects for South Vietnam.

The bishop felt that the cease-fire was part of a Communist strategy. One must remember, he pointed out, that the PRG and the North Vietnamese were one and they shared the goal of a Communist victory in the south. The North Vietnamese were strong and dedicated, but they were tired and needed a respite, so they agreed to the cease-fire. This also afforded the Americans the opportunity to leave South Vietnam without a disaster. President Thieu, Bishop Seitz felt, was too timid and hesitant to rally any effective force to oppose the Communists successfully. The situation was bound to deteriorate and, since the Communists' strategy called for taking the highlands first, in a matter of time Kontum, Pleiku, and Ban Me Thuot would fall. Standing by the window, the bishop pointed to the hills north of Kontum, saying, "Look, Monsieur, all that you see to the north, where so many of the Americans' battles were fought, is in the hands of the Communists."

Leaving Kontum, I went to Pleiku to conduct the final interviews for the herbicide study. Pleiku was filled with ARVN troops and their dependents. There was more of a feeling of life here than in Kontum, but the town had a squalid air. Most of the bars and steambaths were closed, their gaudy façades now faded and dusty. Gone were the heavily made-up girls with their miniskirts (prostitutes catering to ARVN did not bother with such frills) and the petty thieves (there was little to steal). The highland refugees were now housed in a former prisoner-of-war camp near Route 14 and in Camp Enari, the former U.S. Fourth Infantry Division base on the side of the sacred Hodrung Mountain. Tracy Atwood and his Jarai assistant accompanied me there to conduct interviews. ARVN had looted such things as doors and window frames, and the dusty wind whistled through the buildings. The refugees were jammed in the small rooms, where smoke from their cooking fires blackened signs still announcing "Mail Call at 0900" and "Movie Tonite at 2000."

At Cheo Reo the cease-fire had brought calm. The refugees were no longer a problem because many of them had moved back to their villages. Col. Nguyen Van Nghiem (who had been at the MDEM) was now the province chief. He emphasized to me how he had been cooperating with Nay Luett to make the King of Fire better known throughout the highlands. Believing that the King of Fire lived in a house that seemed too impoverished for his status, they had built him a new longhouse with a tin roof. Several celebrations already had been held there. Ed Sprague informed me that Siu Choi, the King of Fire's nephew (and more than likely his successor), had disappeared. Col. Nghiem claimed that the Communists had captured him, but some of the Jarai said that Siu Choi had been talking against Nghiem in villages, so the province chief had had him assassinated.

The Cheo Reo Jarai had the reputation of being the best musicians in the highlands, and Sprague had obtained some electronic musical instruments that some of his young Jarai friends wanted. They liked western rock music, and at Sprague's house in the CORDS compound on the edge of the town (one of the only places with electricity) they gathered to play, calling themselves the Ayun-Ea Pa Rock Band (named for the rivers that converged at Cheo Reo). They also played traditional Jarai music, and many people gathered to dance and hear Ksor Hip (2.31) sing.

The town of Ban Me Thuot seemed normal. At La Souris Blanche, the small French restaurant, the planters still gathered to sip drinks, eat, and exchange gossip. The only disturbing note was that some of the French planters were uneasy about the future of South Vietnam and were trying to sell their estates. The highland refugees were being moved into new settlements with some land for them to farm. The Bru had been in Buon Jat almost a year. Some of them had realized excellent profits, selling their crops of vegetables (maize, potatoes, yams, and white beans) to a Rhadé entrepreneur who transported the produce to Nhatrang. There was still considerable concern among local Rhadé leaders about the continuing encroachment by Vietnamese on highlanders' lands. Y Jut Buon To (1.19), head of the Ethnic Minorities Bureau in Ban Me Thuot, pointed out that during the past year twenty Vietnamese and highlanders had been killed during land disputes in Buon Ho district. Y Char Hdok, director of the Highland Normal School, compared it to the American Indian situation (he had a B.A. from Southern Illinois University), but, he noted, at least the Indians had their reservations. At Buon Ale-A, FULRO leaders Y Preh Buon Krong and Y Dhe Adrong worried about the withdrawal of the American military forces. "Who," they asked, "will be our mother and father when the Americans leave?" They felt that the highland people would be in a worse position than they had been during the 1955–1959 period. They were also concerned about the illegal logging that was destroying much of the forests and the unexploded shells and mines in some of the more remote areas.

In Dalat, Touneh Han Tho was busy organizing the new Highland Research Center, located in Madame Nhu's former villa (which even had a sizable swimming pool). The center already had a small library, and it had

Mnong fleeing fighting at Kien Duc, near Gia Nghia (1973)

embarked on a project to translate into Vietnamese some customs that had been recorded by Sabatier and Antomarchi. Dalat also was the projected site for some foreign investments. Han Tho related that an American businessman and his Vietnamese wife were planning a ranch on 500 acres as the initial phase of a larger beef industry. They encountered difficulties with the province chief and the central government because there already had been a proposal submitted by a consortium of Japanese, American, Chinese, and British business interests in Hong Kong to build a tourist center on the land. The Vietnamese wife had contacted Han Tho and K'Briuh to enlist their support for her project. She complained that everyone in the provincial and Saigon administrations wanted payoffs. Reminders that the cease-fire had not yet brought peace to the highlands, however, still were in evidence. On 4 March 1973 SIL staff members Ellwood Jacobson and Gaspar Makil and the latter's eleven-year-old daughter Janie were killed in a Communist ambush while driving on Route 20 southwest of Dalat.

Saigon was removed from the grim realities of highland towns such as Kontum and there was confidence that Washington was committed to preventing any rash Communist violations of the truce or any attempt by the North Vietnamese to mount any military offensive in the south. Plans were being made for a large influx of tourists (who might want to visit some of the battle scenes of the war) and foreign businessmen were planning to construct new hotels. The Christian Brothers were planning to establish a new university on a site near Saigon. The last American military personnel departed on 30 March. (I sailed for the United States the following day.) A large number of American civilian contractors were arriving in Saigon to replace the American military technicians, and the sizable staff of the Defense Attaché's Office that sponsored them was moving into the enormous former MACV headquarters near Tan Son Nhut airport.

According to Touneh Han Tho, the primary concern at the MDEM during this period was the settlement of refugees in places where they could farm. USAID resettlement funds, however, were not going to the MDEM but to other ministries and to Dr. Pham Quang Dan, the Vice Prime Minister for Resettlement, whose major project was moving Vietnamese refugees from Danang to places in the south. Luett and his staff had to rely on their own sources of money and on the Ministry for Social Welfare for such things as tools and paddy seed. Han Tho also observed that the ministry at this time was plagued with corruption at the lower levels because contractors and suppliers were paying bribes to get preference.

Another serious concern, according to Han Tho, was the possibility that the government might abandon the highlands. Han Tho himself had become convinced that this was a real possibility when in 1971 he had spent a year at the National War College in Saigon. One of the lecturers, retired Australian Colonel Francis P. Serong, strongly advocated a strategy of withdrawing government forces from the highlands in order to concentrate them along the coastal plain. Han Tho had stood up to argue against this. Nay Luett and his colleagues believed that the views of Serong, whom they feared might have some influence in the palace, could be shared with high-ranking leaders like Thieu. This prompted the highland leaders to pursue their plan to concentrate all of their people in seven provinces. They now were beginning to talk among themselves of making the seven provinces an autonomous, neutral state that would function as a kind of "Switzerland" bordered by Vietnam, Cambodia, and Laos. Han Tho claims that the Vietnamese Central Intelligence Organization found out about the plan and subsequently began to create difficulties for the MDEM. Soon after, for example, Hoang Duc Nha, now the Minister for Communications, abolished all broadcasts in highland languages, saying that there was only one national language in South Vietnam.

In October 1973 Touneh Han Tho went to Belgium to receive training in socioeconomic development at the Louvain in order to prepare him for his new role as director of the Highland Research Center in Dalat. At the MDEM, in spite of the uncertain conditions in the highlands, plans were being drawn up for sweeping agricultural development in the seven provinces where everyone would be regrouped. This new Five Year Agricultural Development Plan recognized the shortcomings of the high-landers in using land: "Highland people do not understand the value of land. They cultivate with traditional methods, estimating land value based on present output, and they forget the potential of the land." The authors (Han Tho, K'Briuh, K'Broi, and Kpa Dai—the last two had received degrees in agriculture at the University of Hawaii) outlined a scheme for informing local populations about improved methods and the possibility of farming new crops. There would be demonstration plots, new methods would be taught in the primary and secondary schools, and villagers would be encouraged to make more use of their draft animals. Other subjects in the plan included mechanization, irrigation, cattle production, marketing, processing crops, and transportation. They also discussed credit, capital, banking, and the formation of farmers' associations and cooperatives.

When Han Tho returned to the ministry in March 1974, he found the situation among the staff vastly changed. The "team spirit" that had prevailed among the high-level highlanders was now gone. In effect, the social network that had existed since Nay Luett became minister in June 1971 was now fragmented. Nay Luett had become isolated and his manner in dealing with the staff had become authoritarian. K'Briuh confided to Han Tho that he could no longer approach Luett in an informal and friendly manner as before. Y Thih Eban complained that he was being treated "like a little soldier" whose sole function was to report the attitudes of the Rhadé to Luett. No one visited Luett in his office, except some Chinese and Vietnamese businessmen regarding contracts with the ministry.

Outside the ministry Luett remained close to Senator Ksor Rot, but his relations with other highlanders and Cham in the National Assembly suffered because of Luett's continued support of Thieu. According to Han Tho, late in 1974 Assemblymen Rcom Anhot, Touneh Ton, Y Dhe Adrong, Dinh Van Roi, and Ton Ai Lieng (a Cham who had been a FULRO leader) angrily accused Thieu and his colleagues, particularly General Nguyen Van Toan, the II Corps commander, of having allowed Vietnamese province chiefs and other high-ranking officers to steal lands belonging to villagers and to profit from illegal logging. They too were bitter about the loss of territory to the Communists. This led to an open conflict, and at some gatherings at this time there were harsh words between Luett and some of his former supporters.

RESURGENCE OF FULRO AND THE FALL OF BAN ME THUOT

Among all of the problems that beset Nay Luett in 1974, one that was of growing concern was the reappearance of FULRO. This development was not due to any direction from the FULRO leaders in Cambodia (where the war was going badly for the Lon Nol government), nor was it due to a resurgence of the spirit of ethnonationalism. Rather, it came about as the result of a bizarre set of circumstances. According to Y Jut Buon To and Touneh Han Tho, these events were initiated at the beginning of 1972. Y Chon Mlo Duon Du had lost his bid for the National Assembly in the 1971 elections, and he also had been replaced as secretary general of the MDEM. Early in 1972 he met with John Paul Vann, the Senior Adviser in II Corps, and discussed the possibility of locating missing American military personnel or their remains. The point was raised as to whether this might be done through some cooperation with the Viet Cong. Y Chon agreed to organize this effort and accepted 500,000 piasters from Vann, who also gave Y Chon a camera to provide photographic proof of the survival of missing Americans or their tombs.

Vann was killed in June 1972, so Y Chon got together with Y Blieng Hmok and Y Blu Nie Buon Drieng to start a business selling timber to Vietnamese entrepreneurs. This precipitated a clash with Y Jut Buon To, the representative of the MDEM in Ban Me Thuot, who accused them of logging illegally on village-owned lands. In December 1972, after the elders of Buon Nie Ea Sah claimed that Y Chon had sent his workers in to cut wood in their sacred grove, Y Jut charged Y Chon and his colleagues with having violated the land law providing "main living areas" for highland villages. Y Jut also notified the MDEM, and Nay Luett became very angry. Despite this, Y Chon continued to sell timber to the Vietnamese. As security around Ban Me Thuot began to deteriorate in 1973, however, Y Chon found that most timber was now either in the Communist-controlled zones or in village territories. To cope with this, he contacted Kpa Koi, a Jarai who now was serving as head of the nearly defunct Southern Highlands Ethnic Minorities Solidarity Party (that had been launched in February 1969 by Y Bling Buon Krong Pang), proposing to Koi that he join Y Chon's timber business. Koi agreed, and they used the solidarity movement's seal to stamp papers which they presented to village authorities as valid documents approving logging within the village territory in order to "raise funds for the highland political movement."

Y Chon then embarked on another scheme. Knowing that the Americans were interested in information on their missing military personnel, Y Chon approached Y Preh Buon Krong, a FULRO leader, and informed him that they could make a great deal of money by contacting the Viet Cong to learn about missing Americans. Y Preh contacted Rcom Thok, a Jarai lumberman (who, according to Y Jut, was also a police agent). Thok, like many of the lumbermen in the highlands, had contact with the Viet Cong who, for a fee, allowed them to engage in illegal logging. Thok, in turn, put Y Preh in touch with Y Hong Mlo, a local Viet Cong leader. According to Y Jut, Y Preh presented himself to Y Hong as someone who knew the Americans well. Y Preh assured Y Hong that the Americans were no longer interested in supporting President Thieu and would be willing to cooperate with the Communists. Y Preh also proposed that a revived FULRO join forces with the Communists to overthrow the Thieu government. Y Hong reported this to the H-5 District Committee and the B-3 Liberation Headquarters in Mondulkiri province in Cambodia. After the H-5 committee approved of negotiations between the NLF and FULRO, a meeting of their representatives was arranged in November 1973 at a place near the Mewal coffee estate, northwest of Ban Me Thuot. The FULRO delegation consisted of Y Preh, Rcom Thok, and Kpa Koi, while the NLF was represented by Duc-Kim (the Vietnamese who eventually became province chief after the fall of Ban Me Thuot), Y Hong Mlo, and two other highlanders (a Sedang and a Bahnar). A second meeting took place in December 1973, and Y Preh brought a letter addressed to Y Bih

Aleo stating that the United States would help with the liberation of South Vietnam. Y Preh also gave Y Bih a small camera so he could photograph evidence of missing Americans. At this point conflict split the FULRO group when Rcom Thok, angered at what he considered an unequal sharing of the lumber profits, informed the Vietnamese police and security officials in Ban Me Thuot about the contacts with the Viet Cong. The police put all of the group under surveillance, and Kpa Koi went into hiding.

Y Jut related that, at this time, Koi began visiting villages, declaring that he was the representative of Y Bham Enuol, the president of FULRO. Y Blieng Hmok called a meeting of local Rhadé leaders in his Buon Pan Lam longhouse to convince them that Kpa Koi was the valid FULRO leader in Darlac. Y Blieng and Y Chon had a FULRO stamp made and used it on papers they took to surrounding villages where they told the local leaders that Kpa Koi was launching a revival of FULRO. They succeeded in gaining considerable following, particularly among unemployed young men who had served in the CIDG program and were sympathetic to FULRO. Y Preh also lent his support to this effort. Y Jut attributed a rash of incidents, such as buses being robbed, Vietnamese getting shot while plowing land taken from the highlanders, and ambushes, to this development. He and Nay Luett tried unsuccessfully to organize a leaflet drop to warn villagers that Kpa Koi was not a real FULRO leader.

Y Jut estimated that by March 1974 the Communists began using FULRO as a front. The Viet Cong E-25 Infantry Regiment (one-third of which was composed of highlanders) went into villages, claiming to have Y Bham's support. The villagers generally responded favorably, particularly since the Communist propaganda played on their discontent regarding Vietnamese land-grabbing in Darlac. This Viet Cong unit began to operate more openly around Ban Me Thuot, and one of its objectives was to cut Route 21 to the coast.

According to Y Jut, in order to avoid the suspicion of the police, Y Chon accepted a position as Special Chargé d'Affaires for the MDEM In Darlac. This also would give Y Chon an opportunity to undermine Nay Luett's standing and further his own interests. He wrote several letters to the prime minister and to President Thieu stating that he, Y Chon, was best suited of all the highland leaders to cope with the growing FULRO problem. In June 1974 Y Chon became director of the Highland Research Center in

Dalat and continued to talk against Nay Luett after he assumed this post.

Touneh Han Tho related that in June 1974 Les Kosem's son (who was married to the daughter of the Cham leader Ton Ai Lieng) brought a letter from Y Bham (who still was in Phnom Penh) to Nay Luett. The FULRO leader made no reference to events taking place in Darlac, simply declaring that he would agree to return to Vietnam if the highland people were given control of their own administration and could have their own army and flag.

By August 1974 Kpa Koi was rallying considerable support in the villages around Ban Me Thuot. Y Jut's brother-in-law Y Nguk Buon Krong, a follower of Kpa Koi, related that the Viet Cong had assigned a highlander from Dalat named K'Broi (who had joined the Communists in 1964) to report on all FULRO activities. Y Nguk also claimed that 90 percent of the Regional Forces were supporting Koi. On 2 November 1974 the *New York Times* reported that an estimated 500 men were in the FULRO forces and the movement had been responsible for a wave of violence against Vietnamese, resulting in fifty deaths during the month of August.[1] Regarding it as a revolt, the Vietnamese authorities had deployed two battalions of ARVN Rangers (numbering 800 men) around Ban Me Thuot to check the papers of all young men. The *New York Times* article noted that Kpa Koi was suspected of having been involved in "some shady lumber deals involving Chinese middlemen" and was an unlikely figure to lead any successful revival of FULRO.

Meanwhile important events bearing on Vietnam were taking place in the United States. The Watergate scandal had culminated in the resignation of President Nixon on 9 August 1974 and his replacement by Vice President Gerald Ford. Three days later before a joint session of Congress, Ford declared, "To our allies and friends in Asia, I pledge a continuing of our support for their security, independence, and economic development. In Indochina, we are determined to see the observance of the Paris cease-fire, and a negotiated settlement in Laos. We want to see an early compromise settlement in Cambodia."[2] But despite these reassuring words, Congress was in the process of cutting the large amounts of aid going to South Vietnam.

1. James M. Markham, "Montagnard Uprising Poses a Threat to Saigon Drive," *New York Times*, 2 November, 1974.
2. Leslie H. Gelb, "Once More, Decisions to be Made on Vietnam," *New York Times*, 25 August, 1974.

In Saigon during this period, opposition to Thieu was mounting with student riots and rising criticism of the corruption in his regime. In the countryside, the Saigon forces were losing more posts and district towns. In late July 1974 Mang Buk, some 80 kilometers north of Kontum, was abandoned following a Communist ground attack. In early October the district capital of Chuong Nghia, northeast of Kontum, was captured by Communist forces.[3] On 6 January 1975, after a week long siege, Communist units launched a heavy artillery barrage and a ground assault on Phuoc Binh (Song Be), capital of Phuoc Long province, north of Saigon in the Stieng country.[4]

The events in early 1975 leading to the fall of the highlands to the Communists were described in a series of articles by North Vietnamese General Van Tien Dung, published in the Communist newspaper *Nhân Dân* (The People) between 1 and 21 April.[5] In his article of 1 April 1976 General Dung related that between July and October 1974 the General Staff agencies of the PAVN were assessing their strategy on the basis of continuing victories, particularly in the highlands; he cited places such as Dak Pek, Chu Nghe, Mang Buk, Mang Den, and Le Minh.[6] They also took note of the fact that the two main-force divisions of ARVN were spread over a wide area, and they assessed the highlands as a region where "one could easily build roads, develop his technical and mobile capabilities and bring his strength into full play." In their view, the highlands constituted "an extremely important area strategically." The General Staff therefore decided that the central highlands would be the "main battlefield in the large-scale widespread 1975 offensive." There were political preparations to be made. Early in December 1974, Viet Cong leaders Chu Huy Man and Vo Chi Cong of the Fifth Region (embracing the highlands) were invited to Hanoi to meet with the Standing Committee of the Central Military Party Committee. Subsequently, there was a series of meetings held by the Political Bureau between 18 December 1974 and 8 January 1975. During these meetings (on 7 January), the highland town of Phuoc Binh (Song Be) fell, and all of Phuoc Long province came under

3. "Loss of a Town by Saigon Feared," *New York Times*, 28 July 1974. David K. Shipler, "Saigon Base is Reported Lost," *New York Times*, 5 October 1974.
4. James M. Markham, "Saigon's Forces Lose Phuoc Binh," *New York Times*, 8 January 1975.
5. Van Tien Dung, "Great Spring Victory" (translated by the U.S. Government's Foreign Broadcast Information Service, Asia & Pacific [FBIS-APA]), 2 vols., vol. 1, 7 June 1976; vol. 2, 7 July 1976.
6. Ibid., vol. 2, 7 June 1976, pp 4–26.

Communist control. It was the first province in the south "to be completely liberated."

The following day Le Duan officiated at the concluding session of the conference and announced that, in view of the U.S. withdrawal and lack of any American military response to the Phuoc Long defeat, 1975 was the time to strike a strategic blow. He pointed to the map behind him and said, "Attacks must be unleashed toward Ban Me Thuot and Tuy Hoa." Thus the Fifth Region would form a "liberated area from Binh Dinh province northward, and the Tri-Thien forces will have to control an area from Hue to Danang."

On 9 January preparations for Campaign 275 in the highlands (where there were five PAVN divisions) were put into final form. General Vo Nguyen Giap, secretary of the Central Military Party Committee, established the areas and targets of the offensive. Dung went to Darlac to join General Vu Lang, the field commander of that zone. Dung was accompanied by General Le Ngoc Huyen, deputy chief of the General Staff, and General Dinh Duc Thien, head of the General Logistics Department. The three comprised the Highland Command of the Central Highlands Front. They flew to Dong Ha and on their way south through the mountains, visited several PAVN units. Arriving in Darlac, General Dung and his colleagues established a command post west of Ban Me Thuot. On the evening of 25 February Dung and his staff decided definitely to attack Ban Me Thuot. There would first be diversionary moves to lead the Saigon command to think that they intended attacking Kontum and Pleiku, so the ARVN commanders would divert forces to both places. There also would be a preliminary assault on Duc Lap (Dak Mil) south of Ban Me Thuot to open Route 14 to Communist troops and another attack on Thuan Man district town north of Ban Me Thuot, where Route 14 joins a country road to Cheo Reo.

According to Y Jut, Kpa Koi and his group were aware of the Communist buildup in the vicinity of Ban Me Thuot, but they kept it quiet. Y Jut noted that one of the followers of Y Bham, who did not support Kpa Koi, did inform the province chief. He in turn passed on the information to II Corps headquarters in Pleiku. General Pham Van Phu, the II Corps commander, went to Ban Me Thuot for a brief visit. Elements of the 23d Division (which had been sent to Pleiku) were dispatched to Ban Me Thuot but were ambushed at the Mount Dreh pass (one of the places where Mobile Group 100 had been ambushed in 1954).

On 1 March the 968th PAVN Division destroyed two posts on Route 19 west of Pleiku. On 4 March the PAVN 95th Regiment and the 3d Division of the 5th Military Region attacked posts on Route 19 west of An Khe. Two regiments of the ARVN 22d Division in Binh Dinh were sent as a reaction force. General Phu also sent the 2d Cavalry brigade from Pleiku to An Khe and ordered the 4th and 6th Ranger battalions to move northwest of Kontum and Pleiku to search for the PAVN 10th and 320th divisions. Meanwhile, elements of the PAVN 320th Division moved into a stretch of the road between Thuan Man and Cheo Reo to prevent ARVN from sending reinforcements south from Cheo Reo to Ban Me Thuot. Dung noted that he did not want to cut Route 14 between Pleiku and Ban Me Thuot at this time because it might have revealed his plan to isolate the latter city in preparation for an attack.[7]

Y Jut related that there had been intelligence received in Ban Me Thuot concerning an impending attack on the city. He had been informed by some Rhadé PRU that they had captured a PAVN major who carried orders for a 15 March attack. Y Jut also told how a Rhadé friend went to his farm on the road to Ban Don west of Ban Me Thuot and was captured by PAVN troops. They were staging in that area, and the Rhadé was kept for several days before they let him go to warn the villagers not to come out of their houses when the attack began. He reported to Y Jut that there were a great many PAVN troops in the vicinity of his village.

On 8 March the PAVN 320th Division overran Thuan Man district town, cutting the roads from Pleiku and Cheo Reo. The following day Communist units captured Duc Lap, giving them control of Route 14 south of Ban Me Thuot. At 2:00 A.M. on the morning of 10 March the attack on Ban Me Thuot began with heavy artillery bombardments accompanied by sapper ground assaults on the edge of the city. The electricity plant blew up and the airport was ablaze.[8]

Jay Scarborough, a former IVS volunteer and a law student, was visiting Vietnam and had arrived at Ban Me Thuot on 9 March. He was staying at the Y Ut Technical Training School near the 23d Division headquarters when the attack began. He spent the night on the floor as shells rained on the ARVN installations and the city airstrip. The following morning

7. Ibid., pp. 23–25.
8. Ibid., pp. 26–32.

Scarborough made his way to the house of Paul Struharick, the USAID representative (who had married the daughter of Y Blieng Hmok). There he was joined by Peter Whitlock, an Australian, John and Carolyn Miller and their daughter Luanne, Betty Mitchell, and Lillian and Richard Phillips of the Christian and Missionary Alliance. Later, Norman and Joan Johnson, a Canadian missionary couple, also came to the house. As PAVN tanks and troops entered Ban Me Thuot, the house was surrounded and all were taken prisoner. They were held in various places until October, when they were released.

Y Jut Buon To described how he was flying in a helicopter over Ban Me Thuot during the first day of fighting and saw the PAVN tanks surround the USAID house. He also was in radio contact with Y Tin Hwing, a Rhadé who was an ARVN officer (he had worked with Nay Luett on the scheme for a highland military force). Y Tin had a unit of highlanders southwest of Ban Me Thuot and was trying to mount a defense against the attacking Communist forces. Later, he was reported to have been killed. Y Jut said that the tanks rolling into Ban Me Thuot had "Front for the Liberation of the Ethnic Minorities" written on their sides. He also reported that Kpa Koi had lost control of his FULRO forces and many of them joined the attack.[9] The Rhadé Regional Forces made no effort to mount any kind of resistance.

According to Y Jut, on Monday 11 March VNAF began to bomb, but they mistakenly hit the command post of the 23d Division, effectively ending any organized resistance. VNAF also bombed Buon Ale-A, and among those killed were Y Thih Eban's wife and six children. Buon Pan Lam also was badly bombed and some four hundred villagers were killed. On 12 March people began to stream out of Ban Me Thuot. Hiup, the Bahnar leader, led fifty Rhadé, Mnong, and Cham students to Lac Thien. They encountered some PAVN troops who divided them up and allowed them to return to Ban Me Thuot. Y Char Hdok, Director of the Normal School, fled to his village near Lac Thien but was captured. Senator Y Bling Buon Krong Pang also made his way south to Lac Thien and fortunately was picked up by a helicopter and was taken to Nhatrang. By

---

9. In Jean Lartéguy, *L'Adieu à Saigon*, Paris, Presses de la Cité, 1975, pp. 95–97, it is reported that a Vietnamese priest informed Paul Léandri of the news service, Agence France-Presse, that the Ban Me Thuot attack was carried out by the Viet Cong without any PAVN assistance but with the aid of FULRO. Léandri subsequently was killed by the Vietnamese police in Saigon.

the evening of 12 March the Communists had complete control of Ban Me Thuot. Y Bloc Eban, who had joined the Viet Minh in 1945, was named province committee chairman, a position he held for several months.

Vast numbers of Vietnamese fled Ban Me Thuot, making their way eastward on Route 21 in an attempt to reach the coast. As they went, their numbers were swelled by thousands of Rhadé from villages along the road. Denis Warner reports that a young man who fled Ban Me Thuot on 10 March told him that he had joined a mixed army-civilian group of about 5,000–6,000 people trying to escape. "Four days later they met a small group of Viet Cong, who were too few to stop them. Later on the same day in a clearing they were surrounded by fifteen Molotova trucks that drove at high speed through the crowd, killing fifty or sixty." [10]

LOSS OF THE HIGHLANDS AND COLLAPSE OF THE THIEU GOVERNMENT

In a discussion of these events in Washington in October 1976, former Chief of Staff Cao Van Vien told me that President Thieu had summoned a group of generals to the Independence Palace on 12 March. They had breakfast (*phở*—noodle and beef soup—and coffee) while they discussed the situation in the highlands. Then, standing before a map, Thieu swept his hand over the area north of Ban Me Thuot and declared that it all would have to be given up. Ban Me Thuot and the important plantation area of Darlac would be the only part of the highlands that the government must save, and it must be retaken from the Communists.

Meanwhile, in Ban Me Thuot, General Van Tien Dung and his colleagues made plans for further moves in the highlands. They were deciding which of several options they would choose. Their deliberations, however, were to be rendered unnecessary by a sudden turn of events that began on 15 March. Two days after the palace breakfast, on 14 March, Thieu called a meeting of generals Tran Thien Khiem, Cao Van Vien, Dang Van Quang, and Pham Van Phu at Cam Ranh Bay to decide on a strategy for the highlands. According to the account given the Communists by captured Ranger commander Col. Pham Duy Tat (who had obtained his information from General Pham Van Phu, II Corps commander), Thieu asked

10. Denis Warner, *Certain Victory: How Hanoi Won the War* (Kansas City: Sheed Andrews and McMeel, Inc., 1978), p. 63.

Vien if there were sufficient reserve forces to reinforce II Corps, and Vien said that there were none available. Thieu then asked Phu how long he thought he could hold the area, and Phu replied that he could defend it for a month, adding that he would defend it to his death. Thieu stated that these conditions were not favorable and, given the PAVN strength, the main forces would have to withdraw from Pleiku and Kontum so as to have sufficient strength to defend the coast and the Mekong river delta. Addressing Vien, Thieu inquired if the withdrawal could be accomplished on Route 19. Vien replied that during the Indochina War, no forces were able to retreat along that road without being mauled by the insurgents (an obvious reference to Mobile Group 100). Route 21 also was ruled out because it was cut by strong PAVN forces. The generals concluded that Route 7B, running southeast from Pleiku to Cheo Reo and then down the Ba river valley to coastal Phu Yen, would have to be the avenue for withdrawal. Although the road was in bad condition (it had not been used in years) and the bridges had been blown up, it could be repaired. Also, Route 7B would be an unlikely means of withdrawing, so it would surprise the enemy. Thieu concluded by stating that the Regional Forces should be left to defend the withdrawal. He noted that, since they were for the most part highlanders, they would not find out that the region was being abandoned until after it was over, and then they could fend for themselves.[11]

On the morning of Saturday 15 March, General Phu called his staff together at the II Corps headquarters in Pleiku and gave the order to conduct the evacuation of the highlands the following day. The plan was to get all of the forces down to coastal Phu Yen and reorganize them for a large-scale operation to retake Ban Me Thuot. At this time there were over 60,000 troops in Pleiku and Kontum, including most of the 23d Division, Ranger units, and elements of VNAF. There also were most of their dependents in addition to the civilians left in both Pleiku and Kontum, all of them totaling around 250,000. General Phu and his staff (along with their families) then flew to coastal Nhatrang where they were going to establish a forward command. Troops of various technical units, including engineers to repair the destroyed bridges, began moving down Route 7B with their families. By this time the word had spread through Pleiku that the evacuation was taking place. Officers and enlisted men left their units to

11. Van Tien Dung, "Great Spring," pp. 46–47.

get their families together to leave. There was bewilderment among the civilian population as to what was happening. According to Nguyen Tu, a journalist from the Saigon newspaper *Chinh Luan*, soldiers ran through the streets of Pleiku telling the people to run for their lives.[12] Bewilderment gave way to panic. Mobs of military personnel and civilians flooded into the airport to storm every cargo and military aircraft landing as part of the evacuation. Those with vehicles began to clog Route 7B. The chaotic flight from the highlands, one of the worst debacles of the Vietnam War, had begun.

Meanwhile General Dung and his staff quickly worked out a strategy to take advantage of what they viewed as a retreat. Their goal was to turn it into a rout. Dung contacted the commander of the 320th Division, reprimanding him for not considering Route 7B as a possible line of communication for the enemy troops to use for their withdrawal. He warned the commander, "If the enemy escapes, you will be responsible." Dung then ordered the Central Highlands command to mobilize more armored cars, trucks, artillery, and supplies to assist the 320th Division to "pursue and destroy the enemy." At the same time he ordered the 5th Military Region forward command in Binh Dinh to mobilize the Regional Forces of Phu Yen to block Route 7 and "prevent the enemy from escaping to Tuy Hoa."[13]

The ARVN 22d Ranger Multibattalion moved out of Kontum, going south on Route 14 to Pleiku. The panic spread to Kontum, and everyone began to evacuate. In every kind of vehicle, the civilian population, the civil servants, and military dependents flooded southward to join the masses trying to leave Pleiku. The American Mission evacuated its personnel from Kontum and Pleiku. Pat Smith and most of her staff were flown out of Kontum.

Ed Sprague, the CORDS representative in Cheo Reo, was the only American left in that town in March 1975. He recalled (in a discussion in Washington in April 1977) that around 1 March he had visited Plei Bahrong, the village of the King of Fire, who predicted that there soon would be great trouble in Cheo Reo. It would last six months, after which calm would be restored. On 8 March, PAVN attacked Thuan Man district town. R'mah Wih (3.27) was the district chief, but he had to abandon his

---

12. Gloria Emerson, *Winners and Losers: Battles, Retreats, Gains, Losses, and Ruins from a Long War* (New York: Random House, 1976), pp. 35–36.

13. Van Tien Dung, "Great Spring," pp. 46–47.

post after his Vietnamese officers fled. Wih went to the nearby Jarai village of Buon Blech, and on 10 March Sprague flew there in a helicopter. The highlanders reported that the PAVN at Thuan Man were moving in the direction of Buon Blech, and the Bru (around 2,000) and Katu (1,000) refugees who recently had been settled there were anxious to leave. Wih and the remainder of the Thuan Man defenders led the Bru, Katu, and many Jarai to Cheo Reo, where the Vietnamese authorities arrested Wih as a deserter. (Sprague sent a message to Nay Luett, who arranged to have him released.) The highland refugees moved into the former IVS Agricultural Training Center.

Sprague related that the news of the fall of Ban Me Thuot made everyone in Cheo Reo uneasy. Then, on the afternoon of Saturday 15 March he encountered a convoy of military vehicles—a Ranger unit— coming down Route 7B in the direction of Cheo Reo. The rains had not begun, and the trucks sent clouds of dust into the air. They stopped and the convoy commander told him that Pleiku and Kontum were being evac- uated and they had orders to proceed to Phu Yen on Route 7B. Sprague told them that it was impossible because the road was in bad condition and the bridges were out. The convoy leader said that they were going to repair the bridges in advance of the other units being evacuated. The convoy moved on.

No sooner had the dust from the convoy settled when Sprague noticed that not far behind was a mass of civilian and military vehicles all mixed together. There were military trucks of all types, commercial trucks, buses, automobiles of all sizes and vintages, motorbikes, three-wheel Vespa and Lambretta taxis. They were jammed with soldiers, men and women of all ages, and children, along with belongings of every description (bundles of clothes, furniture, cooking utensils, blankets, and mats) and baskets of chicken and ducks. Cattle, horses, and goats walked alongside. The column stretched along Route 7B as far as the eye could see. At Cheo Reo the mass of refugees stopped when word came that bridges to the south had to be repaired. News of the evacuation rapidly spread through the town, and the residents began to pack their belongings to join the exodus down Route 7B.

By Sunday morning 16 March the civilian populations of Kontum and Pleiku, mixed with a mass of soldiers whose leadership had vanished, were streaming down Route 7B over the undulating plateau and down the pass in the direction of Cheo Reo. Nguyen Tu, the Saigon journalist, reported that Pleiku had become a nightmare. There were "people running around the streets as if they were caught in a trap, clinging to their most precious possessions." Every imaginable kind of vehicle was being used in an effort to flee what they considered a doomed city. Tu described how all order disappeared as the police and officials left and even the doctors and staff at military and civilian hospitals abandoned the patients on their beds. By evening, Sunday 16 March, the mass of vehicles streaming out of Pleiku with their lights on resembled a column of traffic returning home from a holiday weekend. There was shooting all over Pleiku, and thunderous explosions rocked the city as ammunition dumps were blown up. Flames from burning buildings in the town lit the sky. Joining the exodus at 10:30, Tu was bitter, noting that "there was no explanation to the people so they could withdraw in an orderly way, no help for the poor in getting any transport."[14] On the road, Tu observed that all of the highland settlements appeared to be deserted. The refugees pushed on, and he lamented, "It's a pity to see those people who could not afford to ride on cars or trucks. They are miserable. They can use only their feet. They are the largest bunch—women, children, elders—walking as rapidly as they can and not even a drop of water to quench their thirst." The misery of the scene moved Tu to write, "The desolation of the highway gives me an impression I find hard to describe with words. If I had a friend by my side I would tell him: 'Dear friend, the sky has as many stars as the sufferings that wound my heart.'"[15]

Meanwhile at Cheo Reo, Sprague reported that by Sunday morning, 16 March, the town had filled with vehicles and people, including thousands of troops who had now abandoned their units. There were tanks and armored personnel carriers that had run out of gas and were left on the road, cars were crashing into one another in an effort to move ahead, and some overloaded trucks had tipped over. The refugees were jammed in the town, and food and water supplies were running low. Sprague went to see the province chief, who simply looked pained and shrugged his shoulders. Taking some of the back trails he knew, Sprague went to the Thua Manh pass south of Cheo Reo to assess the situation. He found that the Jarai

---

14. Gloria Emerson, *Winners*, pp. 35–36; James M. Markham, "South Vietnam Reported Yielding Most of Central Highlands Area: Main Evacuation Route Cut Off," *New York Times*, 18 March 1975; Malcolm W. Brown, "Vietnam Refugees Stream from Highlands to Coast," *New York Times*, 19 March 1975.

15. Denis Warner, *Certain Victory*, p. 62.

Regional Forces had been abandoned by their Vietnamese officers. They agreed to remain in their positions for at least one more day to try to fend off Communist troops that might try to harass the mass of refugees now making their way slowly south of Cheo Reo.

Returning to Cheo Reo on Sunday afternoon, he found the city almost inundated with vehicles and refugees, many of the latter now arriving on foot. Large numbers of refugees were looking for food and water and ways of getting farther south. Most of the townspeople had fled, and the highlanders living in or around Cheo Reo had gone to hide along the banks of the Ayun river. Suddenly the Communists began shelling the airstrip close to the town, and panic seized the refugees. Sprague described how all order vanished as Rangers began breaking into the shops, looting and burning. The civilians joined in, and the town became one massive riot. The soldiers turned on civilians in automobiles, shooting and dragging them out to take the vehicles. The Rangers attacked buses and trucks. Sprague saw them kill women and children on the main street of Cheo Reo. He witnessed some Rangers fatally shoot the son of FULRO leader Nay Guh.

Sprague hurried to the CORDS compound near the airstrip to radio the headquarters at Nhatrang. At the compound Rcom Ali (3.25) and other Jarai had set up a defense of the perimeter as the confusion became worse and the shelling intensified. The Cheo Reo police captain came to the compound, demanding the CORDS vehicles so he and his fellow policemen could flee. He threatened Sprague with his gun. Ali threatened the captain, who turned and attempted to shoot him. The bullet hit a concrete post next to Ali and Ali responded quickly, shooting the captain dead. The captain's colleagues then opened fire and in the ensuing gunfight seven of the policemen fell to the ground. The remaining police departed.

On Monday morning 17 March an Air America helicopter landed at the compound and Sprague took it to some surrounding villages in order to see what kind of assistance, if any, his Jarai friends needed. At Plei Pa, most of the villagers had gone, and Ksor Hip (2.31) and Ro-o Bleo (5.3), two young leaders, had a force of several hundred Son Thon cadremen they were going to lead into the forest. Sprague bade farewell to them and returned to the helicopter. As they flew over Cheo Reo, he could see that the town was one jumble of vehicles and people. Route 7B to the north and south was an extension of the same scene. As the helicopter landed at the CORDS compound, the shelling began with greater intensity.

Sprague found that several more Jarai, including two girls who had been working in the town, and a young Vietnamese social worker had taken refuge in the compound. They reported that the situation in Cheo Reo had been made worse by news that the column moving southward was being heavily shelled and attacked by Communist forces. General Dung's determination to destroy those evacuating the highlands was being felt.

By Monday evening the situation in Cheo Reo had become very desperate. The town was now gutted, and the masses of refugees, afraid to move south, had fanned out in search of food and water to the surrounding Jarai villages, looting and burning them (the large longhouse that had been built by the famed chief Nay Nui was reduced to ashes). Another Jarai who had come to the compound reported that there were many dead and wounded in the town and chaos reigned. As night fell, a group of ARVN Rangers began attacking the compound, and Sprague and his group fought them off all night. Ali counted around thirty bodies on the perimeter the following morning. Sprague still had radio contact with Nhatrang, and in the morning an Air America helicopter bravely landed in the compound. All scrambled on board while the attacking Rangers opened fire. They flew to Plei Pa where Sprague found Nay Moul (2.17), Nay Honh (2.23), and R'mah Wih (3.27). Nay Moul expressed his desire to leave, but the other two leaders said that they were going to remain.

Flying over Route 7B, Sprague saw an unbelievable sight. There was one long mass of confusion with vehicles jammed together, many of them pushed off of the road. Intermingled among them were soldiers and civilians in a frenzy. As he watched, a Communist rocket hit the column, blowing up three trucks full of refugees, scattering bodies in all directions. As they moved along, he could see bodies and burnt-out vehicles all along the way. Shells and more rockets fell into the tangle of machines and people. At Phu Tuc, the helicopter landed away from the road and picked up the Jarai district chief, after which they flew to Nhatrang. Leaving his group in Nhatrang, Sprague flew back up Route 7B and was stunned at the sight of bodies scattered on either side of the road for the entire stretch between Phu Tuc and Cheo Reo.

Col. Pham Duy Tat, the Ranger officer who had been captured by the Communists, related that he was with the column moving out of Pleiku when the evacuation was ordered. The plan was to establish a defense line at Cheo Reo in order to wait for the heavy mechanized units and technical units to pass the area. But when they arrived on 16 March these units stopped and refused to go farther. He said that "these troops then destroyed property and looted the streets, thus causing great disorder." According to Tat, the Communist shelling of Cheo Reo inflicted heavy losses on the 23d Ranger Multibattalion, and on 17 March the defense completely collapsed. Some VNAF A-37s flew in but bombed their own troops, wiping out almost a full battalion. The 3d Armored Squadron abandoned all its vehicles and fled into the woods. Other troops did the same thing, taking their families with them. Thousands of the refugees followed them, but the Communist troops "constantly pursued and attacked them." Units abandoned their weapons and scattered. The withdrawal had become a rout.[16]

At Tuy Hoa, Bernard Weinraub of the *New York Times* described how "young women, their faces smeared with blood, carried wounded and dying infants off the evacuation helicopters. Old men and women, some swathed in muddy bandages, trembled and wailed."[17] A woman holding a child with leg wounds told how she had been on a truck when the Communist troops came out of the forest and opened fire on them. Proud of his achievement, General Van Tien Dung wrote, "We annihilated them as they fled."[18] Those annihilated included not only the government military forces in flight but also vast numbers of innocent men, women, and children. Of the estimated 200,000 to 250,000 involved in the exodus from the highlands, it is thought that only about one-third made it to the coast. A great many of those who failed to do so perished on Route 7B in what well may have been the worst bloodbath of the Vietnam War.

In Saigon, the news from the highlands produced a shock at the MDEM and among highland leaders gathered for a meeting of the Council for Ethnic Minorities. Events were happening so fast that Nay Luett and his colleagues could not do anything. Han Tho related that, when Ban Me Thuot fell, the staff met to plan aid for the refugees, but their worst fears were realized when they heard that the highlands were being abandoned. By Sunday 23 March, Kontum, Pleiku, Darlac, and Phu Bon provinces were in the hands of the Communists. Everyone was fleeing the city of Dalat as well as the towns in Quang Duc and Lam Dong provinces. That evening Nay Luett called a conference of forty leaders from among the

16. Van Tien Dung, "Great Spring," p. 47.
17. Bernard Weinraub, "Battered Refugees Tell of Attack on Exodus," *New York Times*, 21 March 1975.
18. Van Tien Dung, "Great Spring," p. 47.

highlanders, the northern highland refugees, and the Cham. The highlanders included Paul Nur (1.13), Hiup (1.20), Pierre Yuk (1.12), Y Jut Buon To (1.19), Nay Moul (2.17), Nay Alep (2.29), Siu Klir (3.23), Ksor Rot (3.20), Y Du Eban (3.21), Touneh Han Tho (4.2), Touneh Ton (4.14), Touprong Hiou (4.4), Touprong Ya Ba (4.9), Toplui Pierre K'Briuh (4.11), Y Thih Eban (5.2), Dinh Van Roi, Y Chon Mlo Duon Du, and Y Bling Buon Krong Pang. They drew up a document demanding autonomy for the highlands and the right of the highland people to form their own military force. The response of the government, dated 24 April 1975, was that the "present policy" would be maintained.

By 3 April, Hue, Danang, Qui Nhon, and Nhatrang had fallen and there was a flood of refugees into Saigon. On 4 April, Nay Luett, Touneh Han Tho, Ksor Rot, Touprong Ya Ba, Pierre K'Briuh, and Nay Alep met at the U.S. Embassy with George Jacobson, Lamar Prosser, and Ed Sprague. Nay Luett began by pointing out that he feared the "genocide of the Montagnard race." Touneh Han Tho added that the highland leaders wanted the Americans to protect their people and bring their plight before the Human Rights Council of the United Nations. Jacobson replied that the Vietnamese government intended defending Saigon and he, Jacobson, was confident that they would consolidate their forces to do so. According to Touneh Han Tho, he and Nay Luett then asked that the American Embassy include the highland leaders who desired to leave in evacuation plans.

By 21 April the ruined and deserted town of Xuan Loc northeast of Saigon, where the last defense against the PAVN was mounted, fell. The evacuation of Americans from Saigon increased. At the MDEM, Nay Luett and his staff drew up an evacuation list that included 322 highland leaders and their families who had gathered in Saigon. Touneh Han Tho related that on 27 April Nay Luett told him that at 1:00 A.M. he had received a telephone call from Mr. Newman, an American missionary who had been in Dalat and who now was in the Philippines. Newman told him that he was arranging for an aircraft to come to Saigon that evening to pick up the highland leaders. Luett said that Newman's interpreter, a Lat named H' Jimmy, then repeated the same message in Vietnamese.

On 28 April the Communist forces were closing in on Saigon from the east and north. Han Tho went to Nay Luett's house where many highlanders had gathered awaiting the aircraft from Manila (that never came). Han Tho returned to his house and arranged through an American friend to get his family (a total of seventeen, including his mother and his brothers' families) on a bus to the former MACV headquarters on 29 April. They were caught in a rocket attack that killed some of the refugees and two American Embassy Marine Guards. As their helicopter flew away from Saigon, the MACV headquarters was in flames (some Americans had thrown thermal grenades into the offices to destroy the building). At the aircraft carrier *Midway*, officers took Han Tho's Cham sabers that had been in his family for generations. Other highlanders, such as Y Jut Buon To (1.19) and his family, Y Bling Buon Krong Pang, Nay Ri (4.17), and Ksor Kul managed other means of evacuation. On 29 April, Duong Van Minh, now president (Thieu had fled to Taiwan), asked his troops to lay down their arms as the Communist forces entered Saigon. The first day of May 1975 marked the end of the Vietnam War.

In neighboring Cambodia, Phnom Penh had capitulated on 17 April. The day before the city fell, H'li Nie Hrah, wife of Ksor Kok (5.11), and her children were evacuated by air. She joined her husband in the United States, where he and Y Bhan Kpuor were in a training program for Cambodian army officers at Fort Benning, Georgia. She reported that Y Bham Enuol, Kpa Doh, Ksor Dhuat, and Y Nham Eban were still in Phnom Penh. Later, a Cambodian refugee who knew them claimed that Y Nham Eban had been killed by the Communists.

After the fall of Phnom Penh the FULRO members remaining in the city apparently took refuge with many others in the French Embassy as the Khmer Rouge drove the population out into the countryside. According to Father François Ponchaud, who also was in the French Embassy, on the morning of 20 April 1975 the FULRO highlanders were forced to leave the embassy. The priest relates that "I can still see 150 FULRO mountaineers, men and women who had fought the Saigon regime, the Viet Cong in Vietnam, and the Khmer Rouge in Cambodia to defend their territory. They had counted on France, and she had let them down. They marched away sorrowfully but with their heads high. Y Bam, the founder of the movement, and Colonel Bun Suor, their chief, led the way."[19] "Y Bam" obviously is Y Bham Enuol, president of FULRO, and "Colonel Bun Suor" is Bun Sur, the Mnong Rlam who had fled Vietnam to study in Paris. It was pointed out previously that he arrived in Phnom

19. F. Ponchaud, *Cambodia Year Zero*, trans. Nancy Amphoux (New York: Holt, Rinehart and Winston, 1977), pp. 15–16.

Penh in July 1970 and was named chief of Mondolkiri province in northeastern Cambodia, where the FULRO troops were active.

Father Ponchaud also presents the account of a Cambodian pharmacist who was taken from the French Embassy and later escaped to Vietnam. According to him:

> We were taken to the Lambert Stadium, two hundred meters from the Embassy. There we went through a preliminary "processing": the Khmer Rouge asked us to state our identities and write our names on one of three lists; military, civil servants, people. Then the officers like Major Tanh Chea and Colonel Y Buon Suor, and high-ranking officials like Dy Bellon and Phlek Phuon, were taken away in trucks. The rest of us moved into the huts built around the edges of the stadium by officers' families and spent the night with the rats, sleeping on wooden platforms.[20]

The pharmacist then related how he and the others (presumably the FULRO members) were taken in trucks north of Phnom Penh to Prek Phneuv, where they joined other evacuees from the capital city. Given the pattern of executing former officers of Lon Nol's army, it is likely that Bun Sur was killed. If Y Bham Enuol and his followers were in fact taken north, there always is the possibility that some of them might have been able to make their way into the forests of the northeast and escape back to the central highlands. The highlanders are very adept at survival in such circumstances.

THE HIGHLANDERS UNDER COMMUNIST RULE

While the Communists were asserting their control in South Vietnam, they allowed the MDEM to continue functioning for the month of May. Pierre K'Briuh and Y Chon Mlo Duon Du were reported to have been in charge. In June, however, the ministry was abolished, and as highland leaders returned to their native areas they were arrested and sent to reeducation camps. One refugee reported that Nay Luett had returned to Cheo Reo, where he and Nay Moul were taken into custody. There were reports that Ksor Rot had been executed. Rcom Pioi (2.21), who had been district chief at Phu Thien north of Cheo Reo (and whose brother Rcom Briu was a general in PAVN) was killed, but highlanders reaching Saigon

---

20. Ibid., p. 16.

after Cheo Reo fell told how it had been done by Jarai, who were angered at Pioi's having shown some Vietnamese the King of Fire's sacred saber. Reports of refugees indicate that Nay Luett, K'Briuh, Nay Moul, Y Blieng Hmok, Touprong Ya Ba, Y Chon Mlo Duon Du, and Ksor Dun initially were being held at the Dam San camp east of Ban Me Thuot. One Rhadé who left Vietnam in mid-1976 reported that the prisoners in the Dam San camp were very thin because of lack of food and they were ailing because of lack of any medical attention. Nay Luett was being kept in solitary confinement.

These sources also related that after the fall of Ban Me Thuot Y Bloc Eban, as was noted above, became chairman of the Darlac administrative committee (the equivalent of province chief), but eventually he was replaced by Duc Kim, a Vietnamese Viet Cong (who had met with Kpa Koi in late 1973). Also, Y Bih Aleo, the Communist leader, came to visit Ban Me Thuot and surrounding villages. Wherever he went he was accompanied by a Vietnamese officer who spoke fluent Rhadé. In September 1975 all of the French priests and nuns were expelled. Some of them said later that in July, when Kpa Koi and other FULRO leaders learned they had been duped by the Communists because there were plans to move massive numbers of Vietnamese into the highlands, they went into the forest to organize a dissident movement that also included former Son Thon and CIDG (Y Thih Eban was reported to have joined them). The French missionaries also reported that Pat Smith's hospital had been nationalized, and Sister Gabrielle had been taken into custody.

By the beginning of 1976 it was apparent that the oft-promised autonomy for the central highlands, that had been so much to the heart of Communist propaganda, was not going to be granted. Just as the Communists had duped Kpa Koi and his FULRO followers, they had also hoodwinked many highlanders into supporting them with the promise of autonomy. The first indications of this were the reports in mid-1975 of a Communist program to settle Vietnamese in the highlands. On 25 February 1976 the Saigon Domestic Radio Service announced the reorganization of the provinces in South Vietnam (see map 7) in preparation for reunification with North Vietnam.[21] Quang Binh (in North Vietnam), Quang Tri, and Thua Thien provinces now became Binh–Tri–Thien province. The new Quang Nam–Danang province in-

21. Translated in FBIS-APA, 26 February 1976.

cluded Quang Nam and Danang municipality, while Quang Ngai and Binh Dinh were fused into Nghia Binh. Phu Yen and Khanh Hoa became Phu Khanh. The upland province the Communists always designated as Gia Lai, which was the same as Pleiku in area, was combined with Kontum to form Gia Lai–Cong Tum province. Darlac and Quang Duc were merged to become Dac Lac province, while Ninh Thuan–Binh Thuan and Binh Tuy became Thuan Hai province. Tuyen Duc, Lam Dong, and the city of Dalat were reorganized into Lam Dong province. The new province of Dong Nai was composed of Ba Ria (Phuoc Tuy), Long Khanh, and Bien Hoa provinces, and the new province of Song Be was formed by merging the Communist province of Thu Dau Mot (Binh Duong), Binh Long, and Phuoc Long.

At the same time there were similar changes in North Vietnam, and the autonomous zones of Viet Bac and Tay Bac were abolished.

On the first anniversary of the fall of Ban Me Thuot, an article in the North Vietnamese newspaper *Nhân Dân*, signed by Y Bih Aleo (a member of the PRG advisory council and representative of the central highlands minority in the PRG), gave hints concerning the situation in the highlands.[22] Citing the progress that had taken place since "liberation," Y Bih noted that "at present, people in the Gia Lai–Cong Tung, as well as Dac Lac, are continuing to fight to sweep away reactionary troublemakers while building a new life." (This would appear to be a reference to the resistance movement in these areas.) He also noted that "vast new economic areas of our state have been established and intensive production is under way." Following this was a reference to the new life in the highlands that would be attained by "the people of various nationalities." These remarks would seem to have heralded the implementation of the program to bring Vietnamese into the highlands for economic development and also to relieve the overpopulation in parts of the lowlands.

News releases at this time also contained a rhetoric that was very reminiscent of the Diem era in announcing programs to settle the "nomadic" highlanders in "permanent communities," implying that all of the highland people practice swidden farming which requires that they move their villages constantly in search of new forest that is indiscriminately burned. In 1957 one might have excused such ignorance by pointing out that the Vietnamese at that time had little experience with the

22. Translated in FBIS-APA, 16 March 1976.

highlanders, but in 1976 the Communists could not make such a claim. It would appear that this resettlement is part of a program to assimilate the highlanders in much the same way as Diem had attempted. Given the resistance in the highlands, it also more than likely has some security considerations such as population control.

In a broadcast from Hanoi on 14 March 1976 it was reported that "the people's revolutionary committee of Gia Cong province recently returned tens of thousands of tribal nomads uprooted during the war to their native villages."[23] They were "resettled in 63 units, reclaimed 3,000 hectares of wasteland and 3,000 of fallow rice fields." Another broadcast from Hanoi on 16 May 1976 declared that "in the central highlands province of Dac Lac, the revolutionary administration is motivating thousands of families of Ede, M'nong, and Gia Rai ethnic minorities to reclaim land and settle down to live in the valleys to grow food and industrial crops instead of continuing their unstable nomadic life on the mountain tops."[24]

Such rhetoric is not only an echo of the Diem era but also that of North Vietnam since the 1960s where migratory groups, such as the Meo (Hmong) and Yao (Mien), were being forced to settle in permanent communities. In 1968, for example, it was reported in Hanoi that the government had ordered 1,500,000 "nomadic people" to settle in fixed communities within three years.[25] More recently, in June 1976, Radio Hanoi declared that "83 percent of the villages of the Meo, Dao (Fan Fu), and Xuan Luu tribal compatriots in the mountain areas and along the border have given up their nomadic farming habits for the cooperativization system."[26] On 25 June, Y Bloc Eban, chairman of the People's Revolutionary Committee of Dac Lac province, stated in a speech recorded by Radio Hanoi that there had been a considerable increase in agricultural production in the highlands, adding that "more than 40,000 highlanders have gone to the lowlands to settle for sedentary farming."[27] (It is not clear whether he meant lower elevations in the highlands or the lowlands as such.) He also declared that "we have built many new economic zones and helped 50,000 people to stabilize their lives after settling in the new economic zones."

23. Translated in FBIS-APA, 30 March 1976.
24. Reported in FBIS-APA, 18 May 1976.
25. "Hanoi Orders Nomads to Settle Down," *Japan Times*, 8 June 1968.
26. Translated in FBIS-APA, 22 June 1976.
27. Translated in FBIS-APA, 1 July 1976.

During this period there also were announcements of new economic zones in some upland areas for Vietnamese settlers. On 29 May 1976 Radio Saigon broadcast that the largest group to date had left Saigon for the economic zones and that they included 3,000 who went to Song Be province and 1,250 to Dong Hai.[28] On 1 June the same source reported that 2,340 people had gone from Qui Nhon to new economic zones in Gia Lai–Cong Tum.[29]

Early in June a United Nations team led by Dr. Victor Umbricht, a Swiss International Red Cross official, recommended that $432 million in aid be given Vietnam to assist in a number of programs, one of the most important of which would be resettlement. The report stated that "it is perfectly legitimate" for the Vietnamese government to seek resettlement of some 8 million people in places like the central highlands. It also pointed out that this aid would be in addition to some $72.5 million already being provided by Communist countries, Sweden, and Japan for resettlement programs.[30]

At this time there was the first public admission that there was among the highlanders organized resistance to the Communist regime. On 10 June 1976 Radio Hanoi reported on a South Vietnam Women's Liberation Union conference and one passage in the report stated that "in the ethnic minority areas in the southernmost part of central Vietnam, ethnic minority women guided our troops in tracking down FULRO elements and called on their husbands and sons to return and report to the administration."[31]

During the early months of 1976, preparations for elections for a new National Assembly for all of Vietnam (a preliminary step in reunification of the country) were being made. The elections were held on 25 April 1976. In Lam Dong, of the four assemblymen elected, two appear to have been highlanders—K'H'yieng and Kiche—both of whom probably were from Koho-speaking groups. Of the five elected in Dac Lac, Umong Ngiet Dam, Mrs. Serdien Kla, and Y Bloc Eban were the three highlanders elected. In Gia Lai–Cong Tum, of the six elected, four of the names—Ksor Kron (a Jarai), Kapha Kinh (this might be a deformation of the Jarai name Kpa Kinh), Dinh Up (Bahnar), and Thuong Y Buong—would seem to be

28. Translated in FBIS-APA, 1 June 1976.
29. Reported in FBIS-APA, 10 June 1976.
30. "U.N. Study Urges Heavy Vietnam Aid," *Washington Post*, 2 June 1976.
31. Translated in FBIS-APA, 17 June 1976.

from local ethnic groups. Dieu Thi Loi, identified as "Cahu Ma," was among the six elected from Dong Nai.[32]

The National Assembly convened for the first time on 24 June 1976 in Hanoi. During the plenary session four southern highlanders were named to the National Assembly Commission for Nationalities. They were Y Buong (delegate from Gia Lai–Cong Tum), K'Hyieng (Lam Dong), Y Bloc Eban (Dac Lac), and Ksor Kron (Gia Lai–Cong Tum). Another Communist highlander who followed the Viet Minh in 1945, Y Ngong Nie Kdam, was named to the Public Health and Social Welfare Commission of the National Assembly (he had been sent to Russia for medical training).[33]

Also, during this plenary session Chu Van Tan, the Nung leader and early Communist leader among the highland groups in northern Vietnam, addressed the National Assembly, stating that "because imperialism continued its activities against the revolution and uses its lackeys to oppose it, the lines and policies of our party and state must be intensively disseminated among the national minorities." He also advocated a policy to have "settled nomadic ethnic minority people" and a program for establishing "new populous areas in the mountain region."[34]

On 2 July 1976 the National Assembly proclaimed the reunification of the country and voted to name it the Socialist Republic of Vietnam. A nationalist flag and a national emblem were adopted. Hanoi became the capital of the new nation (the sixteenth largest in the world and the third most populous Communist state). Saigon was officially renamed Ho Chi Minh City.[35] Nineteen days after these proclamations, on 21 July, the twenty-second anniversary of the signing of the Geneva Agreements passed unnoticed.

THE END OF A WAY OF LIFE?

In spite of all that has happened, up to the present time the highland people have tenaciously clung to a way of life that had been transmitted from one generation to another through the long centuries. They have lived in their small communities surrounded by kin and close neighbors, sustaining

32. Reported in FBIS-APA, 3 May and 11 May 1976.
33. Reported in FBIS-APA, 6 July 1976.
34. Translated in FBIS-APA, 25 July 1976.
35. Ibid.

themselves farming the slopes and bottom land, following the never-ending cycles of rainy seasons followed by dry seasons, of fields planted or fallowing. In the nearby streams they drew their water, bathed, and fished. The surrounding forests supplied them with game, wild fruits and vegetables, and the wood, bamboo, and rattan for their artifacts and houses. The highlanders scrupulously observed their ancient, traditional rituals, heeded signs and omens, and tried to keep in harmony with their many deities. Through time, they consistently have been people with a symbiotic, almost mystical, attachment to the green upland. They have been the Sons of the Mountains in every sense.

They could have endured without the world beyond the mountains, but, as the foregoing chapters (and the companion book, *Sons of the Mountains*) have chronicled, with the passage of time the more advanced outsiders encroached on their way of life. This is not to say that they lived in total isolation—historically many of them engaged in trade with lowlanders, although it was not vital to their survival. In the mid-twelfth century, Cham armies were the first penetrating force from the outside. Then there were the Vietnamese with their "pacification" schemes on the eastern fringe of the cordillera. It was the French who in the late nineteenth century brought the entire region under their colonial rule. 9 March 1945 was a fateful day when the Japanese took over the administration, marking the first involvement of the highland people in international conflict. With the ensuing Indochina War, the highlanders became "a people in between," and the Geneva Agreements put the mountain country under direct Vietnamese control for the first time.

The post-Geneva period of peace was all too fleeting, and with the Vietnam War the highlanders again were "a people in between." With its modern weaponry, however, this war had a fury much greater than that of the Indochina War, and much of the fighting took place in the uplands. Highland villagers became the targets of both sides, and whole ethnic groups were swept from their traditional territories as they were enveloped in the violence. By 1973 the existing ethnolinguistic maps were rendered invalid. An estimated 200,000 highlanders died during the Vietnam War, and an estimated 85 percent of the villagers were forced, one way or another, to flee as refugees.

But, disrupting as the ever-increasing contact with the outside was for the people of the mountains, it did over a period of time give them a greater awareness that they shared among themselves a way of life setting them apart from the intruders. It was this awareness that fueled the Python God nativistic movement as it swept much of the highlands during the late 1930s. It also was this awareness that created a bond among many of the elite from different ethnic groups, resulting in a pattern of intermarriage. By the end of the French administration in 1954 there had emerged a definite highlander ethnic identity among the better-educated leaders. It crystallized into ethnonationalism with the Bajaraka movement of the late 1950s and the FULRO movement in the 1960s. During this period, inter-marriage among the elite families increased, resulting in a kin network that spread among the major groups, embracing civil and military leaders on the government and Communist sides alike. By 1970 the highlanders were well on their way to becoming a *people*. As that decade unfolded, however, the war worsened and became wanton, leaving no part of the mountain country untouched. It became painfully clear to the highland leaders that the very existence of their people was being threatened. At this point, the spirit of survival eclipsed the spirit of ethnonationalism.

The Vietnam War has ended, but peace has not returned to the high-lands. The autonomy that the Communists had promised will never be granted and ethnonationalism clearly will never be tolerated. Dedicated leaders such as Y Thih Eban and Ksor Rot have been killed while Nay Luett and all of the others have been incarcerated under harsh conditions. Some of the leaders have fled as refugees while others have gone into dissidence, carrying on the struggle for ethnonationalism in the forests.

By mid-1976 the policy of the Communist government toward the highlanders was clearly spelled out in programs and public statements, both of which were reminiscent of the Diem era. Expressions such as "tribal nomads" and "unstable nomadic life on the mountain tops" are echoes of 1957. Programs to resettle the highlanders in "permanent com-munities" and those involving massive movements of Vietnamese into upland "new populous areas" and "economic zones" are like dreary replays of the Diem schemes. It is apparent that the present Hanoi regime no more than the Saigon regime of the 1950s has any intention of honoring highlander land claims or their right to arbitration based on their own indigenous laws. The inescapable conclusion is that the highlands are to be "developed" by the Vietnamese who will assimilate what is left of the upland population.

So now the highlanders have reached the most crucial phase in the struggle to preserve their way of life and their ethnic identity. They have been abandoned by the French and the Americans to their own fate. The highlanders who remain in their villages will see the old ways disappear as their children become part of the new socialist Vietnamese culture. A few dances and native costumes will be permitted so that visitors can be shown the "national minorities" in the new Vietnam. The highlander ethnic identity, however, will survive with those who have chosen to resist. Their struggle may be futile and they may spend their lives in dissidence, but at least they will be Sons of the Mountains, free in the forest.

AFTERWORD

Following the 1976 reunification of the two Vietnams, Hanoi's efforts at integrating the central highlands into the new socialist state through a process of Vietnamization intensified until the end of 1978, when to all indications the pace slackened. Through 1976 and 1977 large numbers of lowland Vietnamese were resettled in upland economic zones.[1] During that same period there were reports of "nomadic" highland people being regrouped in "permanent" villages where they received a "new culture."[2] A 30 May 1978 article in the *New York Times* reported that since 1976, some 1.33 million people had been resettled (it specified that 100,000 Vietnamese had been sent to Dac Lac province) as part of a grand plan to

1. A 9 December 1976 Radio Hanoi broadcast (translated in FBIS/APA, 16 December 1976) reported that "Nearly 350,000 Ho Chi Minh City dwellers have left for new economic zones," most of which were in upland Song Be and Dong Nai provinces. About the same time it was reported in another broadcast (translated by FBIS/APA, 8 December 1976) that as of late October 1976, Gia Lai–Cong Tum province had received more than 15,000 settlers from Nghia Binh province, and plans were being made for 3,000 laborers to be moved from Ha Nam Ninh province. On 28 March 1977, an article published in the newspaper *Nhân Dân* (translated in FBIS/APA, 2 May 1977) described how 10,000 people from Hue had been moved to Dac Lac province.

2. In a reference to the Rhadé, Mnong, and Jarai, a 1 October 1976 broadcast from Hanoi (translated in FBIS/APA, 22 October 1976) revealed that "More than 50,000 people of the Ede, M'nong, and Gia Rai ethnic minorities, about one-tenth of the population of Dac Lac province, had adopted a settled agricultural life." In a 28 October 1976 Ho Chi Minh City broadcast (translated by FBIS/APA, 2 November 1976) concerning "the development of the cultural movement in the mountain areas," the Vice Minister of Culture posed the question, "Under what circumstances and conditions have we begun to build a new culture in the areas inhabited by the ethnic minority nationalities in the south?" and after discussing this topic he concluded,' "It is necessary to eradicate all of the outmoded customs and superstitions which the Americans and puppets sought to develop and spread among the ethnic minority nationalities while gradually bringing the new culture to each area inhabited by the people of each ethnic minority nationality in accordance with their ability to assimilate this new culture." Two days later, on 30 October, in an additional broadcast (translated by FBIS-APA, 11 November 1976), the Vice Minister of Culture outlined "five ethnic minority zones." The first embraced the groups in the central highlands (the other zones were for the Cham, the Khmer Krom, the Chinese, and northern upland ethnic groups that had come south in 1954). The minister noted that in the first zone, "The great economic potential has not yet been exploited and as a result the material and cultural standards of the ethnic minority are still low."

move 10 million people during a 20-year period.[3] This source also revealed that 260,000 "Montagnards" had been regrouped.

In 1978 the Vietnamese economy experienced a downward turn. For a variety of reasons—including bad weather, the ill-advised attempt to collectivize southern Vietnamese farms, and shortages of fuel and chemical fertilizers—paddy production in the Mekong river delta began to decline seriously. To make matters worse, on 23 March 1978 the government moved against free enterprise in the south, shutting down thousands of thriving businesses, which precipitated the exodus of Chinese entre-preneurs, technicians, and skilled workers, all of whom played vital roles in the economy. The international situation also affected the Vietnamese economy. Deteriorating relations with neighboring China and Cambodia led early in 1979 to conflict with both nations, necessitating a general mobilization. Vietnam was again at war.

By the end of 1980 the Sino-Vietnamese border was still the scene of sporadic fighting. In Cambodia the Vietnamese army of occupation was plagued by harassment from the deposed Khmer Rouge, who had become guerrillas. Hanoi also had assumed the costly and demanding task of coping with the shattered Khmer society.[4]

These developments appear to have contributed to the decision to slow the pace of resettlement. Significantly, in May 1978 the Hanoi govern-ment asked the World Council of Churches for $2 million in aid over a two-year period to support an economic zone in Lam Dong province. In May 1979 when two members of the Church World Service visited the site it had 8,500 residents, and the plan was to have a population of 100,000. The aid funds were approved and used to provide bulldozers, heavy trucks,

---

Reporting on a Ministry of Agriculture conference in Nhatrang, a 16 January 1977 Hanoi broadcast (translated in FBIS-APA, 18 January 1976) described how the "700,000 ethnic minority people leading a nomadic life" would be the target of the revolutionary administration's efforts to have them adopt "a sedentary life and cultivation in new villages." A 23 March 1977 article in the Hanoi publication *Tạp Chí Cộng Sản* (the Communist Journal) concerning "development" of the highlands outlined a scheme for resettling vast numbers of Vietnamese and to "help 1.5 million nomads in the mountainous areas to adopt settled farming and settled living." Also in March 1976 at the Lam Dong provincial party congress it was reported that more than 18,000 "nomadic ethnic minority people have settled and engaged in crop cultivation" (a translation is found in FBIS-APA, 11 March 1976).

3. Fox Butterfield, "Vietnam Plans Resettlement of 10 Million Over 20 Years," *New York Times*, 31 May 1978.

4. "Vietnam," in *Asia 1979 Yearbook* (Hong Kong, Far Eastern Economic Review, 1979), pp. 316–23; Nayan Chanda, "No Peace Without Compromise," *Far Eastern Economic Review* 108, no. 17 (1980): 8–20.

and other equipment. When the economic zone was visited again in June 1980 the population had risen to only 9,300.[5]

Information on both Communist and non-Communist highland leaders during the 1976–1980 period was relatively sparse. On 20 December 1976 it was announced that a new Vietnam Communist Party had been formed.[6] Among its thirty-two alternate members, numbers 31 and 32 were Y Bloc Eban and Y Ngong Nie Kdam respectively. Y Wang Mlo Duon Du was named deputy director of the Central Committee for Nationalities.[7] On 22 April 1977 it was reported in *Nhân Dân* that General Secretary Le Duan had visited Dac Lac province and had been greeted by a committee of highland Communist leaders including Y Bih Aleo, member of the Presidium of the Central Committee of the Vietnam Fatherland Front; Y Bloc Eban, standing member of the Dac Lac Communist Party Committee and chairman of the province Fatherland Front Committee; and Y Wang Mlo Duon Du, member of the Central Committee of the Vietnam Fatherland Front. Le Duan then went to Gia Lai–Cong Tum province where he was met by a delegation that included Ksor Kron, alternate member of the Communist Party Committee in the province and chairman of the People's Committee; Y Pah, alternate member of the Central Committee of the Vietnam Communist Party; and Kpa Thin, commander of the Armed Forces for Gia Lai–Cong Tum province.

For the highland leaders who had been arrested by the Communists in 1975 the situation by 1980 appeared dire. Only a few had been released and there was news of some dying in the prisons and reeducation camps. In May 1978, the magazine *Quê Mẹ* (Native Land), published by Vietnamese refugees in Paris, presented a map showing locations of principal political prisons and reeducation camps in what had been South Vietnam.[8] Prisons containing more than 1,000 inmates were located in Dalat, Ban Me Thuot, Pleiku, and Kontum. Reeducation camps with more than 1,000 were found in Kontum, Pleiku, Duc Lap, and Don Duong, while those with 5,000 or more were in An Khe and Gia Gai.

Early in 1978, Touneh Han Tho encountered a Tho (one of the northern upland groups) who had lived in the central highlands since 1954 and had

5. This information was obtained from William Herod of Church World Service in Washington, D.C., during conversations in October 1980.
6. Reported in FBIS-APA, 20 December 1976.
7. Reported in FBIS-APA, 27 December 1976.
8. *Quê Mẹ* (Native Land), May 1978.

just escaped Vietnam by boat. He reported that in December 1976, Nay Luett's family had been informed that he had "committed suicide" in the prison. The Tho refugee also related that Senator Ksor Rot and Y Thih Eban had been killed around the time of the Communist takeover. The same information was obtained from two young highlanders of elite families who escaped by boat in 1979. One of them reported that Lat leader Lieng Hot Ngheo also had died in prison. This refugee also described seeing Pierre K'Briuh, who had been released from a reeducation camp. Emaciated and suffering from beri-beri, K'Briuh went to Kontum to remain with his wife's family. Both refugees said that life for the high-landers was very hard because Communist troops occupied the villages and confiscated the harvests, leaving little food for the population. They also affirmed that resistance by FULRO was continuing.

Between July 1976 and January 1981 a variety of sources described FULRO-conducted resistance to Communist rule in the highlands. A 25 February 1977 article in the newspaper *Quân Đội Nhân Dân* (People's Army) titled "The Battlefield Is Still Before Them" described military operations in Lam Dong province.[9] It related that troops of the 6th Battalion were stationed in villages, staying in the highlanders' houses and accompanying them to the fields.

Refugees have proven a rich source of information on FULRO activities. In April 1977, Jay Scarborough received a letter from a Cham friend who had just escaped Vietnam that same month. The letter described "four divisions" of Cham and highlander dissidents led by Kpa Koi, the FULRO leader. It also revealed that the Communists had sent several divisions to pacify highland areas considered "insecure."

According to a 1 June 1979 article in the *New York Times*, a former captain (a Vietnamese) of the Saigon army encountered in a Hong Kong refugee camp claimed that he recently had been involved in guerrilla operations with FULRO troops.[10] Using American-made weapons and field radios, they would launch attacks about once a month against the Communists in Lam Dong province. Another Vietnamese refugee reported to have had contact with FULRO was Buddhist monk Thich Thien Quang, who had been a subordinate of Thich Tri Quang, leader of

9. Reported in FBIS-APA, 22 March 1977.
10. Fox Butterfield, "Vietnam Refugees Say Attacks on Communists Continue in Highlands," *New York Times*, 1 June 1979.

Buddhist opposition to the regime of Ngo Dinh Diem and Nguyen Van Thieu.[11] Interviewed in a camp on Bintan Island, Indonesia, on 12 July 1979, Thien Quang described how he and Tri Quang had been imprisoned after the Communist takeover and released in 1977 (by which time Tri Quang had been reduced to a skeletonlike cripple). Forced to go into hiding following a Buddhist protest in March 1978, Thien Quang dressed as a layman and made his way into the highlands. There he made contact with FULRO. He related that in April 1978, FULRO units had occupied the town of Cheo Reo and subsequently had clashed with Communist units, including the "Yellow Star" Third Army Division in the area south of Ban Me Thuot. When asked where the anti-Communist groups obtained their weapons, the monk replied that they purchased many from Communist soldiers, adding, "If you have gold you can buy anything in Vietnam now."

It also was revealed at this time that a link had been established between FULRO and the Khmer Rouge, who now were engaged in guerrilla warfare against the Vietnamese forces occupying Cambodia. The source of this information was Ieng Sary, one of the Khmer Rouge leaders, who was interviewed at Colombo, Sri Lanka, in June 1979 by a journalist from the *Far Eastern Economic Review*. Sary pointed out that, apart from the Khmer Rouge, the Jarai and other rebellious hill people organized by FULRO offered the most serious resistance to the Hanoi regime.[12] "The FULRO approached us for cooperation," Sary reported, "to exchange intelligence, military experience and get guerrilla warfare training." He explained that after the Khmer Rouge were deposed it became difficult to supply the highlanders with food and ammunition. This, however, did not lessen their collaboration. "On the contrary," Sary noted, "they supply us with the powerful poison which only they know how to produce. Once it enters the body it immediately coagulates blood and leads to death." He also claimed that during the February–March 1979 period the FULRO killed some two hundred government troops in the Ban Me Thuot, Pleiku, and Kontum areas.

On 14 November 1979, the Khmer Rouge's clandestine Voice of

11. James P. Sterba, "Ordeal of Famed Buddhist in Ho Chi Minh City Revealed," *New York Times*, 14 July 1979.
12. Nayan Chanda, "Ieng Sary: Unite for Our Country," *Far Eastern Economic Review* 104, no. 25 (1979): 10–11.

Democratic Kampuchea reported that its government had received a letter from "Anuk N'gram" ("Son of N'gram").[13] This pseudonym, derived from the name of a legendary Cham hero, was used by a Cham leader from Phan Rang who had been involved in the FULRO revolt at Buon Sar Pa in September 1964. In the letter he was identified as prime minister of the Dega-FULRO. (It was noted previously that Dega means "Sons of the Mountains" and that it had appeared in Y Bham's letters as "Dega-Cham," another designation for FULRO.) The letter also identified the president of the movement as "Ndrang Hmuol" (which conceivably might be Y Bham Enuol deformed in transcription). The broadcast claimed that the letter reaffirmed the collaboration between the two groups in their "struggle against the Vietnamese aggressors, expansionists, annexationists, and exterminators, who are the common enemy of our two people."

The Voice of Democratic Kampuchea reported on 23 January 1980 that a second Dega-FULRO letter (dated 10 January) had been received.[14] It accused the Hanoi regime of "massacre against our people behind closed doors"—out of the world's view—and it claimed that since 1975, some 150,000 highlanders had perished and many had been jailed. Young highlanders were being pressed into military service "to fight in Kampuchea, Laos, and at the Sino-Vietnamese border." The letter also described how the Communists "have tried to abolish the Dega social traditions and customs through all means. They have deprived the Dega people of their rights, forcing them to speak Vietnamese, and eat and dress in the Vietnamese way." It related that "people in each village must feed a group of ten to fifteen Vietnamese soldiers," and that "families whose husbands, sons, or relatives have joined the FULRO guerrillas are always oppressed, intimidated, harmed, arrested, and killed." Villagers are subject to corvée labor for construction of military roads into Cambodia and Laos, for construction of military installations, and to act as bearers for transporting military goods. The letter ended with an appeal to all in the world "who cherish freedom and justice," for help. It was signed "Anuk N'gram, Prime Minister of the Dega-FULRO Government."

Broadcasts from the clandestine Khmer Rouge radio described FULRO attacks against government posts and convoys in Lam Dong, Dac Lac, and

13. Translated in FBIS-APA, 15 November 1979.
14. Translated in FBIS-APA, 8 February 1980.

Gia Lai–Cong Tum provinces during the 1979–1980 period.[15] The sites of these actions were pinpointed, and there also were claims of many Communist troops "put out of action" and the capture of numerous arms. Interestingly, Khmer Rouge reports of FULRO actions against the Hanoi forces also were reported by the Voice of the People of Burma (in Burmese), broadcast from a Burmese Communist Party facility in Kunming, People's Republic of China.[16]

An 18 October 1980 article in the *Washington Post* describing Chinese military aid to "right-wing guerrillas" in Laos also noted that "with Chinese weapons also flowing to Khmer Rouge and Khmer Serei forces fighting the Vietnamese in Cambodia, and probably to anti-Communist Montagnard insurgents in Vietnam's central highlands as well, Peking appears to be nurturing in all three countries of Indochina a front against domination by Hanoi."[17]

By the end of 1980 the clouds of international conflict were gathering once more over Vietnam, and the highlanders were again becoming "a people in between." Their cultures were threatened by the authoritarian Communist rule, but their spirit of ethnonationalism still lived in the FULRO movement and its struggle. The only refuge for the highlanders' way of life was in the mountain forests, the forests that had molded their cultures and sustained them. Whatever happens, the highlanders know that the mountains and forests will provide salvation as they have ever since a remote time long before the advent of history.

15. Translated in FBIS-APA, 14 and 15 January 1980; 8 February 1980; 21 March 1980; 2, 10, and 14 April 1980; 25 and 26 September 1980; 1, 2, 3, 7, 9, 10, 16, 30, and 31 October 1980; 21 November 1980.

16. Translated in FBIS-APA, 14 November 1980.

17. John Burgess, "Right-Wing Rebels Aided by China Worry Laotians, Vietnamese," *Washington Post*, 18 October 1980.

APPENDIX A

Highland Population Figures

A 1921 census in the French protectorate of Annam where most highlanders were located—there were some in Cochinchina—reported a total
of 405,888.[1] It also revealed that in Darlac province there were 5 French
and 20 Vietnamese and in Kontum province 27 French and 7,000 Vietnamese. Lang Biang province had 24 French and 600 Vietnamese; Haut
Donnai province had 20 French and 500 Vietnamese.

The highlander population of Darlac in 1921 was reported to be 98,000.
In 1930, however, Monfleur estimated that the highlander population was
closer to 150,000.[2] In 1931 a French government source reported for the
first time that the highlander population in the colony of Cochinchina was
100,000, all in the eastern uplands.[3]

In 1943 an official census gave a total of one million highlanders.[4] It also
listed the Vietnamese population in the highlands as 42,267: the distribution was 4,000 in Darlac; 10,000 in Haut Donnai; 7,000 in Kontum;
21,000 in Pleiku; and 267 in Dalat. The French population totaled 5,090,
concentrated mostly in Darlac (199), Haut Donnai (141), Kontum (141),
Pleiku (70), and Dalat (4,461).[5] In that same year the French administrator
Guilleminet estimated that there were 60,000 Rhadé, 150,000 Jarai, and

1. Gouvernement Général de l'Indochine, Direction des Affaires Economiques, Service de la
Statistique Générale, *Annuaire statistique de l'Indochine* (Hanoi: Imprimerie d'Extrême-Orient, 1927),
1:42.
2. A. Monfleur, *Monographie de la province de Darlac* (Hanoi: Imprimerie d'Extrême-Orient, 1931),
p. 32.
3. Gouvernement Général de l'Indochine (Société des Etudes Indochinoises), *Cochinchine 1931*
(Saigon: P. Géstaldy, 1931).
4. *Annuaire des états-associés: Cambodge-Laos-Vietnam* (Paris: Editions Diloutremer et Havas, 1953).
5. Ministère de l'Economie Nationale, *Annuaire statistique de Vietnam*, vol. 1 (1949–1950) (Saigon:
Institut de la Statistique et des Etudes Economiques du Vietnam, 1951), p. 24.

80,000 Bahnar—a total of 290,000 for these three largest of the highland groups.[6]

In 1953 the Social Action Plan prepared by the Bao Dai regime used a total of 500,000 for highland people in the Crown Domain (not including the highlanders in central Vietnam or in the Cochinchina area) and stated that there were an estimated 30,000 Vietnamese living there.[7]

There was a tendency during the Diem era to underestimate the highlander population in order to minimize the importance of that segment of the population. In 1958, the government reported that in Dong-Nai Thuong (formerly Haut Donnai), Kontum, Pleiku, and Dalat (Darlac was not included), the highlanders totaled 162,378.[8] It also noted that the other provinces of central Vietnam had 211,777 highlanders, giving a total of 455,592. In addition, it stated that there were 162,378 Vietnamese as well as 536 French and 14 Americans in these provinces (again, excluding Darlac).

Another report in 1959 estimated that there were 100,000 people living in the highland urban centers of Ban Me Thuot (28,000), Kontum (8,700), Di Linh (5,500), Pleiku (7,200), Gia Nghia (1,700), and Dalat (49,000).[9]

During the 1965–1967 period, I collected data on population by ethnolinguistic groups in the highlands, using estimates of the SIL, missionaries, local authorities, and highland leaders. My figures are summarized in table A.1. Also included in that table are the estimates reported by the Special Commission for Highland Affairs and the FULRO leaders. These figures represent the state of the highlander population before the most serious disruptions of the Vietnam War took place.

In 1968, a government report indicated that the number of highlanders living in the provinces of Darlac, Kontum, Lam Dong, Phu Bon, Pleiku, Quang Duc, Tuyen Duc, and the city of Dalat was 350,898.[10] Adding to that the number of highlanders in other provinces, the total rose to

---

6. P. Guilleminet, "Ebauche d'une classification des Moi au point de vue culturel," *Indochine*, no. 169 (1943), p. 26.

7. Nguyễn Đê, *Plan d'action sociale pour les pays de sud du Domaine de la Couronne* (Saigon: Editions de la Délégation Impériale du Domaine de la Couronne, 1953).

8. Bộ Kinh-Tê Quôc-Gia (Ministry of National Economy), *Việt-Nam Niên-Giám Thông-Kê* (Statistical Yearbook of Vietnam), vol. 7 (Saigon: Viện Quôc-Gia Thông-Kê, 1959), pp. 18–21.

9. Bộ Kinh-Tê Quôc-Gia (Ministry of National Economy), *Việt-Nam Niên-Giám Thông-Kê* (Statistical Yearbook of Vietnam), vol. 8 (Saigon: Viện Quôc-Gia Thông-Kê, 1960), p. 43.

10. Việt Nam Cộng Hòa Nha Tổng Giám-Đôc Kê-Hoạch (Republic of Vietnam Directorate of Planning), *Việt-Nam Niên-Giám Thông-Kê 1967–1968* (Statistical Yearbook of Vietnam, 1967–1968), vol. 11 (Saigon: Viện Quôc-Gia Thông-Kê, 1968), pp. 394–95.

Table A.1

Population Estimates of Highland Ethnolinguistic Groups 1965–1967

Ethnic Group	Unofficial Sources (SIL, Hickey, missionaries, etc.)	Special Commission for Highland Affairs	FULRO
Austronesian-speaking Groups			
Chru	15,000	4,998	15,000
Jarai	150,000	142,171	150,000
Rhadé	100,000	79,595	100,000
Roglai	57,000	27,775	47,000
Rai[1]		2,787	
Mon Khmer-speaking Groups			
Bahnar	75,000	58,833	85,000
Bru	40,000	22,370	43,000
Chrau[2]	15,000	6,428	20,000
Cua	20,000	11,562	20,000
Duan[3]		3,500	3,500
Halang	10,000	2,516	10,000
Kyong[4]		548	
Hre	100,000	43,015	43,015
Jeh	10,000	4,082	10,000
Katu	40,000	23,136	20,000
Koho Language Group[5]	100,000		100,000
Chil		10,525	
Sre		21,778	
Lat		1,271	
Maa		26,070	
Nop		981	
Tring		4,145	
Monom	5,000	2,150	5,000
Mnong	40,000	27,730	35,000
Pacoh	15,000	6,584	
Rengao	15,000	9,123	15,000
Sedang	40,000	26,120	40,000
Stieng	30,000	36,701	30,000
Strieng[6]		1,120	1,120
Takua[7]		2,700	
Totals	877,000	610,314	792,635

[1] The status of the Rai as an ethnic group cannot be determined because the ethnographic research done on them is insufficient.

[2] It was pointed out elsewhere that although the SIL treat the Chrau as an ethnic group, on the basis of the available data, I feel that it constitutes a linguistic rather than an ethnic group.

Table A.1 (*continued*)

[3] The Duan have not been identified as a separate ethnic group.
[4] The Kyong have not been identified as a separate ethnic group.
[5] In 1967, the SIL included Chil in the Koho language group, but later placed it with Mnong. The Koho language group includes the Sre, Lat, Maa, and possibly the Nop and Tring, although neither is definitely identified as an individual ethnic group. The Special Commission for Highland Affairs also listed Chil, Sre, Lat, Maa, Nop, and Tring separately.
[6] The Strieng have not been identified as a separate ethnic group.
[7] The Takua have not been identified as a separate ethnic group.

464,354. The number of Vietnamese in the provinces listed above and the city of Dalat totaled 496,199. The urban populations were estimated to total 266,650, concentrated in Ban Me Thuot (62,092), Kontum (18,687), Bao Loc (19,678), Cheo Reo (5,890), Pleiku (23,720), Gia Nghia (5,181), Tung Nghia (15,760), and Dalat (83,641). These figures were, at the time, generally considered low. There had been no systematic census of the highlanders, and many were in areas not under government control. The government continued to underestimate the population figures for highlanders. Figures for urban populations also were underestimated. By 1966 the population of Pleiku had risen to an estimated 50,000 with a large influx of workers for construction and service jobs on American bases and the arrival of a great many dependents of Vietnamese military personnel.

In September 1970, the Ministry for Development of Ethnic Minorities reported a total of 848,174 highland people with a total of 436,500 in Kontum, Pleiku, Phu Bon, Darlac, Quang Duc, Tuyen Duc, Lam Dong, and Dalat. The higher figure for the highlanders was undoubtedly due to the improved organization of the ministry's services in the highland provinces. The ministry's representatives collected population data, and, since most of them were highlanders, they had better contact with the local populations than the Vietnamese officials. As a result, their figures were more apt to be accurate. The Vietnamese population for the same area was reported to total 448,349, or 50 percent of the total population, giving some idea of the rapid increase of this segment of the population since 1953, when the Vietnamese were estimated at 30,000.

Figures after 1971 were considered unreliable because of the vast disruptions due to the 1972 offensive, followed by the fall of South Vietnam in early 1975.

APPENDIX B

One Hundred Highland Leaders: Ethnic Affiliation, Approximate Birth Date, and Religion

Ethnic Group and Name	Approximate Birth Date	Religion
1. BAHNAR		
Doi, Paul	1935	Catholic
Dong, Michel	1935	Catholic
Hiar (1.7)	1905	Catholic
Hiu (1.16)	1930	Catholic
Hiup (1.20)	1934	Catholic
Nur, Paul (1.13)	1926	Catholic
Yuk, Pierre (1.12)	1919	Catholic
2. BRU		
Anha	1930	Traditional*
Binh (1.29)	1953	Protestant
3. CHRU		
Banahria Ya Don (4.6)	1917	Traditional
K'Kre (4.5, Chru-Sre)	1919	Catholic
Touneh Han Din (4.3) (deceased)	1917	Traditional
Touneh Han Tin (4.13) (deceased)	1922	Catholic
Touneh Yoh (4.10)	1936	Protestant
Touneh Ton (4.14)	1936	Catholic
Touprong Hiou (4.4)	1917	Traditional
Touprong Ya Ba (4.9)	1923	Protestant
Ya Yu Sahau	1923	Catholic
Ya Duck	1933	Catholic

*Traditional means that he adheres to the traditional religious beliefs of his own ethnic group.

Ethnic Group and Name	Approximate Birth Date	Religion
4. HRE		
Dinh Ngo (deceased)	1920	Traditional
Dinh Roi	1935	Traditional
5. JARAI		
Kpa Koi	1934	Traditional
Kpa Doh	1937	Traditional
Ksor Wol (3.5)	1908	Traditional
Ksor Glai (3.10)	1917	Catholic
Ksor Dhuat	1937	Traditional
Ksor Dun (5.8)	1933	Protestant
Ksor Rot (3.5) (reported dead)	1937	Traditional
Ksor Hip (2.31)	1942	Traditional
Ksor Kok (5.11)	1944	Protestant
Nay Der (2.12)	1900	Traditional
Nay Moul (2.17)	1913	Traditional
Nay Phin (2.19)	1916	Traditional
Nay Lo	1919	Traditional
Nay Dai (2.27)	1925	Traditional
Nay Blim (2.25)	1928	Traditional
Nay Honh (2.23)	1933	Traditional
Nay Luett (2.26) (reported dead)	1935	Catholic
Nay Alep (2.29)	1940	Catholic
Rcom Rock (3.11)	1920	Buddhist
Rcom Briu (2.20)	1922	Traditional
Rcom Pioi (2.21)	1925	Traditional
Rcom Hin	1927	Traditional
Rcom Perr (3.13)	1934	Catholic
Rcom Anhot (3.12)	1936	Traditional
Rcom Po (3.22)	1937	Traditional
Rcom H'ueh (2.28)	1941	Traditional
Rcom Nhut (Ali, 3.25)	1947	Traditional
Rahlan Beo (2.14)	1922	Traditional
R'mah Liu	1934	Traditional
R'mah Wih (3.27)	1942	Traditional
Ro-o, Bleo (5.3)	1943	Traditional
Siu Plung (1.23)	1926	Traditional
Siu Sipp (deceased)	1929	Traditional
Siu Nay	1934	Traditional
Siu Ky (deceased)	1943	Catholic
6. KATU		
Kithen	1915	Traditional

Ethnic Group and Name	Approximate Birth Date	Religion
7. LAT		
Cil K'Din (4.16)	1943	Catholic
Lieng Hot Ngheo	1939	Protestant
8. MNONG RLAM		
Y Tang Phok	1936	Catholic
Y Char Hdok	1937	Catholic
Bun Sur (probably deceased)	1937	Catholic
9. RHADÉ		
Adrong, Y Dhe (5.10)	1920	Protestant
Adrong, Y Dhon (deceased)	1933	Catholic
Adrong, Y Klong (5.9)	1934	Protestant
Aleo, Y Bih	1901	Traditional
Buon Dap, Y Dhua	1923	Traditional
Buon Krong, Y Preh	1920	Protestant
Buon Krong Pang, Y Bling	1922	Catholic
Buon To, Y Jut (1.19)	1944	Catholic
Buon Ya, Y Puk	1940	Traditional
Buon Ya, Y Wik (deceased)	1941	Traditional
Buon Ya, Y Ngo (deceased)	1943	Catholic
Eban, Y Sok	1900	Traditional
Eban, Y Bloc	1917	Traditional
Eban, Y Mo (5.7)	1927	Traditional
Eban, Y Thih (5.2) (reported dead)	1932	Protestant
Eban, Y Ju	1935	Traditional
Eban, Y Nham (probably deceased)	1937	Traditional
Eban, Y Du (3.21)	1949	Traditional
Enuol, Y Bham	1913	Protestant
Hmok, Y Blieng	1920	Traditional
Hwing, Y Tin (reported dead)	1944	Traditional
Kbuor Y Soay (1.11) (deceased)	1917	Traditional
Knuol, Y Pem (deceased)	1927	Traditional
Kpuor, Y Bhan	1937	Traditional
Mlo, Y Kdruin (Philippe Drouin, 2.24) (deceased)	1936	Catholic
Mlo Duon Du, Y Toeh (5.1)	1910	Protestant
Mlo Duon Du, Y Wang	1925	Traditional
Mlo Duon Du, Y Say (deceased)	1925	Traditional
Mlo Duon Du, Y Chon	1933	Protestant
Nie Buon Drieng, Y Blu	1923	Traditional
Nie Hrah, Y Ham (5.4)	1930	Protestant
Nie Kdam, Y Dhuat	1919	Traditional

Nie Kdam, Y Ngong	1923	Traditional
Nie Kdam, Y Sen (3.18)	1943	Catholic

10. SEDANG
Peang	1924	Traditional
Kek	1936	Catholic

11. SRE
Toplui Pierre K'Briuh (4.11)	1937	Catholic
Toplui K'Broi (4.12)	1944	Catholic

A. Total Number of Leaders Listed ... 100
  (1) Male ... 99
  (2) Female ... 1

B. Total for Each Ethnic Group
  1. Bahnar ... 7
  2. Bru ... 2
  3. Chru ... 10
  4. Hre ... 2
  5. Jarai ... 35
  6. Katu ... 1
  7. Lat ... 2
  8. Mnong Rlam ... 3
  9. Rhadé ... 34
  10. Sedang ... 2
  11. Sre ... 2

C. Total Number of Leaders on Kinship Charts
  Chart 1 9   Chart 4 11
  Chart 2 14   Chart 5 9
  Chart 3 11   Total 54

D. Totals by Religion
  (1) Traditional ... 55
  (2) Catholic ... 30
  (3) Protestant ... 14
  (4) Buddhist ... 1

E. Age Groups
  (1) Number born before 1920 ... 16
  (2) Number born between 1920 and 1940 ... 65
  (3) Number born between 1940 and 1960 ... 19

APPENDIX C

Perceived Effects of Herbicides Used in the Highlands

In most of the interviews the informants claimed to have seen the actual spraying, although there were some vague responses concerning the timing of the operations. Informants from Dak Mot-Khon (interview 2a in table C.1) and Dak Mot-Tri (2b), discussing the same defoliated area in Dak To district to the northwest of their settlements, reported that they had not seen the aircraft spraying, but they gave similar accounts regarding the effects.

Those who did witness the spraying were able to describe the type of aircraft and the pattern of the spraying. In the Dak To area of Kontum province, informants from Long Djon village (1a) noted that there had been many spraying operations in the vicinity since 1967, and they had seen the "large aircraft, each with two engines" that passed over "three in a row." This was repeated by informants from Dak Rosa (1b), which is not far from Long Djon, as well as by villagers from Dak Tang Plun (1c), Polei-Krong (3a, b), Plei Jar Tum (4b), and Plei Ngol-Drong (5). The Hroy agricultural engineer (6) was a more sophisticated informant since he had been prepared in Hanoi for the possibility of herbicide missions against food production, and he knew that the aircraft were C-123s. At Dak Sieng Ranger Camp (2c), the informants reported the spraying had been done by a helicopter, and this was verified by a former U.S. Special Forces officer who had been stationed at Dak Sieng and was employed as a civilian with the USAID mission in Kontum. Villagers from Polei Kleng (4a) also reported that the spraying was carried out by helicopters.

Some informants were very explicit about seeing the spray leaving the aircraft. An elderly lady from Long Djon village (1a) said that "it looked like smoke" and it came from both sides of the aircraft, and this was repeated by villagers from Dak Rosa (1b). Informants from Polei Krong (3a, b) reported that the spray looked like water, and one man from Plei Ro-O (1d) in the Polei Kleng area noted that "it looked like rain" but when it reached the ground they found it looked black. Informants from Dak Siang (2c) even noticed that a tube protruded from the helicopter, and it turned and began to spew a liquid. At Polei Kleng (4a) the villagers said that they watched the spray descend and that they could smell it.

In none of the interviews did it appear that there was a deliberate attempt to spray the settlements themselves, although in some instances the villagers' swiddens appear to have been targets. In most cases, however, the spray drifted into the settlements. Informants from Long Djon (1a) noted that during one of the many missions in that area (Dak To district, Kontum province), their swiddens were sprayed, and herbicide was carried into the settlement. Villagers from Dak Rosa (1b) complained that they and villagers from neighboring Kon Briong farmed about 30 swiddens in the area, and all were sprayed several times over a period of several months. The villagers from Dak Siang (2c) described the way some of the spray drifted into their housing area following the accidental spraying of their fields.

One informant from Polei Kleng (4a) noted that the spraying took place over a thickly forested area northwest of village and farming area. It was an area the villagers avoided because it was known to be Viet Cong-controlled. Villagers from Polei Krong (3a, b) watched the aircraft spray both sides of the Dak Bla river near the settlements. Informants from Plei Ngol-Drong (5) reported that the spraying was along Route 19. According to the agricultural engineer (6), the first spraying took place in September 1969 and was aimed at the swiddens in the area, some of which were being farmed by villagers. Most, however, were part of an area where there was concentrated food production for the Viet Cong. The second spraying in March 1970 was along a trail used exclusively by the Viet Cong.

With the exception of two villages—Dak Mot-Khon (2a) and Dak Mot-Tri (2b)—where no spraying was observed by the residents, the first effects reported concerned humans, domestic animals, and aquatic life.

PERCEIVED EFFECTS ON HUMANS

There was a definite pattern in the perceptions regarding the effect of the herbicides on those residing in or near the sprayed areas. The most

Table C.1

Characteristics of Persons Interviewed in the Highlands Herbicide Study

Location of Interviews	*Original Village of Respondents*	*Ethnic Group*	*Characteristics of Principal Interview Subjects, Principal Respondents*
1. Dam San Refugee Center, Darlac Province	a. Long Djon, near Dak To District Headquarters, Kontum Province	Sedang	Two young men, one older woman
	b. Dak Rosa, near Dak To, Kontum Province	Sedang	Older man
	c. Dak Tang Plun, near Tan-Canh, Dak To District, Kontum Province	Halang	Several older men, several women, two younger men
	d. Plei Ro-O near Polei Kleng, 30 km west of Kontum City	Jarai Arap	Young man (NLF defector), several women
2. Mary Lou (Ngok Long) Refugee Center, Kontum Province	a. Dak Mot-Khon, west of Tan-Canh, Dak To District, Kontum Province	Sedang	Village chief
	b. Dak Mot-Tri, west of Tan-Canh, Dak To District, Kontum Province	Sedang	Hamlet chief
	c. Dak Siang Ranger Camp Dependents' Settlement, northwest of Dak To District Headquarters, Kontum Province	Halang	Young woman, her father, older man, older woman
3. Plei Don Refugee Group	a. Polei Krong cluster of villages, west of Kontum City	Jarai Arap Halang Rengao	Man Man Man
	b. Polei Krong cluster of villages, west of Kontum City	Rengao Jarai Arap	Older men Older men

Table C.1 (*continued*)

4. Prisoner of War Refugee Center, Pleiku Province	a. Polei Kleng, west of Kontum City	Jarai Arap	Young hamlet chief, older woman, older man
	b. Plei Jar Tum, west of Kontum City	Jarai Arap	Two men, three women
5. Camp Enari Refugee Center, Pleiku Province	a. Plei Ea Tung Hamlet, Plei Ngol-Drong Village near Edap Enang Resettlement Center, Rte. 19	Jarai To-Buan	Two men
6. Highlander	Phu-Bon and Phu-Yen	Hroy	Man, follower of Viet Minh, moved to North in 1954, trained as Agricultural Engineer in Hanoi University, returned to highlands area astride Phu-Yen/Phu-Bon border in 1969, organized food production for NLF, had "rallied" to Government at time of interview

common symptoms reported were abdominal pains and diarrhea. Informants from Long Djon (1a) also reported that in addition to these symptoms the villagers complained of experiencing a stinging sensation in their nasal passages just after the spray drifted into the settlement. Many developed coughs that lasted more than a month. At Dak Rosa (1b), according to some residents, many villagers went into the swiddens following the spraying and, in addition to the common symptoms noted above, they broke out with skin rashes that lasted many weeks. Dak Tang Plun (1c) residents also reported widespread skin rashes, cramps, diarrhea, and fevers. A Plei Ro-O (1d) informant reported these same symptoms, noting that some villagers coughed blood.

Polei Krong (3a, b) informants stated that the villagers suffered these same ailments and that the skin rashes made them look "like they had been

Table C.2

Illness Perceived by Highlanders Following Herbicide Spraying

Location	Symptoms	People Affected, Deaths
1.a Long Djon	Abdominal pains, diarrhea, nasal irritation, coughs lasting more than a month	More children than adults were affected; "many children died"
1.b Dak Rosa	Abdominal pains, diarrhea, skin rashes looking like insect bites following contact with sprayed vegetation	Several children died; "unusual number" of stillbirths among exposed mothers
1.c Dak Tang	Diarrhea, cramps, skin rashes, fevers	Many children became ill, an estimated 30 died
1.d Plei Ro-O	Diarrhea, cramps, rashes, fever, coughing blood	Thirty-eight children reported to have died as a result of eating sprayed crops
2.c Dak Siang	Diarrhea and abdominal pains after drinking water from stream in sprayed area, dizziness and vomiting after eating bamboo shoots from sprayed area	Some children died after drinking water from sprayed area
3.a,b Polei Krong	Diarrhea, cramps, fever, rash looking like burns with small blisters over red areas	Higher than usual number of children died after spraying
4.a Plei Kleng	Diarrhea, vomiting, fever within one day of spraying	About 40 adults and children died with these symptoms
4.b Plei Jar Tum	Diarrhea, vomiting, fever	Four children and one adult died
5.a Plei Ngol-Drong	Abdominal pain, diarrhea, vomiting, skin rash	Some people died two days after spraying; rash resembled chicken pox
6. Kontum-Phu Yen Border	Abdominal pain, diarrhea after eating manioc harvested after spray, with inadequate cleaning	Illness only among those not following instructions given to agricultural engineer in Hanoi; no deaths

burned, with small blisters all over the red areas." Dak Siang (2c) informants noted that after some of the villagers drank from the stream that was
in the sprayed area they became ill with abdominal pains and diarrhea that
lasted for days. They also reported that some villagers had eaten bamboo
shoots from the sprayed area, after which they became dizzy "like you feel
when you have drunk too much from the wine jar," and later started
vomiting. Polei Kleng (4a) residents, according to one informant, fell ill
with abdominal pains, diarrhea, vomiting, and fever within one day after
the spraying. Plei Jar Tum (4b) villagers with the same symptoms went to
get medical assistance at a local dispensary.

The agricultural engineer (6) had been prepared in his Hanoi training for
the possible use of herbicides by the Americans and the South Vietnamese.
The principal propaganda theme was that the Americans had no regard
for human life and were using dangerous chemicals to kill plant and
animal life. He had been instructed what to do if herbicides were sprayed;
he was told to obtain a gas mask, and, if one was not available, to cover his
face with a wet cloth. To save some of the food crop he was to instruct the
villagers to cut the manioc roots as soon as possible and wash them well
before cooking. When the spraying did occur he followed the instructions
regarding salvaging the manioc roots, and the only villagers who became
ill with abdominal cramps and diarrhea were those who had not been told
what to do. Some of the Viet Cong cadres who came into the area after the
spraying ate some manioc roots and drank water from the affected areas,
and they also developed abdominal cramps and diarrhea.

Dak Tang Plun (1c) informants reported that "many children" became
ill with abdominal pains, diarrhea, fever, coughs, and skin rashes after the
spraying, and they estimated that 30 had died. A Plei Ro-O (1d) informant
described all these symptoms, with the exception of the skin rash, as having
affected many children in the settlement following the spraying. He
claimed that 38 children died, and villagers thought that they had eaten
plants from the sprayed areas.

Informants from Polei Krong (3a, b) reported that a higher than usual
number of children in their villages died within a short period following
the spraying, but they could not say how many. One Rengao village chief
said that in the week after the spraying "two children died one day and two
died the next day." Their symptoms were abdominal cramps, diarrhea,
and skin rashes, which, as noted above, were described as having the
appearance of burns "with small blisters." Dak Siang (2c) informants felt

that the children who died were the ones who drank from the stream following the spray mission. They fell ill the first day and died the following day. "Their skin was the color of green in the leaves," one woman noted, and another added that their faces swelled "as if they had been in a fist fight."

Informants from Polei Kleng (4a) reported that many villagers of all ages fell ill with abdominal pains, diarrhea, and vomiting within one day after the spraying. They estimated that around 40 people—adults and children—died after manifesting these symptoms. One old woman said that she had seen four children die. Plei Jar Tum (4b) villagers described these same symptoms, and they claimed that five residents—four children and one adult—died. At Plei Ngol-Drong (5), according to informants, some people died within two days after the spraying. They could not say how many, but they had the symptoms noted above, and they broke out with skin rashes that resembled chicken pox.

PERCEIVED EFFECTS ON ANIMAL LIFE

Most of the informants interviewed reported widespread deaths among their domestic animals following the spraying. The Long Djon (1a) informants noted that since they were refugees they had few animals, but most of their chickens and pigs died shortly after the spraying, and the Dak Rosa (1b) villagers reported the same thing. Informants from Dak Tang Plun (1c) said that all their chickens, most of their pigs, and some of their cattle died, and the young man from Plei Ro-O (1d) reported the same thing, specifying that this occurred within four or five days after the spraying. He also noted that villagers found a number of dead wild animals, particularly wild boar, in the nearby forests. Polei Krong (3a, b) informants also pointed out they found dead wild boar in the forest. They, too, saw all their chickens, pigs, dogs, and small cattle die, although the big cattle survived. Both the Polei Kleng (4a) and the Plei Jar Tum (4b) villagers said that their pigs, dogs, and chickens died, and the latter added that they also lost cattle. Plei Ngol-Drong (5) informants reported that all their pigs, chickens, dogs, goats (they noted that goats are "very strong"), and cattle died. One man observed that the cattle that died first were afflicted with sores around the mouth. They also said that they found dead deer and wild boar in the nearby forests.

PERCEIVED EFFECTS ON AQUATIC LIFE

Highland villages normally are located near streams or rivers from which the residents draw water for drinking and cooking. They also wash clothes and bathe and water their domestic animals in the nearby watercourses, which also provide fish, an important part in the highlander's diet. Responses concerning perceived effects on the aquatic life in the streams varied more than did those regarding the effects on humans and animals.

Long Djon (1a) villagers were not sure whether the dead fish floating on the surface of the neighboring stream was the result of the spraying. Since many soldiers in the area commonly threw grenades in the streams to get fish, the abundance of dead fish was not an unusual sight. Dak Rosa (1b) residents said they did not perceive any changes in the nearby stream. The interview with Dak Tang Plun (1c) villagers was interrupted before any questions could be posed regarding fish. One Plei Ro-O (1d) informant, however, reported that there were a great many dead fish seen in streams close to the settlement following the spraying. Most of the fish appeared to be swollen, and villagers who ate them became ill with abdominal pains and diarrhea. Residents of Dak Mot-Khon (2d) had not witnessed any spraying nor did they report an effect on humans and animals, but they did see an unusually large number of dead and dying fish in the Dak Kla river near the village. American military personnel from Tan Canh warned them not to eat the fish, and subsequently, they said, the Americans put some "medicine" in the water. Then they were informed they could eat the river fish, and they did so with no ill effects. Informants from Dak Mot-Tri (2b) had not seen any spraying nor did they experience any ailments or deaths among the villagers or their stock, but they, too, noticed a great many dead fish in the nearby river. Some villagers did cook and eat some of them but they reported no ill effects.

The informants from Polei Krong (3a, b) reported that after the spraying they noticed a large number of dead and dying fish floating on the surface of the Dak Bla river, and they specifically noted that the gills of some dead fish were blackened or reddish in color. Some villagers ate fresh dead or dying fish, and most of them became ill with swollen abdomens and diarrhea. Villagers at Polei Kleng (4a) said that there was a small stream near the settlement but there were no dead fish in it following the spraying. Plei Jar Tum (4b) villagers, however, said that the aircraft sprayed the banks of the Dak Bla river near the village, and afterward a very large number of fish began to float to the surface. They noticed blood and a reddish discoloration around the gills, and when some villagers cut into them there was a strange explosive effect which they likened to the striking of a match. This frightened them, and they did not eat these fish. Some villagers did eat fish that were dying, and they experienced no ill effects. Informants from Plei Ngol-Drong (5) reported that dead fish appeared on the surface of the nearby stream, and those who ate them became ill with abdominal pains and diarrhea.

PERCEIVED EFFECTS ON PLANT LIFE

Responses regarding the perceived effects on plant life were highly patterned. Long Djon (1a) informants noted that over a period of weeks following the spraying they observed plants wilting and dying. Where the spray fell directly, all the crops in the swiddens died, and in kitchen gardens where some herbicide drifted the plants wilted and stopped thriving. They said they did not know what was causing this but they suspected it was the "medicine" that had come from the aircraft and stung their nasal passages. They only gathered wild roots and tubers from areas not sprayed, and they washed them before eating them.

Dak Rosa (1b) informants reported that some of the spraying occurred over their swiddens, and very soon afterward the banana plant leaves wilted and the plants died. This also happened to the manioc plants and the eggplant. Some villagers dug up the manioc roots, which seemed to be unaffected, but when they cut into them, they were "rotten." Some villagers gathered manioc leaves that had not wilted and boiled and ate them, but they became ill with abdominal pains and diarrhea. Rice plants that had not died continued to grow, but they did not produce buds. At Dak Tang Plun (1c) the informants noted that there was spraying over some of the swiddens in which they cultivated upland dry rice, maize, manioc, eggplants, and pumpkins, and all these crops died. One old man pointed out that in the forests to the west of the village, in the vicinity of the Ben Het Camp (which had been a Special Forces camp and was converted to a Ranger camp), there were "many Viet Cong" and the spray killed the smaller plants and brush but, while the leaves on the larger trees wilted and died, the trees remained alive. They had never seen anything like this before, and they decided that they could not eat any of the surviving plants (the rice had just begun to bud and the manioc was tall) or roots in the affected area.

The principal Plei Ro-O (1d) informant reported that the villagers grew upland dry rice, maize, manioc, eggplant, and cucumbers in their swiddens, and that all of the crops died where there had been air drifting of spray. At Dak Mot-Khon (2a) and Dak Mot-Tri (2b) there had been no spraying, but the area to the northwest of the villages had been sprayed, and the informants noted that all of the vegetation had "dried and died." It was an area where residents of both villages hunted and gathered forest products, but following the spraying they avoided it. One elderly man from the Dak Siang (2c) dependents' settlement described how he had two swiddens in which he cultivated upland dry rice, manioc, maize, sugarcane, and banana trees, and with the spraying all wilted and died. All of the crops where the spray fell "dried and died." As noted previously, informants reported that some villagers ate bamboo shoots from the sprayed area and experienced dizziness followed by vomiting.

At Polei Krong (3a, b), according to the informants, villagers cultivated upland dry rice, maize, manioc, bananas, sugarcane, and pineapples in their swiddens. In kitchen gardens they grew tobacco, chili peppers, eggplants, papaya trees, and orange trees. The spray drifted over the fields and gardens, reaching them in varying degrees of strength. Where it was strongest, all of the plants and trees died within about one month. The leaves on the fruit trees "rolled up," while the plants appeared to be drying up in both swiddens and gardens. In the swiddens and gardens where the spray was not strong the rice did not thrive as it normally would have, and the fruit trees did not bear edible fruit. It was indicated previously that some villagers went into the fields to cut manioc roots and bamboo shoots, which they ate, and subsequently they got diarrhea. At first the villagers thought a natural blight was affecting the plants but a highland soldier from Kontum informed them that the Americans and the government were spreading "medicine" from aircraft to kill forest where the Viet Cong were hiding and crops the Viet Cong were growing.

Polei Kleng (4a) informants reported the same pattern as that noted above; where the spray was strong all the crops in the swiddens and kitchen gardens died, but plants survived in the less affected areas. Still the rice did not flourish, and ripening fruit fell from the trees. Informants from Plei Jar Tum (4b) simply reported that all the crops in the fields on which the spray fell died.

Villagers from Plei Ngol-Drong (5) reported that they cultivated upland dry rice, maize, manioc, yams, pineapples, bananas, and papaya in the swiddens, and in kitchen gardens they grew chili peppers, several varieties of green leafy vegetables, and cabbage. Where spray fell directly, the leaves on the trees and plants "rolled up" and died, and then the plants died. One man noted that in some swiddens the yams died but some of the rice plants did not wither, although they produced no buds. The agricultural engineer (6) reported that in the sprayed areas all the trees were affected, and the first change was that their leaves died. He added that the low brush survived. Big trees, however, died, and later they were cut for firewood. All or most of the crops in the sprayed swiddens died; this even precipitated a serious food shortage for the Viet Cong. They moved farther to the north where there was a manioc crop, but it caused a delay in some of their planned operations.

ADJUDGED EFFECTS ON SOILS

Responses concerning the adjudged effects on the soil varied considerably. Villagers from Long Djon (1a) said that about one month after the spraying they noticed sprouts appearing in affected areas where the plants had died. They were not convinced, however, that this meant they could replant, so they shifted their farming to new swiddens. Dak Rosa (1b) informants saw the sprouts appear in "two or three months" and they felt that it was a sign that they could farm the swiddens again. Some of the Dak Tang Plun (1c) villagers tried to refarm their affected swiddens, but the leaves that sprouted on the plants were shriveled, and they know that such plants do not produce good fruit or vegetables. Most villagers, they said, felt that since all of the crops had died in some fields, the soil would not be good for a long time. One Plei Ro-O (1d) informant reported that the villagers judged that since the effects were so bad, the soil could not be good, so they shifted to new farming sites.

Polei Krong (3a, b) informants reported that the villagers, who had been told the source of the spray by a highland soldier from Kontum, in some cases did replant their swiddens. The crops were not good, but some still replanted again. When the March 1972 offensive began, however, they had to abandon their fields.

The agricultural engineer informant had done some study in Hanoi on the chemicals being used in the herbicides, and he said he knew which affect plants and which affect humans and animals. He judged that the chemicals being used in the food production area in which he was located were intended for plant destruction and, while some people became ill, it would only be a temporary event without lasting effects. He thought that one type of herbicide being used contained a chemical that actually had a beneficial effect on the soil. It remained in the soil as a residue and broke down so that the soil fertility increased.

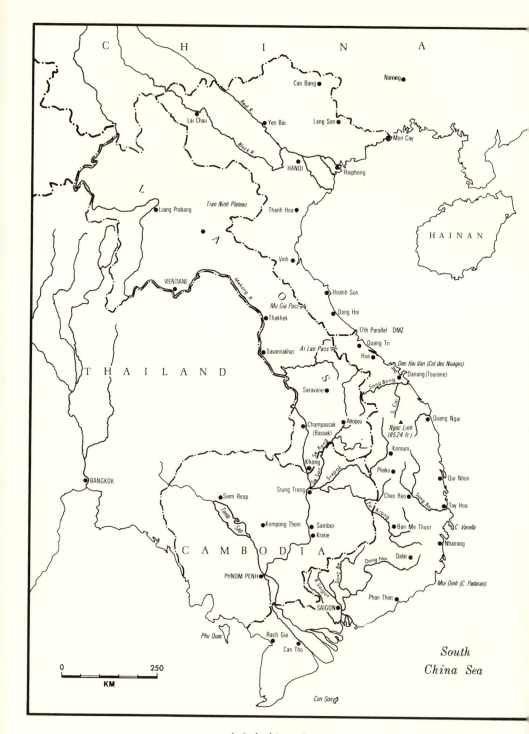

1. Indochinese States

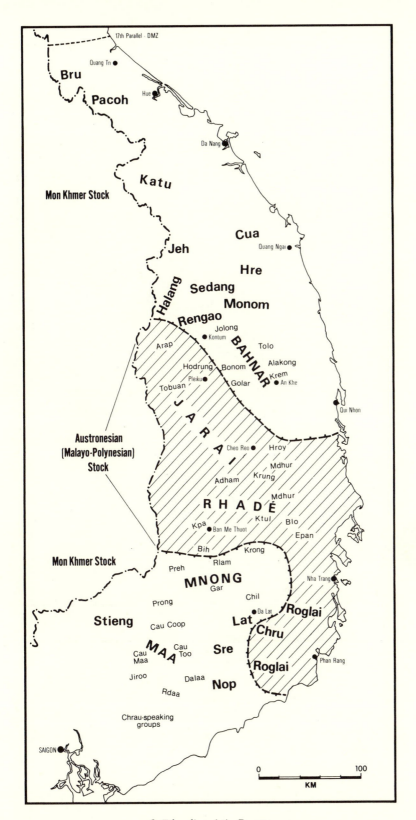

2. Ethnolinguistic Groups

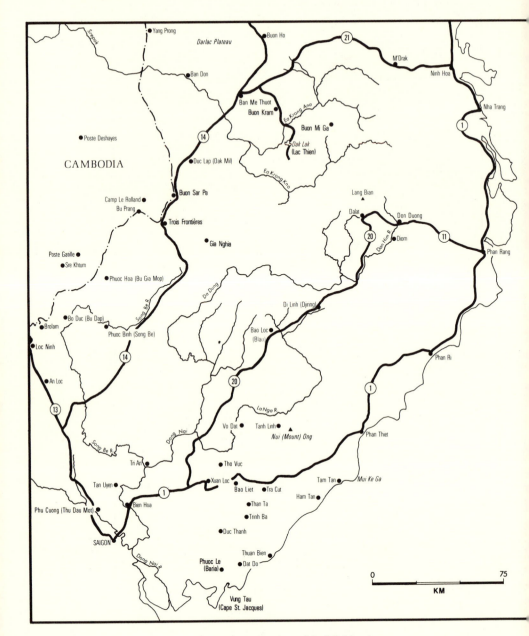

3. Southern Portion of the Highlands

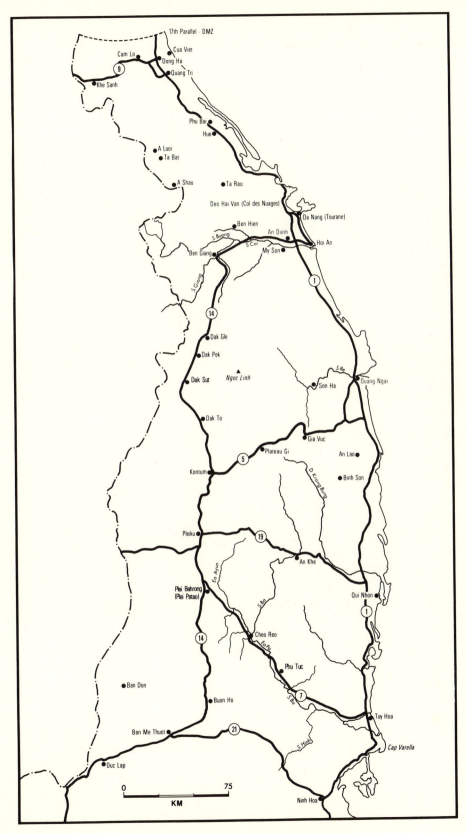

4. Northern Portion of the Highlands

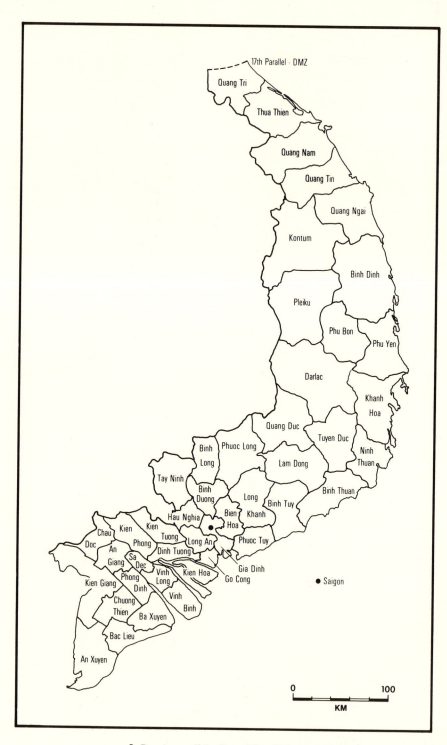

5. Provinces of the Republic of Vietnam

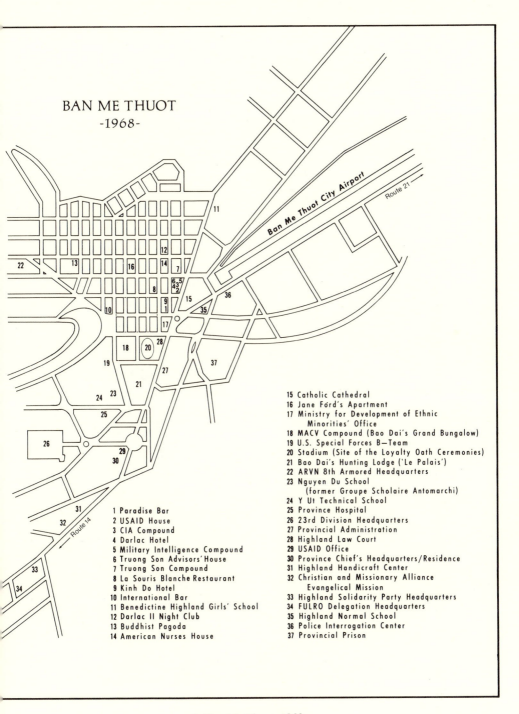

BAN ME THUOT
-1968-

Ban Me Thuot City Airport

Route 21

Route 14

1 Paradise Bar
2 USAID House
3 CIA Compound
4 Darlac Hotel
5 Military Intelligence Compound
6 Truong Son Advisors' House
7 Truong Son Compound
8 La Souris Blanche Restaurant
9 Kinh Do Hotel
10 International Bar
11 Benedictine Highland Girls' School
12 Darlac II Night Club
13 Buddhist Pagoda
14 American Nurses House

15 Catholic Cathedral
16 Jane Ford's Apartment
17 Ministry for Development of Ethnic
   Minorities' Office
18 MACV Compound (Bao Dai's Grand Bungalow)
19 U.S. Special Forces B—Team
20 Stadium (Site of the Loyalty Oath Ceremonies)
21 Bao Dai's Hunting Lodge ('Le Palais')
22 ARVN 8th Armored Headquarters
23 Nguyen Du School
   (former Groupe Scholaire Antomarchi)
24 Y Ut Technical School
25 Province Hospital
26 23rd Division Headquarters
27 Provincial Administration
28 Highland Law Court
29 USAID Office
30 Province Chief's Headquarters/Residence
31 Highland Handicraft Center
32 Christian and Missionary Alliance
   Evangelical Mission
33 Highland Solidarity Party Headquarters
34 FULRO Delegation Headquarters
35 Highland Normal School
36 Police Interrogation Center
37 Provincial Prison

6. Ban Me Thuot, 1968

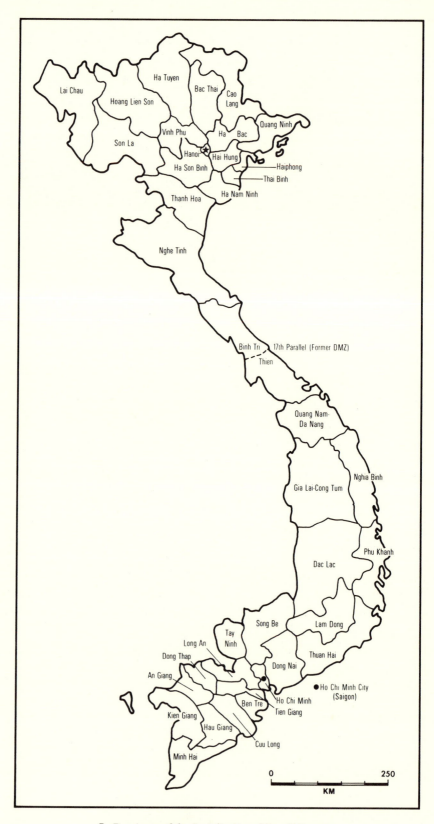

7. Provinces of the Socialist Republic of Vietnam

CHART 1

ELITE KIN NETWORK IN THE DAK TO-KONTUM-PLEIKU AREA

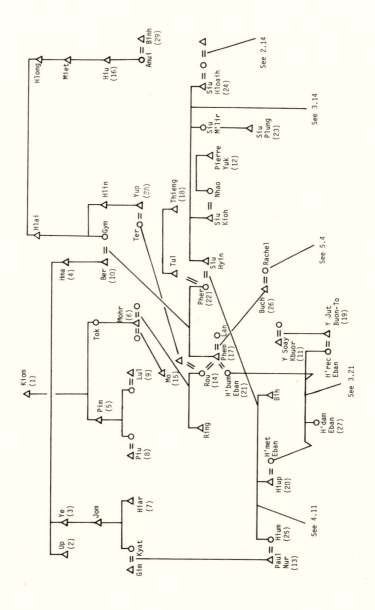

CHART 2

SEGMENT A OF THE ELITE KIN NETWORK AT CHEO REO

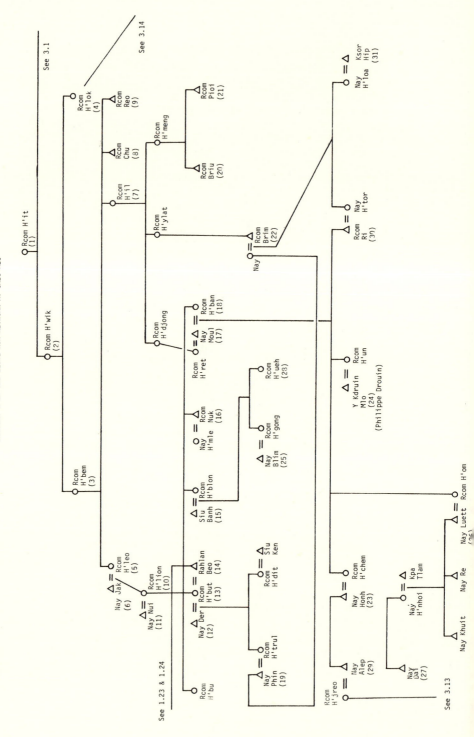

SEGMENT B OF THE ELITE KIN NETWORK AT CHEO REO

CHART 4

CHRU-LAT-SRE KIN NETWORK

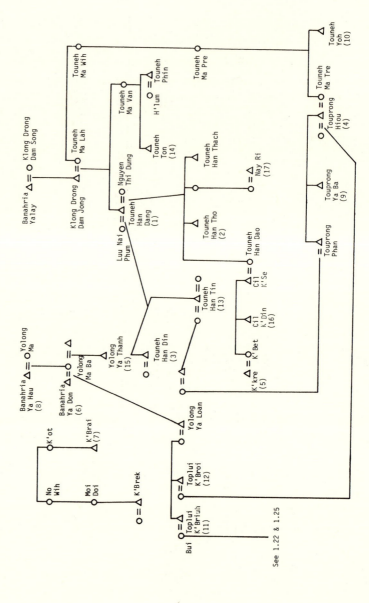

CHART 5

RHADÉ KIN GROUP IN THE BAN ME THUOT AREA

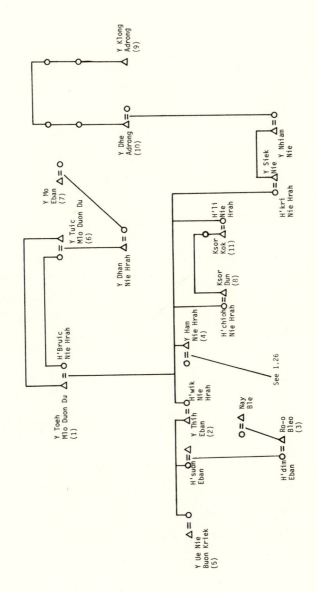

A NOTE ON BIBLIOGRAPHY

Since the early 1950s, most publications on the highlanders have been the result of what might be called wartime ethnographic and linguistic research. French researchers conducted fieldwork during the Indochina War and a few remained longer. Americans, Canadians, Australians, and English carried out most research during the Vietnam War. Prior to the Indochina War those who wrote on the highlanders included missionaries, military personnel, administrators, and explorers, whereas the more recent group of authors is for the most part composed of scholars with formal training in anthropological disciplines. There is nothing to indicate that any anthropological research has been carried out in the highlands since the 1975 Communist conquest of South Vietnam.

Of the French works, one of the best known is Georges Condominas, *Nous avons mangé la forêt de la Pierre-Génie Goo* (Paris, Mercure de France, 1952), an ethnological journal of the author's 1948–1949 field research in the Mnong Gar village of Sar Luc. Later his experiences were recalled in Georges Condominas, *L'Exotique est quotidien, Sar Luc, Viet-Nam central* (Paris: Plon, 1965). Pierre-Bernard Lafont produced three works based on his 1953–1954 Jarai research. Information on Jarai law is found in Pierre-Bernard Lafont, *Toloi Djuat: Coutumier de la tribu Jarai* (Paris: Ecole Française d'Extrême-Orient, 1963), and a collection of prayers is contained in Pierre-Bernard Lafont, *Prières Jarai* (Paris: Ecole Française d'Extrême-Orient, 1963). Pierre-Bernard Lafont, *Lexique Jarai* (Paris: Ecole Française d'Extrême-Orient, 1968) is a dictionary. Two French researchers who lived and worked in the highlands during the Indochina War and part of the Vietnam War produced monographs on the Maa and the Jarai. They are Jean Boulbet, *Pays des Maa domaine des génies Nggar Maa, Nggar Yaang* (Paris: Ecole Française d'Extrême-Orient, 1967); and Jacques Dournes, *Coordonées structures Jörai familiales et sociales* (Paris: Travaux et Mémoires de l'Institut d'Ethnologie, 1972).

Some of the articles resulting from research of this period can be cited. Two on the Mnong Gar are Georges Condominas, "The Mnong Gar of Central Vietnam," in *Social Structure in Southeast Asia*, ed. George P. Murdock (New York: Viking Fund Publications in Anthropology, no. 29, 1960), pp. 15–23; and Georges Condominas, "Schéma d'un Mho séance shamnique Mnong Gar," *Asie du Sud-Est et Monde Insulindien* 4, no. 1 (1973): 61–69. Two articles on the Mnong Rlam are Georges Condominas, "Notes sur le Tam Bo Bae Baap Kuong (échange de sacrifices entre un enfant et ses père et mère) Mnong Rlam," *International Archives of Ethnography* 47, part II (1955): 127–30; and Pierre-Bernard Lafont, "Notes sur les structures sociales des Mnong Rlam du Centre Vietnam," *BEFEO* 53 (1967): 767–78. Jacques Dournes, *La culture Jörai*, Catalogues du Musée de l'Homme, Série K, Asie, II (Paris, 1972) is an ethnographic catalogue on the Jarai with a brief text but many photographs and sketches. Maa swidden farming techniques are the subject of Jean Boulbet, "Le *miir*, culture itinérante avec jachère forestière en pays Maa," *BEFEO* 52 (1966); 77–99. Maa weaving techniques and motifs can be found in Jean Boulbet, "Modes & techniques du pays Maa," *BSEI* 39, no. 2 (1964): 169–287. Light is shed on the Cham presence in the highlands in Jacques Dournes, in "Recherches sur les Haut Champa," *France-Asie* 24, no. 2 (1970): 143–62. The historical role of the King of Fire is treated in Jacques Dournes, "Patao, les maîtres des états," *Asie du Sud-Est et Monde Insulindien*, 4 (1973): xix–xxxvi, and Charles Meyer, "Les mystérieuses relations entre les rois du Cambodge et le 'Potao' des Jarai," *Etudes Cambodgiennes*, no. 4 (1965), pp. 11–26.

Research conducted during the Vietnam War has yet to produce ethnographic monographs on the highland people, but there is a growing list of articles on ethnology and linguistics.

A 1972 issue of the short-lived journal *Southeast Asia* was devoted to ethnographic research by members of the Summer Institute of Linguistics. Articles on the highlanders are Marylyn J. Gregerson, "The Ethnic Minorities of Vietnam," *SA* 2, no. 1 (1972): 12–15; Nancy Costello, "Socially Approved Homicide among the Katu," *SA* 2, no. 1 (1972): 77–87; Vurnell Cobbey, "Some Northern Roglai Beliefs about the Supernatural," *SA* 2, no. 1(1972): 125–29; Dwight Gradin, "Rites of Passage among the Jeh," *SA* 2, no. 1 (1972): 53–61; John Banker, "Bahnar Religion," *SA* 2, no. 1 (1972): 88–124; John Miller, "Bru Kinship," *SA* 2, no. 1 (1972): 62–70.

Staff members of the Summer Institute of Linguistics focused primarily on Mon Khmer languages, and results of their research have been published in their *Mon Khmer Studies* series as well as in other journals. Some of their findings and analyses based on comparative linguistics and lexicostatistics have produced valuable historical insights and new linguistic groupings, which have a bearing on ethnic group differentiation. Some articles reflecting these developments are David Thomas and R. K. Headley, Jr., "More on Mon Khmer Subgroupings," *Lingua* 25, no. 4 (1970): 398–418; and David Thomas, "A Note on the Branches of Mon Khmer,' *Mon Khmer Studies IV*, Language Series no. 2, Center for Vietnamese Studies and Summer School of Linguistics (Saigon, 1973), pp. 138–41. An additional article drawing upon this research is Isidore Dyen, "The Chamic Languages," in *Current Trends in Linguistics*, ed. E Sebeck (The Hague and Paris: Mouton, 1971), 8: 200–10.

Several Vietnamese works on the highlanders have been published since the late 1950s, but none is based on field research. A North Vietnamese source is Nhóm Nghiên Cứu Dân Tộc (People's Study Group), *Các Dân Tộc Thiểu Số Ở Việt-Nam* (Minority Peoples of Vietnam) (Hanoi: Nhà Xuất Bản Văn Hóa, 1960), and a South Vietnam work on the highlanders is Nguyễn Trắc Dĩ, *Đồng Bào Các Sắc-Tộc Thiểu Số Ở Việt-Nam* (Vietnamese Ethnic Minority Compatriots), Bộ Phát Triển Sắc-Tộc (Ministry for Ethnic Minority Development) (Saigon, 1972).

A few sources have treated the historical role of the highlanders in the Vietnam War. Two are Howard Sochurek, "Americans in Action in Viet Nam," *National Geographic* 127, no. 1 (1965): 38–65, which describes the initial phase of the 1964 FULRO revolt; and Colonel Francis J. Kelly, *U.S. Army Special Forces 1961–1971* (Washington, Department of the Army, 1973), which contains information on the role of the highlanders in the U.S. Special Forces program.

Highland ornithology is reported in: Philip Wildash, *Birds of South Vietnam* (Rutland, Vermont and Tokyo: Charles E. Tuttle Co., 1968). Highland soils are described in F. R. Moorman, *The Soils of the Republic of South Vietnam* (Saigon, Ministry of Agriculture, 1961).

INDEX OF HIGHLANDER NAMES

GENERAL INDEX

Abrams, General Creighton W., and resettlement policy, 195

Administration, highlands: French, xv–xvi; Vietnamization of, xviii, 1, 7–10, 45–46; autonomy question, 55, 57, 65–67, 135, 139, 161, 258, 264–65, 282, 291; effects of Bajaraka Movement on, 59–60; under Communists, 258, 285–86, 293

Agreement on Ending the War and Restoring Peace in Vietnam, 257–58

Agriculture: tools, 26–28; cotton, 27, 45; swidden, 27–29, 32, 38, 42, 125, 157, 161, 193, 213–14, 309, 317–18; paddy, 27–29, 38, 213; kitchen gardens, 27–29, 45, 214; division of labor in, 28; terracing, 28; secondary crops, 28–29, 317–18; tree crops, 29, 37, 45, 96, 168, 212; truck gardening, 29–30, 214; rainfed permanent ricefields, 30; in Land Development Centers, 44; cash cropping, 212–15, 262; high-yield rice, 213; MDEM Agricultural Development Plan, 265; herbicides, 309, 313, 316–19. *See also* Coffee; Enterprises, highlander

Animals: wild game, 27, 314; domestic, 30, 314

An Loc: seige of, 234, 249–50; and Stieng refugees, 234, 249–50

Army of the Republic of Vietnam (ARVN): National Army of Diem administration, 3–4, 11–12; highlanders in, 11–12, 54–55, 59, 135; highlanders' complaints against, 50, 54–55, 246; National Military Academy in Dalat, 74; FULRO, 107, 134, 139–40; proposal of highlander force, 112, 133, 153, 187, 189–90, 246, 269; highlander resettlement, 165–66, 221–23; defeat of Operation Lam Son *719*, 168, 227–28; Tet Offensive, 176, 180, 182–84; *1972* offensive, 234–35; and Minh Quy hospital, 248; highlander draft, 252; *1972* ceasefire, 259–60; Communist defeat of, 272–83 passim. *See also* People's Army of Vietnam

(PAVN); U.S. Military Assistance Advisory Group (MAAG); U.S. Military Assistance Command Vietnam (MACV); Viet Cong

Artisans, village, 27

Asia Foundation, and highland student scholarships, 123, 200

Atwood, Tracy, 224–25, 261; cited, 99–101; FULRO revolt, 99–102; *1972* offensive, 241–45, 247

Austronesian languages, xiv, 22, 24

Autonomous zones (North Vietnam): and Chu Van Tan, 12, 15–16: abolition of, 286

Autonomy, highlands: Y Bham Enuol and, 55, 57, 135, 139, 269; Communist promise of, 65–67, 161, 258, 285–86, 291; MDEM scheme for, 264–65, 282

Bahnar: leaders, xvii, 5, 9, 136; bilateral descent, 22, 30; jars, 24; farming, 30; house types, 30; land tenure, 40; primer in, 200; elite network, 206–07, 209–10; refugees, 238, 240

Bajaraka Movement, 142, 291; derivation of name of, 47; ethnonationalistic roots of, 47–49, 291; initial stage of, 49–52; and Front pour la libération des Montagnards (FLM), 50–54; leadership structure of, 53–54; ideology of, 54–55; government reaction to, 55–60; revival, 83–84, 86–88, 91–92, 97–98, 111; and KKK, 98

Ball, George W., and FULRO revolt, 110

Ban Me Thuot, 8, 10; French administration of, xvi–xvii; PAVN capture of, xxi, 258, 271–74; in Land Development Program, 19–20; in *1957*, 33–34; highlander law court, 37, 199–200; Bajaraka Movement demonstration in, 58; FULRO delegation, 135, 139, 153, 169–72; Tet Offensive, 168, 173–83; *1972* offensive, 242, 244

Bao Dai, xiii–xiv, 29, 34; Crown Domain, xiv, 7–9, 51, 301; highlander education, xvi–xvii,

341

of, in *1958–61*, 74

U.S. Military Assistance Command Vietnam (MACV), 121, 155, 186, 188, 264; replacement of MAAG by, 79; and U.S. Special Forces, 80; and Village Defense Program, 80–81; FULRO, 171–72; Tet Offensive, 175, 181, 183–84; *1972* offensive, 238; *1973* cease-fire, 260. *See also* U.S. military troop strength

U.S. military, major highlands operations of· Gibraltar (101st Airborne), 137; battle of Ia Drang Valley, 137; Lincoln (1st Cavalry), 156; Matador (1st Cavalry), 156; 25th Infantry Division, 156; Hawthorne (101st Airborne Division), 156–57; 4th Infantry Division, 157; Francis Marion (4th and 25th Infantry Divisions), 164; Prairie Fire (3rd Marine Division), 164; Paul Revere IV (4th Infantry, 1st Cavalry, 173d Airborne), 165; Niagara II (26th Marine Regiment), 173; Delaware (1st Cavalry), 186; Pegasus / Lam Son *207* (1st Cavalry, 1st Marine Regiment, ARVN), 186; Massachusetts Striker (101st Airborne), 216

U.S. military troop strength, by: end of *1964*, 189; May *1965*, 130; November *1965*, 137; June *1967*, 164; mid-*1968*, 186; end of *1969*, 216; April–May *1972*, 239; 30 March *1973*, 264

U.S. Operations Mission (USOM). *See* U.S. Agency for International Development (USAID)

U.S. Special Forces, 83, 95, 157, 166, 185; and FULRO, xix, 90, 99–107, 110, 134, 136, 140, 142, 162–63, 169–72; in Village Defense Program, 77, 79–80; in Mountain Scout Program, 78; and MACV, 80; CIDG, 80, 82, 84–87, 110, 157; Operation Switchback, 80–82, 85–87; and Bajaraka Movement, 84, 87–88, 97; King of Fire, 150; Tet Offensive, 176, 179–80, 184; education, 201–02; PAVN, 216; withdrawal of, 216

Van Tien Dung, General, and conquest of South Vietnam, 270–81 passim

Vann, John Paul: Office for Highland Affairs, 223; and Nay Luett, 233, 240; *1972* offensive, 235, 240, 242–43, 246–47; death of, 247; and missing Americans, 266

Viet Cong: 17, 121; regroupees, 12–16, 36–37, 49, 64–67, 119, 216–17, 308; defectors from, 13–14, 217; derivation of name, 47; proclamation of NLF, 47, 65–66; activities in villages, 63–65, 69, 95, 120, 123n, 139, 222; highland

autonomy, 65–67, 258; highlander leaders in, 66–67, 93; formation of PRP, 67; Bajaraka Movement, 86; Diem and Nhu, 88–89; FULRO, 116–17, 170, 216, 267–69, 273n; and PAVN, 119–20; post-*1962* approach, 128–29, 157; *1973* cease-fire, 157; political program, 161; Tet Offensive, 175–86; People's Court, 182; Provisional Revolutionary Government, 191; food production, 216–17, 313, 318. *See also* Southern Ethnic Minorities School; Highland Autonomy Movement

Viet Minh, xvi, 47; and Geneva Agreements, xiii; and Diem, 2; highlander regroupees, 12–16; 36–37, 49, 64; highlander village activities, 13–16, 36–37, 63–64

Vietnam Christian Service, 221, 234; and resettlement program, 222; Ronald Ackerman, 234, 242; *1972* offensive, 244

Vietnam Communist Party: proclamation of, 295; highlanders in, 295

Vietnamese Air Force (VNAF), 86: bombing of highland villages, 70–71, 125, 129; *1972* offensive, 237; *1975* Communist offensive, 273, 281

Village Defense Program, 73–77, 79; CIA sponsorship of, 74–77, 80; U.S. Special Forces in, 77, 79–80; MACV takeover of and change to Civilian Irregular Defense Group (CIDG) of, 80; Operation Switchback, 80–82, 86–87; and Strategic Hamlet Program, 82; and Bajaraka Movement, 83–84

Vinh Loc, General, 159; cited, 133; FULRO, 134, 138–43, 153–56, 161–62; land titles, 137; highlander resettlement, 165–66

Vo Nguyen Giap, General, and *1975* Communist offensive, 271

Warner, Denis, cited, 64–65, 274

Weapons, traditional, 27

Weaving, 27; Jarai Arap, 249

Weinraub, Bernard, cited, 281

Westmoreland, General William, 102, 130, 186; FULRO, 103–04; bombing of North Vietnam, 113; bombing of highlands, 114; cited, 119, 137; government-highlander relations, 143

Wickert, Frederick 32

Williams, Lt. General Samuel T., and insurgency, 65

Zorthian, Barry, and FULRO revolt, 104